Martin Travers
1886-1948

An Appreciation

SSPP Trust

Martin Travers
1886-1948

An Appreciation

by

Rodney Warrener

&

Michael Yelton

Published by UNICORN PRESS from their offices at Number 76 Great Suffolk Street in London

To the memory of
Edward Otway Humphrey Whitby, Priest
1883-1948

Unicorn Press
76 Great Suffolk Street
London SE1 0BL

email: unicorn@tradford.demon.co.uk

Copyright © Rodney Warrener and Michael Yelton 2003

First published 2003 by Unicorn Press

All rights reserved. Without limiting the rights under copyright reserved above, no part of this publication may be reproduced, stored in or introduced into a retrieval system, or transmitted, in any form or by any means (electronic, mechanical, photocopying, recording or otherwise), without the prior written permission of the copyright holder and the above publisher of this book.

ISBN 0 906290 70 8

Typesetting by Ferdinand Pageworks, Surrey
Printed in Great Britain

Chapter		Page
	Acknowledgements	
	Foreword	vii
1	Travers the man: a short biography	1
2	Travers' work in context: the Back to Baroque Movement in the Church of England	31
3	Travers the designer: I The early years 1909–1924	51
4	Travers the designer: II Six London churches	79
5	Travers the designer: III The middle years 1925–1938	110
6	Travers the designer: IV Seven country churches	155
7	Travers the designer: V The later years 1939–1948	178
8	Travers the designer: VI Work abroad	207
9	Travers the church builder	219
10	Travers the graphic artist	241
11	Travers: a modern perspective	259
12	A gazetteer of Travers' actual and projected work	269
	Footnotes	334
	Index	337
	Colour plates 1–16 between pages 88–89 17–32 between pages 248–249	

This book could not have been completed without the assistance of very many people who answered our often esoteric questions, allowed us in to churches at inconvenient times to take photographs or poke about looking for candlesticks, and searched out correspondence. We are particularly grateful for the information given by Jeanne Travers and her children Michael Travers and Julia Candlish, and Lawrence Lee, who talked to us about working for Travers, and also for assistance from the staff of the Cambridge University Library, the Council for the Care of Churches (especially Janet Seeley), the National Monuments Record Centres in Swindon and London, the RIBA, the Guildhall Library (especially Sharon Tuff), the London Metropolitan Archives of the Corporation of London, Lambeth Palace Library, the National Library of Wales, the Borthwick Institute at York, the Record Offices at Canterbury Cathedral, Aylesbury, Brighton, Bristol, Bury St. Edmunds, Chelmsford, Exeter, Hertford, Huntingdon, Ipswich, Lewes, Maidstone, Margate, Matlock, Newcastle, Norwich, Nottingham, Oxford, Plymouth, Southwark, Stafford, Taunton, Trowbridge, and Truro, and very many clergy and members of their congregations, with particular thanks to John Greenhalgh of St. Mary Bourne Street, Gavin Stamp, who provided many photographs, Violet Howe, who rediscovered the lost reredos at Steeple, Barbara Giles of Littleton, Richard McEwan and Peter Ward, indefatigable enthusiasts for Travers, and Father Kenneth McNab, parish priest of St. Barnabas Tunbridge Wells, for help in the proof reading. Our most profound thanks are however due to the Trustees of the Society of SS. Peter and Paul, without whose generous assistance this book could not have been published. There could be no more appropriate sponsor of this book. The views expressed are of course the authors' own, and they are well aware that there may be more to discover. Any supplemental information or corrections are most welcome.

R.W., M.Y.

Martin Travers is something of a cult figure among church-crawlers, but very little has been written about his life, and while many know of his high profile London work in St. Mary Bourne Street and St. Augustine Queen's Gate, few are aware of his wider output. There are many myths about Travers: many suppose that because much of his work was associated with the Back to Baroque Movement and the Anglo-Catholic Congresses Travers must himself have been sympathetic to those causes. This book aims to show that Travers is an underrated and misunderstood artist whose work is in fact frequently of high quality, and rarely less than interesting. It also deals for the first time in detail with his life, assisted by information from his family, and places the man in the context in which he worked.

Rodney Warrener, Michael Yelton
Feast of St. Ignatius Loyola: 31st July 2002

Self portrait

Chapter 1

Travers the Man: A Short Biography

Howard Martin Otho Travers was born on 19th February 1886 at his parents' home, Foley House, Brewery Hill, Margate.

In what little has been written about him previously, it has generally been asserted that he was born in Norwich, but in fact his early connections, as well as his later schooling, were in Kent rather than in Norfolk[1]. It is interesting that among his last commissions was a hanging rood for All Saints, Westbrook, in his home town, and indeed throughout his life it happened that he designed work for places with which he had been associated in one way or another.

Martin Travers took two of his christian names from his family. He was called Howard after his father Howard William Travers (1854–1905) and Otho (always thus spelled) was a family name going back several generations. Although in later years he was always known as Martin, on some of his pre-First World War designs he used the style 'Howard M. Travers', and certainly he never forgot his other names; many of his stained glass windows are signed 'HMOT' with the letters entwined. One of his notebooks, which start in 1903 and span most, although not all, of his professional life, shows that he was using the entwined letter device as early as 1907.

The Travers family was originally part of the Anglo-Irish Ascendancy[2]. They traced their line back to Sir Robert Travers, MP for Clonakilty 1634 and 1639, who was killed in the battle of Knockarness, County Cork, on 13th November 1647. Many members of the Travers family served in the Army or the Navy and they thus acquired the name 'the fighting Travers'; a number of others were doctors. Martin Travers' great-great-grandfather, Robert Travers of Round Hill, County Cork, Captain in the Bandon Cavalry, died in 1826. His great-grandfather Robert Otho Travers, Major

I

in the 86th Regiment of Foot, predeceased his father, dying in 1814. He married Frances Elizabeth Steele, daughter of Captain John Steele of Sutton Court, Surrey. The Sutton Court estate, now built over with hundreds of houses, was also important in relation to the next generation. By another coincidence, many years later Martin Travers was to design a window for the church of St. Barnabas, Sutton New Town.

Martin Travers' grandfather, Otho William Travers (1813–1895), son of Robert Otho Travers, married Henrietta Ann Vernon, daughter of the Vicar of Sutton, in 1852, but she died in 1868.

Otho William Travers ran Church Farm, part of the Sutton Court Estate, apparently without great success. He and his wife had 8 children, 4 boys and 4 girls, and a picture has been preserved in the family showing Henrietta Travers with her 4 sons, Otho Robert (1852–1916), who was a surgeon, Howard William, Martin's father, Vernon (1859–1915) who died in what was then the Gold Coast, and Ernest Aston Otho (1864–1934), who became State Surgeon in Selangor, in what was then the Federated Malay States.

Tradition within the family suggests that Otho William Travers' attempts to run the farm were in the end so unsuccessful that he moved to a small cottage on the estate before it was finally broken up and then built over.

The Travers family in the nineteenth century thus presents a fairly typical picture of service to the Crown, at home and abroad, through the armed forces and the medical profession, but with no apparent sign of the artistic talent which was to be so evident in the next century.

Martin Travers' father Howard was also something of an exception to the family tradition, whether from lack of talent or of ambition. Surviving pictures show him as a rather effete looking man, whereas his wife, Lucy Gertrude (née Hunnybun) has a much more formidable look about her. Martin Travers' son Nicholas prepared some draft notes on his own early life, in which he remembered her as a particularly unpleasant woman, whom he had to visit weekly when he was in this country.

Howard Travers was a brewer – indeed he is described on his son's birth certificate as a 'practical brewer'. On 3rd June 1885 he married at St. Mary's Church, Godmanchester, then in Huntingdonshire, now in Cambridgeshire. Gertrude Travers (as his wife was known) was the daughter of Martin Hunnybun, solicitor, who was then in practice in the adjoining town of Huntingdon, and her brothers also went into the firm, which is still in existence today, although now without any representative of the

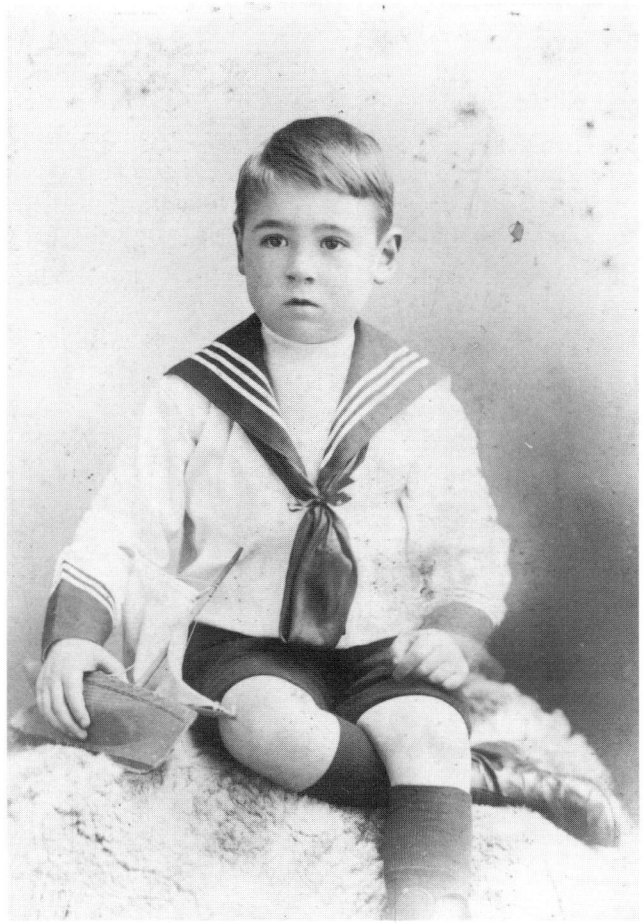

Martin Travers aged about 4, taken in Margate 1890

family. It may well be that such prosperity as the couple enjoyed came from the Hunnybun connection rather than from Howard Travers' earnings.

At the time of Martin Travers' birth his parents were living at Foley House, in Brewery Hill or Lane (sometimes called The Mount) in Margate. Foley House was a reasonably substantial property belonging to Cobb's Brewery and normally housed a senior employee. Brewery Hill was a tiny lane running from behind the brewery into King Street, near Margate harbour and town centre. In 1967 the brewery was sold to Whitbreads and in 1971 there was a comprehensive redevelopment of the area which removed the brewery, Foley House, and even the lane itself.

It will be seen from the dates set out that Martin Travers must have been conceived immediately after his parents' marriage. Unusually for the time they were to have no other children. He was baptized at Godmanchester Church, near his mother's former home. Early pictures of Martin show him as an attractive baby and toddler, dressed in the fashion of the time, and taken at studios in the Thanet area. In conversation with his son in later years, he was to remember a very strict and conventional childhood; in particular he recalled that when the family went to Church on Sundays he had to walk behind his parents, carrying a prayer book.

In about 1897 the family moved to Norwich, where Howard Travers took up further employment in the brewing trade as a manager. They lived at 4, Chapelfield Grove, a substantial Victorian house near the City Centre, which was demolished many years ago when the area was redeveloped. A picture taken towards the end of the century shows a tall, bespectacled boy washing his dog in the garden of the family home. A posed photograph of the same era shows an alert, pleasant-looking, youth facing the camera.

Martin Travers aged about 14, taken in Norwich c 1900

In 1899 Martin Travers went to board at Tonbridge School, thus returning to the county of his birth[3]. There does not appear to have been any family connection with the school save that his cousin Otho Boyle Travers, son of Otho Robert Travers FRCS, was at the school 1893–7, immediately before Martin. Tonbridge School was to play a considerable part in Travers' subsequent career: one of his first recorded designs was for the chapel, although that was never executed, but later he designed further work for the chapel which was carried out. Also in later life Travers became a Freeman of the Worshipful Company of Skinners, which has close connections with the school.

An almost exact contemporary of his at Tonbridge was Guy Brown (later Revd Guy Bryan-Brown) who was killed in action in 1917 and in whose memory Travers was to design a window in Christ's College, Christchurch, New Zealand: see Chapter 8.

In 1904 Martin Travers left Tonbridge and went to the Royal College of Art, then in part of the Victoria & Albert Museum Building[4]. That institution was to play an even more significant part in his later career, and it is unfortunate that it appears that in its archives there are no photographs or significant references to him. It is clear from his choice of further educational establishment that his artistic talent was already apparent.

The Royal College of Art had been founded in 1837 as the Government School of Design, to make the training of designers for industry a national responsibility. In 1896 it changed its name to the Royal College of Art, and in 1899 the Board of Education took over responsibility for running it.

When Travers went to the College in 1904 its primary responsibility had shifted to the training of teachers, but many of its students in fact went into the practice of various forms of art. One interesting contemporary of his was the later suffragette Sylvia Pankhurst, who was at the College from 1904 to 1906.

Entrance to the Royal College of Art was by competition. At the time when Martin Travers entered, short-listed candidates had to sit a 6-day examination in the College on 4 set subjects: architecture, sculpture, painting, and ornament and design. On entry all students had to take a preliminary one-term course in architecture under the direction of the distinguished architect Arthur Beresford Pite (1861–1934). After 1900 each of the main schools in the College had their own instructor, titled 'Professor' after 1901, and Beresford Pite was the head of the architecture school. The head of design was W.R. Lethaby, who had brought with him Christopher Whall to teach stained glass and Henry Wilson to teach silverwork and jewellery. All these men, distinguished in their own fields, were followers of the Arts and Crafts Movement with its emphasis on individual, as opposed to manufactured, work.

Certainly by 1905 practical stained glass painting was on offer to students, and in the same year Whall published his book *Stained Glasswork* in which he articulated an Arts and Crafts philosophy firmly rooted in workshop practice. Lettering was also taught, and Travers' skill in lettering is self evident from much of his work; his spelling however remained erratic. His notebooks for this time show that he was a conscientious student, and that he had early developed the technique of sketching buildings and parts of buildings which interested him. In between the buildings are odd notes such as addresses and train times and also line drawings of friends and people he met.

He left the College in 1908, having been awarded its Diploma in Architecture. This did not qualify him to register as an architect when the Architects (Registration) Act 1931 came into effect, and indeed after the similar Act of 1938 was passed, a person not so registered committed a criminal offence if he described himself as an architect. Therefore when in due course Travers was involved in the design and construction of new work, as opposed to the furnishing of buildings which already existed, he normally needed the assistance of an architect properly so called. Nevertheless, he had in earlier years frequently described himself on his drawings and elsewhere as 'architect'. He could however, and did, properly describe himself as an Associate of the Royal College of Art (Architecture).

On 1st December 1905, Travers' father died in Norwich. He left an estate of less than £500, which was not substantial even at that date. At some point thereafter Travers' widowed mother moved to London and he lived with her.

The exact dating of events in the period between Travers' leaving the College and the First World War is not easy. It appears that initially he acted as an assistant to Beresford Pite, who was much influenced by Byzantine precedents, and the earliest known work attributed to Travers is by Pevsner, who says that the cartouches on the arcaded panelling at the Paget Memorial Mission, in Islington are 'probably designed by Travers, pupil of Pite'[5]. The Mission itself, in Randell's Road, in a derelict area near King's Cross, is worth visiting for the extraordinary wooden interior, left virtually untouched since it was constructed; there are certainly many Travers-like cartouches with the initials VP for Violet Paget, whose photograph still hangs on the wall, and whose husband constructed the building in her memory.

Although Travers was undoubtedly influenced by the Byzantinism of Pite, he stayed with him only a short time. He next worked for Ninian (later Sir Ninian) Comper, and again that period was not long. Although sometimes described as being his pupil, in fact it appears that he was his assistant, or more exactly an 'improver', a qualified employee who was not a pupil and was superior to a draughtsman[6]. Comper had by that time already established a reputation for his exquisite Gothic Revival work and in 1897 at Cantley in Yorkshire he had designed the first revived English altar, with drapes and riddel posts. Such altars became within a few years the stock in trade of every ecclesiastical furnisher, including Travers himself, and were installed in all manner of churches and cathedrals, as adding dignity and colour to the fabric without straying outside the bounds of loyalty to the Established Church.

It is not clear exactly how long Travers stayed with Comper; certainly he cannot fail to have been influenced by Comper's skills and knowledge. It is said that some years later, when Comper entered the chapel of the Benedictine Community at Nashdom, he remarked 'I see young Martin has been messing around here', a remark which tends to suggest some disdain on his part for Travers' baroque altar in the former ballroom. However they seem to have remained on reasonably good terms, perhaps because Comper always showed more respect for former associates who did not merely imitate him. He is also reported to have said 'I always tell my pupils not to copy their master and I can safely say that Martin [Travers] has followed my advice'. Again there is perhaps a note of disdain in the comment. In 1935 they both submitted competing designs for a reredos at St. Mark, Prince Albert Road, Regent's Park, and Comper's design was chosen.

In about 1937 Travers introduced John Betjeman to Comper, and all three had dinner together at the latter's house in South London. Betjeman recorded 'We went on talking about architecture, literature and people till the lights twinkled out over Croydon in the summer evening.' This is an interesting sidenote, in that Betjeman had become a great devotee of Comper and did much to publicize his work. That meeting lead to an important article by Betjeman in the *Architectural Review*, which put Comper's work before a wider public for the first time[7].

There is no doubt that by 1911 at least Travers had left Comper's employment and was in practice on his own. The commentary to the catalogue of his drawings in the RIBA indicates that he set up on his own in 1911, but on the other hand the note in the same publication to his first design for Tonbridge School Chapel, dated 11th June 1909, is said to have

High altar Tonbridge School, unexecuted design of 1909

been drawn 'immediately after he left Comper's office.' This and another contemporary design bear the address 149 Albert Palace Mansions, Battersea, which is also on a notebook of that period. However, by the time that Travers designed a rood screen for St. Julian's Norwich on 26th September 1909 he had moved to 3, Priory Road, Bedford Park, and he remained there until about 1916.

Bedford Park had been constructed in the late nineteenth century specifically as an artists' suburb. Travers lived with his widowed mother in a pleasant house just off the Bath Road, now called 3, Priory Gardens. Behind the house at the end of the garden are premises then known as 1 (now 1A), Bath Road, which he used as a studio. The Travers' house at 3, Priory Road was opposite the vicarage of the Norman Shaw designed church of St. Michael and All Angels, and just round the corner from the church itself, for which he later carried out work.

In the years between 1911 and the First World War, Travers sometimes worked in partnership with George Elton Sedding, son of John Dando Sedding, the architect of Holy Trinity Sloane Street, Holy Redeemer Clerkenwell and of other churches, and another proponent of the Arts and Crafts Movement. They designed not only ecclesiastical furnishings and glass, but also enamelled jewellery, exhibiting at the Exposition des Arts Decoratifs de Grande Bretagne at d'Irlande in Paris in the summer of 1914; that Exhibition was literally overtaken by the outbreak of the First World War and the exhibits were placed in store for the duration.

George Sedding was an important figure in Travers' life and of course was well connected in the artistic life of London through his family. He was a pious Anglo-Catholic attending St. Mary Magdalene, Munster Square, one of the first churches in London regarded as correct by the Ecclesiologists, and also assisting with the scout troop at the very 'advanced' church of St. Saviour, Hyde Road, Hoxton, where Travers was later to carry out work. Sedding had in fact been introduced to St. Saviour through assisting with a hostel in the area in company with the later Prime Minister, Clement Attlee. Sedding was born in 1882 and had been apprenticed to Henry Wilson, who as mentioned above later taught at the RCA, and in about 1904 he himself went to the College and studied under Pite; doubtless that is where he met Travers.

In 1907 Sedding opened a workshop at 11, Noel Street, near Oxford Circus, and from there carried out a number of important ecclesiastical commissions, such as a crucifix for the monks of Caldey, processional crosses for St. Frideswide, Poplar, and St. Mary Magdalene, Munster

Square, an altar for Zanzibar Cathedral, and a lady chapel altar for his father's Italianate church of the Holy Redeemer, Clerkenwell. The work for Poplar and Zanzibar may well have come through his brother Edward, who was a curate at St. Frideswide 1908–12, and thereafter was in East Africa for a time.

There is no evidence that Travers was involved in those specific works, but in later years he was involved on his own account in work for both Zanzibar and Holy Redeemer, and in his notebooks for those early years is a design for the front cover of the parish magazine of St. Frideswide, Poplar. At the same time of course Travers was commencing his own design work, especially in stained glass, which is discussed more fully in Chapter 3.

One of the surprising aspects of Martin Travers' character is that it is quite clear, certainly by the inter-war period, that he was an agnostic; indeed he was known in later years for displaying cynicism over some of his output. That appears to lie ill with a career which was spent almost exclusively furnishing Anglican churches.

Although a certain amount of conjecture is required, it is a plausible hypothesis that he was disillusioned by the First World War, and lost a faith he had earlier held.

Anglo-Catholicism in the first decade of the Twentieth Century was not only vibrant but also appealed to the aesthetic and romantic sensibilities of a young man like Travers. Many of his early designs were for churches in Norwich, and specifically for those churches in Norwich which had embraced the Catholic Revival – All Saints, Westlegate, St. John the Baptist, Maddermarket, and St. Julian, King Street. It may well be that he had met the clergy from those churches in his holidays from Tonbridge and the RCA. Certainly he absorbed not only a wide knowledge of iconography, which he needed for all his work, but also a specifically Anglo-Catholic form of devotion to the saints and to Our Lady in particular.

It would also appear logical that a deeply committed Anglo-Catholic such as Sedding would want to work with a partner who adhered to the same beliefs.

In 1910, possibly while he was still with Comper, Travers designed a stole for the wealthy Humphrey Whitby, then a deacon at St. Columba, Haggerston. In 1911, probably with assistance from Sedding, he was given what turned out to be a most important commission: Whitby had him design a High Mass set and card for his first mass. This work is described further in Chapter 4, but it represented an introduction to a most important patron, and in addition one to whom cost was of little moment. Again, the likelihood is that it was Sedding, with his connections, who introduced Whitby to Travers. Sedding had made a chalice and ciborium for Father Whitby, both of which are now in St. Mary Bourne Street.

During 1912 Travers designed a window for Chesterblade Church, Somerset. In his notebooks is a first draft of an invitation to his friends and family to come and see the design at his studio at 1, Bath Road, with a little map of the area which foreshadowed those he later designed for the Anglo-Catholic Priests' Convention in Oxford. He invited among others Father Whitby, Father Whitby's mother Evelyn, Samuel Gurney, who was by then sending him graphic work for the Society of SS. Peter and Paul (see Chapter 2), Sedding, and Father Magnus Laing, a noted preacher of the time who was a curate at St. Saviour, Hoxton 1909–20 and later at St. Mary, Bourne Street, 1921–5. Laing was said to have great influence on the young and was something of a shooting star in the Anglo-Catholic firmament, before later marrying and settling down to life in the country. It may be that Travers, like others, came under his spell; however there is some evidence on the other side that during those early years Travers was not immune to the pleasures of the flesh. In his notebooks, amid the sketches of friends, are a number of studies of the same girl, both dressed and undressed: we are even given the name, Ethel Harwood, and an address at 11, Westwick Gardens, West Kensington, which suggests that she was more than just an artist's model.

With the outbreak of the First World War in 1914, many young men rushed to join up. Sedding joined the Norfolk Regiment, and died on 23rd October 1915 in Hampstead General Hospital, after being wounded in action in Flanders. A memoir of him entitled *George Elton Sedding: the life and work of an artist soldier* was edited by his brother Revd Edward D. Sedding and published by the Letchworth Garden City Press Ltd. in 1917. Martin Travers drew the title page, displaying items designed by Sedding, together with pictures of St. George slaying the dragon, a favourite subject for his own stained glass windows of that period, St. Dunstan, patron saint of metal-workers, and willow herb and honeysuckle, with which the dead man had decorated his dugout in the trenches. He prepared a heart-shaped block from a piece of jewellery designed by Sedding and this was reproduced in the book also. It seems likely that his death had a devastating effect on Travers. Sedding clearly made a great impression on many people and he was the only modern subject in Kenneth Ingram's series of talks entitled *A Portrait of Six Christian Heroes*, published by SSPP in 1926.

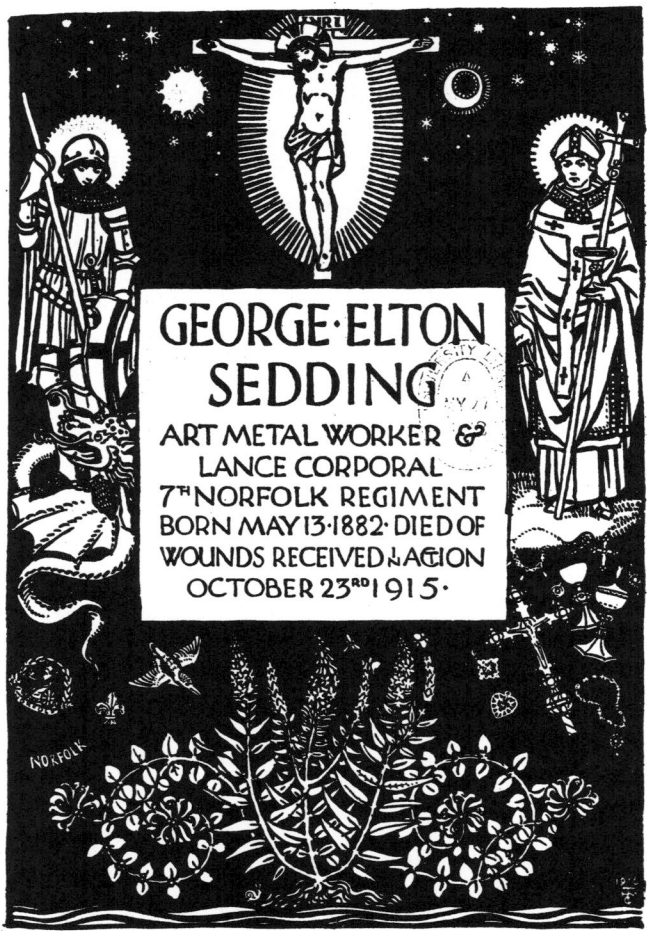

Title page from G.E. Sedding book, 1916

Sedding is buried in the churchyard of St. John the Baptist, West Wickham, Bromley, next to his parents. His father had carried out work in the church, and so did Travers at a later date. This was not to be Travers' last connection with the Sedding family, as in 1934 he illustrated a book by Edward, who was by then a member of the Cowley Fathers: see Chapter 10.

Travers himself had not joined up, and remained in England designing stained glass, as well as memorials for Father Whitby's family in the churchyard of All Saints, Wyke Regis, Dorset. In September 1916 he designed glass for Southwark Cathedral, although this commission never proceeded; this is his only documented output for that year, which happened to be the year when conscription was introduced.

In addition to his friend Sedding, Travers had seen many of his extended family with their military background die young. His cousin Otho, who had preceded him at Tonbridge, was in fact drowned in 1917 when his ship went down.

That year, 1917, was a decisive one in Travers' life. He refused to be conscripted into the armed forces, citing conscientious objections to military service. He was not however an 'absolute' conscientious objector, many of whom were imprisoned, and so he agreed to work as a driver in the Red Cross ambulance service. This decision was not only a break with the family ethos, but it also marked him out, and perhaps isolated him, from many men of his age. In his papers is a letter stamped as received on 10th February 1917 from the Society of Friends commending the work of those who had had the courage to stand up for liberty of conscience and work in the ambulance unit rather than be conscripted; there is no evidence however that Travers himself ever became a Quaker.

Travers also married in 1917. His wife, Christine Berthe Antoinette Wilson (née Willmore) was born in 1891. Most of what we know of Christine Travers' short life arises from the fact that her younger brother Alfred Willmore became well known as an Irish actor and stage manager under his self-adopted name of Micheal Mac Liammoir, and wrote extensively about himself and his family. The name Mac Liammoir was itself a rough self-Gaelicization of Willmore, and is not a form found elsewhere.

It seems that Travers had let his studio at the bottom of the garden to Christine on or after the outbreak of the war. There are many myths surrounding the marriage: it may well have been secret, in the sense that Travers' mother did not know of it, but it has also been said that it was conducted by Revd T.P. Stevens, then a curate at St. Michael, Bedford Park, in a deserted waiting room at a railway station in Birmingham and further that Mrs. Travers senior did not know of the marriage until some years later, and that Christine returned to the studio with Martin remaining in his old house with his mother.

It seems clear however that Mrs. Travers senior must have known of the marriage immediately, not least because of the birth of the couple's first child, Nicholas (often known as Nick) on 15th July 1917; later they had Sarah (always known as Sally) on 15th June 1920. Further, it is clear from examination of the documentary evidence that the couple did not return to Bedford Park for any significant period after the marriage.

It is certainly true that Martin and Christine Travers were married in Birmingham, but the certificate points to the rather more conventional location for the nuptials of King's Norton Register Office. Whether or not any religious ceremony took place in addition is unclear. The date of the wedding was 27th September 1917, which of course was *after* the birth of Nicholas, which took place at 19, Carpenter Road, Edgbaston, Birmingham, an address which has been redeveloped since, but was presumably a nursing home. The birth was not however registered until after the marriage of the child's parents, so that they were named on the certificate as man and wife. However, in an age when matters of this nature were treated with far more gravity than today, having a child outside matrimony was another unconventional step. Further, until the Legitimacy Act 1926 the subsequent marriage of the parents of an illegitimate child did not legitimate the child.

It is certainly plausible to conclude that Travers' mother did not approve of the relationship, and that the pregnancy forced the couple to run off to Birmingham, where it would appear his Red Cross training took place. There is no record of any design work being carried out in 1917, save possibly for one window in St. James, Riddlesdown, Purley.

It would appear also that a rather cavalier attitude was taken to the necessity to give accurate information on registration. On the marriage certificate the groom's address is given as 272, Alcester Road, Moseley, Birmingham, and the bride's as 71, Callcott Road, Brondesbury, London. Gertrude Travers was not one of the named witnesses. By the time Nicholas' birth was registered both parents were said to have been living together at 272 Alcester Road, but the father's address at the date of birth is given as 71 Callcott Road! It is not a difficult conclusion to reach that in fact they were living together throughout at the Moseley address, a pleasant semi-detached Victorian house well out of the City. It seems that the Brondesbury address was in fact that of Christine's parents, and certainly it was the address of her younger brother when he was at the Slade at that time.

The other unconventional feature of the marriage, seen from the perspective of 1917, was that Christine had already been married and divorced, and indeed a considerable air of scandal and mystery surrounded her. This of course makes it the more unlikely that a conventional clergyman of the age, such as Stevens' autobiography shows him to be, would have had any part in their marriage ceremonies.

It is perhaps instructive at this point to look at the characters of the two parties to this marriage.

Martin Travers appears to have been a somewhat quiet, reserved man. Both the photographic evidence and contemporary recollection indicate that he was tall, and slim, with dark hair and steel rimmed glasses. He is said to have dressed more like a civil servant than an artist, but well. A self-portrait from the notebooks of the 1920s shows the very high forehead and swept back hair which were two of his characteristics.

Former clients recall that Travers became completely absorbed in what he was doing, and that eating meals was simply ignored when he was taken with a project. He was a perfectionist, constantly designing and redesigning work, regardless of deadlines to be met, which often led to increasingly frantic correspondence from the client. The most extreme example of this dilatoriness in completing work was the extraordinary saga of the First World War memorial window for New Zealand, which was just ready before the outbreak of the Second World War, and is discussed at some length in Chapter 8. In later years, especially after Christine's death in 1934, the word cynical is frequently applied to his attitude to his work. Lawrence Lee, who knew him as well as anyone since he was taught by him and then worked with him, says however that Travers disguised his deep sensitivity with outward cynicism and flippancy, which put off some students. However, once that was penetrated he was a rewarding man to know. He also made the point that Travers reacted adversely to pompous and superior art critics and museum experts, whom he described as 'sleep walkers'[8].

Francis Stephens, another of his students who got to know him well, says that money was not important to him (unlike Comper, who was certainly in his later years notoriously mercenary)[9]. It is often said that Travers under rather than overcharged if he was interested in the work in hand or was sorry for the parish in question. He was also regarded as an outstanding teacher, willing to go to any lengths to explain to his students. While he was generally patient by nature, he was capable of sharp correspondence when the need arose, and in particular when his ideas were not appreciated; there was an element of the autocrat beneath the gentlemanly veneer, and his comments were sometimes sardonic in tone. In 1924 he left a draft of a letter to a client who had asked him to enter into a competition for work, saying that he was too busy to do that, and that competitions were for men of leisure. That lies ill with the fact that on a number of occasions there survive designs by him for a particular project, but the work was in fact executed by another, which suggests that the client did chose from a selection of schemes; one in particular is the reredos at Ickham, Kent, which was actually carried out in 1924, the same year as that comment was made, by other architects whose design was preferred to that of Travers. A similar situation occurred in a number of other cases, such as a memorial chapel in Aldeburgh (1929), and the first entry in the gazetteer in Chapter 12, a lectern for St. Paul, Barking (1933).

There is extensive correspondence from 1939–40 in the Council for the Care of Churches over Travers' design for a screen for South Collingham Church, Nottinghamshire, when his frustration with his critics becomes clear, and an undated memorandum over the building of St. Cuthman, Whitehawk, Brighton, just before the Second World War ends with the caustic conclusion that the changes implemented by others had led to chaos. On the other hand, although generally quiet and serious, he was known to have a subtle sense of humour, which sometimes came out in his work. In his obituary notice in the Southwark Diocesan Gazette, which is anonymous but almost certainly contributed by his friend Canon T.P. Stevens, this trait was described as 'mediaeval'. When he designed the new daughter church of the Good Shepherd for the Papalist Rector of Carshalton, W. Robert Corbould, he played on the name of the incumbent by incorporating in one window a rook, and some bails which had been hit by a cricket ball.

It is also clear that Martin Travers had an ingenious mind, which delighted in neat solutions to problems of design. He was particularly fond of models to demonstrate what he intended to build, and pictures exist of the completed models of the Carshalton church and also of the Holy Redeemer, Streatham Vale. He exhibited a model of Emmanuel Church,

Model of Holy Redeemer Streatham

Leyton, at the Royal Academy Exhibition in 1934. On one occasion, the same obituarist recalled, a committee were not happy with the original design for a church, presumably either Carshalton or Streatham Vale, but were won over when Travers produced a working model with lights and a bell, both of which functioned. The committee forgot their earlier criticisms once they began playing with the miniature.

He is said not to have been interested in many of the conventional recreations of his time: he did not dance, play cards, enjoy music, hunt, shoot, or even fish. He did apparently collect souvenirs from his travels, and, perhaps rather surprisingly for a shy man, liked a drink in his local pub. Lawrence Lee, one of the few still alive who knew him well, says that he was a very private man, who rarely opened up and never talked about his family to employees.

Christine Travers seems to have been a far more demonstrative, if not theatrical, character; some might say unstable. Her brother Alfred/Michael wrote in *All for Hecuba: an Irish Theatrical Autobiography*, published in 1946[10], that she was:

> 'the sorceress of my childhood. Often she used to frighten me with bogy stories and displays of uncanny skill; and always I was under her spell.'

He later confirmed to Travers' grandson in conversation that he was actually frightened of her. *All for Hecuba* was of course written while Martin Travers was still alive, and a certain reticence may have been exercised in dealing with Christine, but in 1977 Mac Liammoir wrote an extraordinary book entitled *Enter a Goldfish, Memoirs of an Irish Actor, Young and Old*[11]. That is considerably less discreet, but on the other hand it is a source which must be approached with some caution. Christopher Fitz-Simon, the biographer of Mac Liammoir and his partner Hilton Edwards (*The Boys*, published 1994) refers to 'the cloudy half-world of pseudonyms and false trails' in *Enter a Goldfish*[12]. Martin Travers is referred to as 'Mervyn Treacy', which is not a difficult disguise to penetrate, but one difficulty with Mac Liammoir is that he had reinvented himself as Irish, whereas his family in fact came from Kensal Green; he cannot be accepted uncritically. He does say however, that Christine (Tina) was very musical, especially at the piano, and given to caustic criticism. When he was young she read him Shakespeare plays but he says[13]:

> Her considerable talent was lurid and tempestuous, her strength was sheer passion, her weakness sheer melodrama, and both of these qualities she

Christine Travers

carried with her all through her life. They made her at once a vivid yet limited personality, for although her imaginative insight was sensitive and powerful, her interpretation, whether she read aloud or acted some short scene in poetry or prose, was marred by over-emphasis, and her scorn for any form of what was merely pretty, or fanciful, or humorous, would have been fatal for her development in the theatre if she had chosen it for her profession.

He also describes her as having dense sombre hair, deep olive skin, and enormous eyes, which changed colour according to her mood.

The description does not suggest that she was an easy person with whom to live and her own family despaired of her, especially when she declared, again according to her brother[14]:

Have I ever in my life expressed a wish for a good husband? ... A bad one would amuse me a thousand times more. I think I've something of the lion-tamer in my make up.

Christine had always been interested in magic, and that together with a strong devotion to the Celtic Revival and Irish Nationalism, drew her into the Golden Dawn, a mystical quasi-religious order in which W.B. Yeats was prominent. The order involved progression in knowledge into the higher grades of the organisation.

However, Christine then became involved with the much more sinister Aleister Crowley, who had also been involved with the Golden Dawn and was also a supporter of Irish independence. By coincidence, Crowley had spent a short time at Tonbridge himself, but that was before Travers entered the school. He was a charlatan, who thrived on his reputation for immorality; he combined assertions as to his magical power with the consumption of copious quantities of what are now illegal drugs and the promotion of sexual freedom. In about 1911 Christine is said to have had run off with a man named Hawkins, but returned 10 days later announcing that he was a crashing bore and a married alcoholic. There is ample evidence to verify Mac Liammoir's next story, namely that she married a man called Wilson; this certainly occurred in 1913, as the records show. He says that she swept back in to the family and announced 'Here's the Bad Girl of the Family', having left Wilson, whom she had met through Crowley. She then broke free of Crowley, had a nervous breakdown, and took up art; hence her meeting with Martin Travers, which is said to have occurred at the Slade. Her son however thought that part of her subsequent restlessness arose because she could not completely free herself from the demons of the past. Her parents cut her off, and she seems to have had little to do with the rest of her family. One of her sisters, Marjorie, married Andrew (Anew) McMaster, another well-known Irish actor and impresario.

There is no doubt that initially Christine and Martin Travers were happy together. Mac Liammoir says that when he saw Christine shortly after Sally's birth, she had taken on the role of a devoted wife and mother[15],

> and the only detail to suggest that the eternal Tina had not succumbed forever to a decent sense of British decorum was that her slim ankles were bare but for the golden bangle on each one, and that her feet were clad in golden sandals which had nothing to do with the rest of her conventional toilette.

He records her as saying, in complete contrast to her earlier pronouncements: 'There's nothing more lovely than a plain gold wedding ring and all that it means'[16]. Martin Travers' reaction to this was to stroke her hair affectionately.

During the early years of their marriage, the couple were somewhat itinerant. They moved in about 1918 to 46, Cambridge Road, King's Heath,

Birmingham, a Gothic villa in a pleasant side street just round the corner from their Moseley address, and then to 'Wyvenhoe' (sic) at Rotherfield, Sussex. In 1918–9 they were in Spain for a long visit, probably near Madrid, but from early 1919 onwards a steady stream of new designs issued from Travers' new workshop in the Glass Works at Fulham (see Chapter 3). Sally was born at a nursing home in Paddington, at which time her parents were living at 35, Earls Court Gardens. There is a draft letter dated 6th May 1920 in Travers' notebooks indicating a desire to exchange the lease on the Rotherfield property for a sub-tenancy in Earls Court Gardens.

Design for centre light at St. Augustin, Tynemouth, exhibited at Paris, from an advertisement in the Report of the Anglo-Catholic Priests' Convention, 1921

About 1921 the family moved to a pleasant and substantial end of terrace house at 48, Upper Mall, Hammersmith, which looks out on the river, and stayed there until at least 1924. The house bears a 'blue plaque' to the artist Eric Ravilious, who lived there 1931–5, but no reference to Travers' occupation of it. However in 1922 Christine took the two children to Diano Marina, Italy, for a long period, which awoke in Nicholas an intense lifetime admiration for that country.

In 1924 Nicholas had double pneumonia and nearly died. At one point all hope was abandoned for him, and it was decided to baptise him; his mother wanted him baptised into the Roman Catholic Church, which she must have joined at some point, perhaps as a result of her Irish sympathies, and his father wanted him baptised as an Anglican. The child's condition became so worrying that they put aside their religious differences and the local Roman priest baptised him in the house using water from a teacup. Martin Travers' son later recalled his father as having no time for the Roman clergy and a real fear of children being corrupted by them, which again lies odd with his work for those who wanted the Church of England to become ever more ultramontane.

By 1925 the family had moved to 25, St. Peter's Square, Hammersmith, very near to Upper Mall. Both these were very pleasant houses and at that time the Travers were reasonably well off, with two live-in servants and a car each.

The marriage however became somewhat stormy, not least because Christine had a number of lovers. Nicholas Travers' first memory was of howling in his cot while his parents threw china at each other. In fact it appears that they spent increasingly little time together once the children were no longer babies. It is said that as time went by Christine ridiculed her husband and put him down at every opportunity.

Despite these problems however the couple were fairly well known in social and literary circles. They frequented some fairly 'fast' establishments, such as Mrs. Meyrick's club, and had many friends from the stage and artistic life. They moved out from London at some point in the 1920s and lived at Bridge Close, Marlow, Buckinghamshire, where Nicholas could recall the visitors as including Dorothy L. Sayers, the writer and novelist, A.P. Herbert, the humorist and crusading independent M.P., J.C. Squire, the editor of Punch, and G.B. Stern, the writer, whom Christine had met in Italy. The Marlow house, which still exists, is in a very pleasant location on the riverbank and is a moderately large detached property, which was then quite new.

Travers was an astonishingly versatile designer and artist from the beginning of his professional life, and from 1911 onwards he frequently exhibited designs and models at the Royal Academy. In addition, the surviving records show that he was able to design vestments, and material for covering antique furniture, as well as graphic design and illustrations and monuments. His output in secular architecture was very small, although it appears that he had a few commissions for glass in private homes, none of which seems to survive. He designed at least one vicarage that was built (Emmanuel, Leyton), and probably a small number of houses.

1925 was however to be a particularly memorable year for Martin Travers. He was a busy and fashionable designer of church furnishings, especially to those churches which were leading what appeared to be an irresistible advance by the Catholic-minded wing of the Church of England: see Chapter 3.

In that year also Travers was awarded the Grand Prix for stained glass at the International Exhibition of Modern Decorative and Industrial Arts in Paris. It is somewhat unexpected to find that, although every short biographical reference which refers to Travers mentions this prize, there was so little mention of it in the artistic press at that time; perhaps the importance of the prize has been exaggerated retrospectively. However, his entry, which was the centre light from St. Augustin, Tynemouth, and was entitled Mater Dolorosa, was depicted in the Government Report on the Exhibition, dated 1927; this report indicates fairly strongly that the British showing in general was not as strong as it should have been[17].

The Paris Exhibition was an event of great significance: the purpose was to show work of a modern, as opposed to derivative or copied, style, and it was an enormous undertaking, covering about 70 acres, with many pavilions representing the work of different countries. The Exhibition can now be seen in retrospect as the high point of the Art Deco style of furnishings: Travers was later to borrow ideas from that style for his ecclesiastical work[18].

Unfortunately the most detailed information about the event is difficult to garner at present, as the library of the Musée des Arts Decoratifs in Paris is closed for long term renovation. It is clear however that a number of those well known to Travers participated in the British Section, including Henry Wilson, by then President of the Art Workers' Guild, who designed the decoration of the ceiling and walls of the Pavilion.

It was also in 1925 that Travers was appointed as head of stained glass at the Royal College of Art, and was thus entitled to the honorary title of 'Professor'. This appointment was a consequence of the policy of the then principal, Rothenstein, to develop within the school the concept of the part-time tutor who was also a practising artist or designer. It revitalized the College; among a number of distinguished contemporary tutors was the sculptor Henry Moore, who taught at the College from 1925 to 1931. In Travers' own case, it meant that he had an enormous influence upon a generation of stained glass painters: see Chapter 11. It also of course ensured some security of income when commissions dried up.

Unfortunately in 1927 Christine Travers was diagnosed as suffering from tuberculosis, and that necessitated even more frequent stays in a warmer climate. It may be that during those trips Martin Travers carried out further observation of continental Baroque architecture, the forms of which he was adapting in the course of his practice. He had certainly been to Holland, Belgium, Italy and France before the First World War, and then he went to Italy and France again and also to Spain in the decade after the War. There appears to be no note of trips to Austria or Germany, but the records are incomplete.

In 1929 it was suggested by Martin Travers' uncle Ernest that for the sake of her health Christine should live in Kenya for a couple of years with some distant relations of her husband. She took the Grantully Castle from Tilbury with the two children, intending to travel out via the Cape. Travers had in fact designed some glass for churches in South Africa, but there is no evidence that he himself ever went there, and he certainly did not go on this trip.

The vessel had scarcely left harbour when Nicholas was diagnosed (wrongly) as having smallpox, which later turned out in fact to be chicken pox, and kept in isolation for the voyage. His mother used the time to make the acquaintance of a Boer farmer named Koos, and when the ship reached Durban she disembarked with the children and went to live with him on his farm in Swaziland for some time. Kenya was abandoned as a destination. Koos was then left behind, and Christine took the two children to Zululand and then to Transvaal and later Natal, with a trip to Rhodesia. They returned in 1931.

Ironically in the light of these shipboard activities, in 1932 Martin Travers designed a splendid window in St. Nicholas, Brockenhurst, Hampshire, in memory of G.K. Gandy, a captain on the Union Castle Line, showing the route taken by its ships to the Cape.

Christine is said to have spent her husband's money fairly prodigiously, but she also supported herself by becoming a ferocious card player. In later years her bosom companion was a lady known as 'Poker' Hartley, who adored her and followed her about. After Christine's death she ran a theatre in London.

It is not clear what effect this marital disharmony had on Martin Travers and in particular on his work. It may be that he withdrew somewhat into himself and so far as he could absorbed himself in his practice. The family was certainly becoming somewhat dysfunctional.

In 1933 and 1934 Martin Travers produced relatively little outside work. This may have been a consequence of the Great Depression, or a result of his wife's illness, or caused by both of these.

Christine Travers died at Marlow on 16th September 1934 at the early age of 43. Her children were then respectively 17 and 14. The death certificate indicates that Martin Travers was present at the death, but Nicholas recalled that he was not there and she was with 'Poker' Hartley, who had nursed her. The death certificate indicates that the causes were cardiac failure and pneumonia, and since neither post-mortem nor inquest was required, the death cannot have been unexpected.

In *All for Hecuba* her brother says that he was aware of her death through telepathy, although he had not seen her for 10 years[19]. In *Enter a Goldfish* he says that Christine's death was an indirect consequence of a monkey bite she received in South Africa, and that it had been foretold by Crowley when she left his cult. He goes on to say that Crowley's followers tried to remove her body from the cemetery, but were prevented by the police[20]. Perhaps both versions represent the least reliable part of Micheal Mac Liammoir's reminiscences.

In 1926 Martin Travers had moved his studio from the Glass Works to 8, St. Paul's Studios, Hammersmith, which was later renumbered 48, Colet Gardens. The terrace in which that address stands was named after the adjoining St. Paul's School premises and backs on to the Underground near to Baron's Court station. The studios had been built at the end of the nineteenth century specifically for artists, with high projecting windows to let in light. The premises which he used are at the western end of the terrace, and both end studios are different in design to those in the centre. At that time the area looked very different from today: Colet Gardens is now cut off at the south end by the approach road to the Hammersmith fly-over, and the studios, instead of being in a quiet residential backwater, have been renumbered again as part of the extended Talgarth Road.

Martin Travers left the Marlow property very soon after Christine's death, and at some point thereafter moved into 51, Colet Gardens, in the centre of the terrace; eventually that was used mainly as the stained glass studio, with living accommodation below, and 48 was used for carving and other work. Correspondence in later years came from 51. His son recalled the living areas, which were in the basement, as dark, dusty, and dreary. Lawrence Lee recalls that there was a very clear division between the living and working accommodation, and those who were employed were scarcely ever invited into the other part of the property.

It appears that Travers was not without female consolation during the years between 1934 and the Second World War, in the form of a lady called Eva Yeats, who was not popular with Nicholas, but his future daughter-in-law, who met him first in the late 1930s, thought him a lonely man, although she liked him immediately, and he was kind to her.

It is also clear that from 1935 onwards Travers' practice revived itself: see Chapter 7. However, the work which originated from the ultramontane wing of the Church had largely disappeared, and his clientele were more widely based within the spectrum of churchmanship.

It cannot have been at all easy either for Martin Travers or his children to cope in the situation in which they found themselves after 1934.

Nicholas was in a particularly difficult position, as when he came back from Africa he had had very little formal education, spoke Italian almost as well as English, and had not worn shoes for two years. This last state of affairs had an interesting consequence as his father thought that this had resulted in his son having feet of perfect shape, and thereafter used them as a model for his designs of the Christ figure on the Cross. He also ensured that after Christine's death Nicholas was confirmed in the Church of England, so even if he was an agnostic by that time, Travers was clearly an Anglican agnostic.

On his return home, Nicholas was sent to a 'crammer' in Cricklade, Wiltshire, another place where his father carried out commissions. In 1932 he went on to Baddingham College, a Dickensian establishment which specialised in late starters. There he discovered the delights of education, passed matriculation and went on in 1934 to the Royal College of Science to study entomology. In 1935 he was persuaded by his father, who wanted him to follow in his footsteps, to enrol at the LCC School of Building in Brixton to learn architecture; interestingly Travers' old mentor Beresford Pite had been architectural director of this School from 1905 to 1928. This was an odd step on which to insist for a man who had rebelled against his own background, but Nicholas himself was showing a rebellious streak: while at Baddingham he had joined Oswald Mosley's Blackshirts, which was not an enthusiasm welcomed by his father. They fell out, and eventually Nicholas literally ran away from home and from the School of Building to go to sea, starting as a stoker. After a year, he was selected by the Naval Authorities for training for a commission – an extremely rare decision at that time in the case of a man on the lower deck. However, his father bluntly refused to sponsor him, telling the Navy in terms that if they wanted him they should pay for him themselves. It was left to another relative (an Admiral's widow) to assist, but Nicholas was desperately short of money during his training, and had to save to pay for his own uniform. This episode does not reflect well on his father, and seems out of character, although it appears that he had began to put down Nicholas constantly in the same way that Christine had put him down. It is ironic to note in the light of his attitude towards the naval training that during the war Travers designed a wooden plaque for H.M.S. Chesterfield, commemorating the raising of funds for the vessel by the people of Tonbridge.

Nicholas reverted to the family's older traditions, subsequently being awarded the DSC as a submariner, and rising to the rank of Lt. Commander in the Navy. In due course there was a something of a rapprochement between father and son, and when Nicholas became engaged in 1939 Martin Travers wrote a delightful letter to his fiancée:

> I very much want to give you something as a suplement (sic) to Nick's ring, so I hope this little trinket will be to your liking and that it will suit you, although of course the lily needs no gilding.

The trinket was a family heirloom – a brooch with hand mounted diamonds. He travelled down to Devon to present the couple with this, and took them out to dinner, toasting them in his favourite wine, Lacrima Christi. Later, there is a relaxed photograph of Martin Travers in about 1944 in the garden of Nicholas' wife's parents in Plymouth, holding his first grandchild.

Another of Micheal Mac Liammoir's doubtful stories is that immediately after his sister's death he was approached by 'a wild young man who had been under the spell of ... Christine' with a message from the dead woman that she wanted Sally, whom he had not seen for 10 years, to go to him in Ireland[21]. Whether or not that recollection is accurate, certainly by

Martin Travers aged about 60 with his first grandchild, Julia, in Plymouth, c 1946

1938 Sally had gone to Ireland and joined her uncle's company. She elected to stay in Ireland when the war began, although worried about her father in London. It appears that again there was a rift between them for a time, because on 7th June 1941 Travers wrote to his friend John Betjeman, who was then acting as Press Attaché to the British Ambassador in Dublin, a rather plaintive letter: 'It would be nice if you could get in touch with my daughter, who I have not seen for two years. You could then, if so minded, write and tell me what sort of creature she has developed into'[22]. Travers cannot of course have known that earlier that year Betjeman had written to his friends John and Myfanwy Piper: 'Martin Travers' daughter Sally who acts here with a repertory company is pro-German and sleeps with my opposite number [a man called Karl Peterson]. He is so unpopular here except among politically minded tarts and stockbroking and lawyer place-hunters that he does his cause more harm than good'[23].

The letter which Travers wrote to Betjeman is an odd one for a father to write about his daughter, but Sally and he were frequently at odds. She did not have a good word for her father. Indeed, because of her physical dissimilarity both to her father and her brother, and because of her mother's promiscuity, there were even mutterings in the family that Martin Travers was not actually her father.

Travers did indeed stay in London during the 1939–45 war; in fact, although too old to join up, he was Civil Defence Warden for Hammersmith 1942–5. Despite the war, commissions from churches continued, including some for memorial windows which were required even before the cessation of hostilities. In 1940 the Royal College of Art was evacuated to Ambleside; Travers did not ever move there, but resumed his teaching duties when the College returned in 1945.

On 15th July 1946 Martin Travers remarried. He was then 60 years of age; his bride, Mollie Greenwood (née Jones) was 35 and herself widowed. She had been acting as his housekeeper, and her late husband had been a great friend of her new husband. On this occasion, the ceremony certainly took place in church; the officiant was the now Canon T.P. Stevens, who may or may not have assisted with the first marriage. Stevens was by then an old friend of the bridegroom and had been connected with him for many years; he had been a curate at St. Michael Bedford Park when Travers lived at 3, Priory Gardens and carried out work at that church during the First World War. The bride's residence on the marriage certificate is given as 57, Colet Gardens, but the bridegroom appears to have established an address of convenience for the purposes of the ceremony. He was said to be living at 100, Augustus Road, Wimbledon Park, within the parish of Canon Stevens' church of St. Paul. There was obviously a very substantial age difference between the two parties to the marriage, and Lawrence Lee thought that the new Mrs. Travers was not unduly sympathetic to her husband's work.

At the time of his remarriage Martin Travers was well known and respected both as a practitioner and as a teacher. However, the prestige which comes from 'establishment' commissions had largely eluded him up to that date. The last two years of his working life were however marked by a number of more prestigious projects, such as altar furniture for St. Helier Church, Jersey, on the gift of the then Queen, and an altar cross for the Temple Church, and an uncompleted refurbishment for Gibraltar Cathedral: see Chapters 7 and 8. The work which could have culminated his career, a magnificent new east window for the lady chapel at Ely Cathedral, was rejected by the Dean and Chapter in 1946 on the grounds of cost.

Martin Travers died suddenly of a heart attack in the night of 25th July 1948. He was only 62, but had been under considerable strain over the years since the end of the War, with a greatly increased workload. Lawrence Lee looks back and with hindsight remembered thinking that the effort Travers required to turn the starting handle on his Ford Popular, which always refused to fire first time, might affect his heart in due course.

Francis Stephens recorded that when he arrived at the studio on the following morning (a Monday) he was met by a white-faced Alf Noe, Travers' long-time assistant with special responsibility for decoration and gilding. Mollie Travers was obviously distressed, but on the other hand was disconcertingly delighted at being allowed into the studio, from which she was normally excluded. It is clear that Travers himself had had no premonition of the heart attack: he had been designing work the week before his death and indeed his last design, for glass for SS. Peter and Paul, Temple Ewell, Kent was dated 20th July 1948. The design was carried into effect after his death and the glass installed in 1950.

Travers had been involved for some years in a comprehensive refurbishment of the church of St. Edward, Corfe Castle, Dorset, in the course of which he had had many dealings with local antiquary Dr. G. Dru Drury. With some poignancy, he wrote to him on 22nd July 1948 indicating that he and his wife would be on holiday in the area for a fortnight starting on 10th August, a holiday he was of course never to take.

On 26th July 1948 a notice of the death appeared in *The Times*, rather pointedly stating that the deceased was the 'beloved husband of Mollie' without mentioning his children. The address was corrected the next day and the funeral announced for 2.30 p.m. on 28th July 1948, at Godmanchester Parish Church. Later there was a memorial service.

It was fitting that the funeral should be at Godmanchester, as not only had Travers been baptised there, he had also designed some distinguished furnishings for the side chapel in 1937. Within the rails designed by him, and very close to the altar, is a floor plaque to his memory, which indicates that he is buried within the churchyard; there appears however to be no separate gravestone.

There was a short obituary in *The Times* for 4th August 1948 by Maj.-Gen. R.J. Blackham, Clerk of the Worshipful Company of Glaziers and Painters of Glass. He referred to the outlines of Travers' career and to his being a Fellow of the British Society of Master Glass Painters as well as a Freeman of the Skinners' Company and a liveryman of his own Company, for whom he acted as a judge for scholarship competitions. He described him as a 'charming personality'. Travers had in fact only recently become a liveryman of the Worshipful Company, and was indeed one of the few in his sphere who was involved both in that and in the British Society of Master Glass Painters. There was a further obituary in The Times for 30th August 1948 by Martin Buckmaster, who had been a friend of the deceased since school days, and the notes already quoted in the Southwark Diocesan Gazette, in which the author refers to Travers' intense dislike of 'weak kneed young men and weak chinned young women.' There was also a short obituary in *The Builder*.

John Betjeman wrote in notes preserved in the Council for the Care of Churches that Travers was 'a most charming and inspiring companion and a man of infinite kindness … He was quietly amusing and a good friend.' Betjeman of course used Travers' name in his poem *Anglo-Catholic Congresses*.

Martin Travers died intestate and Hunnybun & Sykes (as they then were), the family solicitors, wrote round to that effect on 12th August 1948 and then acted in the administration of the estate. Letters of administration were granted to his widow Mollie and daughter Sally, and the estate was sworn at £11500 odd. It is not clear whether he had ever made a will, or whether an earlier will had been revoked by his remarriage. His characteristic dilatoriness may have been reflected in his attitude to this matter also. One consequence of the intestacy was that his son was disinherited, as he was born before his parents' marriage and therefore was not at that time treated as his child for the purposes of inheritance.

The conclusion of work in hand and execution of work designed by and in the style of Martin Travers is dealt with in Chapter 7. However, there was a large mountain of letters, many of which had lain unanswered for months, to be dealt with, and Lawrence Lee and Mollie Travers were occupied with sorting these out for about twelve months.

Mollie Travers, twice widowed before she was 40, remarried again shortly after Martin Travers' death, and, under her new name of Mrs. Stonor, presented an assortment of his notebooks, drawings and photographs to the predecessor of the Council for the Care of Churches, who in turn deposited them on permanent loan to the RIBA. The drawings have been catalogued, but the notebooks do not appear to have been read for many years, and the photographs are largely unsorted.

Nicholas Travers had married Jeanne Victoria Stevens in 1942. When he retired from the Navy, he went to live in Canada, where he died in 1997, although after his retirement from the Royal Navy he became bored and joined the Merchant Marine for a further six years; his widow, one of the few people who remembers Martin Travers personally, still lives there. Nick Travers had three children, all of whom survive him: Julia Candlish, Michael Travers, and Christine (Tina) Bonkowski.

Michael Travers is himself an artist, living in Ireland, and has two children: his son, another Martin Travers, is a muralist living in California. Tina, the youngest granddaughter of the subject of this book, lives on Vancouver Island, and for many years practised as a stained glass artist herself.

Sally Travers became an accomplished actress in the Gate Company of her uncle Micheal Mac Liammoir in Dublin. She married author Alan Sharpe in 1962, but had no children, and died young on 7th May 1986. Micheal Mac Liammoir remained very attached to Sally throughout her life: he left his estate to his partner Hilton Edwards, and he in turn left half his estate to Sally Travers.

It can be seen that the artistic side of the family has reappeared in Travers' grandchildren and great-grandchildren and his family has been most helpful in the preparation of this book.

Chapter 2

Travers' Work in Context:

THE BACK TO BAROQUE MOVEMENT IN THE CHURCH OF ENGLAND

The term 'Back to Baroque' appears to have been first used by the late Peter Anson, for a chapter heading in his seminal book *Fashions in Church Furnishings 1840–1940*[1]. He meant by it that movement among some within the Catholic wing of the Church of England to reject Gothic, and even more so modern, art and design in favour of continental Baroque forms; it is a movement with which Martin Travers' name is always connected. The aim was to make the Church of England less English and more like the Roman Catholic Church as it appeared to the traveller in Europe. This tendency ran its course for about 30 years from 1910, and had a profound influence on Travers' work.

It is instructive to remember that by the early years of the Twentieth Century the Catholic Movement in the Church of England had already been in existence for some 70 years. It had made very considerable progress during that period in terms of raising the standards of the priesthood and restoring dignity to the services of the church, but with a few exceptions the ceremonial used was still fairly simple. Those priests who were prosecuted under the Public Worship Regulation Act 1874 were in fact carrying out their services with less ceremonial than could be seen in many moderate churches one hundred years later.

As the new century began however, the pressure within the Catholic-minded groups for increasingly elaborate ceremonial grew, as did the opposition from those who wished to preserve what they saw as the Protestant nature of the Church of England. The Royal Commission on Ecclesiastical Discipline, which reported in 1906, concluded that the law of public worship was too narrow for the religious life of the day and that the machinery of discipline had broken down. In the light of those conclusions, the Bishops took 21 years to formulate a Revised Prayer Book, only to find it

'I am the living bread' from People's Mass Book, 1921

rejected by a House of Commons swayed by anti-Catholic prejudices, and they failed to bring about any effective reform of the internal disciplinary procedures of the Church of England.

The result was a power vacuum, within which those who wished to do so could press forward with practices which went far beyond those which the Church would officially allow. This was particularly the case in the Diocese of London, under the long and benign episcopate of Bishop A.F. Winnington-Ingram (1901–39); he was a moderate Anglo-Catholic himself by inclination, and adopted a lax attitude to discipline, which contrasted strongly with that of some other bishops of the time. The Diocese of Southwark for example was far more efficiently 'policed' between the Wars than was that of London north of the river.

The advances in ceremonial at the end of the nineteenth and beginning of the twentieth centuries were not co-ordinated and certainly were not all in the same direction. On the one hand, one group favoured the so-called Western Use; in practice this meant a close copy of contemporary liturgical practice in the Roman Catholic Church. The various local customs which had grown up, with priests, choir and servers wearing whatever took the incumbent's fancy, began to be replaced by what was originally called the 'Plymouth School', after the system introduced at All Saints, Plymouth by Father C.R. Chase in the years following his arrival as vicar there in 1878. It was said that there were more services in his church than in any other in the Anglican Communion, and perpetual reservation of the Blessed Sacrament was introduced at least by 1882. The influence of the Plymouth School continued after Father Chase's resignation through ill health in 1898 and his subsequent secession to Rome in 1900. He had been Master of the Society of the Holy Cross, usually called SSC, its initials in Latin, between 1889 and 1891 and again from 1895 to 1897 and this increased the influence of the proponents of the Western Use.

The opposing group – and the conflict between the two groups was often fierce – were those who looked back to the Prayer Book of 1549. This was the English or Sarum Use, whose advocates argued that the ceremonial which they used was not only legal, but required.

As is often the case however, ritual differences reflected deep-seated differences towards the nature of the Church. The proponents of the Western Use took the view that the Church of England was a part of the Latin Church, which had unfortunately been separated from full communion with Rome by local political differences in the Sixteenth Century.

The proponents of the English Use took the view that the Church of England was a branch of the Catholic Church with its own local ritual which owed nothing to the Counter-Reformation or developments since.

As time went by, there appeared also a division within the Western School. Some took the view that the Church of England was the only true representative of the Catholic Church in this country, well reflected by the statement[2] by Father Embry, historian of the Society of the Holy Cross, that:

> the attempt to establish a hierarchy in opposition to the lawful occupants of the ancient sees must be a schismatic one, and ... the Roman Catholic bishops in England and the priests under them must be in the position of schismatics.

Others, the true Papalist party within the Church of England, took the view that the Catholic Church in England had bifurcated at the Reformation, and that both the Church of England and the Roman Catholic Church were parts of the Church; there could therefore be no question of regarding the Roman Church in England as an 'Italian Mission.' That view took account of the recusants and in particular the English Martyrs, who tended to be ignored by the protagonists of the theory that the Church of England was the only true branch of the Catholic Church in this country.

It is also of importance in considering the impact of the Back to Baroque Movement to remember that, until it commenced, the Catholic Movement in the Church of England identified itself almost exclusively with the Gothic style in architecture. There were very few exceptions to that generality, one being John Dando Sedding's Holy Redeemer, Clerkenwell.

It is instructive to bear in mind that in the first decade of the Twentieth Century, the brightest star in the sky of advanced Anglo-Catholicism was the Community on Caldey Island. Abbot Aelred Carlyle had the most grandiose ideas for the Monastery on the island, but the chapel was furnished in the Gothic taste. When, in 1924, the successors to that part of the Community which had not seceded to Rome came to decorate their new property at Nashdom, Buckinghamshire, there was no question but that the décor should be Baroque, and this resulted in another commission for Travers. That was the extent of the change of taste brought about by the Movement. After Ronald Knox went over, he wrote that[3]:

> [Roman] Catholics will not easily realize the extent to which in the Church of England the mediaevalist movement has been captured and exploited by a comparative moderate party. Broadly speaking, 'Gothic' and 'Renaissance' accessories symbolize a difference not of taste, but of view; the 'Gothic' belongs to the 'loyal' Churchman who takes his stand on the practice of the early Church and fulminates against 'Roman' innovations.

SSPP monogram

The Society of SS. Peter and Paul was an attempt to disseminate within the Church of England continental devotions and to change taste in favour of the furnishings of the Counter Reformation. The two moving spirits behind the Society, Samuel Gurney and Father Maurice Child, each individually became important patrons of Travers, and the Society collectively employed him as their house designer for literature and objets d'art.

It appears that the catalyst for the formation of the Society was a holiday in Bruges in the summer of 1910. Gurney had known Ronald Knox, son of the ultra-Protestant Bishop of Manchester, both at Eton and at Oxford. They went to Bruges together to study Belgian spirituality, and there they met Child. The effect of the religious life in Bruges was profound in the case of all three of them.

Samuel Gurney, like Travers, has a mention in John Betjeman's poem *Anglo-Catholic Congresses* ('and has Sam Gurney poped?'). He was the youngest son of a branch of a well known Norfolk banking family and indeed one of his brothers was the squire of Walsingham, and an opponent of Father Hope Patten's restoration of Marian devotion there. Gurney's mother remarried after his father's death and became Lady Talbot de Malahide; in 1935 he wrote a glutinous memoir of his mother, which appears to have been his only venture into print, although the SSPP published some of her addresses to the Mothers' Union of the Church of Ireland[4]. He was a director of the Medici Society but was able to use his substantial private resources to support the SSPP and other such ventures.

Maurice Child too either was, or appeared to his contemporaries to be, a man of means, and he always retained a flat in Eaton Square even when living out of town. In early editions of Crockford he is listed as having the additional or alternative christian names of Charles Francis Hugh Dominic, but he was always known as Maurice. Child was ordained deacon in 1909 and priest in 1910. He was curate of St. Andrew Haverstock Hill, Hampstead, 1909–12, although during that time he was a missioner at St. Silas, Kentish Town, then curate of St. James the Less, Plymouth, 1912–4, Holy Trinity Sloane Street, 1914–7, and St. Mary Bourne Street, 1917–23, before other posts which will be discussed later. Many of the supporters of the SSPP were connected with or served at St. Mary Bourne Street, a church important enough in Travers' work to deserve extended treatment later: see chapter 4. Father Ronald Knox on his ordination took the additional name of Hilary (which appears on a number of his books of that time), and said his first mass at Bourne Street on 12th September 1912.

Gurney provided the money for the SSPP, Child the aggressive marketing techniques and the sarcasm, and Knox, who became Chaplain of Trinity College, Oxford and Revd Norman (usually known as 'N.P.') Williams, a Fellow of Exeter College, Oxford, provided the intellectual ammunition. Other supporters were Father J.C. Howell, vicar of St. Mary Bourne Street from 1909 until his early death in 1916, his successor Father Humphrey Whitby, Father W.G.V.C. Baker, who was a curate with Child both at Haverstock Hill and in Plymouth but later seceded to Rome, Niall Campbell, Duke of Argyll, who devoted much of his life to the promotion of the Catholic faith in the Episcopal Church of Scotland, and Ronald Knox's brother Father Wilfred Knox.

The central premise of the SSPP was set out by N.P. Williams in a pamphlet entitled *Too Much Stiffness* in 1917[5], to the effect that the Catholic movement must be conceived of

> *not* as a return to the past, but as *a resumption of arrested development.* It is not an attempt to get back to where we were before the Reformation; *it is an attempt to get forward to where we should have been if the Reformation (in its more destructive aspects) had not happened.*

Maurice Child installed two neo-Baroque altars in St. Michael Plymouth (a daughter church of St. James the Less)[6] in about 1913 while he was in charge of it, and St. Michael Ladbroke Grove acquired a continental Baroque altar in the early years of the First World War, but in fact it was after the war that the impetus built up for altering the interiors of Anglo-Catholic churches, especially in London, to resemble what could be seen abroad. Travers was the perfect artist for this, as he had a fine eye for the detail of architectural styles and could adapt the details to present day (often cheap) materials. There was an element of stage dressing to the movement, and in later, more cynical, times Travers spoke of himself as an ecclesiastical stage dresser.

Indeed there was an element of trompe l'oeil about the whole of the SSPP attitude towards liturgy. There had before their influence began to be felt been a tendency to interpolate parts of the Roman Canon silently into the Anglican Communion service. The SSPP attempted to show that it was possible to use the whole of the 1662 Communion service, perhaps with some internal rearrangements, but make it look to the observer as though the Roman Mass was being said or sung by importing the externals of the Tridentine liturgy. One of the earliest SSPP manifestos *Decently and In Order*, which was issued reprinted from *Pax*, the magazine of the Caldey community, spoke of 'a way of saying mass which, so far as what is *heard* is concerned, simply is a perfectly straightforward Prayer Book rite, and so far as what is *seen* is concerned, is the customary living use of the Western Church.'

The Elevation of the Host from Christ's Chronicle

One of the great masters of this technique was Father Humphrey Whitby, who succeeded Father Cyril Howell at St. Mary Bourne Street in 1916, and who already knew Travers because the latter had designed the set of vestments for his first mass in 1911.

The SSPP appears to have been formed in 1910, but it announced itself to the outside world only with a meeting at the Medici Society on 24th February 1911, after which the Church Times carried an advertisement for altar and servers' cards. It initially operated from 7, Bruton Mews, Bond Street, which was in fact the back entrance of the Medici Society. It soon attracted adverse comment from the Church Times, but by September 1911 had opened premises of its own at 32, George Street, Hanover Square; later that was used only as offices and the shop premises were at 302, Regent Street, near All Saints, Margaret Street. Ironically their first publication was a copy of the Mass of 1549 for Lord Halifax, who used that liturgy in his private chapel at Hickleton. A veritable flood of publications followed, many designed to be provocative; there were advertisements, devised by Child, for Lambeth incense and Ridley and Latimer votive candle stands. The Society promoted 'fiddle back' vestments in the Roman style and short, lace trimmed cottas. In December 1912 they began calling themselves 'Catholic publishers to the Church of England' on some of their literature and later 'Publishers to the Church of England' was displayed above the shop window at the Regent Street premises. Some of their productions were regarded as too ecclesiastically risqué by more respectable publishers such as Mowbrays, who kept them 'under the counter' as if they were pornographic, but on the other hand even such venerable pillars of Catholic orthodoxy as Lord Halifax had a considerable regard for the SSPP; Halifax admired in particular Child's drive. It was partly because of the refusal of other booksellers to sell their products that the SSPP (or 'Porter and Peel' as some called it) had to run their own shop. That and the fact that they published a very large number of items made their financial state perpetually unstable.

Gurney was responsible for the design and type of publication, and used Seventeenth and Eighteenth Century illustrations with appropriate type faces; an elderly retired engraver named W.M.R. Quick was recruited for this purpose. In 1913 Ronald Knox published, under the title *Naboth's Vineyard in Pawn*, a series of sermons he had delivered at St. James the Less, Plymouth that summer. Maurice Child and Vincent Baker were both curates at the church, and Sam Gurney went down to the West Country in a huge Talbot car known as 'the Light Ford'. A publisher on West Hoe, near St. James the Less, was used for some of the early publications.

Things to know, 1915, in Practical Prayers series

It all seemed great fun, and Child in particular revelled in the conspiratorial side of it all; however that aspect alienated some of those who might otherwise have been potential customers. Knox then wrote his satires *Reunion All Round* and *Absolute and Abitofhell*, both of which were published by the SSPP, and followed these with *Some Loose Stones*, a serious refutation of *Foundations*, a book which was causing some considerable stir at the time.

Another aspect of the Society was the holding of an annual High Mass at St. Thomas, Regent Street, in Bourne Street style, that is the Book of Common Prayer to Roman rubrics. Latin vestments and long lace albs were de rigeur for the priests; Sir Hubert Miller, squire of Froyle, Hampshire, sang the Ten Commandments from the west gallery and Samuel Gurney fasted from the night before in order to be the sole communicant required by the Prayer Book. The later Canon Frederic Hood was a torchbearer at one of these Masses, before his ordination.

It seems clear that Travers began illustrating SSPP publications from the very start, and he also designed emblems for the Society. He certainly designed the first mass card for Father Whitby, which bears the SSPP name, and which is dated 12th June 1911 (See Plate 2).

The catalogue of 1914 advertises an almanack for 1915 designed by him. The next year's catalogue and prospectus features the 'Martin Travers series' of Christmas cards, the Canterbury almanack 'with fine design by Martin Travers' and a sailor's mortuary card, also designed by him. It was said that the People's Mass Book was available and 'the pictures have been drawn by MARTIN TRAVERS, whose work for the SSPP is now so well known.' The 1916 report carried many advertisements for works with Travers' drawings and also included one for votive candlestands and candlesticks for paschal candles, to a 'new design by Martin Travers'; in addition, it illustrated his windows for St. Clement Barnsbury and St. Mary Hoxton. (See Chapter 3.)

Also in 1916 the SSPP published Volume II of Pictures of the English Liturgy, dealing with Low Mass. This and the accompanying Volume I on High Mass, which was often promised but in fact did not appear until 1922, are one of Travers' finest monuments in graphic design and are

Pictures of the English Liturgy, Low Mass: 'The Lord be with you'

further discussed in Chapter 10. The long gap was no doubt caused partly by his usual dilatoriness, and partly by the disruption of his Red Cross service. The books are found in various different formats, sometimes together and sometimes apart and with subtle variations on Volume I called Pictures of the American or Roman Liturgy. They were also available as loose unbound sheets. It is also somewhat confusing that Volume II appeared such a long time before Volume I.

Volume II carried an introduction headed *The Lost Opportunity*, a play on an earlier piece of propaganda from the Sarum side; the 'Westerners' decried the English use as 'British Museum Religion', and this introduction said that the Sarum Use 'barely survives'. They were correct about that, albeit that in the long run the English Use had a very considerable indirect influence on the wider Church of England.

In 1921 the SSPP published its *Anglican Missal*, which perhaps surprisingly, was not illustrated by Travers, but had many engravings by Quick.

By 1922 the SSPP lists were full of works illustrated by Travers, including the Martin Travers calendar, and also carried advertisements for 'WINDOWS, TABLETS, CALVARIES, AND WAR MEMORIALS designed and erected by Mr. Martin Travers'.

The affairs of the SSPP became somewhat labyrinthine after 1919, when a private company, the Society of SS. Peter & Paul Ltd., was incorporated, with Gurney holding most of the shares. A note to the 1923 lists indicates that the Society as such did not trade, but simply disseminated literature: the Company dealt with all trading and publishing and did not control the Society.

In about 1924 there was a move to Abbey House, Westminster, and a new catalogue was issued which made it clear that the company had been reconstructed with Kenneth Ingram, a well known religious writer, as managing director, and that the Society, but not the company, had been amalgamated with the Catholic Literature Association under the title of 'Catholic Literature Association of the Anglo-Catholic Congress'. The secretary of this Association was Miss Muriel Cazenove, daughter of a churchwarden at Holy Trinity Sloane Street; Maurice Child, when a curate at that church, had introduced her to N.P. Williams, who subsequently abandoned his advocacy of priestly celibacy and married her.

In fact the work of the SSPP was largely amalgamated within the Anglo-Catholic Congress by this time, and on 31st December 1929 the Company was wound up; the Congress issued a statement to the effect that the liquidation was voluntary, all creditors had been paid in full, and no

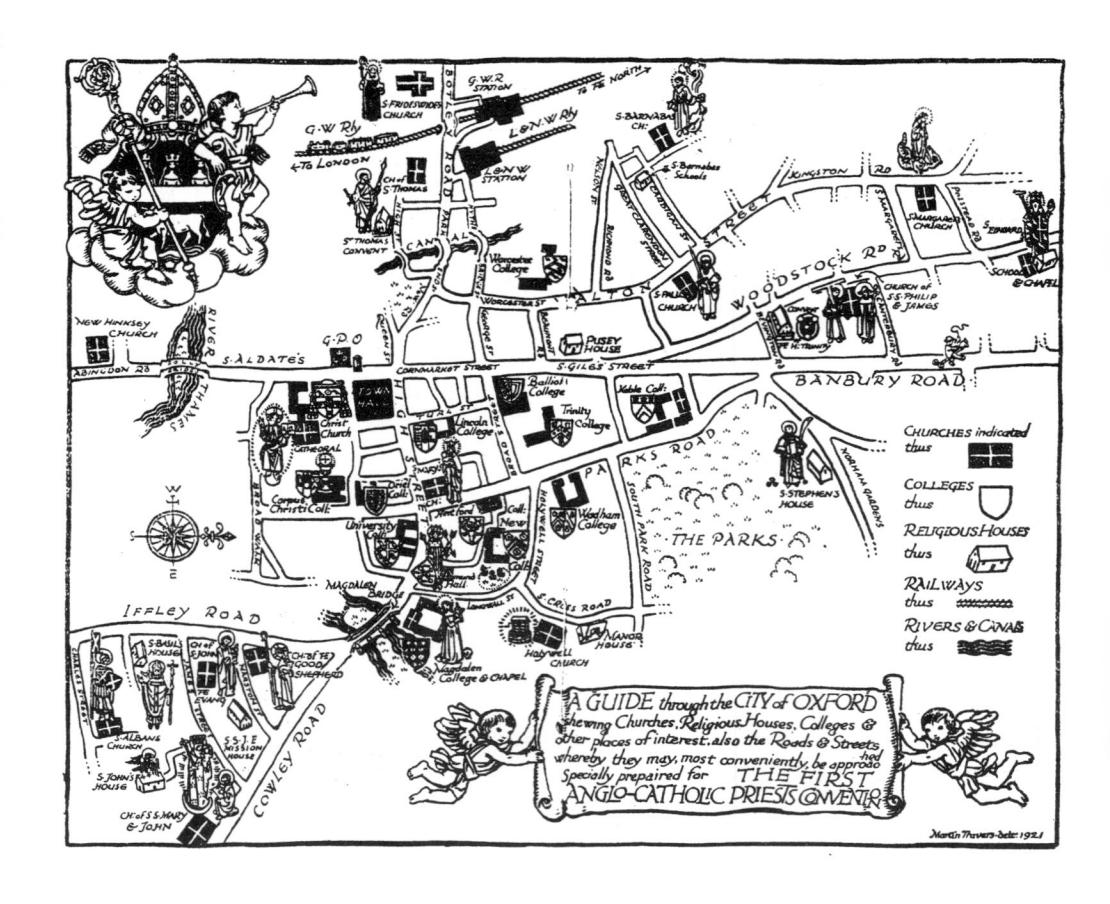

Catholic Oxford (from 1921 Anglo-Catholic Priests' Convention Handbook)

ACC funds had been used to support the company. The name was perpetuated in a trust set up by Father Whitby in 1940, the Society of St. Peter and St. Paul Charitable Trust, which has published work from time to time, particularly the Anglican Missal; it also assisted during one period with the publication of works for the Church Union. Most appropriately, it has sponsored the publication of this book.

The SSPP brought Martin Travers' work before a much wider audience than would otherwise have been the case. It also harmed him to the extent that it caused some people to believe, quite wrongly, that he was prepared only to work for those to whom the SSPP appealed, and it made him appear unreliable in the eyes of the establishment. It has also caused some to believe that he personally believed in the ideals of the Society: in fact, his use of the Baroque seems solely to have been as a response to those who required work in that style for their churches and publications, and did not result from any convictions of his own.

One particular feature of SSPP literature was the printing of reports and handbooks for the Anglo-Catholic Congresses, which were held in London and provincial cities between 1920 and 1933. The SPCK printed the report of the 1920 London Congress, but the SSPP prepared those for the 1921 Priests' Convention in Oxford and the 1923 and 1927 London Congresses. These volumes all have advertisements for Travers' work. The 1930 and 1933 Congress Reports were produced by the Catholic Literature Association, as was that for the 1932 Priests' Convention, the SSPP having by that time ceased to exist, as set out above. However, they continued to carry advertisements for books illustrated by Travers. A number of the reports have cover designs by Travers and these are discussed in Chapter 10.

The style of furnishing which emerged as a result of the Back to Baroque Movement is sometimes called 'Anglo-Catholic Congress Baroque.' It now appears as a period piece and Travers' name is closely linked to it; hence the reaction against his work followed closely on the reaction against excessive ceremonial which resulted from the Second Vatican Council. As time has passed, it is perhaps possible to look at the work more objectively.

The Anglo-Catholic Congress movement arose from a casual remark by Father Carrick Deakin, who was in due course to be a most important patron of Travers: see Chapter 4. Father Deakin was then the incumbent of Christ Church, South Hackney. From 1910 onwards a number of dining and discussion groups, each limited to 12 members, had arisen among the Anglo-Catholic clergy in the London area, the first being 'Friends in

MARTIN TRAVERS: AN APPRECIATION

Cover of report of 1921 Anglo–Catholic Priests' Convention

Council'. From time to time they all met to discuss a particular problem; in November 1916 at one such meeting Father Deakin suggested holding some kind of conference 'as the Protestants do at Islington'[7]. From that, the idea grew for a Congress, which initially was to be for priests only. However, an advertisement in the Church Times drew such an enthusiastic response from the laity that it was decided to throw the meetings open, and eventually the Albert Hall was not only booked but also filled. Further, the first Congress was so successful that it was decided to repeat the event, and in due course a permanent organization was set up, the Secretary of which after 1925 was none other than Maurice Child. There were also a large number of Congresses in various provincial centres.

It is salutary now to read of the enthusiasm which all observers saw at the Congresses, from the young in particular. One consequence of course was that literature was sold and ideas were exchanged. Consequently the ideals of the SSPP permeated further, and the years of the Congresses (1920–33) coincided with the tide of renovations away from Gothic and in favour of Baroque.

After the 1933 Oxford Movement Centenary Congress it was decided that there should be a gap of seven years, and indeed a youth group called the

Anglo-Catholic Congress 1927: triptych in the Albert Hall

Seven Years Association was started. Events of course overtook any thought of a 1940 Congress and by the last Congress, in 1948, there was less support.

It also appears that by 1933 the initial wave of enthusiasm for Baroque had run its course, and there were relatively few further renovations in that direction thereafter, although the work for Father Child himself at Cranford was a notable exception. It may also be that the whereas immediately after the First World War it was relatively easy to raise money for memorials and the like, which could then be carried out in accordance with the prevailing fashion, as time passed that became more difficult, and when the 1930s approached the economic situation became such that there was little surplus available for work which did not strictly need to be done.

The Congress Movement itself, apart from the indirect benefits brought to Martin Travers' practice, also resulted directly in some very important work. He was commissioned to design work for the Albert Hall for the 1923 and 1927 Congresses and the altar for the outdoor mass at Stamford Bridge Football Ground for the 1930 Congress. In 1927, he designed a gigantic triptych with the crucifixion in the central panel and lettering on each side, with huge lights in front of it. In 1930 the outdoor mass was celebrated at a long low altar with a tentlike canopy and six enormous candlesticks and matching crucifix. For the largest gathering of all, the 1933 Centenary Congress, for which 70,000 enrolled, he designed the outdoor altar and baldachino for the culminating mass, held at the White City Stadium, and also, in conjunction with Father Eric Cheetham, vicar of St. Stephen Gloucester Road and the landlord of T.S. Eliot, the décor for the Albert Hall, featuring a high altar with a reredos of green brocade within a gilded baroque frame including volutes at the sides. Travers and Father Cheetham were also responsible for the presentation of the impressive Pageant in the Hall. These were important and prestigious commissions to be given.

It was decided by the Anglo-Catholic Congress Committee in 1923 to have a year of continuous intercession in churches across the country, commencing on 1st January 1924, and that a Fiery Cross would be taken from church to church as part of this devotion. This appears to have been yet another successful idea by Father Child, who saw it as an alternative to the Devotion of the Forty Hours, but the rough sketch for the Cross was made by Father Cecil Russell.

Travers was chosen to transform the rough sketch into a finished design; the Cross was made of wood and featured gilded flames sprouting from a Sacred Heart at its base. On it was the inscription 'Sic enim Deus dilexit mundum.'

TRAVERS' WORK IN CONTEXT

High altar at White City Stadium for Anglo-Catholic Centenary Congress 1933

The Fiery Cross was taken to the Holy Land on pilgrimage in 1924, and then taken round from parish to parish with successive watches of 24 hours each being maintained in each church. This venture was so successful that it was extended for a second year, in 1925, and thereafter became a permanent feature of devotion. It appears indeed that at one time there may indeed have been several such crosses. A Fiery Cross Association was set up with Father Russell as secretary, and three circles of intercession were maintained, one by religious communities, one by between 600 and 700 parish churches, and the third by individuals. The proceeds of collections taken in connection with the

Fiery Cross at Whitstone, Cornwall

devotion were given to the Anglo-Catholic Ordination Candidates Fund.

At about the same time a magazine appeared styled *The Fiery Cross*, which was intended as an insert for parish papers, and this continued up to the end of the 1940s. Travers' illustrations often appeared in the magazine. For use with the intercessions the SSPP produced a book entitled *The Hour of the Fiery Cross*, which ran into a third impression, making 25000 copies in all. The illustration used at the beginning of each section would appear to be by Travers, but this cannot be authenticated, as there is no signature.

A photograph in the Green Quarterly Magazine, Volume 1 Number 2, April 1924, shows the Fiery Cross being received at St. Saviour Ealing, and a slightly modified picture of the Cross appeared on the cover of the 1933 Oxford Movement Centenary Congress Handbook.

Martin Travers died just after the 1948 Anglo-Catholic Congress, and Francis Stephens, who was himself involved with the décor for that event, put on a small exhibition of his work.

Travers was not of course the only designer of baroque style furnishings, but he was the best and also the best-known; it is perhaps to the long-term

Receiving the Fiery Cross at St. Saviour Ealing 1924

detriment of his reputation that excessive concentration on this part of his work has obscured his great talents as a stained glass painter.

It would be fair to say that by the end of the Second World War, the Back to Baroque Movement had run its course in the sense that although thereafter there were some churches where the particular incumbent wished to continue with the process of furnishing the church in accordance with Counter-Reformation principles, there was no concerted movement to that end. One example of a church which was refurnished after the Second World War to remove the Warham Guild influences and make it baroque in style is St. Augustine, Tonge Moor, Bolton, where a great deal of work was done after Travers' death by his former pupil Douglas Purnell.

The Back to Baroque Movement was part of a school of thought quite commonly found in the wider Anglo-Catholic Revival, which held that the Church of England, in order to prove its Catholicity, must possess the same attributes as the Roman Church. In particular, some seized on the revival of communities of men and women living the religious life, which took effect in the latter half of the nineteenth century, as showing that the Church of England was capable of the spiritual discipline which they admired in Rome. The revival of the Walsingham shrine under Father Hope Patten brought both these strands of thought together: the shrine proved Anglican devotion to Mary, but it also looked like a Continental place of pilgrimage, although in rural Norfolk. Walsingham was in many ways, as Anson remarked so presciently, the culmination of the Back to Baroque Movement[8]: it is unfortunate that Travers' work there is so limited, but equally it seems difficult to believe that there would not have been a clash of wills between Hope Patten and Travers, both strong minded men. The continued popularity of the Walsingham devotion perhaps belies the scorn which it is nowadays fashionable to bestow on the Congress Baroque style.

It is also of course the case that the furnishing of Anglo-Catholic churches before the Second World War was designed for a liturgical system in which the emphasis was on the sacrificial nature of the mass, with communion taking place only at early celebrations. One of the more revealing autobiographies of the time is that by Prebendary E.D. Merritt (*The Erratically Drafted Memoirs of Edmund Douglas Merritt*, 1951). In it he says of his time at All Souls, St. Margaret's on Thames, that by Easter 1917 'there were for the first time no communicants at the Sung Mass ... it was a great joy to me when the last of the mid-day communicants disappeared'[9]. This was a typical attitude of the time. Thus altars became more elaborate, and provision was made for adoration or benediction of the

Blessed Sacrament, usually with the strong disapproval of the bishop, because the fasting rules made evening communions impossible.

After the Second World War, the combination of the relaxation by Rome of the fasting rules and the onset of the Liturgical Movement, represented in its Anglican strand by the advocates of the Parish Communion, changed the entire focus of the mass from a sacrifice offered to a sharing between all the faithful, even before the revolutionary changes effected by the Second Vatican Council. These changes obviously necessitated different furnishings, and led in particular to the pulling out of many altars to allow the celebration from the westward position, and the dismantling of reredoses; many of Travers works which survived the Second World war bombing were mutilated after it.

Whether insights will again change so as to revert to previous liturgical practice remains of course to be seen. What is clear is that the new orthodoxy is thought by those who spread it to require the dismantling of many of the shrines which Travers and his contemporaries designed.

Anglo-Catholic Congress Logo

Chapter 3

Travers as Designer:

I THE EARLY YEARS 1909–1924

Martin Travers' early training has already been set out in Chapter 1. During the period discussed in this chapter, he worked initially from Albert Palace Mansions, Battersea, and then after the summer of 1909 from Bedford Park. He left there when he moved to Birmingham in 1917 for his Red Cross work, and in due course returned to London married.

When Travers returned to full time practice, which appears to have been in early 1919 or possibly late 1918, he rented a room at the Lowndes & Drury Glass House, 11, Lettice Street, Fulham, and he practised from there until about June 1926.

The Glass House was set up in 1897 by Mary Lowndes and Alfred Drury, who were promoters of the revival of stained glass as an art instead of an article of mass production. That revival owed a considerable amount to the support of John Dando Sedding, father of Travers' erstwhile partner. By the post-First World War period, the Glass House had a dual function: there were facilities for the firm to fire the glass for others, and in addition rooms on the floor above were let out to individual artists as studios, obviously in the expectation that they would use the facilities of the firm for their firing. There were obvious conveniences in that course, but in fact Travers continued to use the Glass House for firing even after he moved from their accommodation.

It is not always easy to date Travers' work accurately. In the case of plans held and catalogued by the RIBA, there is at least an initial date from which to work. In his notebooks is a hand-written list, which can be internally dated to 1923, in which he sets out his work to that date, which is of very great use in discovering whether work was ever carried out. Even that is not entirely accurate, in that he lists Petham, Kent, in the list, and he

The seven sacraments

must recently have designed work for that church, which was gutted by fire in 1922; however his work was not chosen.

In the case of some of his work, the plans have been lost; moreover, while his windows are sometimes dated, his other furnishings are neither signed nor dated. Further, much of his work has been altered or moved since it was executed, and of course the air raids of the Second World War and the ravages of fire have taken their toll. There was often a significant gap between the design and the work, caused either by Travers' habitual delays or by the need to obtain a faculty. Then many schemes were carried out only in part or in a different way from the design, and in some cases the reverse applies, namely that plans exist for part only of that which was carried out.

Unexecuted design of high altar for Petham, Kent, c 1924

The dates upon which work was carried out can in many cases therefore only be an informed guess. In this and the following chapters work is dealt with on a roughly chronological basis according to the plans, if their date is known, and there is extended discussion of certain important work in separate chapters.

This chapter therefore covers Travers' output up to the end of 1924. Obviously reference is not made in the main text to every piece of work with which he was concerned, but it is intended that the gazetteer (Chapter 12) cover every such project, together with notes and references, which are not therefore additionally attached to the chapters.

Martin Travers' first surviving designs as from independent practice are dated 11th June 1909. Shortly before then, there had been a fire in the old and rather small chapel of his old school, Tonbridge, and it was decided to build a much larger chapel at the rear of the main school buildings. Travers prepared an elaborate scheme for furnishing the sanctuary of the new chapel; above the east window hung a large rectangular canopy and on either side of the window were statues of St. Gregory and St. Augustine in Gothic niches. The walls were painted with much foliage and plants, amongst which were images of various saints. Behind the altar stood a large Gothic triptych with projecting tester, and in the centre panel was a painting of the Risen Christ, Our Lady, St. John, and various English saints. That part of the scheme was obviously influenced by Comper, but the altar candlesticks and crucifix and the two large standard candlesticks were in Baroque style. The scheme would have been extremely expensive for the school to undertake, and it is uncertain whether the drawings were even submitted for approval. The reredos which was in fact erected in 1928 to Travers' later design bore no resemblance to this earlier scheme and even then the School had difficulty raising the money for it. (See page 8, Chapter 1.)

A few days after the Tonbridge School design, Travers produced the first of a number of designs for altar frontals and vestments for All Saints Westlegate in Norwich. This church is still standing, although it was made redundant in about 1976, and is now a social centre. One of the frontals and a chasuble were taken for further use elsewhere, but the most important piece of his work in the church (for which there are no finished drawings, but sketches in his notebooks) was a beautiful Virgin and Child on crescent moon in the east window, surrounded by clear glass in the manner of Travers' later work, and said to have been executed in about 1910. Fortunately, this glass was removed in 1976 to the nearby, flourishing, church of St. John Timberhill, where an engraving beneath it sets out its history and provenance, and it joins a fine statue of Our Lady, also by Travers, from later years (See Plate 1).

During 1909, but just after his move to Bedford Park, Travers designed a rood screen, lectern and vestments for another Norwich Anglo-Catholic centre, St. Julian, King Street, which was damaged by enemy action in the Second World War and has since been rebuilt. The drawings show a priest with biretta in front of the screen, but the furnishings are not on Travers' hand written list and it does not appear they were ever carried out; there is no information about the vestments.

In 1911 Travers was involved with the design of Father Whitby's first mass set, which is dealt with in the chapter 4. At some time before the First World War, Travers designed a small hanging rood for the mortuary chapel at Father Whitby's then church of St. Columba, Haggerston. The rood has been restored and now hangs in the south aisle of St. Gabriel Pimlico. It is possible that at St. Columba he designed the fine wrought iron screen in the mortuary chapel (which had been consecrated only in 1906), and also a confessional for the main body of the church, which has now been taken over by Pentecostalists.

Before the First World War Travers was given the first two commissions for glass in Somerset, a county where his windows are well represented. In about 1912 he designed a magnificent east window of the Ascension for the church of that name in South Twerton, Bath. Fortunately, while the Baedeker raids on that city caused considerable damage to windows in the church, the Travers window survives, although it required extensive repair work after the war. It is an important example of his early work; the window has a predominantly yellow tone, with the ascended Christ shown against an ochre background and a similar colour used for the wings of the supporting figures and for the painting of a walled city with buildings beneath.

At the tiny church of St. Mary, Chesterblade, near Shepton Mallet, there is an extremely fine window showing the Nativity with the child Christ at the feet of his mother, and other children around, which again is an important early survival, showing well detailed figures and well integrated into its setting. He threw a party for his friends to celebrate the completion of this design, as set out in Chapter 1. It is signed HMOT with entwined letters and dated 1913.

In the same year Travers designed glass for the well-known Anglo-Catholic church of St. Aidan, Small Heath, Birmingham, but it appears that it was never made.

At about this time, although the date is unclear, Travers designed the

Chesterblade Church Window

three light window in the baptistery of St. Columb Notting Hill. The centre light showed Our Lady with the child Christ on a crescent moon, rather similar to the Norwich window, and the design was exhibited at the Royal Academy as late as 1922. The church is now used by the Serb Orthodox and has been rededicated to St. Sava. The lean-to narthex containing the baptistery has recently been demolished, and the windows are no longer there.

In July 1914 Sedding wrote to his brother 'I went to see Travers' window this afternoon'[1]; unfortunately he does not say where the window was, but since he was in London it appears likely that it was at St. Columb, Notting Hill.

The striking church of St. Michael, Bedford Park, lay only a few yards from Travers' new residence. In 1914 Thomas Primmitt Stevens, who was to get to know Travers well over the years and who was destined to officiate at his second marriage, arrived at the church as a curate; he in fact came from St. Columb Notting Hill. The same year Travers was commissioned to design a reredos and altar and also a window in the Chapel of All Souls at St. Michael. The commission consisted of a fairly simple classical reredos with stencilled painted columns of fruit on each of the pilasters. In the pediment was a knot design; the centre panel contained an aumbry with brass grill door. Travers intended a semi-relief of two angels on either side of the aumbry and a tasselled ribbon below, with two large Baroque candlesticks on the altar.

The reredos has been renovated and unfortunately this was not done in accordance with the artist's intentions. The new stencilled panels are of lilies and work well, but around the aumbry is a painted country scene with figures, which is garish and quite out of keeping with the original design. Travers also designed for this church a wooden gilded processional cross, and an outside rood above the south west door. Some years later he designed the internal door case for the same door.

In the All Souls' chapel is a striking, strongly coloured window by him dated 1915. It shows St. Michael killing the dragon over London, and is an early example of a characteristic Travers device: putting extra detail in a window to interest the viewer. In this case, not only can St. Paul's Cathedral

Design for reredos St. Michael Bedford Park, 1914

be seen beneath the figures, but also at least one identifiable local house. Adjacent to the window is a commemorative tablet by Travers which opens out and is in memory of Robert Haynes Barrow, priest. The east window in the church, which replaces one blown out in the Second World War, is in Travers' later style, but is in fact by his pupil Lawrence Lee in about 1952.

Travers also carried out other work in glass in London at this time. At St. Clement Barnsbury he designed a chapel window of Our Lady with the Child and at her feet two cherubs, one playing the pipes and one the lute, with St. Clement, holding the church, and other saints in the side lights. This was exhibited at the Royal Academy in 1915. The church is now used for housing and unfortunately the stained glass was stolen after the church was declared redundant.

At St. Mary, Britannia Walk, Hoxton, Travers was responsible for a memorial window of about the same date to the former vicar, Nicholas Devereux, showing the Holy Spirit as a dove descending, and certainly designed a tablet to him in addition. That church was bombed in the Second World War and demolished.

He also carried out work at this time at St. James Riddlesdown (then called St. James Coulsdon), near Croydon. His glass in this church, of which there is a great deal, is less well known than that at St. Andrew, Catford, although equally important. The new church was consecrated in 1915, and in 1916 two south aisle windows by Travers were dedicated, both in his contemporary style involving much deep colour. The first depicted St. Elizabeth of Hungary, St. Joan of Arc, and St. Patrick, the second St. Swithun, St. Francis of Assisi, and St. Hugh. In 1917 a missionary window was dedicated to the memory of Mary Bloxam, showing children of all races, but with particular reference to the diocese of Zanzibar,

St. Mary Hoxton, window of the Holy Spirit

then under the episcopate of Frank Weston, the star of the 1923 Anglo-Catholic Congress. At some point it appears that he also designed two very small windows in the porch, showing St. Cecilia and St. Francis de Sales. Further work was done at this church later, and is described in Chapter 5.

In 1916 Travers prepared a design for a window for Southwark Cathedral, which unfortunately was not carried out. He later did a considerable amount of work in the Southwark Diocese, and it may be that the Chapter felt embarrassed by their failure to commission that work, which was referred to in his obituary in the Diocesan Gazette as 'an administrative error.'

The church of St. John Maddermarket in Norwich had been in the forefront of the Catholic Revival in that City, and the mediaeval church was also much altered during the long incumbency of Canon William Busby (1898–1923). In particular, he discovered an early eighteenth century English oak canopy stored in a house near Lowestoft, bought it an auction, and installed it as a baldachino in the church. Beneath it, fluted Corinthian pilasters frame a painted altar piece of the Last Supper in Italian seventeenth century style. In 1914/5 a lady chapel altar and reredos were installed, which were almost certainly decorated by Travers. It appears that the altar was of continental origin; there is a central niche for a statue of Our Lady, which has itself disappeared. Photographic evidence shows that the statue which has gone was definitely of European provenance, and not by Travers, but the entire piece is beautifully gilded and has designs of blue lilies, which are attributed to him. Above is stencilling with a sentence in Latin from the Magnificat. There is further stencilling attributed to Travers over the vestry door and he carried out work to the lectern. The church also has, on the high altar, a crucifix by him, which came from St. George Tombland, also in Norwich.

St. John Maddermarket is redundant, but is kept open several days a week by devoted friends. Travers had actually designed a completely different reredos and altar for this church, in much more restrained style with a lamb and flag device in the centre, but that was not carried out.

In 1915 he designed a north aisle window for St. Andrew, Curry Rivel, Somerset, which had a Norwich connection in that the vicar was Revd H. Maude-Roxby, a relative of Father Roxby then of Stratton Strawless, and later for many years vicar of St. John Timberhill. Although the aisle was reconstructed, the window was not put in.

In about 1915 Travers designed a reredos for the high altar of the small and remote church of St. Michael, Winforton, Herefordshire. It shows a seated figure of Our Lady with the Holy Child on her knee and two cherubs above, all gilded in semi-relief. The relief is in the centre of a deep red reredos with lettering, and a gilded edge with decoration. The work is little known, but was well restored in 1994 and is in fine condition. In addition to the reredos, Travers supplied riddles, which he himself termed 'side rods and curtains with candles at the ends of the rods'; in his notebook is a draft bill for these accessories dated April 1915. A very similar design was used for the reredos of the Chapel of the now demolished Battersea General Hospital and Winforton was a precursor of better-known later work by Travers in Liss and Romsey.

By 1916 Travers, then 30, had established a growing reputation in a number of fields, although at that time he was probably best known through his graphic work for the SSPP. His practice was then interrupted by the need for Red Cross work as an alternative to conscription, and he did no artistic work during 1917 save the missionary window for Riddlesdown, or in 1918, save for one design for a tablet.

It would be a cliché to say that the world to which Martin Travers returned to practice in 1919 had changed after the cataclysm of the First World War. One minor consequence of the enormous loss of life was the substantial demand for war memorials of all types, in stone, glass, and wood, both for individuals and communities or parishes.

It is ironic that Travers as both an agnostic and a conscientious objector was employed so much in the ten years after the First World War in the production of such memorials. He was always an adaptable artist, and was perhaps assisted in his work, rather than hindered, by being unencumbered by religious principles.

The early post war period saw Travers involved with the work for Father Whitby at St. Mary, Bourne Street, and Father Fynes-Clinton at St. Magnus the Martyr, City, both described in Chapter 4, but it also saw him carrying out a number of generally undistinguished commissions for the Warham Guild, an organization whose ideals were diametrically opposed to the Society of SS. Peter and Paul: they generally supported the English Use and a much more conservative, subdued approach to church furnishings.

Thus in 1919 Travers not only began work at Bourne Street, he also designed outside stone calvaries as war memorials for St. Augustine, Slade Green, Bexley; St. James, Friern Barnet and All Saints, Poplar; a double sided lectern as a war memorial for St. Andrew, Clifton Campville, Staffordshire, and a Gothic screen with cross, not crucifix, above, for SS. Peter and Paul, Stoke, Kent.

As well as the stone and wooden work, there were a number of commissions for windows to commemorate the fallen, such as St. Michael, Runcorn, Cheshire, which was probably his first commission after returning to full time practice, although the chapel he drew in 1919 was never carried out. He did however produce two fine windows, one showing St. Joan of Arc, to commemorate the French contribution to the war, and St. Michael the Archangel slaying a dragon, the other, dated 1921, depicting St. George and St. Nicholas of Myra. Between them is a memorial plaque.

Travers also provided a well-regarded window for St. Andrew, Swanwick, Derbyshire, on the instruction of the Warham Guild. This shows Christ with Our Lady and St. John the Baptist on either side of him, and towers of a city beneath; it is similar in style to that at Tynemouth, discussed below.

Travers designed a very fine west window for St. John, Broadstone,

War memorial design for St. John the Baptist, Broadstone, 1920

Dorset, signed and dated 1920, which is full of colour. As with many of his designs of this period, the window is crowded, and there is little of the clear glass which so distinguishes many of his later windows. At the foot of the window are a soldier and a sailor kneeling on either side. The following year he designed a wooden lettered memorial tablet, which is on the chancel wall, and is very similar to that at Runcorn. In 1920 he also designed the Good Shepherd window at Holy Cross, St. Pancras, in similar style to the Broadstone commission, but using fine rust red colour for the cloak of Our Lord, and at about the same time a war memorial window at St. Clement, Notting Dale, which again features a kneeling soldier. This last window is of interest in that it is less crowded than that at Broadstone, and Travers used squares of various colour glass as the background, rather as he did in windows carried out at the end of his life, instead of full colour or a clear background.

In 1921 Travers produced a small but high quality war memorial triptych, which remains in good condition in the church of St. Thomas, Clydach Vale, in South Wales.

Travers frequently used the same design ideas more than once, indeed many times. Nearly all the work he carried out was in the south east of England, but in 1922–7 he executed a series of fine, and little known, windows in the east end of St. Augustin (sic), Jackson Street, Tynemouth (sometimes referred to as being in North Shields). Here again, he used the soldier and sailor at the foot; as this was a poor parish, the work was carried out over a number of years, with a centre light in 1922, the two outer lights in 1925 and the oculus in 1927. The windows show Our Lady robed and crowned in the rays of the sun, with a sceptre of lilies and the Christ Child, and a pieta at the foot. On the left are St. George and St. Augustine, on the right St. Nicholas of Myra and St. Oswald. In the oculus is the risen Christ. The whole is full of colour, although the oculus shows a development of style away from the boldness of the earlier windows. The design of Our Lady from that window should be better known: it was shown in *The Studio* magazine in 1923[2], and was then Travers' winning exhibit at the 1925 Paris Exhibition (see Chapter 1). He later used it extensively for advertising purposes. This is a church which is in danger of closure and which deserves to be saved for the windows alone.

In 1920 Travers designed a chapel for SS. Peter & Paul, Kettering, Northamptonshire, which was the forerunner of a number of such schemes. The date of installation is not clear but was certainly in the 1920s. There is a fine wooden screen painted black with flowers and the like on it

War memorial window designs for St. Augustin, Tynemouth, 1925: these were for the lights either side of the design of Our Lady exhibited at Paris

and cherubs above with the words 'Venite Adoremus' in gold. Behind it are two small rails and kneelers, also by Travers, although the pews are not. The altar itself is simply a wooden table, perhaps unfinished through lack of funds, but on it is a splendid gold tabernacle with Our Lady and St. John on either side of it in large figures in characteristic Travers style. It was a trick employed by Travers to use bas-relief to make his figures appear in the correct perspective to the observer from the direction in which one would normally look. The scheme also incorporates a cross with sun behind. It is possible that the tabernacle roof has been altered since its installation. There are rails behind the altar with the Good Friday words in Latin, also by Travers, as is the sanctuary lamp, which is now at the high altar. The slightly smaller lamp in the chapel is in fact a replacement. The glass in the chapel is however by Comper. It is fitting that Father Peter Blagdon-Gamlen, a long-time devotee of Travers, should in his retirement sometimes say his mass at this altar.

In 1920 Travers designed a war memorial for SS. Peter & Paul, Mitcham, then in Surrey, which, as with many such, shows St. George slaying the dragon in a small gilded triptych on the south aisle wall. It remains there, but is now worn in appearance. This figure was produced from a standard mould, which was also used by Travers for a war memorial triptych at St. Columb, Notting Hill in about 1931, and for work in St. John the Evangelist, Upper Norwood about 1935.

In about 1920, Travers also executed an important commission for four windows at St. Michael and All Angels, Cheriton, Hampshire. His patron here was Mrs. M.A.P. Egerton, four of whose nephews had been killed in the War. He depicted each of them in knight's armour as representative of a particular virtue, and around them showed scenes from the Bible, the lives of the Saints and the legends of King Arthur, with appropriate badges (See Plate 3).

One of the more difficult aspects of tracing Travers' work lies in discovering whether or not work which he undoubtedly designed was ever carried out. This is particularly acute in the case of his elaborate design for the

Detail from designs for St. Michael & All Angels, Cheriton, c 1920

Unexecuted design for window, Mercers' Hall, City, 1920

Chapel of the Mercers' Hall in the City of London, which he produced in 1920. It shows the crucifixion, with cherubs around a sunburst above, and a pile of skulls beneath. There are saints on either side of the window. Not only was the design exhibited at the Royal Academy in 1927, but it features in an article in the Journal of the RIBA dated 19th December 1931, to illustrate an report of a talk by F.C. Eden, along with the window of the Coronation of Our Lady in St. Mary, Kettering, which Travers carried out about 1925. Since the Mercers' Hall was entirely destroyed in the blitz, the unsuspecting researcher might conclude that the work was done, but has joined a large body of Travers' work which fell victim to German bombs. However in fact, it is clear from Jean Imray's detailed history of the Mercers' Hall that a war memorial window was carried out in the chapel by others in 1923 and that Travers' work was never in fact put into effect. This episode shows that he was perfectly prepared to use a design for advertising purposes when it had never in fact been carried out. There is an additional complication, which is that he also produced at least two other designs for the same chapel, which were less widely circulated.

On the other hand, Travers certainly did execute a memorial window to the 23rd Signals, which he exhibited at the 1920 Royal Academy; it was placed in St. John the Baptist, Barham, Kent. This single lancet memorial window shows St. George slaying the dragon, and is in vivid colours, especially using red glass.

However the magnificent east window, by contrast, dated only five years later, shows a dramatic change of style, with much use of clear glass around the figures of Our Lady and the Infant Jesus. There is clever detailing of the life of St. John the Baptist in the panels beneath. The concept of Our Lady and the Child Jesus, backed by drapes, held up by cherubs, as used here, was obviously influenced by Travers' design for the Handbook and Reports for the First Anglo-Catholic Priests' Convention of 1921. Below the east window is a fine high altar and reredos in what may loosely be termed as the English style, but with a strong classical influence. The riddel posts are in the form of fluted columns and support small urns. The original design shows artificial flames in these urns, but in fact they are used as normal candleholders. The whole is executed in green and gold; stencilled on the reredos in typical Travers lettering is the text 'O Lamb of God that takest away the sins of the world, Grant us thy Peace.' A pair of silver leaf baroque candlesticks and matching cross stand on the altar. A panelled wooden

Design for window of St. George, Barham, Kent, c 1920

Design for window and altar at Barham, Kent

frontal in a blue marbled effect, bordered in gold, was included, although the design showed one in the ordinary Roman style. Completing the whole ensemble are matching green and gold communion rails (See Plate 5).

There are two memorial plaques by Travers in Barham: one is near the St. George window and the other, in a more florid baroque style, is in the vestry. It is in gilded wood and has at its base a typical Travers putti head with wings.

A rather macabre design for an unexecuted memorial window is also kept at this church. It features scenes from the Book of Job and was to have been made in amber gold and clear glass. It is most unusual, even if somewhat gruesome.

Many years later, Francis Stephens made the screen to the vestry in plain wood and its spindles at the top echo those of the communion rails from the Travers scheme designed originally in 1923.

Barham is one of the best churches in which to see Travers' versatility and fine workmanship, and all the work is in fine condition.

Shortly thereafter he designed another regimental memorial window, this time for St. Edmund King and Martyr, Lombard Street, to the 26th Battalion Royal Fusiliers. Unfortunately his design was passed over in favour of an inferior artist, but in fact the church does contain some work by Travers, in that in 1931 he designed a fine, well-lettered tablet to the well known former vicar, G.A. Studdert-Kennedy ('Woodbine Willie').

In about 1920 Travers also began designing windows for St. Andrew Catford, where eventually there were a number of his designs in place covering almost 20 years. The first was for the east window, showing Christ in Majesty. The figures in the lower half of this window are all life size, and of a strong, masculine appearance. In the centre Christ sits crowned in Majesty and surrounded by the 12 lamps from the Book of Revelation, with many saints around, including St. Joan of Arc. On either side of this large east window are tall single lancets containing the figures of St. Michael and St. Gabriel. The clerestory above the chancel has windows with the themes of the canticles at Matins and Evensong. On the north side is one of Simeon, and next to it another of Our Lady entitled Mater Salvatoris, whilst on the south is one of St. Ambrose, representing the Te Deum. The window recess next to this was bricked up, and was originally to have contained a window of the composer Purcell. For the recent tercentenary of his death two parishioners expressed their desire to complete the scheme by paying for this window to be installed as a Diamond Wedding commemoration. The window was completed in about 1998 thus adding to the splendid collection of glass in the church.

In the lady chapel are three windows from the 1920s showing King David, in memory of P.W. Kennett, Our Lady, in memory of the Patten family, and St. Teresa of Avila, in memory of a lady named Theresa Violet Hughes. Again there are strong facial expressions with luxuriant colours. King David wears a sumptuous robe covered with a DR monogram and plays the harp. Two small lozenges depict him slaying Goliath and being anointed King respectively. Our Lady is surrounded with stars; above her head are the Star of Bethlehem and a lozenge illustrating the Annunciation.

The south chapel has a coped figure of the Infant Christ in a children's window from 1936, which shows Travers' changing style by that period.

TRAVERS AS DESIGNER I

Design for Lady Chapel windows at St. Andrew, Catford

Another east window with the theme of Christ in Majesty was designed in about 1920 for St. Nicholas, Plumstead, nearby in south east London. Many more were to follow, but this has particular appeal because of the strength of the characters portrayed. The saints in this window included

Detailed design of centre three lights for East Window, St. Nicholas, Plumstead, c 1920

Design for St. Joan of Arc and St. George, East Window, St. Nicholas, Plumstead, c 1920

St. Nicholas, St. Michael together with St. Joan of Arc, and St. George, to reflect French and English contributions to the war effort.

Travers' reputation was beginning to spread outside the metropolis, and apart from the Tynemouth work already described, he also received commissions for glass from St. Stephen, West Bute Street, Cardiff (now closed) and for glass and furnishings from St. Stephen, Buckland, Portsmouth, which was demolished after being bombed. There were two designs for the Cardiff work, one showing St. Nicholas of Myra and St. Oswald, in which that saint is shown with a strong chiselled chin and cheekbones, characteristic of this period of Travers' glass, and another showing St. Nicholas with a boat; that with the two saints was eventually used. The east window at

Design for window at St. Stephen, Cardiff

Design of lady chapel window for St. Stephen Portsmouth (bombed in war), 1921

Buckland shows Christ the King on horseback surrounded by various English saints all of whom have strong determined faces, as do the figures in the window of the Via Dolorosa in St. Gabriel, Walm Lane, Cricklewood, of the same era. The Buckland work was a particular loss in that Travers obviously thought highly enough of it to exhibit designs for windows there at the Royal Academy in 1921 and 1923 and the Royal Scottish Academy in 1922. The lady chapel window at Buckland, designed later in memory of Dr. Richard Emmett, showed St. George and the dragon (again) with St. Luke, for the medical connections of the man commemorated, and St. Barnabas, and there was also a window of Our Lady.

The motif of St. Nicholas and the ship, seen in one of the Cardiff designs, was repeated at Plumstead, at Holy Trinity, Southwark, at The Good Shepherd, Carshalton, at St. Nicholas, Denston, Suffolk, and most successfully at St. Sampson, Cricklade, Wiltshire, discussed further in Chapter 6.

It is also possible to see amidst the baroque altars which Travers was designing in the early 1920s some signs of later developments. In about 1920 he designed an altar and window for the particularly ugly early nineteenth century church of Holy Trinity, Blackford, Somerset, which was not in fact executed. It shows a very simple reredos with crucifix and virtually no other decoration, two restrained candlesticks, and a fine window of St. Mary Magdalene and Our Lord. Particularly significant also was a scheme for a lady chapel and window at Clifton Campville, Staffordshire, a church for which he had already designed a lectern. He set out his proposals in a letter to the vicar dated 26th March 1922. The scheme was not adopted, but it shows a simple retable of an ogee shape, a crucifix on the retable, and a text on either side of the crucifix. He also designed a similar scheme for All Saints, Petham, Kent, which was also not adopted. Many similar reredoses were to be supplied in later years as the tide in favour of baroque began to ebb. The windows designed for Blackford and Clifton Campville too are precursors of what was to come, with far more clear glass around the central figures.

In 1920–1 Travers supplied a hanging rood of Christus Rex design to the small early nineteenth century classical church of St. Thomas, Clapton Common. This was supplied through the Warham Guild and cost £183.3.6d., a considerable sum for that time. In 1923 he prepared a scheme for a baroque high altar on which were to stand six candlesticks in matching style and a tabernacle with very large throne behind. In fact, the tabernacle and throne were not supplied and an aumbry was provided in the north side of the apse behind the altar. The church was damaged in the Second World War and was rebuilt, but the east end with its apse survived.

The rood, high altar and candlesticks are still in the church, but the altar is now freestanding in order to accommodate modern liturgical requirements.

Travers was asked in 1923 to design a new lady chapel for the church of St. John the Baptist, Spencer Hill, Wimbledon. It was to be a memorial to the son of a parishioner who had been killed in the First World War while serving in the Navy. Two schemes were provided and were similar in style. The first was a triptych containing a large semi-relief panel of Our Lady, the boy Jesus, and his cousin John the Baptist. This was set against a blue and gold panelled screen in which were set two doors, one to the vestry and one a cupboard. In front was a simple altar on which stood two squat wooden baroque candlesticks. The second scheme included a rood and triptych surrounding a painting of the Madonna and Child.

The first was chosen and installed. Although the candlesticks have disappeared, the remaining work is in good condition and this is fortunate in that virtually no other furnishings by Martin Travers have survived in the South London area from his best period in the 1920s (See Plate 4).

In addition to the work which was actually installed, Travers designed a turned wood screen with gates between the chapel and the nave, and also panelling for the north wall of the chapel. Neither of these was carried out.

1923 was of course the year of the Second Anglo-Catholic Congress, for which Travers had designed much graphic work. Nearly all the well known Catholic churches in London took part, either holding services or providing visiting clergy with an altar at which they could say mass.

One such was St. Mary Magdalene, Paddington, and in readiness for the Congress Travers produced a charming little map of the parish showing houses and streets. Church property was marked with black roofs and small drawings of the patron saints.

It was this year also that he redesigned the Lady Chapel in that church as a memorial to Father Bleadon, the former vicar. The RIBA Catalogue aptly says, 'As no Anglo-Catholic church was complete in the first half of the Twentieth Century without a work by Travers, a Lady altar was installed …' The memorial consisted of a large gilded wooden triptych framing a painting of the Coronation of Our Lady in Heaven. The baroque altar below is in gilded wood and on it stands a large tabernacle with double doors. A small crucifix is attached, and four baroque candlesticks plus two ornate kneeling rails in a lily design complete the scheme. Unfortunately two of the candlesticks have recently been stolen (See Plate 7).

It is interesting to note that the parish had contemplated a memorial reredos to Father Bleadon some ten years earlier. A faculty application had

Parish Map of St. Mary Magdalene Paddington

been made back in 1913 submitting a design by Comper, but the interruption caused by the First World War forced that scheme to be shelved and its cost would have been a major consideration in the post-war years.

In 1929 Travers designed an unusual and striking outside calvary as a memorial to the War dead of the parish, which was erected outside at the east end of the church, and is now in need of renovation.

Another commission from 1923 was an unusual one geographically: he designed a painted and gilded reredos for the church of St. David, Maenordeifi, near Cardigan, which remains in place. It depicts the three women at the empty tomb after the Resurrection. He also at some point (and the date is uncertain) made a window of Our Lady for St. Cynfelin, Llangynfelin, at the other end of the County of Ceredigion.

In 1924 Travers was commissioned to assist the Benedictine Community when they moved into their new home, Nashdom, Burnham, Buckinghamshire. He had already made two statues for the Community in about 1922, while they had been at Pershore, one of St. Benedict and one of Our Lady, a maquette of the well known statue of Our Lady Queen of Peace at St. Mary Bourne Street. Both of these survive and are at the Community's present home at Elmore, Berkshire, although Mary's crown was replaced in 1956. They now have on each side Comper candlesticks from the High Altar at Nashdom.

The former 'Noble Salon' at Nashdom was converted into a chapel ready for the arrival of the Community in 1926; this provoked Comper into making disdainful remarks about Travers' work. Travers designed a sarcophagus shaped altar with two console tables and a canopy; the whole was intended, and did, give the impression that the monks were in communion with Rome, as did the liturgy. The candlesticks were replaced after the war when a new set, designed by Comper, was given in memory of a lay brother. The canopy was renewed in 1962. In addition, in the Chapter Room was an Italianate altar given by Father Whitby, behind which Travers erected a Baroque reredos.

Colby memorial reredos at Maenordeifi, West Wales, 1923

High altar, St. Paul, Shadwell, as installed by Father Ferrier, 1924

In the *Jubilee Book of the Benedictines of Nashdom* (1964)[4] it is suggested tactfully that the quality of the workmanship was not up to that of the design, and that it was surprising that the altar had lasted even to that date. In due course a new altar was installed and in 1986 the Community vacated Nashdom and moved to Elmore.

The Travers high altar with its console tables is now in the lady chapel of Holy Trinity, Oxford Road, Reading. With it is the crucifix, now attached to a white wall behind the altar, and the original set of candlesticks designed by Travers, which are in baroque style and are three-sided, gold, red, and black, so they can be turned in accordance with liturgical arrangements. They are kept in excellent condition among what must be the most eclectic collection of church furnishings in any parish church, mostly collected by the erstwhile parish priest, the late Canon Brian Brindley (See Plate 6).

The Chapter House altar and reredos were not taken to Elmore; they went to St. Agnes, Ullet Road, Liverpool, but were never used there and are now believed to be in private hands.

In 1924 the parish of St. Anne, Derby, was considering a sanctuary re-ordering and Travers prepared drawings of a most attractive baroque scheme comprising a triptych surmounted by the Holy Spirit represented as a descending dove. In the centre panels Our Lady and St. Anne were shown and above them the Christ Child stood on a globe; it was all backed by vast sunrays and on the altar below stood a baroque tabernacle with crucifix attached. Six baroque candlesticks were included together with an ornate Roman style frontal with a scalloped antependium edged with fringe and tassels. Unfortunately, the scheme was never put into effect.

The final project from 1924 again took Travers outside his usual geographical area. Father Douglas Ferrier, vicar of St. Paul, Shadwell, just outside Leeds,

Unexecuted design for reredos at St. Anne's, Derby

asked Travers to give the sanctuary of his little church a more ultramontane atmosphere. In a manner similar to his design the following year for the Annunciation, Brighton, he incorporated a small window within the centre of the reredos. The shape of the reredos was similar to that he designed also the following year for St. Saviour, St. Albans. Framing the panels of St. Peter and St. Paul were moulded drapes and tassels. A large baroque tabernacle, which was almost identical to that installed in St. Mary Magdalene, Paddington in 1923, stood in the centre of the gradine. Six baroque candlesticks completed the scheme, which was the subject of a great deal of controversy locally at the time, although not from the parish, who supported their priest. In addition, Travers designed a statue of Our Lady, which was placed robed in the church.

In about 1962 the altar was pulled out and to allow for westward celebration. The tabernacle was removed in about 1967 and the reredos has been repainted several times, destroying the original effect, even though that may have been somewhat overpowering.

Some vestments were designed for Father Ferrier by Martin Travers, and after his death in 1939 his widow gave them to the Shrine of Our Lady of Walsingham, but regrettably in the 1960s Canon Stephenson, the then administrator, gave them away.

Travers' practice had recovered well after the War, and he was about to embark on a very busy period, dealt with in the main in Chapter 5.

CHAPTER 4

Travers As Designer:

II SIX LONDON CHURCHES

ST. MARY, BOURNE STREET, PIMLICO
ST. SAVIOUR, HYDE ROAD, HOXTON
ST. MAGNUS THE MARTYR, LOWER THAMES STREET, CITY
HOLY TRINITY, LYONSDOWN, NEW BARNET
ST. MATTHEW, GREAT PETER STREET, WESTMINSTER
ST. AUGUSTINE, QUEEN'S GATE, SOUTH KENSINGTON

This chapter looks in more detail at six important examples of Travers' designs in London, four of which survive in full today, and one in part; three come from the period dealt with in chapter 3, and three from the period dealt with in chapter 5.

MARTIN TRAVERS' WORK AT ST. MARY, Bourne Street, Pimlico, is so well known, and the church was so important to the development of his practice, that it certainly deserves that extended treatment[1]. In fact that description of the church is anachronistic as at the time in question it was known as St. Mary, Graham Street, and Bourne Street was still named Westbourne Street.

As already set out, many of the supporters of the SSPP were connected in one way or another with the church. Travers' great chance came however with the appointment of Father Humphrey Whitby as parish priest upon the early death of Father Howell in 1916. Not only was Father Whitby an existing patron of Travers, he was also a man of very considerable private means, and was prepared to use those means to forward the Catholic faith in the Church of England. He also had a very strong devotion to the Book of Common Prayer, which he regarded as perfectly compatible with a Catholic interpretation. On the other hand, he supported extra-liturgical devotions to the Blessed Sacrament, including Benediction, which was itself the subject of tremendous controversy between the wars as the Bishops attempted to ban any such service. Even Bishop Winnington-Ingram attempted to prevent Benediction with a monstrance after the rejection of the Revised Prayer Books, and it is noteworthy that Father Whitby was one of 'The Twenty-One' who openly defied him.

Father Whitby is also important in the spread of Travers' work in that, in company with Father Atlay and Father Cornibeer at St. Matthew Westminster and Father Deakin at St. Augustine Queen's Gate, the curates at those churches were introduced to Travers through their respective incumbents, and later commissioned work on their own account once they were in charge of their own parishes.

Our Lady holding Church of St. Mary, Bourne Street

Martin Travers appears first to have encountered Humphrey Whitby in about 1910, when he designed for him a white silk damask stole; the damask itself had been designed by Comper in 1893 and it seems that this commission took effect while Travers was still working for Comper, although as set out earlier the dating of the end of their association is difficult.

This introduction was very significant. Father Whitby was a deacon at St. Columba, Haggerston and was about to be ordained as a priest: he then commissioned Travers (probably with George Sedding's assistance) to design a High Mass set of vestments for his first mass, which was celebrated on 12th June 1911; Travers also designed the card for the mass. The vestments, which are now in the possession of St. Mary Bourne Street, are in good repair, and are still used. As Timothy Ashurst says in his chapter on vestments in the history of the parish, *Streets of Heaven*, '[Father Whitby's] first mass ... must have been an amazing sight'[2] (See Plate 11).

The vestments incorporate a clever amalgamation of an historic style with a contemporary form of late Edwardian Art Nouveau embroidery. The chasuble is of a basic Sixteenth Century Austrian style and the dalmatic and chasuble are complementary. These have traditional sleeves, which are sometimes called 'English' as opposed to the later continental style with flap sleeves. All the orphreys and monograms are embroidered directly on to the fabric, which is red Italian silk damask. The chasuble has conventionalized flames symbolizing the Holy Spirit in gold jap couched embroidery. The monograms also incorporate blue silk floss and gold jap thread (See Plate 11).

On the dalmatic and tunicle the trails of leaves and flowers forming the orphreys are in an Art Nouveau style, which was still fashionable in 1911, and the workmanship is of the highest quality. The leaves are not embroidered in the more conventional long and short stitch, which would have been easier to execute, but are couched in an eau de nil silk with a gold jap edge. This gives a high quality stylized effect rather than attempting to produce a more naturalistic copy of a leaf. No attempt was made to reproduce shading – in accordance with Art Nouveau principles. Once again the monograms are in blue silk floss and gold jap thread. Glass beaded tassels on these two vestments complete the over all effect of opulence. Even the stoles have couched crosses intermingled with the words Veni Creator Spiritus.

The cope has an ornate hood embroidered in silk floss depicting the descent of the Holy Spirit on Mary and the Apostles, but the orphreys are plain with gold bullion braid. To have embroidered these would have added much to the manufacture of an already extremely expensive and sumptuous set of vestments.

Father Whitby was obviously pleased with these splendid vestments, and in about 1915 he commissioned Travers to design a graveyard cross and gravestones for the churchyard at All Saints, Wyke Regis, Dorset, in

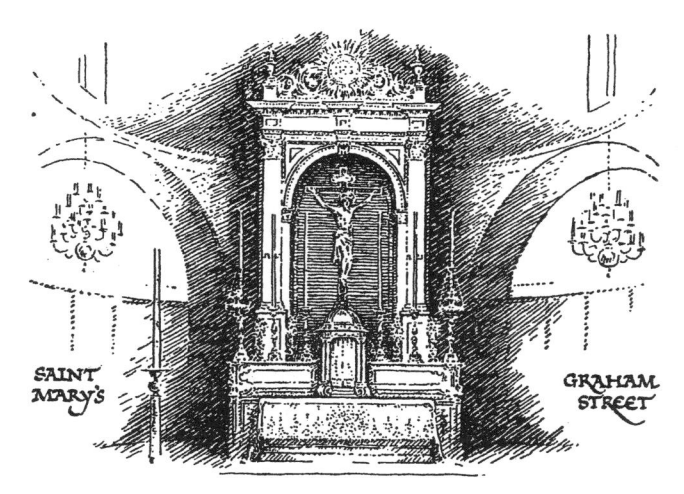

St. Mary Bourne Street: sketch of high altar, from Anglo-Catholic Congress Handbook, 1923

memory of his grandparents, Sir Arthur Otway, Bt., and Henrietta Otway; Father Whitby's christian names were Edward Otway Humphrey. The graves remain in the churchyard, but the very large cross has disappeared, although the elaborate plinth with inscription on it is still there. In 1916 Whitby's mother (Henrietta) Evelyn (Marianne) Whitby also died and Travers designed the gravestone for her too: it has a rood set on it, carved in stone, but recognizable as a typical Travers production.

Father Whitby himself died in September 1948, just after Travers; he is also buried at Wyke Regis, next to his mother and grandparents.

Having been more than satisfied by these two commissions, he then decided to entrust to Martin Travers on the latter's return to practice the responsibility of carrying out considerable further work, this time in the church itself.

St. Mary Bourne Street is a small brick church built by R.J. Withers in 1874 as a daughter church to St. Paul Knightsbridge. In 1897 Mary Lowndes of Lowndes & Drury, stained glass artists, added a west window; that firm was to feature considerably in Travers' life in the 1920s.

In 1909 Father Howell commissioned S. Gambier Parry to replace the Gothic reredos and to replace it with an Elizabethan style arch in dark wood with strapwork, cresting and, above, a sunburst device (often used by Travers himself in other places). He also designed the organ case and loft in a similar style, which might be described as a revival of the restrained English Baroque used by Wren. On Father Howell's death however it was Travers who designed the gravestone for him in Brompton Cemetery.

The first work designed by Travers for St. Mary Bourne Street itself was a memorial tablet for Edward James ('Ted') Kay-Shuttleworth, who had died in the War, and was a friend of Ronald Knox and many others associated with the church; however no tablet in his memory is in this church, and it appears that it was hung instead in Gurney's church at Compton Beauchamp (see Chapter 6). The designs for the Bourne Street tablet are dated 21st January 1918. He then designed a wooden tablet to Father Howell, the designs for which are dated 20th February 1919; this records not only his death but also the dedication of the reordering of the sanctuary set out below and is on the north side of the chancel. In later years Gavin Stamp copied the lettering for a memorial tablet in resin to Father F.E.P.S. Langton, parish priest 1948-64, which is opposite Travers' plaque.

Travers then turned his attention to the high altar and to the reredos, which of course was only 10 years old at that time. It is a measure of the way in which he was able to alter and adapt that which was already there

St. Mary Bourne Street: high altar showing Travers frontal from 1924

that this remains one of his best-known pieces of work, despite the fact that his contribution over all is relatively small.

Travers produced a design dated 20th June 1919 for the new high altar and tabernacle, and a further design dated 16th August 1919 for alterations to the reredos; the schemes represented a memorial to Father Howell.

Once this work had been carried out, St. Mary had a sarcophagus shaped altar in gilded wood, a wooden gilded and painted gradine, and six very large wooden baroque candlesticks. In the middle of the altar was an ornate tabernacle of considerable size with a dome. The reredos was altered so that the arch and strapwork cresting of Gambier Parry remained, but the decoration was removed from the arch and the brick background in the centre of the arch was cut out to allow blinds to be inserted and to cover the figure if necessary. The sides of the reredos were altered so that the new arrangement did not curve in at each side.

The new rood had only the central figure of Jesus on the cross, which was altered by Travers so that the arms were straightened. The cross itself was new, and it was intended that the figures of Our Lady and St. John left by Gambier Parry should be re-erected on either side, but this was never done.

The whole scheme as carried out by Travers at that time subtly changed the original restrained English style to a more flamboyant European Baroque, but without incongruity. His notebook for the time contains a draft specification dated 2nd August 1919 in his own handwriting, which indicates that where possible existing material was to be utilized. The existing altar slab was in fact framed in mahogany to form the new sarcophagus, and although Travers agreed to lay board floor in front of the altar, he was told to reuse the existing wood blocks outside the altar rails. Two additional steps were inserted and their corners chamfered, and the altar rail extended to the same design as had previously been employed. The wood screen at the side of the sanctuary was raised and some new work carried out to it.

The reredos was subsequently altered yet again, this time by H.S. Goodhart-Rendel. It was not until about 1934 that it reached its final form: the volutes at the side and the cartouche of the Coronation of Our Lady are by him, not by Travers, although Goodhart-Rendel again was able to adapt what was already there so that the whole was congruous (See Plate 9).

The reredos contained a wind-up throne for exposition of the Blessed Sacrament, and two built in veils to cover the crucifix, one in purple for Lent and one in gold and white brocade for use during Benediction. Hidden in a rosette on the gradine was a bell to signal to the organist, so all eventualities were catered for in the structure.

SIX POSTERS BY MARTIN TRAVERS

Church Literature Association, Faith House, 7 Tufton Street, S.W.1.

St. Mary Bourne Street: Our Lady Queen of Peace, poster using Travers design c 1973

The high altar candlesticks were in due course replaced after one disintegrated, but the replacements are themselves almost exact copies of Travers' originals. It appears that four of the originals were subsequently passed on to Christ the King, Gordon Square, Bloomsbury.

In about 1920 Travers designed the statue of Our Lady Queen of Peace, which is now in the new north aisle, having been moved there when the church was extended. Here again, Travers' ingenuity can be seen. The shrine of Our Lady was based on a mediaeval Gothic statue at Amiens, which may well have been seen by some of those fighting on the Western Front. A combination of gilding with a large sunburst behind turns the effect into Baroque rather than Gothic, and time has not taken away its appeal. It has been suggested that he used his wife as the model for the statue, which is perfectly plausible bearing in mind his frequent use of her and other members of his family in various works. There are no extant designs for this statue, but the maquette was given to the Benedictine Community, then at Pershore, and has stayed with them ever since, moving to Nashdom before finally being placed in the striking new chapel at Elmore (See Plate 10).

On 17th January 1922 Travers designed the walnut sedilia for the sanctuary, and on 12th March 1924 a magnificent white embroidered altar frontal with a motif of the pelican feeding her young, covered in flowers and swags. It has recently been beautifully restored and remains a spectacular piece.

Travers carried out further work for the church, also in about 1919: he designed six large hearse lights, a Paschal Candlestick for use at requiems, a set of requiem candlesticks for the high altar, and a smaller set of candlesticks, also for the high altar. The large Paschal Candlestick was inscribed to the memory of Father Whitby's mother. Travers also designed a ciborium cover of white silk, embroidered with the Sacred Heart of Jesus surrounded by thorns and surmounted by a crown and flames, drops of blood and a glory, enclosed in volutes of gold thread. All is bordered in couched gold and silver threads with a cloud design, which was a typical Travers device of this period. Finally, there was a tablet of about 1923 to Wilfred Herbert Gore-Ewart, which is now adjacent to the statue of Our Lady, and at some point a processional cross was made. The tablet on the other side of the statue of Our Lady is similar to that to Gore-Ewart and appears also to be by Travers (See Plate 12).

All this work remains in place and the various items are still in use at the church.

However, that was not the whole of Travers' involvement with St. Mary, Bourne Street.

There had at one stage been a suggestion that he might design a pulpit for the church, and in his specification he mentions a temporary pulpit. The church certainly had a temporary wooden-framed pulpit for many years until the late 1960s, but it is not clear if it was designed by Travers.

One obstacle which always stood in the way of Travers' further advancement in his field was his lack of formal architectural qualifications, which were vital where structural work was required. In January 1922, when Travers was still engaged in work in the church, the parish called in Goodhart-Rendel, a qualified architect and a practising Anglo-Catholic; he later seceded to Rome. He was asked to convert a former public

St. Mary Bourne Street: scheme for enlargement, 1924

St. Mary Bourne Street: design for shrine of Our Most Holy Redeemer, 1925

house, 'The Pineapple', adjacent to the church, to a presbytery. This he did.

After the internal alterations already described, Father Whitby was anxious to enlarge the church. It appears that a competition was held for this, and Goodhart-Rendel's design, dated about November 1924, was successful. The faculty for the work, dated 1925, records that the parish adopted this design at a meeting on 1st December 1924. Goodhart-Rendel added an ingenious seven-sided porch leading to a new north aisle with altar of the Seven Sorrows; Travers' statue of Our Lady was repositioned into this aisle in due course.

It is said that Travers was extremely offended by the decision to award this work to Goodhart-Rendel when his own earlier work had been so successful; that would accord with what we know of his character. Travers himself had designed an extension to the church, which involved plain arched windows in the north wall, a new confessional box, and the moving of the statue of Our Lady Queen of Peace into the chapel of the Seven Sorrows. Unfortunately the design for this extension is undated, but the logical conclusion is that it was before the parish at the same time as Goodhart-Rendel's, and was not preferred.

However, on 11th July 1925 Travers designed a triptych for a shrine of Our Most Holy Redeemer showing Christ in agony with outstretched arms. His torso is covered in droplets of perspiration, and blood from the crown of thorns. It was intended as a memorial to those of the parish who had died in the First World War, and a version was exhibited at the Royal Academy in 1924, but it was unfortunately never executed. The church in fact, most unusually, never has had a proper Great War memorial.

The design for the Holy Redeemer triptych was well *after* the decision to employ Goodhart-Rendel for the extension, which suggests that Travers' feelings of rejection may have been overstated. It also seems clear that he and Father Whitby remained in touch, as after the latter revived the name of the SSPP for his own publishing ventures in 1939, Travers illustrated the Missals which were produced.

Goodhart-Rendel went on, not only to add to the reredos, as already mentioned, but also to add other furnishings to the church in an unusual early re-revival of Gothic.

It seems quite possible that Travers would have whitewashed the interior had he been permitted to work further. Whitewashing was fashionable at that time and was most famously carried out at the nearby St. Augustine, Queen's Gate, although Travers has been wrongly blamed for that. Goodhart-Rendel, on the other hand, purposely used expensive brickwork for his extension. There is also the consideration that Travers was less than successful with his building work (see Chapter 9).

The co-authors of this work on reflection regret the decision to reject Travers' scheme; the reader may take his or her choice.

Travers also prepared at some point an artist's sketch for the transformation of the whole church; this drawing was in the possession of the late Father Milburn of St. Paul, Brighton, but was left by him to a priest in the United States of America. It showed a number of shrines and a particularly ornate baroque canopy and triptych for the statue of Our Lady Queen of Peace.

The confessional in the church at present was designed by Goodhart-Rendel in the Gothic style and installed in 1936. In Holy Trinity, Shepherdess Walk, Hoxton, is a confessional with tall Corinthian pilasters, by Travers, which came from St. Mary Bourne Street; presumably it was made at the same time as the other artefacts installed during the 1919-24 period.

Brian Brindley, in his description of the interior of the church published as *Infinite Riches in a Little Room* (1970s) and Leonard Buckley, in his short pamphlet on Travers published in 1992, both say that St. Mary's 'must be accepted as a masterpiece of Martin Travers'[3]; that may be overstating the

1. *Window of Our Lady, now in St. John Timberhill, Norwich: Travers' first known stained glass*

3. *Window to Basil Christy in St. Michael & All Angels, Cheriton, c 1920*

2. *Father Whitby's first mass card, 1911*

4. *Lady chapel in St. John the Baptist, Wimbledon, c 1923*

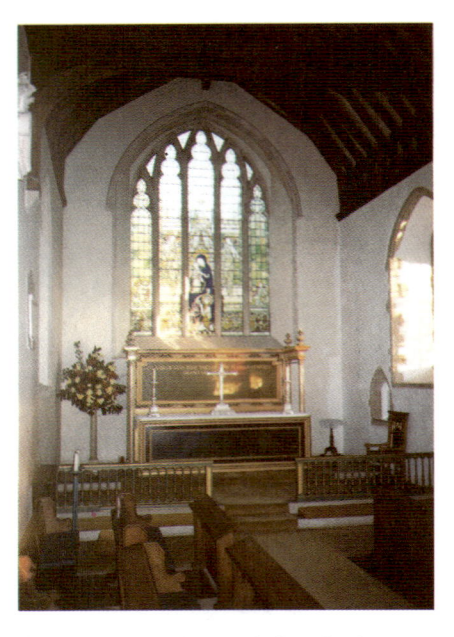

5. *High altar and east window, Barham, Kent, 1925*

7. *Lady Chapel, St. Mary Magdalene, Paddington, 1923*

6. *High altar from Nashdom Abbey, c 1925, now in Holy Trinity, Reading*

8. *Weston Memorial altar before the fire, St. Matthew Westminster*

9. High altar, St. Mary Bourne Street as altered by Travers and completed by Goodhart-Rendel

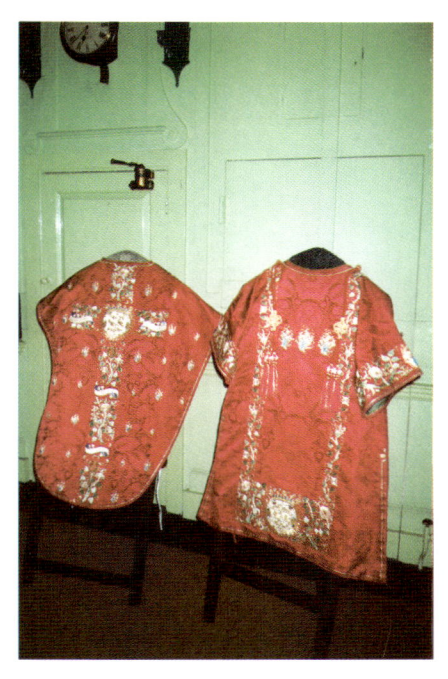

11. Chasuble and dalmatic from Father Whitby's first mass set, now in St. Mary Bourne Street

10. Our Lady Queen of Peace, St. Mary Bourne Street

12. Ciborium cover, St. Mary Bourne Street

13. *High altar, St. Magnus the Martyr, City*

15. *High altar and reredos St. Augustine Queen's Gate, 1928: probably Travers' best known work*

14. *North altar, St. Magnus the Martyr*

16. *Chapel of Our Lady, St. Augustine Queen's Gate, 1938*

case, but his work there is important, well-integrated, and, most importantly, still well regarded and preserved. It is unfortunate that the relationship between Travers and the church ended in the way it did, whether or not the decision taken to pass him over was the correct one.

AT ABOUT THE SAME TIME, Travers began working at St. Saviour, Hyde Road, Hoxton. Fortunately there is a great deal of material available on St. Saviour, as many of the parish magazines have survived and those which are available contain a serialized history of the parish written by the late Lawrence Jack, one of the last churchwardens, in 1938-40.

St. Saviour was a thorn in the side of the usually tolerant Bishop of London, Winnington-Ingram. Ironically it was the Bishop himself who had intervened to procure the living for Father Ernest Kilburn in 1907, after it was proposed by the Crown, who held the right of presentation alternately with the Bishop, to introduce a Low Church incumbent from Leeds.

Kilburn was inducted as vicar on 26th October 1907. Initially his views appear to have been quite moderate, and he followed the English Use. However, by 1910 incense was being used, and by 1911 the magazines refer to 'Mass' instead of 'Holy Communion.' By the end of the First World War he had turned the church into a working replica of a Roman parish. Mass

St. Saviour Hoxton, engraving of church

after 1919-20 was always said in Latin, and all the usual Roman devotions were observed; the Sunday evening service was normally Vespers and Benediction. Dom Anselm Hughes, in his personal history of the Catholic Movement in the Twentieth Century, a sympathetic observer, wrote: 'occasionally an individual has made the mistake of moving too far ahead of the front line and so losing contact altogether. This is almost certainly true of E.E. Kilburn ...'[3]. The problem facing the authorities was that Kilburn himself was a saintly figure, and the church was always full when others were not.

The church itself was a typical red brick building with apse, designed, as with so many other churches in that area, by James Brooks, in this case in 1866.

Originally the church had an alabaster reredos by W.R. Ingram, which was left behind the work which Travers carried out. In 1915 the Marquis de Tournay d'Oisy, representing Louis Grossé, carried out some work to the high altar including a sacred heart motif on the figure of Christ, and added some curtaining, originally on a temporary basis for Corpus Christi Day.

In 1919 Travers designed a new altar, but the parish magazine for August that year ('the month of Our Lady in Heaven') said that there were insufficient funds to start work, and then the next month indicated that he had been too busy at St. Mary Bourne Street. The cost of the work was then quoted as £28 for a new tabernacle, £135 for a new altar and gradines and mensa of marble, £12 for steps to the throne, £15 for a plinth, £65 for removing the existing levels and £31 for new steps to the altar.

The work was carried out in stages, the first being the installation of the new altar and removal of the curtain screens, which was completed in time for a Solemn High Mass of Exposition on 13th March 1920. In the parish magazine for April 1920 is a short note by Travers himself, indicating that gilding and a new set of candlesticks was required to complete the work. He also explained that he had provided a proper Western Use altar, with a sepulchre in the centre for relics; the church later placed in the altar relics of St. Anthony and St. Francis.

The altar was of sarcophagus shape, and had a baroque gradine in front of the original Gothic reredos, which was built into the apse. A photograph on the front pages of the Parish Magazines of 1921 shows that six brass Puginesque candlesticks and four smaller brass candlesticks were in use. For a short period a dossal curtain was hung behind this altar.

In 1922 Father Kilburn resigned because of the strains arising from the hard work required and the poor financial position of the parish, which had resulted in Travers himself not being paid in full until September of that

St. Saviour Hoxton: high altar before erection of reredos

year. It is quite clear from his farewells that at the time of leaving the parish Father Kilburn was not intending to secede to Rome, but a year later he and his former curate Father Holland did so, and both later joined the Oratory. He was permitted to nominate his successor, Father J.F. Bloxam, who had at one time been at Bourne Street, and he continued the same liturgical policy, and continued to employ Travers.

In 1924 Travers gilded the altar, and this was made ready for Corpus Christi Day, 19th June of that year.

The next stage of the work was the erection of a reredos and canopy, the plans for which formed part of Travers' exhibits at the Royal Academy in 1927. This work was carried out ready for the Midnight Mass at Christmas 1926.

A large gilded and decorated calvary was erected within an ornate frame surmounted by a pediment containing a representation of a chalice and host. On either side were figures of Our Lady and St. John, rather similar to the effect which was intended for St. Mary Bourne Street, although the figures there were never reinstalled. As completed, six wooden baroque candlesticks stood on the top gradine, six smaller on the middle and four on the lowest shelf. Above the altar hung an ornate octagonal canopy complete with tassels all in gilded and coloured wood. Around the apse were six long strips of brocade suspended from baroque cartouches matching the reredos. An unusual feature of the 'Big Six' candlesticks was that they were one-dimensional, and were propped up from behind by iron rods. This may have been a cost-cutting exercise; it has been suggested that they were intended only as a temporary set until others were made, but that seems unlikely from the contemporary notes, and some similar examples can be found in continental Baroque churches. They must have appeared very theatrical from the side, and according to Lawrence Jack the reredos was built up at the rear with boxes on which the brand name of Tate and Lyle could easily be seen! Travers was much criticized for this type of 'Baroque on a Budget' but it provided a poor parish with what they wanted at a low cost.

MARTIN TRAVERS: AN APPRECIATION

Interior of Church of St. Saviour Hoxton on Dedication Festival, 10th May 1936 showing Travers high altar, canopy and cartouches

In 1927 Father D.A. Ross became vicar; he had to promise before his institution to revert to the vernacular for his services, although the church continued to be Papalist in tone. It housed the offices of the Confraternity of Unity from its establishment in this country in 1929. In 1932 Travers returned to tile the sanctuary.

In 1940 the church was severely damaged in an air raid and, being in an area which was rapidly being depopulated, was not rebuilt. One of Travers' exotic but cheap schemes from this period was thus lost for ever, and it is fortunate that there is some photographic evidence of what was done there.

IN 1921 HENRY JOY FYNES-CLINTON was instituted as rector of the Wren church of St. Magnus the Martyr, Lower Thames Street, in the City of London, where he was to stay until his death in 1958. Father Fynes-Clinton was an inveterate founder of organizations, including the Catholic League, the Community of St. Augustine of Hippo (later the Servitors of Mary and St. Austin), and the Canonesses of Our Lady of Victory, and throughout his life carried on an extensive correspondence with many other clergy all over Europe[4]. He was the son of the vicar of St. Giles, Cromwell, Nottinghamshire, although the Clinton in his name spoke of connections with the Duke of Newcastle, and he behaved like an aristocrat. He lived for some years in the St. Ermin's Hotel in Westminster and entertained foreign visitors there. He also became a considerable presence in the City of London, and in later years started lunchtime masses in the City long before they became commonplace. The church records show that when he first began to exercise his ministry at St. Magnus, there were 2500 weekly attendances, of whom 600-700 were on Sundays.

He and Father Corbould of Carshalton, another patron of Travers, were among the leaders of the Papalist wing of the Church of England, and neither ever deviated from an uncompromisingly pro-Roman position.

It is not surprising that Fynes-Clinton asked Travers to refurnish St. Magnus, since he knew other clergy for whom Travers had worked, but the church presented particular problems not to be found in the case of a stock brick Gothic building such as Bourne Street. The church is well known not least because of the reference to it in T.S. Eliot's *The Waste Land*, where the poet, a committed Anglo-Catholic himself, refers to it as an 'inexplicable splendour of Ionian white and gold'; this is always quoted whenever Travers' work in St. Magnus is discussed, but in fact it does not refer to it at all. Immediately after his institution Father Fynes-Clinton had the interior repainted in white, and it is that to which The Waste Land refers: the work was first published in 1922, two years *before* Travers started work in the church.

It is generally agreed that this was one of Travers' most successful refurnishings, not least because there were not the severe constraints on cash found in many of his schemes, and also because the scheme was thought through and brought into effect as one, in 1924-8, with only a few later additions. Further, despite bomb damage which blew out many of the windows (none of which were by Travers) all the work survives and has been beautifully maintained.

The main part of the work was carried out in 1924, and a dedication service took place on 15th December of that year. Travers remodelled the church, formerly a black preaching box, into something rather like an Austrian Baroque interior of the Seventeenth Century. St. Magnus as refurnished was designed to foster the illusion that the Reformation in England had not taken place, in accordance with the teaching emanating from the pulpit and the ceremonial at the altars of the church.

Travers altered the high altar reredos, which has been attributed to Grinling Gibbons, by restoring most of the upper story, which, with the exception of the central section and its painting, had been removed in the nineteenth century. At that time the angels had been placed further in from the corners and were silhouetted by an ugly neo-Norman Victorian stained glass window. The reredos as altered by Travers was surmounted by a painted and gilded rood, complete with Our Lady and St. John. On either side were two urns with their gilded flames and the angels were set further down on the outer corners in newly gilded splendour. The two panels of

Dedication service at St. Magnus the Martyr, City after completion of the Travers work, December 1924

Moses and Aaron together with those of the Ten Commandments, the Creed and the Lord's Prayer were added, as previously the lower section was completely unadorned and very sombre in plain wood. Above the two panels of the Commandments, the pelican in her piety feeding her young was also gilded. A cartouche of the Holy Spirit as a descending dove hung above the putti heads under the rood; this now hangs above the sacristy doors and its original purpose seems a mystery when one considers that the Holy Spirit is already in the painting (See Plate 13).

When the faculty applications were made in 1924, a second scheme modifying the existing reredos less drastically was also submitted. It showed an integral tester with wooden tassels in place of the Ten Commandments, and three cherubs holding the Bible open with its appropriate text, above the pelican motif in the centre of the reredos. Travers had matched the lady chapel reredos columns in a Corinthian style with those of the high altar reredos, whose central section and upper part containing the putti heads and the Holy Spirit were flanked by ornate scrollings terminating with two angels. Three more cherubs surrounded the Holy Dove just below the rood, which surmounted the whole ensemble. Only one flaming urn appeared on either side at the top of the central pediment.

This second design was not as heavy and overpowering as the chosen reredos with its large panels of stained wood on either side of the central section. However, in view of all the litigation which was taking place at St. Magnus over the reordering and also the services of Benediction and Vespers of Our Lady being held there, it was probably thought that to omit the Ten Commandments from a 17th century reredos in a City of London church was inappropriate.

Travers cleverly constructed two side chapels out of old door frames and placed them diagonally across the north east and south east corners of the church. The chapel on the north east is the Lady Chapel, which was completed in 1925 and is dedicated to Father Fynes-Clinton's parents. In the recess above the altar is a painting of the Madonna and Child. The second scheme had included a statue in the niche instead of a painting. This was also the subject of litigation during the faculty applications in 1924, but the Chancellor found in favour of Father Fynes-Clinton, and evidence of a statue in this position exists, although it only remained there for a short time. On the left of the altar hangs an unusual silver sanctuary lamp to Travers' design, showing that the Blessed Sacrament is reserved here. Originally, Travers had designed a Baroque aumbry for reservation, which is situated on the east wall near the Lady

Unexecuted design for St. Magnus the Martyr, City

Chapel, below a monument which Father Fynes-Clinton had covered with a painting of the Handkerchief of St. Veronica. Later a large tabernacle was installed on the altar, and the aumbry now houses a relic of the True Cross (See Plate 14).

The south east chapel is that of Christ the King, a devotion only instituted in the Roman Church in 1925. In the 1924 litigation referred to above, the Chancellor felt he could not sanction the use of a third Holy Table at St. Magnus, but as he was aware that there was a need for balance to the lady chapel in the opposite corner, he said that a shrine could be considered. Many years later, the figure of Christ the King was boarded in and the table used as an altar. It is only since the restoration a few years ago, following the fire, that the Travers statue has once again been uncovered and is now part of a chapel and not just a shrine.

The church also features a large statue of St. Magnus by Travers; he stands resplendent with Viking axe holding a model of the church in his left hand. In Travers' original drawing St. Magnus was shown holding a sword and not an axe, and his helmet sported magnificent wings. This was how the finished statue arrived at the church and so remained for several years. However after subsequent war damage the sword was replaced by the axe and the wings were substituted by the present horns.

As well as extending the sanctuary floor area by enlarging the steps and moving the communion rails, Travers provided a new altar with console tables at the side. He added two new columns in the nave next to the gallery to enhance the effect of the arcade, opened up the pulpit and designed a crucifix for it, and provided a new soundboard to complement what was already there. Travers also designed a new baptistery, a bishop's throne, a confessional, a wrought iron paschal candlestick, a thurible and boat stand, and constructed the sacristy screen under the organ loft, as well as installing the side benches in the aisle. He had a Benediction throne and enormous torches made for the church. Travers also made the interior look far more continental by removing the box pews and installing new pews with cut down ends. The front kneeling desks have characteristic Travers moulded tassel ornamentation, very similar to those he provided for the Embassy Church in Madrid: see Chapter 8.

In 1931 Travers designed a very fine statue of Our Lady of Walsingham for St. Magnus; Father Fynes-Clinton was a guardian of the shrine and an old friend of Father Hope Patten, and was among the first in London to revive the devotion. At some point Travers also framed the icon of Our Lady of Perpetual Succour, which Father Fynes-Clinton had had specially painted for him in Russia. When he established the Community of Our Lady of

Statue of St. Magnus as originally erected in St. Magnus the Martyr, with winged helmet and sword

St. Magnus the Martyr: Shrine of Our Lady of Walsingham, 1931

Victory in 1915, he gave them the icon for their house; the Community did not prosper and in 1928 they moved to the grounds of the Convent of St. Mary at the Cross, Edgware. Later the icon returned to St. Magnus.

In 1935 Travers was called back. One of the less obvious improvements effected in 1924 was the creation of a parish room in the crypt. In 1935-6 Travers superintended further work underground, in which a servers' room was built. The project turned out to be more complicated than was envisaged when it commenced, and a number of new walls had to be erected under the church.

All the work at St. Magnus the Martyr can still be seen, and the furnishings are used; some restoration took place after a fire in the gallery and has been very well executed.

There is no other surviving example of a City church so remodelled by Travers; he carried out a considerable amount of work in St. Augustine, Watling Street, shortly before the Second World War, but that was bombed and his furnishings lost. He also carried out work on the reredos at St. Antholin, Nunhead, which came from a City church, and designed a reredos along the model of a City church at Holy Cross, Greenford: see Chapter 7.

The work carried out by Travers at St. Mary Bourne Street and St. Magnus the Martyr is very well known: that at St. Saviour, Hoxton, has many evocations for those of an Anglican Papalist frame of mind.

HOWEVER, IT SEEMS THAT VERY few know of Travers' work for the Evangelical parish of Holy Trinity, Lyonsdown, which being in New Barnet has always been in the Diocese of St. Albans, although well within the suburban sprawl of London. This church however has a very large quantity of work in wood by Travers.

Holy Trinity Lyonsdown is a simple brick church by Ewan Christian, built in 1864-5. It has always been towards the lower end of the Anglican spectrum, and in recent years has had close links with Oak Hill Theological College. Prior to 1925, it had a rather poor stone altar with cross and reredos.

In 1923 Revd G.E. Gardner, vicar of the parish from 1885 to 1917, died. It was decided to commemorate his ministry and after a sum of £310 had been raised, Travers was instructed. The vicar then was Bishop G.H. Lander, formerly of Hong Kong.

The initial scheme, put in place under a faculty of 1925, was for an Austrian oak reredos and panelling behind the altar. Travers designed a plain, somewhat modernistic piece, which was very different from his usual output, and also panelled right around the chancel. There were in addition curtains around the altar, an oak credence table, and a gilded or silver cross. Other members of the congregation then provided further gifts, which resulted in a further faculty in 1927. Travers added a plain altar, a pulpit, and communion rails, and at some time also he supplied a vicar's stall and bishop's chair; all these were in oak. The church ordered three windows, also in 1927, and for some reason did not employ Travers for this, with the result that those which were installed were inferior to his products.

In 1931 Travers was again employed at the church, on this occasion to erect a screen, also in oak, but this time rather lighter, between the main church and what was then the vestry. The screen was presented by the children of Dr. Arthur Perigal, and is inscribed to his memory. The area behind the screen was later converted to form a chapel, and in it is Travers' last

Screen for Holy Trinity, Lyonsdown

contribution to the church, a Perigal family hatchment designed in 1943 and painted on a lozenge-shaped wooden board.

This work is an interesting and salutary antidote to those who see in Travers only the Anglo-Catholic pantomime dresser he sometimes pretended to be. In fact of course it shows the versatility of his output, and it is not the only instance where he provided such wood work: another is the contemporary St. George, Madrid (see Chapter 8).

In 1968 the reredos was repainted and the curtains were removed. In 1992 the chancel was refurbished: this involved pulling out the altar from the reredos, and angling the communion rails while at the same time for some reason turning them round, so that the more elaborate inside ends were on the outside. The church therefore still retains a very great store of Travers woodwork in unusual and somewhat atypical style.

ONE OF THE LEADING CHURCHES in the Catholic Movement in London in the first half of the twentieth century was St. Matthew, Great Peter Street, Westminster. Situated in the middle of what used to be a very heavily populated area, the work load of the curates was heavy: see the description by H.A. Wilson in *Received with Thanks* (1940)[5]. There were 20000 communions a year at the church in the early 1920s, when the vicar was the outstanding Marcus Atlay, the chairman of the 1920 Anglo-Catholic Congress, who resigned the living in February 1922, and died suddenly a few years later. Bishop Frank Weston of Zanzibar had been a curate at the church from 1896 to 1898.

Bishop Weston died in 1924, shortly after his remarkable performance at the 1923 Congress, galvanizing those present with his rhetoric.

Travers' work in the church, including the memorial to Bishop Weston, was commissioned by Father A.E. Cornibeer, the then incumbent, between about 1926 and 1930. The altar and reredos in memory of Weston were exhibited at the Royal Academy in 1929; they consisted of a triptych with a large calvary, on the doors of which were St. Francis Xavier and St. Adrian the African, which was erected in the south aisle near the entrance porch. The triptych was similar to that in St. Saviour, Hoxton. The altar had an embossed and gilded wooden frontal and on the mensa stood two large baroque candlesticks. The accompanying altar rails were in wood and painted red and gold; on the south wall hung a memorial plaque showing Frank Weston in his bishop's cope and mitre. In addition, Travers carried out other work at the church including alterations to the existing rood screen to include typical decoration around the figures and also lettering,

TRAVERS AS DESIGNER II

St. Matthew Westminster: Frank Weston Memorial Chapel, 1928

St. Matthew Westminster: rood and loft after Travers alterations

and a baroque tabernacle on the high altar. The overall effect in this otherwise somewhat architecturally undistinguished church was very pleasing (See Plate 8).

In 1977 however the church was seriously damaged by fire, and unfortunately the alterations to the chancel screen were lost, but the baroque tabernacle and the work in the memorial chapel survived. The church was rebuilt and the chapel furnishings with the Weston plaque have been resited under the tower in cramped conditions. They are no longer used as an altar and have become simply an ornament to be gazed at through the glass doors. It is very unfortunate that these fine fittings from Travers' best period should now be in this position, although it is difficult in the rebuilt church to see an alternative.

At least however they were not destroyed in the fire, and the monument to Bishop Weston is an important and impressive item of church furnishing and well constructed.

THE FOURTH LONDON CHURCH WHICH is well known for Travers' work within it is St. Augustine, Queen's Gate. Here it would be fair to say that Travers' contribution was more controversial.

St. Augustine is a large Butterfield church with that architect's characteristic polychromatic brickwork. It became a prominent centre when in 1923 Carrick Ransome Deakin was instituted as vicar. Not only was Father Deakin the originator of the concept of the Anglo-Catholic Congress, but the position of his church, near the Albert Hall, meant that it was much used in the course of the meetings. Father Deakin obviously knew Father Whitby at Bourne Street, Fathers Atlay and Cornibeer at St. Matthew Westminster, and Father Child, who in 1925 became Secretary of the Congress.

St. Augustine represents a change of style by Travers from St. Mary, Bourne Street. The latter was intended to embody the ideals of the SSPP; St. Augustine on the other hand was aptly described by Sir John Betjeman in his *Collins Pocket Guide to English Parish Churches* as 'the apotheosis of the Anglo-Catholic Congress movement'. Most observers would agree with that conclusion, but some might not agree with his next, namely that it is 'a period piece of rare delight.'

1926 saw the first of Travers' furnishings for the church arrive. This was the calvary memorial to the departed of the parish. It consisted of a large gilded triptych with blue, dark green, gold, and ivory colouring in a mahogany frame. The colouring was intended to harmonize with Butterfield's brickwork. It was provided with its own kneeling desk, and two large baroque candlesticks, and stood in the first arch on the south

St. Augustine Queen's Gate: watercolour of war memorial, 1926

west side of the nave, before being moved to the entrance porch in 1975. Father Deakin's name and that of others have been added to what was originally a war memorial. There is an interesting letter to the Chancellor from Dr. Eeles on the subject of this memorial. On 16th February 1926 he wrote that 'It is a brilliantly clever piece of work, but to my mind it is overpowering in size and is of the ghastly realistic character which is characteristic of the crucifix as used in the period of the Counter Reformation abroad … In confidence I may add that the present vicar of St. Augustine's Queen's Gate is an out and out Romanist … The tract case near the door contained literature of a thoroughly Roman and disloyal type. The Roman priest in cotta and beretta (sic) which Mr. Travers has so cleverly suggested in the sketch is quite typical of the church.'

Also in 1926 George Tuckerman, who was then still a deacon, joined Father Deakin's staff. Father Tuckerman trained as an architect but had entered the priesthood instead of pursuing an architectural career. He felt Butterfield's brickwork did not do justice to the interior, which he described as looking like a Neapolitan ice cream and containing a hideous chancel screen. Indeed early photographs taken before the Travers transformation do show a dark cluttered church with a very heavy iron chancel screen.

It was apparently Father Tuckerman who managed to persuade Father Deakin and Martin Travers to whitewash the interior as the backdrop to the furnishings, although Travers himself, in a memorandum dated 20th January 1927, said that the church needed whitening as it was far too dark. It is this aspect of the work which has invoked the ire of many critics, but it is only fair to say that at the time the vast number of the informed, including such as Ninian Comper, were strongly in favour of whitewashing, and Goodhart-Rendel at Bourne Street was a voice in the wilderness. Travers later whitewashed another, much less well-known Butterfield interior, the chancel of Holy Saviour, Hitchin, Hertfordshire, and after the war he was also involved in the whitewashing of another polychromatic interior, although not by Butterfield, at St. Jude, Courtfield Gardens, South Kensington.

In 1927–8 Travers prepared drawings for a fairly restrained reredos, influenced by Low Countries Baroque, between two lancet windows at the east end of the church. Above the chancel arch was to be a rood with Our Lady and St. John. The reredos was surmounted by a representation of the ascendant Christ over a panel containing a chalice and host. Below this was a pelican in her piety and in the lowest section St. Augustine of Hippo and

St. Augustine Queen's Gate: second unexecuted design for High Altar

St. Augustine of Canterbury flanking a representation of the Holy Trinity. The altar was provided with six baroque candlesticks and a tabernacle.

This scheme was not chosen, and neither was a second proposal showing a large reredos surmounted by a rood on a pediment containing a chalice and host, wooden pendants, and the Risen Christ in the midst.

A third design was chosen. It appears that this is in fact a variant of a scheme proposed by Travers for the church of the Holy Trinity, Reading, which as it happens later acquired two Travers altars. This third scheme is reminiscent of South American Baroque; there does not appear to be any evidence that Travers ever visited Latin America but he had certainly been to Spain, and there he would have seen the extraordinary excesses of the ultra-Baroque Churrigueresque style. The vast reredos, measuring 37 feet

St. Augustine Queen's Gate: final design for High Altar, 1927

by 23 feet 6 inches, has a rood as the central feature set below an integral tester with its own wooden tassels. Above, the Holy Spirit is represented as a dove, and at the very top the whole is surmounted by the Hand of God appearing from heaven. On either side are large panels, which imitate pleated material. It was these panels which caused certain wits to refer to the church as 'The Essoldo, Queen's Gate', and they do in fact bear a certain resemblance to the curtain drapes found in cinemas at that time. However the pleated material effect was yet another change in the final design, as the drawing submitted with the faculty shows two ornate panels with SA monograms in their centres, and also two flaming urns above the scrolls situated two thirds of the way up the reredos. The faculty papers also reveal that the estimated cost was £1200, which was an enormous sum of money at that time, and well out of the financial reach of most parishes. While the inspiration for the reredos is thoroughly Baroque, it has a look of the 1920s as well (See Plate 15).

The design as executed was not the same as that prepared but never executed in Reading. Travers' drawing for that church shows a similar reredos but the side panels are open with turned wooden spindles, and the distinctive pleats are absent.

St. Augustine Queen's Gate: interior facing east when church whitewashed

Travers himself said of one of his reredos schemes that it was 'a free adaptation of the Renaissance manner more in keeping with the style now generally in use but following to some extent a traditional English type [such as] St. Magnus the Martyr'.

The reredos is a monument to a theatrical way of regarding the Church of England which relatively soon was regarded as passé. The wood was covered with silver foil and then varnished over with gold tints. The whole piece is actually rather flat, but the trompe l'oeil effect makes it appear much more three dimensional than it is. At certain points the feet of the priests have worn away the varnish, revealing the silver beneath, but the whole is in excellent condition. Because of its size, it was difficult to install and there was a great deal of scaffolding in the church, on which Alf Noe and another employee play acted, pretending to be about to fall to the ground far below.

In 1928 the tabernacle and six Italian baroque candlesticks were installed on the altar and during the following year the alterations to the pulpit, including a crucifix and sounding board, were commissioned. In that year also Travers created the wooden communion rails with their pierced knot designs, and, certainly one of the finest and most impressive items at St. Augustine, the double sided wooden frontal for the High Altar. The front resembles a pleated gold brocade Roman style frontal, whilst on the reverse is a more striking black one for requiems. In the centre is a gilded pieta on a black background powdered with gold and silver teardrops, which looks extraordinarily spectacular under the spotlights. Travers used a similar design in the Chapel of the Seven Sorrows in the Shrine of Our Lady at Walsingham after the Second War, and also for an unexecuted design intended for Christ Church Ealing in about 1935.

Travers also designed the Stations of the Cross for St. Augustine at about the same time. Their simplicity and boldness have received much admiration over the years and in about 1935 his assistant and chief carver, John Crawford, made an almost identical set for the church of the Holy Redeemer, Clerkenwell, the vicar of which was then Father Langton, who later moved to Bourne Street. The impact of the Stations is subtle owing to Travers' concept of making the background of each successive representation darker up to the Crucifixion scene; the last Station however has a lighter background suggesting the impending Resurrection. All the figures are in Travers' usual finish of silver foil varnished in yellow and daubed with umber.

In 1932 a memorial to one Elizabeth Fleming in the form of a backing to the shrine of Our Lady appeared, and the kneeling desk at this shrine was also included.

St. Augustine Queen's Gate: design for lady chapel, 1935 (Due to folds in the original Travers drawing some dark horizontal patches have resulted in this reproduction for which the authors apologise)

There was then a gap of a few years, and in 1938 Travers designed the lovely Lady Chapel altar and triptych complete with its wooden frontal bearing the AM monogram, together with a crucifix and two baroque candlesticks. The cherubs on the triptych hold silver ropes, which resemble peppermint creams, on which hang tassels, and for some this all seems to sum up Congress Baroque as pure high camp; others simply admire it. Here again the cost was high, some £435 (See Plate 16).

The east window was designed by Travers but not completed until 1950, after his death. It replaced a window by Butterfield which had been destroyed in the war, and because the reredos had covered part of the original window, the new window was only half the size of that which it replaced.

In 1975 the parish cleaned the church and decided to remove the whitewash, which was very dirty after nearly 50 years exposure. Some could not be taken off the brickwork as it was too deeply ingrained, and therefore a resemblance of the Butterfield brickwork was painted on the pillars of the nave and on the east wall. At that time, it was said that Butterfield's work and Travers' furnishings were each strong enough not to overpower the other.

It is not necessary to agree with Elizabeth and Wayland Young, who in their *London Churches* (1986) say 'perhaps the huge flat 'baroque' altarpiece by Martin Travers can some day be removed. It is quite a good piece but jars in this church ...'.[6] The opposite view was taken by Gavin Stamp and Colin Amery in *Victorian Buildings in London 1837-1887* (1980), when they say that Travers' fittings are 'just as worthy of preservation in their own right [as Butterfield's work]'.[7]

There are some, who include both the authors, who prefer the Travers furnishings against a whitewashed interior. The Stations of the Cross in particular were far more impressive when they hung in the white recesses rather than among the newly re-exposed tiled panels. Perhaps Father Tuckerman had been right after all!

However, of more importance perhaps is that the parish did not remove the furnishings and they are all still there to be seen.

Chapter 5

Travers as Designer:

III THE MIDDLE YEARS 1925–1938

The year 1925 was a high point for Martin Travers in many respects. In that year he was awarded the Grand Prix at the Paris Exhibition, and he was also taken on the staff of the RCA as head of stained glass. In addition, although he had had the setback of being passed over for further work at St. Mary, Bourne Street, he was completing his work at St. Magnus the Martyr, which was both successful and prestigious: see Chapter 4. He was in demand both for the baroque pastiches required by Anglo-Catholics and for stained glass required by a wide range of churches. His reputation was growing largely through personal recommendations from clergy and patrons and was spreading outwards from London.

As set out in chapter 3, Travers remained at the Glass House in Fulham until mid 1926, at which point he moved his workshop to 8, St. Paul's Studios, Hammersmith, which in 1931 became known as 48, Colet Gardens; he would still be using that address at the end of his life.

Travers' work continued at a high level throughout the 1920s, and included schemes which require extended discussion such as St. Augustine, Queen's Gate (Chapter 4) and Ashbury, Compton Beauchamp, and Cricklade (Chapter 6). However, by 1933 the baroque style was less in demand, and the world economic situation was poor. The combination of these factors with the illness and then death of his wife Christine in 1934 meant that his practice had reached a low ebb by the end of that year, and required to be rebuilt. In addition, he had attempted to diversify into designing new churches, a venture which had occupied a great deal of his time in the early 1930s, and that had not been a success: see Chapter 9.

It is fair to say that Travers managed the rebuilding very successfully. From 1935 to the outbreak of the Second World War his order book increased again, but on the whole the clientele was different. Travers began

Cover for An Office of Our Lady

to be seen as a man who could fulfil the requirements of any parish for either furnishings or stained glass. The files of what is now the Council for the Care of Churches show that he was greatly assisted by recommendations given on his behalf by Dr. F.C. Eeles, the then Secretary, who was himself a liturgist of some note and writer for the Alcuin Club, the stronghold of moderate English Use against the Romanisers. Travers even designed a personal bookplate for Eeles. Curiously, Eeles and Comper had a strong mutual dislike, although in some ways Comper's work would have seemed more naturally appealing to him than much of Travers' output; Comper however had deep and principled objections to the Diocesan Advisory Committees and even more to the Central Council for the Care of Churches. Travers' lack of personal convictions enabled him to deal with committees more easily, despite occasional problems.

As the 1930s went on, the standard Travers refurnishing scheme, often obtained by way of the Warham Guild, usually involved an English altar, with or without riddel posts, and often a plain reredos with a crucifix at its centre and sometimes rood figures in bas relief, and then a well lettered text on either side of the figures. The background was often blue or a characteristic deep red, almost terracotta, colour. No finer example exists of this form of decoration than the side chapel at St. Mary, Godmanchester, where, fittingly, Travers was later buried.

However, although Travers' work became more conventional, it retained both quality and distinction. He showed some influence from Italy, especially Mediaeval Lombardy, and even when working for the Warham Guild his altars incorporated some baroque embellishments, often with some Art Deco influence as one might expect at the time, particularly bearing in mind Travers' involvement with the 1925 Exhibition, although elsewhere that movement was regarded as somewhat passé by the 30s. It may be thought that the Art Deco influences emanated in part from John Crawford, who began working for him in about 1931 and was a considerable artist in his own right, but in fact those who knew the Travers method of working believe that all the new ideas came from Martin Travers himself.

Travers' stained glass shows significant changes in this period, with perhaps the really influential window being that for St. Mary, Tyneham, Dorset, designed in 1925 and installed in 1927.

It may perhaps be appropriate to commence this chapter with Travers' work at Tyneham, a village which has become well known because of its history over the last 50 years. Martin Travers designed for the small village church on the coast a simple reredos, which was to be the forerunner of many more executed in the 1930s. It is wooden, oblong, and dark red in colour. In the middle is a rood in bas-relief with a text across it. For the east window above he designed a delicate Madonna and Child backed by a willow tree, representing the Tree of Life. Travers' widow Mollie told the writer on stained glass, E. Liddell Armitage, that this was his favourite work; he exhibited it at the Royal Academy in 1927.

In later years it may be that the design became somewhat of a cliché; he used the same figure at various other places, such as Cricklade, Haddiscoe, Northiam, Nettlecombe, Iver Heath, and Riddlesdown, sometimes reversed. However the combination of the figures, the tree, and the clear glass is a powerful one. The window at Tyneham was given in memory of Grace Draper (1874–1923) by her husband.

The notoriety attached to Tyneham results from the Army taking over

Design for window and altar at Tyneham, Dorset, 1925

the village for training during the Second World War and forcibly evacuating the inhabitants. They then refused to allow them back, despite clear assurances given to the contrary, with the result that the village remained deserted. The church, unlike other buildings, was not used for target practice, but lay unused for many years. It can now be visited most weekends and every day in August. Lilian Bond set out a vision of the village as a lost idyll: *Tyneham: a lost heritage* (1955). She says of the window[1]:

> It represents Our Lady seated in the shade of a weeping willow with the Holy Child upon her knee. The side lights show, as distant background, miniature scenes of daily life at Tyneham, fishermen putting out to sea and labourers

busy in the fields. The figures are surrounded by clear glass, allowing the trees and hills to be seen beyond them. On sunny days the painted butterflies which flutter around the central group appeared to have floated in, that very moment, from the outside air, ready to drift away into the blue.

It appears from Mrs. Bond's book that for a time the window may have been stored at Corfe Castle, where Travers also did extensive work. However, it is now in its proper place. It also appears from her book that the reredos was taken out and placed in another nearby church, Steeple. However, that too has returned, but unfortunately not in its proper place. It has been attached to the west wall in the gallery, but is in good condition. Steeple church also had its own rather similar reredos designed by him, which has been removed and is now hidden in the tower. Another similar reredos was erected at this time at All Saints, Laleham, then in Middlesex, now Surrey, which sadly has been removed since, resulting in a cold bare sanctuary.

In the same year, 1925, Travers executed a commission which was totally different in ethos from Tyneham, on this occasion in Sussex.

On 6th November 1924 a new parish priest was inducted to the living of the Annunciation, Washington Street, Brighton. This was Father John Tiley, who had come from The Ascension, Lavender Hill, Battersea, where he had served a curacy under the well-known Arthur Montford, who had been the Chairman of the Committee organizing the 1923 Anglo-Catholic

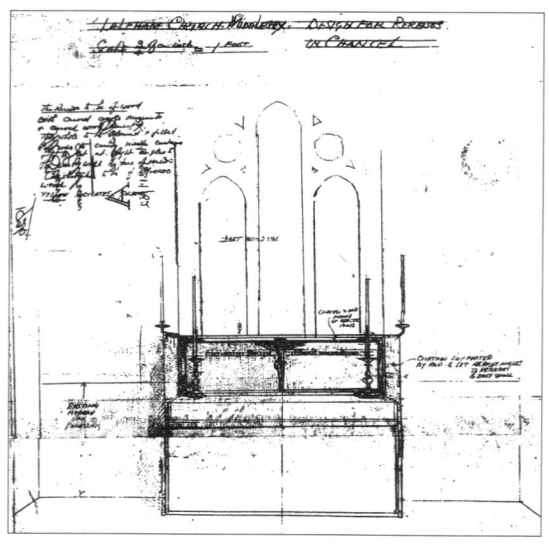

Laleham Reredos

High altar, Church of the Annunciation, Brighton, 1925

Congress. Early in 1925 Father Tiley commissioned Martin Travers to refurnish the sanctuary at The Annunciation. The previous altar was a Gothic design of no great merit, which is pictured in H. Hamilton Maughan's *Some Brighton Churches* (1922)[2]; that book itself is an interesting period piece with its sustained advocacy of the Western Use. Travers produced an imposing Spanish-style reredos, altar with frontal, and a large tabernacle flanked by six baroque gilded wooden candlesticks. This reredos cleverly incorporated the east window, which contains glass by Rosetti and Burne Jones. On either side he provided two baroque frames for a pair of Della Robbia plaques which portray the Annunciation. Above the high altar with its gilded frontal hung one of Travers' ornate octagonal canopies also in gilded and painted wood complete with tassels. Several of his designs for the more 'advanced' parishes included these canopies during the 1920s. This work remains in the church today.

Brighton was a new area for Travers: he had in fact designed a chapel and windows the previous year for St. Patrick, Hove, including an English altar with riddel posts supporting boy cherub candleholders, with a simple rectangular reredos with a rood within it, like that for Tyneham, but this never came to fruition. In 1932 he was to design a series of windows in the narthex of All Saints, Hove, in memory of the former vicar, Canon Peacey, and his wife, showing the Annunciation, the Incarnation, the Three Kings, and the Presentation, with two smaller windows showing the patron saints of England, Scotland, Wales, and Ireland; these were executed.

It is likely that through Father Montford's earlier connection with the church of St. Saviour, St. Albans, Martin Travers was asked in about 1924

Unexecuted design for High Altar at St. Saviour, St. Albans, mid 1920s

to produce two sets of drawings for major refurnishings for that parish. One was for the high altar and the other for the lady chapel. The high altar scheme was for a vast triptych with various saints portrayed on the doors; in the centre was a semi-relief of The Resurrection and below this stood a baroque altar with six candlesticks, but all within riddel posts. High above hung a large gilded wooden canopy complete with tassels. Unfortunately this exotic idea did not materialize, but the Lady Chapel was furnished from his second scheme in 1925-6. This scheme comprised a tall Spanish-style reredos with two large panels depicting the Annunciation. Above hung an octagonal tester. On the altar stood a large gilded wooden tabernacle and two candlesticks. The chapel was enclosed by a turned wooden screen painted blue and gold. At the top of each panel was a moulded putti head and all was surmounted by a freeze of fretwork lilies. In 1926 Travers added the chapel windows, and in 1931 he added clergy stalls at the rear of the chapel. This work still survives, although it is beginning to show its age somewhat and needs some attention. The screen looks somewhat artificial and is not of the quality of the one at SS. Peter and Paul, Kettering (See Plate 17).

Travers of course continued to work in the London area. In about 1925 he designed a trompe l'oeil surround for the tabernacle in Old St. Pancras. The flat board appears to be a concave box. Following a reordering after a desecration, the surround is now in the tower and is used as a backing for the shrine of Our Lady of Walsingham.

In the 1925-8 period Travers carried out five significant renovations in the diocese of Southwark; unfortunately only one remains in place today. They can perhaps be dealt with as a group at this point.

In 1924 Revd T.P. Stevens, an old acquaintance of Travers from his days at Bedford Park, became vicar of St. Matthew, New Kent Road, Newington. According to his autobiography, *Cassock and Surplus* (1947), Stevens 'had a passion for decorating churches'[3]. He asked Travers to transform the interior of the rather ugly church, which was near the Elephant and Castle. It was dark and overcrowded with the roof supported on heavy iron pillars, and across the chancel arch was a heavy wooden gothic screen.

Travers covered the iron pillars with cement casing, raised the roof and inserted ten rectangular windows to form a new clerestory. He colourwashed the church and installed two new chapels in the north and south aisles. The old screen was remodelled into two parclose screens between the new chapels and the chancel and the organ was repositioned into the west gallery.

He moved the existing four-panelled Gothic high altar reredos into the lady chapel on the north side, and inserted behind the two centre arches a

St. Matthew New Kent Road: lady chapel after alterations of 1927

plaque of the Annunciation. On either side and surrounding it was a frieze of painted oranges and pears entwined with ribbons. A new frontal (designed later) and two baroque candlesticks completed the chapel furnishings.

Across the apsidal east end of the chancel Travers placed a screen containing a door at each end, leading to a sacristy behind. The upper panels of these doors were constructed of turned wood spindles. He brought the new chancel forward into the first bay of the nave providing more space. In order to achieve this some of the pews were discarded. In front of the new screen stood a reredos in his own idiosyncratic baroque style representing the Holy Spirit sending forth tongues of fire to a Christus Rex on the altar cross below. Two gilded wooden candlesticks and a double-sided wooden altar frontal completed the new chancel refurnishing (See Plate 18).

Although this new scheme was fairly extensive, there had in fact been another set of drawings for the high altar, but as St. Matthew's had been involved in such costly alterations for the clerestory and nave it is likely that the cheaper sanctuary plans had to be chosen. The other set had shown a vast triptych and ornate chancel screen.

However, in addition to the other work, the pulpit was provided with a sounding board decorated with putti heads. A rood with Our Lady and St. John was later designed to hang over the chancel arch; this was not in his usual style, as Our Lady was shown trampling down the Devil in the form of the serpent. A gilded 'lily' crucifix was also provided for the Lady Chapel (see previous page). Travers lit the church with new plaster light fittings shaped in the form of star and wheat ear embossed medallions. Similar fittings were used at St. James, Watford, and the Good Shepherd, Carshalton: see Chapter 10. When seen from the west end they must have had the appearance of Christmas decorations, but as the bulbs were exposed on the other side the effect from the chancel must have been glaring and rather ugly. Revd B.F.L. Clarke, antiquarian and inveterate church crawler, remarked in his usual laconic way: 'I saw this work being done, and admired it at the time: after nearly 40 years, it does not look as enterprising as it did'[4]. The RIBA Catalogue says: 'Travers' design for rendering less unpalatable a cheap and aggressive Gothic church ... is typically resourceful and theatrical.' Travers' skill in this church was to take a very unpromising building and make something of it without spending too much money.

This church is in an area which has been rebuilt in the last thirty years and

St. Matthew New Kent Road: sanctuary and pulpit, 1927

it has itself recently been demolished and replaced by a mediocre modern building. The reredos has been moved to St. Agatha, Landport, Portsmouth for use there. The hall, also by Travers, has been demolished.

Nearby at Holy Trinity, Southwark, a classical church designed and built by the architect Bedford in 1823, Travers produced an altar in English style within a riddel framework of linenfold panelling. On each corner stood an urn sprouting flames. Two classical candlesticks and a cross were included in his drawing, but an old photograph shows that the church used a standard Victorian cross and candlesticks. Above hung a vast octagonal canopy of painted and gilded wood with its own stylized wooden tassels. The east window had an impressive representation of the Trinity in grey, yellow and gold and was framed to match the riddels and canopy. On the window sill was a pelican feeding her young, executed in painted and gilded wood. Two other stained glass windows of Our Lady and St. Nicholas are to be seen in his plans, and he also designed a memorial tablet to a former vicar. John Betjeman says of this church: 'The interior was made dramatic and catholic by Martin Travers ...'[5].

Holy Trinity was closed for many years and the glass may well have been taken out, before it was gutted by fire in 1973, when all the furnishings were too badly damaged for further use; it was then converted into a recording studio and rehearsal room for musicians.

These two churches were examples of Travers' skill when dealing with difficult commissions in a diocese where his work of a more extreme nature would not have found acceptance with the Advisory Committee.

High altar and window, Holy Trinity Southwark, 1928

Not very far from Southwark, in Nine Elms, was St. Andrew, Dashwood Road, Battersea, (sometimes known as St. Andrew, Stockdale Road) which was a dull redbrick church designed by a local architect, Henry Stone, in 1875. Its intended tower with a spire in the south east corner was never completed. In 1927 the incumbent, Father James Humphries, embarked on a refurnishing project and asked Travers to prepare a scheme for the high altar. It consisted of a large ornate gilded triptych with a centre panel of Christ in Glory. On the doors were Our Lady and St. John. The altar was provided with a crucifix and two candlesticks which, unusually, were not in the baroque style. All was within simple riddels, the curtains of which hung on iron brackets supporting candlesticks.

Being a poor parish, St. Andrew's was probably unable to afford the triptych and altar which Travers had originally planned; the furnishings which eventually appeared were much simpler and bore a resemblance in shape to the contemporary reredos at St. Matthew New Kent Road. This depicted Christ's resurrection and on the altar were six wooden baroque candlesticks. The altar had a double sided wood frontal in the form of pleated material, another Travers device. Fortunately there is photographic evidence of the arrangement when new.

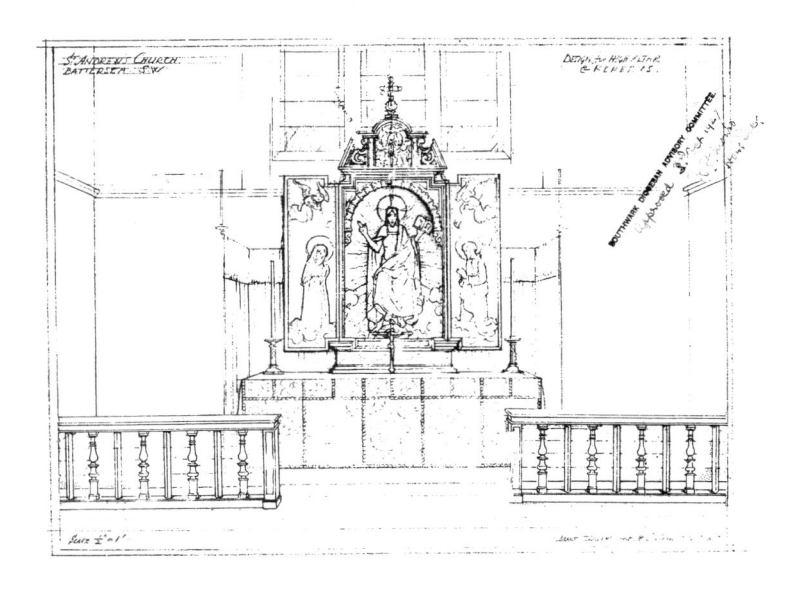

St. Andrew Battersea: design for sanctuary, 1927

High altar and reredos, St. Andrew Battersea, now demolished

In a manner similar to that used at St. Magnus the Martyr, City, a door frame was transformed into a reredos for a side chapel. Here the altar was also given a double sided wooden frontal and a large sacrament house was installed. It has been said that the old Victorian pews were cut down and refashioned, but photographic evidence in a parish magazine from the 1930s shows this not to be the case.

During the blitz of September 1940 the church and many of the houses in the parish were obliterated in one night. St. Andrew was never rebuilt and the parish is now part of St. Saviour and St. George, Battersea, which uses a small modern building for worship; the Catholic tradition has long since disappeared.

Further west in Battersea, on the borders of Balham, is the majestic basilica church of St. Luke, Ramsden Road. This parish was in a more prosperous area than the three earlier mentioned Southwark parishes and was able to afford much embellishment within the building. The parish history describes as 'short but brilliant' the incumbency (1924-8) of Revd W.T. Havard, later Bishop of St. Asaph and later still of St. David's. It was

Lady chapel, St. Luke, Battersea, mid 1920s

he who was instrumental in the production by Travers of an elaborate lady chapel in 1925, which is approached through an Italianate screen designed in the same year. In this chapel is a triptych of Our Lady with the infant Jesus in a typical Travers moulded shape. At the top of this central relief are two cherubs holding a small cartouche. On the walls on either side of the triptych are two baroque plaques of the Annunciation, the Angel Gabriel on the left and Mary on the right. These are identical to the plaques in St. Matthew, New Kent Road, and St. Mary, West Wickham and would have come from the same moulds. In 1927 he installed the window of King David playing his lyre.

Two font cover designs had appeared in 1926. The first resembled an open church tower with the infant Christ inside. The second was a tall open spire structure on several columns in gilded and red painted wood, loosely based on the church of St. Stephen Walbrook in the City. This was the chosen scheme, and it is still in place over the font.

The communion rails at the high altar were also designed by Travers, and are in his own inimitable baroque style bearing Latin inscriptions; the ends contain angel faces sprouting from scrolls shaped to resemble clouds. He also designed the fine superfrontal in 1928. It has an intricate knot design which has recently been restored in new gold threads and looks majestic on the high altar. This church alone of the group continues to have its Travers work in original condition: the only

St. Luke Battersea: design for font cover, 1926

changes have been that the rood crucifix from the lady chapel now stands in front of the altar rather than on it, and the Travers silvered plaster candlesticks are also no longer on the altar, their place being taken by two small blue painted ones.

Finally in the Southwark area at that time, Travers carried out extensive internal work at the famous church of St. Agnes, Kennington Park. This consisted of alterations to the chancel levels and high altar and decoration of the chancel roof, as well as the provision of furnishings. The roof stencilling cannot be described as a success: it shows stylized angels, which Comper called 'almost Scandinavian'. In 1926 the vicar applied for a faculty

Interior of St. Agnes, Kennington, showing the stencilling on the roof and the two altars in front of the screen: the work was carried out in 1925

to insert two further altars in the church, both on the nave side of the rood screen, one to the left to St. George, with familiar statue, and one to the right to St. Joan of Arc, also with a statue. The Chancellor was dubious about the insertion of a further two altars into a church which already had three, and Travers had to appear, with the vicar, before him; the faculty was only granted on condition that an existing altar was removed. This church was also badly damaged in the war and later demolished amid much controversy.

There is a small modern church of the same name, which has a crucifix, two candlesticks, and a statue of Our Lady by Travers from the old church. The rood beam was taken to Holy Spirit, Southsea, but the rood itself, would not fit that church, so was hung in St. Peter's, Streatham. That rood is not by Travers (whose draft account for work done at the church shows that he merely cleaned it), although it has been attributed to him. It was in fact designed by Temple Moore in 1885–9.

Travers also carried out other work in South London during this period, including a window of the Presentation in the Temple in the south aisle at St. Andrew, Garrett Lane, Wandsworth, (1926), windows at St. Mark, Woodcote Village, Purley (1928 and 1931), an elaborate doorcase at St. Mary Balham (1933), a window at St. Barnabas Sutton (1934) and a chapel at St. Mary Lewisham (1934), which included a reredos with pleated wood effect and a painting of Our Lady. Unfortunately in 1996 this church was reordered and the reredos fixed to the ceiling of the north transept, where it is obviously out of place: on the other hand, it is still there. The remainder of the work set out still exists, but a memorial reredos in the side chapel at St. Mary, Shortlands, Bromley (1928), which was said by Dr. Eeles to be the best piece of work in the church, was lost to bombs in the war.

A Travers reredos at St. Lawrence, Catford (1932) was removed to St. Paul, Woodford Bridge, when the Catford church was demolished in about 1970,and has now been removed from that church also. A chapel at St. Peter, Walworth (1929) with a reredos depicting St. Christopher and the Holy Child was also destroyed by bombs and was later rebuilt in a pale imitation of Travers' style and to a different design. There is a cartouche of cherubs over the doorway to the chapel which looks like his work, but in fact was not part of the earlier design.

In West London at this time (1927) Travers designed a series of small windows for the lady chapel of St. Saviour's Church for the Deaf, Old Oak Lane, Acton, in memory of Bishop Pereira, who had been much concerned with work among the hard of hearing. The windows are well lettered, as usual, and in a predominantly yellow ochre colour.

Design for window at Burbage, Derbyshire

One rather backward-looking commission for the time was a First World War memorial window for Christ Church, Burbage, Derbyshire, which was executed as late as 1925. Not only was this later than many such memorials, but although the work was designed in the same year as the Tyneham window, it was in an earlier style, with a bright blue background to the rood figures depicted rather than the clear glass which he was increasingly using.

In 1925 Travers turned his attention to his old school. His first scheme for the chapel at Tonbridge, from 1909 and showing a strong Comper influence, had never been taken up, and he prepared two further sets of drawings. The first of these, which was rejected, was for a baroque triptych showing the Transfiguration with Moses and Elijah in the centre and St. Gregory and St. Augustine on the doors. Below was an altar similar to that installed in Barham, but with two boy cherubs on the riddels. The candlesticks and cross were identical to those at Barham. The third and accepted design was a free rendering in the Renaissance manner and was a large impressive reredos, incorporating a cupboard behind for storing altar frontals. At either end was a concave door with open turned wooden upper panels.

The reredos was known as the Lowry, Lucas, and David memorial; it was erected in memory of Charles Lowry, Headmaster 1907-22, Revd Arthur Lucas, Assistant Master 1878-1909, and Martin David, Assistant Master 1899-1916. The latter two would have been known to Travers when he himself was at the school, from 1899 to 1904.

The centre relief, which was unfortunately not ready when the reredos was erected in 1928, was of Jesus appearing to the two disciples during the evening meal at Emmaus. A photograph from 1929 in the Tonbridgean shows that the flanking panels were not completed until later, when sufficient funds were available. However in due course the money was found, and the reliefs installed. They were of St. Augustine, St. Gregory, St. Alban, and St. George. Above each panel a pair of cherubs held a cartouche bearing the monogram appropriate to the saint. Angels and cherubs sprouted everywhere, and at the top, in the centre of the cornice, two more held an IHS monogram within a sunburst. This was flanked by the arms of the following: The Skinners' Company, St. Augustine, St. Andrew, Sir Andrew Judd, St. Gregory, and Tonbridge School.

Travers' plans for this altar included only two candlesticks, and a cross in gilded wood; there were also two standard candlesticks. Altar rails were shown but never materialized.

In due course, the altar was provided with six silver candlesticks and riddel curtains, in similar manner to the high altar at York Minster.

The reredos at Tonbridge School was Travers' only work using these concave doors, which were most attractive, although the idea of using open panelled doors was itself much favoured by him in the 1920s, as at St. Matthew, New Kent Road and an unexecuted design for St. Swithun, Compton Beauchamp.

In 1925 he had prepared a drawing for memorial tablets around the west door which commemorated the donors of the chapel windows. These tablets, in red and gold, were linked by an intricate knot pattern culminating in large gilded tassels. Once again, this took some time to materialise.

Travers did further work in the chapel in 1947-8, described in Chapter 7. Unfortunately, in 1988 the chapel was completely burned down and all his work was destroyed.

In many of the churches where Travers installed his neo-baroque furnishings, they did not match the Gothic style of the church, and therefore looked somewhat artificial. However, in 1926 Travers was called in by Roger Wodehouse, parish priest of St. Paul, Walton Street, Oxford, and a scion of the nobility: a contemporary letter of his drops the name of his mother (Lady Sandhurst). St. Paul was a small classical building which Father Wodehouse wished to transform into something resembling a French or Belgian parish church. He was a strong supporter of the SSPP, and in 1917, while a curate at St. Thomas the Martyr, Oxford (another church for which Travers was later to carry out work) he had had the high altar transformed into a replica of an eighteenth century continental shrine, including commissioning a reproduction of an Italian painting in the Vatican. He was also known for his keen sense of humour. Travers produced

TRAVERS AS DESIGNER III

High altar, Tonbridge School, as originally installed and prior to completion of panels, 1928

High altar, Tonbridge School, as completed

for this client a scheme for the high altar which was both ornate and theatrical, suiting Father Wodehouse well. It had a reredos with baroque frame simulating drapes and tassels and was capped by gilded cherubs holding a cartouche inscribed 'Sic enim Deus dilexit mundum.' In the centre, behind the baroque crucifix and tabernacle, hung red drapes. All of this ensemble was in painted and gilded wood with an ornate octagonal canopy with its own wooden tassels. Unfortunately, this exuberance never materialized, probably due to lack of finance, and the design which was subsequently adopted was much simpler and consisted of a gilded wooden gradine with baroque scrolled ends which resembled the dolphin tails on the furniture in the Brighton Pavilion; this was done very much later, after Father Wodehouse had left the church.

There was a large tabernacle in the centre of the altar, which Father Wodehouse had obtained in Belgium and contained an ingenious device which must have appealed to Travers: by turning a key the tabernacle turned round so that it became a throne for benediction.

Once the interior was completed by introducing further genuine continental furnishings to complement Travers' work to the altar, the church looked, as it was intended to, completely alien to the Church of England.

In about 1964, St. Paul was closed, but the altar and gradine were saved and installed in Holy Trinity Reading, where it was later joined by the Travers altar from Nashdom. The St. Paul's work begins to show its age and perhaps the inadequate materials used in its construction, but at least it is there to be seen, and it is still used.

Revd T. J. Jalland became parish priest of St. Luke, Swindon, in 1925. The church is and was strongly Catholic in teaching; very few Anglican parishes have authenticated relics of St. Pius X and St. Theresa of Lisieux in the high altar. In 1926 Father Jalland commissioned Travers to design a crucifix for a new south aisle chapel. Although the altar for which it was designed has now disappeared, the crucifix remains in the church as part of a war memorial. In the same church, in 1928, Travers was again able to exercise his ingenuity. It was a poor parish, and when they required the rood to be hung from the ceiling rather than to stand on a beam, Travers was able to reuse the existing figures, but replace the cross itself with a more suitable design.

At All Saints, Fulham, in 1928, Travers provided a small baroque triptych war memorial. He also prepared drawings for a new lady chapel altar with riddel posts at this church in the same year, but another artist was commissioned to carry this out. In 1925 he had designed a memorial tablet for the church for one Matthew Morrison, which remains on the wall near the triptych. The candlesticks and crucifix in this church, which resemble Travers' work, were executed by Laurence King through Faith Craft in 1949.

Travers continued during this period to design glass for a wide range of churches across southern England. In 1928 he provided for St. Bartholomew, Burwash, East Sussex, a fine triple-lancet east window in memory of Revd R.L. Martyn-Linnington, vicar of the parish 1909–25. This has some similarities to the fine east window in Barham, discussed in Chapter 3. In the centre are Mary and her Child, on the left St. Bartholomew, and on the right St. Richard of Chichester. There is a great deal of clear glass, and much excellent detail, including some typical cherubs.

The splendid church of St. Mary, Woodbridge, Suffolk was enhanced in 1930 by an east window depicting the Adoration of the Magi with clear glass around it enabling light to flood into the interior. John Betjeman

Design for east window at St. Mary, Woodbridge, 1930

rightly commented: 'The interior has been wonderfully improved ... by a beautiful east window by Martin Travers'[6].

In the same year, he fulfilled one of his rare non-ecclesiastical commissions, with a window in the house of the Warden of St. Edward's School, Woodstock Road, Oxford, showing the saint on horseback; this was a gift from the then president of the School Society and his wife.

Also in this year he also designed the north transept window for Christ Church, Swindon Old Town, in memory of local dignitary Fitzroy Pleydell Goddard. Betjeman in his contribution to *Studies in the History of Swindon* (1950) calls this[7] 'a most interesting modern window ... It is a transparency done in the eighteenth century manner of enamelled glass with three coats of arms and a view of Liddington painted as seen in a frame of hollyhocks and foxgloves from 'The Lawn' [Goddard's house]'. It is indeed an unusual window, as there is no religious content to it and much is landscape.

In 1931 Travers designed and executed a three light window at St. Mary the Virgin, High Easter, Essex, showing the Annunciation, the Nativity, and the Presentation in the Temple. This church has no catholic tradition and demonstrates the wider appeal of his work by this time. He had earlier designed a variation on the 'Tyneham' pattern for this church, but the eventual design was more detailed and contained more figures. In fact, the faculty papers show that the window was only installed after an earlier design by another artist for a mosaic floor was rejected, which led to litigation over the terms of the will in which the legacy to enhance the church had been left. Fortunately, the court ruled that there was power to use the money for a window.

The next year, he contributed a memorial to the painter Mia Arnesby-Brown, who died in 1931, to the Norfolk church of St. Mary, Haddiscoe. This window adapts the standard 'Tyneham' design of mother and child, both by adding a picture of the church itself, and by including references to the flowers which the deceased used to paint.

He also designed three separate panels for two windows at St. Nicholas, Brockenhurst, in the New Forest. One, installed 1932, has already been mentioned in Chapter 1; it commemorates a former captain with the Union Castle line. In 1926 he had again depicted St. Nicholas in a schooner, but on this occasion incorporated in the design the three legs of Man, a reference to the origins of the subject, the former vicar, Revd C.H. Gill. The third, the least distinguished, was installed in 1936 and shows St. Francis preaching to the birds, in memory of H.N. Bowden-Smith.

During 1931 Travers designed two small windows at one of the more

Design for St. Mary, High Easter, 1931

obscure London churches, St. Bartholomew, Dalston, which was closed in 1945 and later converted into housing. A scheme to commemorate a previous vicar, Revd E.S. Bruhl, by putting in stained glass in part only of a window was rejected, and Travers was brought in. He portrayed St. Bartholomew in one window and the lion of St. Mark in the other, and his scheme received a faculty.

The following year he executed a small window at St. John the Evangelist, Kilburn, which has now been demolished: this was also in memory of a former vicar, Revd George Martin, and showed a saint receiving a message coming from above on a scroll.

1932 saw Travers design a window for St. George, Littleport,

Cambridgeshire, which was installed in 1934 in memory of C.C. Defew. It shows the appearance of Our Lord to the Apostles after the crucifixion, and is in good condition; unfortunately a wall has been erected between nave and aisle to form a vestry, which means this fine window cannot be seen by the congregation.

A similar one off commission resulted in a window of 1934 in the remote Broadland parish of St. Edmund, Thurne, Norfolk, showing Jesus' appearance to St. Mary Magdalene, with much clear glass around.

Within the 1930–4 period there were relatively few commissions for furnishings, as opposed to glass, although Travers was concerned during this time with building new churches at Streatham and Leyton: see Chapter 9.

In 1931 he produced a war memorial triptych behind an altar at St. Columb, Notting Hill, for which he had previously designed some of his first glass. The altar was given a frontal of painted and gilded wood representing pleated material and was decorated with a knot design. On the

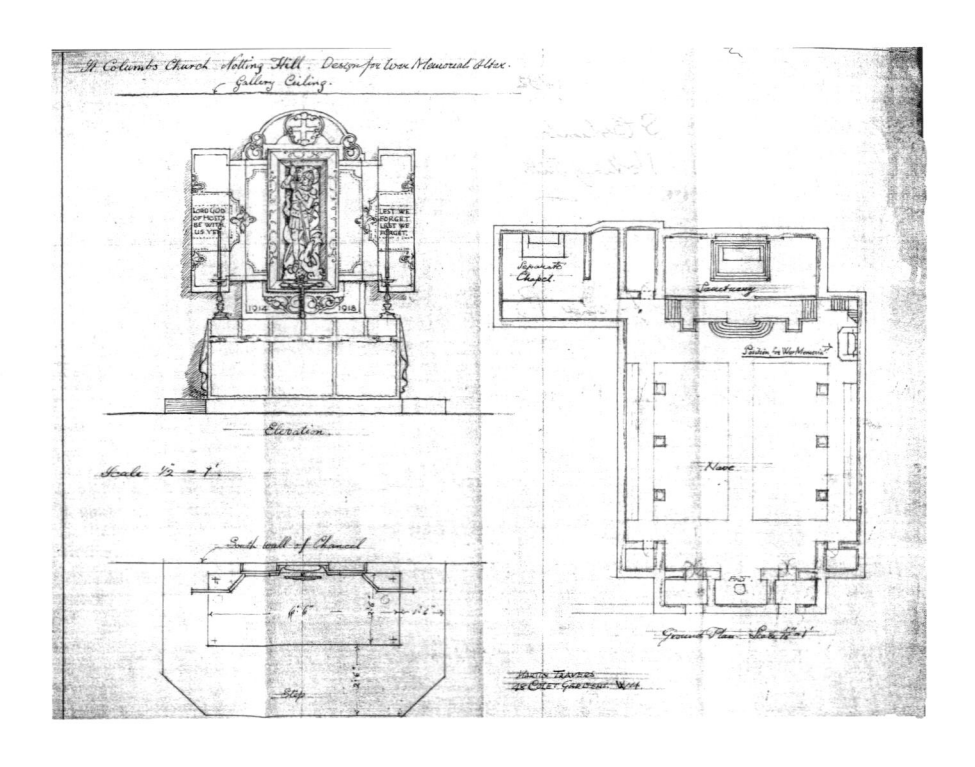

St. Columb Notting Hill: design for war memorial altar

mensa stood two silver wooden Baroque/Art Deco candlesticks. These furnishings are now in All Saints, Notting Hill, as St. Columb, now St. Sava, is used by the Serbs.

However, Travers again began receiving work through the Warham Guild, and was on their list of approved designers, thus again broadening his client base. In 1932 he received, through the Guild, a commission from the church of St. Dionis, Parson's Green, Fulham. He provided a fine, if loose, rendering of the English altar, which included a small ogee shaped reredos in characteristic terra cotta colour representing pleated material on which was displayed a crucifix with a sunburst and the inscription 'Sic enim Deus dilexit mundum'. The riddel posts supported the usual boy cherubs holding candles. On the altar stood two Baroque/Art Deco candlesticks.

Parish magazine cover, St. Dionis Parson's Green

This work was also featured in the English Churchman's Kalendar that year; the editor said it was a 'stately altar ... more or less, though not perhaps wholly, in the manner of the Renaissance.'

The viewing of the new altar necessitated heightening of the chancel screen, which was then provided with a large rood and its own loft. New communion rails appeared to Travers' designs and on 29th October 1933 the completed sanctuary was dedicated by the Bishop of Kensington. It had been paid for by a Mrs. Walter Jones in memory of her husband. Travers carried out further work for this church just after the end of the period dealt with in this chapter. For the Golden Jubilee of the church in 1935, he produced the following: a banner of St. Dionis, and three memorial plaques, one to Miss Charlotte Sullivan, one to Mr. S.H. Gardiner, and the third, a semi-relief of St. Dionis, commemorated Revd J.S. Sinclair, the first vicar of the parish. In appearance it recalls those at Ashbury and Compton Beauchamp dealt with in Chapter 7. Three years later he designed a font cover in the form of the tower from the City church of St. Dionis Backchurch, which had been demolished in 1878, at which time the font and pulpit had been given to St. Dionis Parsons Green. This cover was a memorial to Dr. Carter, a former vicar, and his wife. Travers also designed the gilt hymn boards, each with a scroll above.

Sometime in the 1970s the vicar removed the reredos and dismantled the English altar. It was replaced by a plain silver cross set against a dark blue velvet dossal curtain below the east window; some think the effect is more akin

Font cover, St. Dionis Parson's Green, mid 1930s

to a local authority crematorium. The Travers reredos now hangs forlornly on the south side of the chancel near the relief of St. Dionis. This has not enhanced the church at all; a simple English sanctuary has been destroyed.

Another altar from this period was that at St. Mary, Liss, Hampshire, erected in about 1930. Travers produced an English high altar within riddel posts, which supported his usual boy cherubs holding candles. On the altar itself stands a gilded triptych of Our Lady, rather similar to his earlier design for Winforton, Herefordshire, and to it was fixed a simple cross. Two candlesticks completed the scheme. This work was featured in the English Churchman's Kalendar for 1931, where it was said that Travers had solved a difficult problem – how to fill the space beneath the east window 'very adroitly upon sound English liturgical lines.' The centre panel of the triptych is also a precursor of those at Beaulieu and Romsey discussed in Chapter 7 (See Plate 19).

At the same church, but in about 1942, Travers designed two small stained glass windows in memory of a former Rector and his wife, one of Our Lady with St. Anne and one of St. Joseph and Our Lord at the carpenter's bench. He also at some point stencilled the ceiling of the bell-ringing room in the tower.

In 1934 Travers designed a plain gilded and pleated reredos with crucifix and also an east window in 'Tyneham' style for St. Margaret, Iver Heath, Buckinghamshire, which remain, although the reredos has recently been dismantled and stored, and also work at SS. Mary and Sexburga, Minster-in-Sheppey, Kent, most of which has been removed. The Minster work is interesting as showing Travers' ingenuity and also the effect of changing liturgical fashions on his designs. The Abbey is a mixture of styles, and at that time there was a heavy eighteenth century reredos behind the high altar. Travers was originally asked to move the reredos to the tower arch at the back of the church. However, papers with the faculty application make it clear that, within the budget given, he devised a scheme which he then persuaded the parish to adopt. He provided a new, longer, high altar with candlesticks and crucifix, he renovated the reredos by removing poor Victorian lettering, gilding it, and painting panels in his trademark deep red with lacquer and in addition he completely restored the main rood screen and loft, of which only the base remained. However, in 1964 the church obtained a faculty to remove the reredos, which eventually went to St. Lawrence, East Donyland, Essex; it proved unpopular there also and has since been removed and sold. In 1969 the rood screen itself was dismantled (restoring the church to its pre-Travers look) and was adapted to

Interior of the church of SS. Mary & Sexburga, Minster-in-Sheppey, showing the chancel screen as restored and the high altar and reredos. None of this work, carried out in c 1934, is now in place.

cover the entrance to the tower, where the reredos had originally been intended to stand in 1934. The altar remains, but with modern furnishings on it, and there is little to show of the Travers work.

The decade 1925–34 had seen a promising career apparently falter towards the end of it, but the next decade was to bring further successes.

In 1935 Travers was asked to design a sanctuary reordering for Christ Church (now Christ the Saviour), Ealing. He provided two schemes for a new high altar and reredos. One was of an ogee shaped reredos within riddel posts and cherub candlesticks; on the altar stood six baroque candlesticks and a dome tabernacle. The second set of drawings depicted a Sacred Heart emblem on a simple castellated reredos, with candlesticks and tabernacle as in the first scheme. Two frontals were also designed, or possibly he used his usual double-sided version; one showed an Agnus Dei backed by sunburst and made to resemble pleated material, which was bordered in an intricate knot design. The other was as requiem frontal in black powdered with silver teardrops, similar to the one he had made for St. Augustine, Queens Gate. He also designed a new oak high altar.

In 1935 a faculty was granted for the new altar, and also for alterations to the sanctuary step levels and repaving. At the same time an application was made for a new reredos, also designed by Travers, which in fact had a risen Christ figure extending his blessing in the centre, with the four evangelists around on the corners of the side panels, and was thus different again from the two original schemes. In fact, the parish could not afford it at that time and so that part of the application was withdrawn. However, the triptych, tabernacle, crucifix and six candlesticks arrived some time later. The tabernacle and the triptych have since been removed and in recent years the original Victorian reredos has been renovated, and looks in tune with the rest of the building. The altar, crucifix and candlesticks remain.

Travers also designed a rood and loft for the chancel screen in 1935, but these never materialized, presumably also owing to lack of funds.

The fine church of St. John the Evangelist, Upper Norwood, was Ninian Comper's parish church, and he regularly worshipped there. It was interesting therefore that it was to Travers that they turned when work was required in the 1930s. In 1935 he produced a statue of Our Lady. 1937 marked the fiftieth anniversary of the building of the church, and to celebrate the event the parish decided to create a First World War

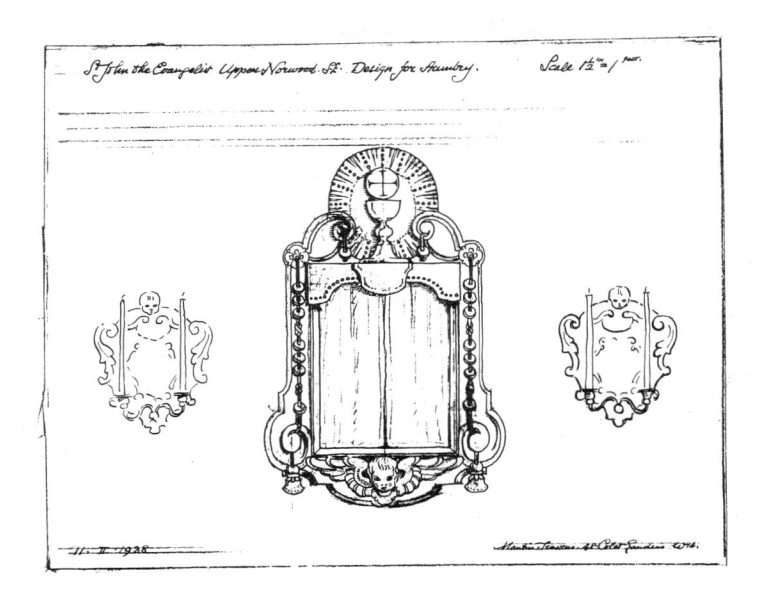

Unexecuted design for aumbry, St. John, Upper Norwood

Design for chapel of St. George at St. John, Upper Norwood

memorial chapel of St. George for those who had been in the Royal Naval Volunteer Reserve and the Royal Naval Division at Crystal Palace. Travers made a plaque of St. George and the dragon, which hung on the wall above a baroque crucifix. Below was an altar on which stood two large wooden candlesticks; this altar was provided with a double-sided wooden frontal made to resemble pleated material and bordered in a knot design. This was situated in the south aisle, and a wall was built across the aisle in front of the south transept and lady chapel, which also has a Travers altar frontal in blue and gold. The new wall was painted with whitewash, thus providing an ideal background for the furnishings. On 22nd April 1937 it was dedicated by Bishop Cary and the Bishop of Croydon, and later the same year, on 4th July the Bishop of Nassau blessed Travers' statue of Our Lady.

In recent years the walls of this chapel have been stripped back to the brickwork in an attempt to match the rest of the church, but unfortunately neither the bricks nor the pointing are of the quality used in the rest of Pearson's majestic church, and the result is somewhat rough. The crucifix has also been raised far too high above the altar, which consequently has been provided with a silver plated crucifix between the two Travers candlesticks, which it does not match. The plaque of St. George has been moved to the south aisle wall of the chapel, and Travers' original concept of St. George as patron of England above the altar has been completely spoilt.

In the north aisle is a window of Our Lord, Our Lady, and St. John. This was designed by Travers in late 1947 and executed in 1948; it is said to be the last work completed by him in his lifetime.

A drawing exists for a baroque aumbry designed by Travers in about 1938 for the church, but this was never made.

Apart from his furnishings, Travers continued to design good quality glass in 1935-6. Among the work designed in those years was a further window for St. Andrew Catford to join those he had carried out in the 1920s and a fine, strong-coloured, Virgin and Child for St. George, Bicknoller, North Somerset. In the remote nearby church of St. Mary, Nettlecombe, a rather similar setting to Tyneham, Travers designed another variation of the window used there. It was in memory of Sir Walter Trevelyan (1866–1931), whose family owned the adjoining Nettlecombe Court for many generations, and his daughter Urith (1906–29). As well as the Mother and Child, the window depicts (none too accurately) the church and Court, and the four seasons of the year. Travers also designed a small dark red reredos, and replaced the original stone altar, which had been left in the churchyard. A rather hideous Victorian altar and reredos were removed, and the ancient church much improved by his work.

Also in Somerset, and executed during this period, was a memorial window to Archdale Palmer Wickham at St. Mary, East Brent, a church known for its Tractarian disputes under Archdeacon Denison. Prebendary Wickham was a keen entomologist and cricketer, and the window reflects these interests. Unusually, there is no central portrayal, but rather a number of small pictures. Prior to taking up his appointment at East Brent, Preb. Wickham had been vicar of the fine church of All Saints, Martock, also in Somerset, and after his death Travers commemorated him in this church also, with a striking wooden gilt altar crucifix and candlesticks.

Near to Martock is St. Catherine, Drayton, where there is a fine window in the Lady Chapel by Travers. This shows Our Lady surrounded by scenes of local arts and crafts with vigorous character depiction; basket making is particularly featured. In addition to the window however the church also has other work by Travers: high altar furnishings very similar to those at Martock, a candlestand or trundle which hangs above the high altar and a most unusual rood. The crucified Christ hangs in the chancel arch, but the supporting figures are not part of the rood, as is the normal pattern, but on either side of the arch, near the ground. There are also lozenge shaped text boards on either side of the altar in this church.

In Surrey, Travers designed a window of St. Christopher, for the church dedicated to him at Haslemere; it displays fine characterization of the figures and deep colours, and shows again his skill at making the subject of a glass design look like a real person. Travers later designed a rood figure for the church, which was probably carried out by others after his death.

In 1936 Travers carried out the three light east window for the modern church of St. Paul, Furzedown, between Tooting and Streatham, which had originally been designed for the church of St. Andrew, Langley Mill, Derbyshire, and had been exhibited the previous year at the Royal Academy. The Langley Mill design was preferred for Furzedown to the slightly different design which had actually been prepared for that church. Both were of three lights, and both depicted Christ in Glory in a familiar way, but the detail was different in a number of respects. He also installed the same design at Langley Mill itself, so there are virtually identical windows in the two places. At Fordwich, Kent, the fine old church was enhanced at this time by an east window of the Annunciation in memory of a previous vicar.

Travers also designed a further distinguished window to add to those already possessed by St. Margaret, Ilkley, a church well out of his usual area, but a stronghold of the Catholic Revival in the West Riding, and this was installed in 1937. It shows the Incarnation, with on either side St. Margaret of Antioch, holding the church, and St. Hilda of Whitby, complete with seagull.

It will be remembered that Travers had carried out work at St. Andrew Battersea for Father Humphries. He later moved to the church of the Holy Spirit, Narbonne Avenue, Clapham, at which, in the 1930s, he again employed Travers, but on this occasion to carry out less radical work, including a triptych of the Holy Child, minor alterations to the rood, work to a pulpit with elaborate inlay, and a banner.

Another old friend also asked Travers to carry out a simple scheme during the 1930s – this was Father George Tuckerman, who had been at

Design for window for St. Margaret, Ilkley, 1937

St. Augustine Queen's Gate when Travers had worked there. In 1932 Father Tuckerman was inducted as Vicar of Wrotham, Kent, and was also in charge of the daughter church of The Good Shepherd, Borough Green. As an Anglican Papalist Father Tuckerman had been used to what used to be termed 'full Catholic privileges' at St. Augustine's, but the Diocese of Rochester was a different matter all together. It was only at the little church of The Good Shepherd that that he felt he could get away with any catholic externals of the type to which he had been accustomed. It is probable that he had to pay for the improvements himself, and Travers provided him with an inexpensive, plain wooden reredos, painted red, on which was mounted a crucifix. Above projected a small tester in wood, resembling pleated material and decorated with a gilded knot design. Six baroque wooden candlesticks completed the scheme together with a 'pleated style' painted and gilded wooden altar frontal. It was installed in 1935 and dominated the little church, as Father Tuckerman had intended.

It is also interesting to note that one of the churches which Father Tuckerman often visited during his time at Borough Green was St. Barnabas Tunbridge Wells, for which Travers later carried out work, and where several years later one of the authors served mass for him in his retirement.

After Father Tuckerman left Borough Green the tradition gradually changed and the six candlesticks disappeared. In the early 1970s the altar was pulled forward from the reredos to allow the westward position to be adopted and thus the whole effect was ruined. By the 1980s the reredos was very shabby and after great difficulties in finding it a home it was eventually destined for the new owner of Hammerwood House near East Grinstead, where it was to be used as a backdrop to display an antique cello which had previously belonged to the famous cellist Beatrice Harrison. The story does not however end there, as the reredos has recently been purchased for the

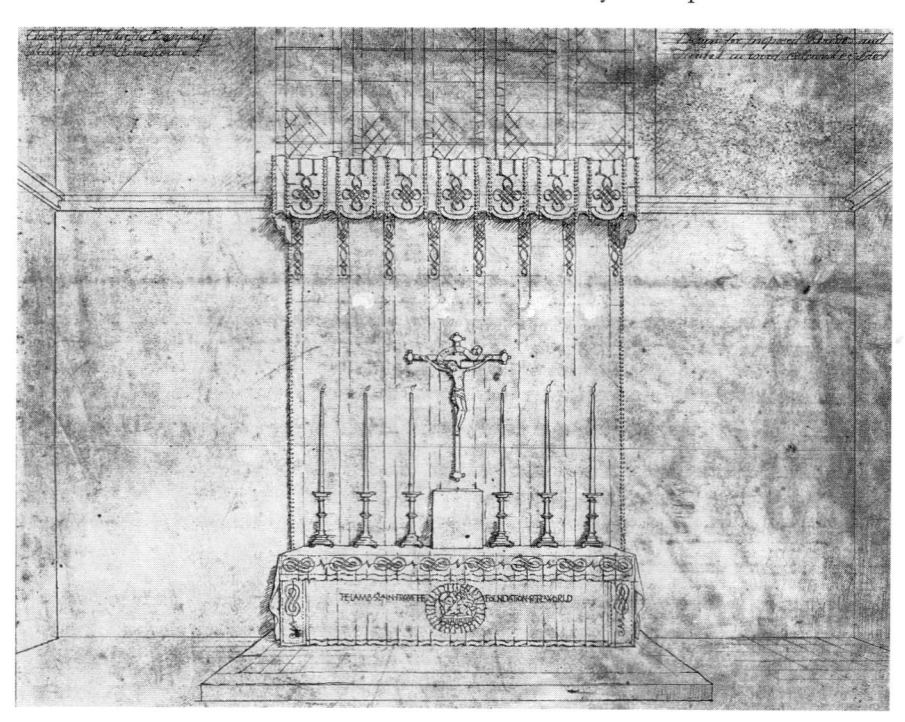

Design for high altar, St. John, Limehouse

high altar in St. John, Larcom Street, Walworth, thus returning to its proper use again; it has been repainted, and has Comper fittings in front of it.

Travers used a similar set of drawings to those used at Borough Green for a commission in 1936 for St. John the Evangelist, Haley Street, Limehouse. The work here consisted of lengthening the existing high altar, using the tabernacle and candlesticks already in the possession of the church, and providing a more elaborate double sided frontal containing an Agnus Dei in a sunburst, yet again bordered in the ubiquitous knot design. Behind the altar was a tall reredos in wood imitating pleated material with a pelmet-like canopy. A faculty for this work was granted in 1938, but the church was bombed in the Second World War and demolished, so his work had a very short life.

When Father Hobbes left Compton Beauchamp (see Chapter 6), he moved to the church of All Souls, South Ascot, where he again employed Travers. This church then had a most definite Catholic tradition; Father Hobbes' replacement as incumbent was to be Bishop Vibert Jackson, a veteran Anglo-Catholic who had started his ministry in Newcastle upon Tyne, where he suffered under a most narrow minded Evangelical bishop, N.D.J. Straton. Jackson later became Bishop of the Windward Islands, and retired to South Ascot, where he was prominent in Reunion Movements and became Visitor to the Benedictines of Nashdom. In 1936 Travers prepared a scheme for the church with an altar of English design within curved riddles and a simple reredos. In fact however, all the work which Travers did for the church was an elaborate surround for a piece of sixteenth century Flemish carving, which was blessed by the Bishop of Oxford on 18th July 1937. The reredos was not installed and the present reredos, of antique Spanish leather, was installed in 1964. The tabernacle immediately beneath the carving, which has baroque style scrolls, had in fact been installed earlier.

Also in 1936 Travers designed a very large painted and gilded statue of the patron saint with tall canopy above for the fine Victorian church of St. Stephen, Bournemouth.

It will be recalled that one of the earliest churches for which Travers had carried out work was St. James, Riddlesdown. The church had been enlarged, and he carried out further work in the 1930s, consisting of a lady chapel window similar to that at Tyneham, showing Mary with her Child in front of an emerald green Tree of Life. On the left is depicted Southwark cathedral, on the right St. James' Church itself. In 1937 a baroque/Deco aumbry and ornate sanctuary lamp bracket were provided in this chapel,

Design for sanctuary, St. James, Riddlesdown

which were designed by Travers but actually carved by Douglas Purnell. Travers designed further work for this church after the Second World War; in 1946 he drew a four light window of the Annunciation for the north aisle, but this was not carried out. The following year he proposed alterations to the sanctuary, including a chancel rood. The high altar was within riddel posts with plain candleholders; the reredos was rectangular with a stylized border of pomegranates and in the centre was a crucifix. Included in the design was a new five light east window with Christ vested in an alb and stole, holding a chalice and paten. Above him descend vast rays from the Holy Spirit shown as a descending dove, whilst below are scenes from his resurrection appearances.

The scheme for the rood was never taken forward. It is not clear whether the altar was ever installed, but certainly, although the reredos and riddels are not now in evidence, a silver painted crucifix and two candlesticks to a Travers design remain, but the altar now stands in front of a plain blue dossal curtain. Travers also designed and made for the high altar an Art Deco sanctuary lamp, which was a complete departure from his usual style, and has been likened to a flying saucer.

The new window was installed in 1949, having been slightly modified by Lawrence Lee after Travers' death. Douglas Purnell then designed a Second World War memorial on the south wall with St. George and the Dragon within it.

St. James thus has windows from right throughout Travers' professional life, and is comparable in that regard to St. Andrew, Catford. It is fitting that his name is commemorated in the Book of Remembrance in the church.

During 1937 Travers prepared two schemes which harked back to his work at St. Magnus the Martyr in the City, discussed in Chapter 4. He designed work to the reredos of St. Augustine and St. Faith, Watling Street, just behind St. Paul's Cathedral. This involved six baroque candlesticks with a matching crucifix in front of the existing elaborately decorated reredos, which he re-embellished and recoloured. It had saints in the side panels and scrolls around, and stencilling evident. Fortunately this was photographed on completion. This work is little known, as the church was bombed out in the Second World War and so the new work, like that in Limehouse, lasted only a short time. It has been suggested that a crucifix alone of his work was saved and put in St. Paul's, but it does not appear that that is the case; all that the Cathedral has from St. Augustine is a processional cross, which antedates Travers' work. In 1939 Travers designed further extensive renovations to this church, including new flooring, the restoration of the west gallery, a new pulpit, and a new altar, but although a faculty was granted in that year for all the work save the altar, it appears most unlikely that it was ever carried out, as the war broke out so soon afterwards.

The other site was St. Antholin, now St. Anthony, Nunhead, in south east London, where Travers was asked to reorder the sanctuary and the chancel and to embellish the seventeenth century reredos, which had been saved from the City church of St. Antholin Watling Street when that was demolished in 1875; in the same year the new church opened in Peckham Rye and the reredos was transferred. In its centre are two panels containing the Ten Commandments. Travers heightened the reredos in a similar way to his work at St. Magnus, the addition containing a painting of the Holy Spirit in the form of a dove. On top of the pediment was an IHS motif within a sunburst medallion, flanked by two candlesticks complete with false candles. Four additional candlesticks were placed on the top of the side panels. In front of the Ten Commandments Travers placed a rood

High altar SS. Augustine & Faith, Watling Street, as decorated by Travers, 1937

High altar St. Antholin, Nunhead, as completed by Travers 1937, and prior to bombing

and below on a Laudian covered altar stood two large baroque candlesticks. Travers' final scheme included a new pulpit, and new rails to the organ loft and also the gallery on the opposite side of the chancel. Outside, he erected a new calvary.

Cheltenham College assisted with an appeal for funds for this project as their mission in Nunhead Grove was within the parish and they knew Travers from his work there (see Chapter 9). In the appeal documents it is said '[The] problem has been to take a fine but spoiled church and a charming but mutilated reredos, not in keeping with each other, and make from them a setting more helpful for Christian worship. The problem has been solved as only Mr. Travers could have solved it. Mr. Travers' proposals are an extraordinarily able pastiche ...' Certainly the work was an enormous improvement on what had been there before: Travers reconciled the Wren/Gibbons reredos to an ugly Victorian church.

In 1940 the church was gutted by bombing. It was restored in the 1960s by Lawrence King, who lowered the roof and returned the reredos to its original shape, retaining Travers' rood figures. On the altar he placed six candlesticks rather than the two which Travers had provided, thus giving the sanctuary a more Roman appearance. Again, fortunately, there is photographic evidence available of the Travers work as it was completed. At the time of writing, the reredos is to be restored for use in a new parish church. Travers also designed for this church an outside calvary, which is now so dilapidated that it has lost its figure of Christ.

Travers was asked in 1937 to refurnish the lady chapel of All Saints, Notting Hill, by the vicar Father J.H.C. Twisaday, another well-known and flamboyant Anglo-Catholic. Here he designed a reredos backing a relief of Our Lady; it included a small tester with a fleur de lys cornice in fretwork. The tester and the side panels of the reredos were decorated in an intricate knot design with tassels. During the following year he made the communion rails for the high altar in a modified baroque design. In the damage to the church in the War, the lady chapel furnishings were destroyed and the present fine triptych is by Comper. In the south transept of this church is the Travers St. George's memorial altar and triptych, which was previously in St. Columb Notting Hill. He had made another reredos for the north chapel of All Saints, backing a statue of the Sacred Heart by Dupont of Bruges. However when St. Columb closed, the fine Comper reredos of the life of the patron saint was moved to All Saints and put in this chapel. Travers' reredos was moved to hang above the north door.

It was in 1937 also that he designed the side altar for St. Mary, Godmanchester, the church where he had been baptised and where he was to be buried. Here he installed an altar reminiscent of the high altar at Cricklade, in the same deep red, almost terracotta colour, with crucifix and equally well-proportioned wooden altar and rails in front of it. On the south wall is a small scroll tablet of standard design relating to the altar. Unfortunately, although the church has many fine windows, there are none by Travers.

In the same year Travers designed the organ gallery, altar with associated furnishings, and the font cover, at St. Peter's, Newlyn, Cornwall, a rare example of his furnishings outside the South East of England. The small church is dominated by the high altar and reredos with tester; Travers designed for the reredos a relief of Our Lady but the vicar of the parish, Allen Wyon, was himself an artist of some distinction and made a large crucifix for it.

Lady chapel (destroyed in War) at All Saints Notting Hill, designed 1937

Beneath the crucifix is a representation of the Last Supper in terracotta.

Travers also designed work for the church of Our Lady, Warnford, Hampshire, with a large new hanging crucifix, and a smaller altar crucifix which is now on the north wall.

At Northiam, Sussex, he designed the east window of the south aisle, again in 'Tyneham' style, but on this occasion with oast houses and sheep in the background, so that it appears that the Nativity took place in Sussex. The living of this church has for many years been in the hands of the Martyrs' Memorial Trust, so it would not at first sight appear suitable ground for Travers' work. Lawrence Lee now lives in this village.

Near Warnford and also in Hampshire is St. Mary and All Saints, Droxford, for which Travers exhibited a lady chapel window at the 1938 Royal Academy Exhibition, and later installed it. It is a three light window with Our Lady in the centre and scenes of four other saints around.

Travers returned to Cornwall in 1938, with a commission for the east window in the then new church of St. Thomas of Canterbury, Camelford. The people of Camelford had had for many years to walk for some miles out of the town in order to attend the ancient parish church. In due course, a small but charming building was provided in the town in mediaeval idiom. Travers' first design for the east window was rejected, and according to the church guide he was told to 'sink himself in apathy, disease and immorality, and then cover himself with the Love of God.' His second design , which was installed, is a very fine example of his work; he obviously took the injunction to heart. It shows the Crucifixion, but instead of the usual rather static supporters it depicts St. Thomas on one side, and St. John on the other supporting Our Lady of Sorrows. At the foot of the cross is St. Mary Magdalene. The window is particularly impressive against the white of the barrel roof (See Plate 29).

Travers then prepared designs for All Saints, Marazion, in the same county, initially providing an organ gallery and a screen and eventually installing a north aisle altar and associated furnishings after the war.

His only other work in Cornwall at this time was refurbishment at SS. Maunanus and Stephen, Mawnan, where Dr. Eeles again showed his strong support for Travers. A query was raised about work being done at this church, which in fact followed a faculty in 1938 to remove images and the like from the church, and on 18th August 1939 he wrote that what Travers was providing were 'good and simple fittings'. A further faculty was granted in 1940 to carry out a comprehensive refurnishing of the church along lines suggested by Travers, which began with screens for the new organ, but the whole scheme was not completed partly because of Travers' death and partly because of shortage of money. This was yet another example of Travers designing rather simple but fine fittings for a country church, in this case to replace furnishings of an overtly Anglo-Catholic nature which had been removed. The high altar would have had English fittings with a cross on the backboard and two squat candlesticks. He proposed a new barrel roof for the chancel with characteristic stars on it and a wrought iron candelabrum hanging from it; none of these were carried out. Travers also worked in Helston, but this comes within Chapter 7.

Travers designed a very large Te Deum east window for St. George, Pinner View, Headstone, Harrow, in 1937 and exhibited the design at the

All Saints Marazion: side chapel altar

Royal Academy in 1938. Not only is this one of his finest and largest windows, we have the advantage of his own contemporary thoughts on it: he contributed to the parish magazine for April 1937, explaining the window. The hand of God is shown at the top, with Our Lord in majesty below on the Emerald Rainbow (see the Revelation). Beneath his feet is the Holy Church throughout the world, which comprises a panorama of churches and cathedrals including St. Paul's, Canterbury, Notre Dame, Paris, and Florence. Our Lady and St. John the Baptist are on either side and beneath are Apostles, Prophets, and Martyrs, with various texts from the Te Deum. The money for the window was given anonymously by a member of the congregation. When the window was first put to the P.C.C. they approved it, subject only to the deletion of King Charles the Martyr from the window. That decision was approved, ironically, on 30th January 1936, the anniversary of King Charles' execution (See Plate 28).

This church is also discussed in Chapters 7 and 9, as further work was done later and yet further work has been acquired recently.

Chapter 6

Travers as Designer:

IV SIX COUNTRY CHURCHES

ST. SWITHUN, COMPTON BEAUCHAMP, OXFORDSHIRE
ST. MARY, ASHBURY, OXFORDSHIRE
ST. SAMPSON, CRICKLADE, WILTSHIRE
ST. MARTIN, LONGMOOR CAMP, LISS, HAMPSHIRE
ST. DUNSTAN, CRANFORD, HILLINGDON
ST. MARY MAGDALENE, LITTLETON, SURREY
ST. EDWARD, CORFE CASTLE, DORSET

Samuel Gurney was, as we have seen, a wealthy layman who was passionately interested in promoting Anglo-Catholicism. It was he who had provided the funds for the SSPP and its enterprises, and even before then he had shown himself willing to patronize building work, when he paid for the bells for the Caldey Community's monastery. Gurney was one of a number of such lay patrons of the Catholic Movement in the first half of the twentieth century who were prepared to expend money in the promotion of that cause, such as Athelstan Riley, who paid for the pyx at Caldey and much else besides, Lord Halifax, who paid for an entire new church at Goldthorpe, Yorkshire, and Sir Hubert Miller, who decorated the church at Froyle, Hampshire.

In about 1924 Gurney bought the Old Rectory, a substantial property at Compton Beauchamp, a minute village in the downlands of what was then North Berkshire, but is now Oxfordshire. The previous name of the village was Compton Regis, which referred to a gift of the Manor from Edward the Confessor. A previous vicar had lived in the house, but after 1922 the living was held with that of Ashbury by Revd A.J.F. Hobbes. Father Hobbes remained vicar of the two parishes until 1934, when he was replaced by Revd E.G. Mortimer.

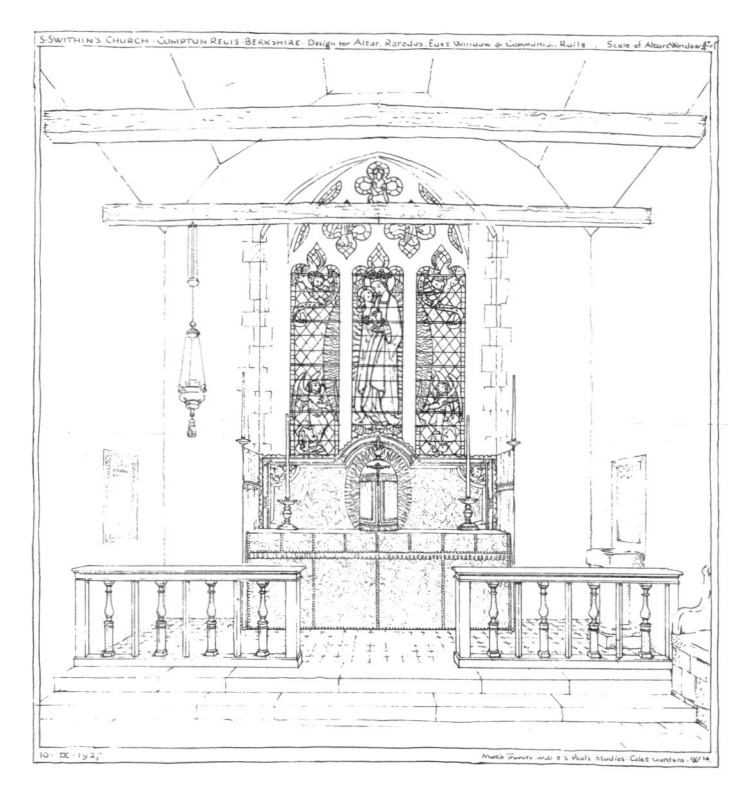

Design for altar and window, Compton Beauchamp

Gurney set himself up as in effect the village squire. He organized outdoor services on Compton village green for the patronal feast of St. Swithun, and he decided to beautify the interior of the little whitewashed church, and move the churchmanship firmly into the Catholic tradition. From the outside, it is an unremarkable but pleasant small country church, of the sort which can be seen everywhere. Inside however, as a result of Gurney's money and Travers' ingenuity, it is almost unique.

Compton Beauchamp, drawing of church

Compton Beauchamp: interior prior to installation of Travers communion rails

Travers considered this his second best interior after the work done for Father Child at Cranford, which is discussed later in this chapter, but some may consider it is actually the finer scheme, although at Cranford better quality materials were used for the high altar, which has lasted well in comparison with Compton.

Travers in fact provided various schemes for St. Swithun, and as he and Gurney knew each other well he had virtually a free hand. The refurnishing was completed between 1925 and 1951.

The scheme for the high altar that eventually materialized was relatively simple; the sanctuary was completed with an altar within plain iron riddels and curtains. The reredos and frontal were decorated with gold painted, varnished, embossed wallpaper from Sandersons, which is now wearing badly. Betjeman and Piper call it a 'golden altar'. Upon the altar was a large veiled domed tabernacle, and two baroque silver gilded candlesticks. The altar is in scale with its surroundings, unlike for example that which was installed at St. Paul, Shadwell, Leeds. It contains relics of SS. Vital and Victorinus of Assisi, authenticated by Bishop O'Rorke, formerly of Accra, who was a neighbour and supporter of Hope Patten at Walsingham.

The rejected designs for the high altar were more complex. One showed a new high altar in front of a screen with a door at each end leading to an altar frontal store. These doors had turned wooden spindles in the upper panels. On the altar stood a baroque tabernacle in gilded wood with crucifix attached, similar to the one at St. Mary, Bourne Street, and on either side stood a large gilded baroque candlestick. Above hung a large octagonal tester.

Travers added new stained glass to the existing mediaeval stained glass which remained in the east window. It shows a figure of the Virgin and Child with angels and within a sunburst, and is signed MT 1937. The altar and the window behind were designed to complement each other, although the altar was installed before the window (See Plate 22).

On the tympanum, Travers installed a painted and gilded rood in 1927. In 1933 Travers designed a font canopy, which was specifically intended to be after the manner of those at Great and Little Walsingham. This was a memorial to Gurney's mother and bears the inscription: 'Of your charity pray for the repose of the soul of Isabel Charlotte Baroness Talbot de Malahide, 20 XII 1851–22 II 1932'.

In 1934 Travers created a tiny lady chapel at the west end in the old porch, under the tower, with a small altar above which sits a typical shallow moulded relief of Our Lady with the infant Jesus. This is now beginning to show signs of decay after having been subject to damp conditions for some 65 years.

Compton Beauchamp: lady chapel

As well as the new east window, in 1937 Travers designed a very fine plaque of St. Swithun, which is on the south side of the chancel arch. The plaque depicts the saint wearing a cope, which is cleverly divided to represent the sun and the rain. The morse shows the sun and St. Swithun holds a model of the church (See Plate 23).

The communion rails were designed by Travers, but were not in fact installed until about 1951, after his death. They are in his later, slightly modified, baroque style.

Travers carried out other work at St. Swithun over the years, including a baroque missal desk, specially made to hold a leather bound copy of the Anglican Missal, as published by the SSPP. On the south side of the nave is the vesting chapel, which is dedicated to St. Edward the Confessor. Here, across an old blocked window, Travers placed a wrought iron grill worked with monograms of ER and RC. On this is fixed a beaten copper figure of St. Edward. There are two wrought iron candlesticks on what was intended as another altar, and a small copper Christus Rex attached to the wall; matching the candlesticks are six hearse lights, also in wrought iron.

Travers also designed two screens in turned wood and these were placed between the nave on the one hand and the two chapels, St. Edward on the south and the Good Shepherd on the north. Gurney provided the vesting chapel with a complete vestment press and cupboard in oak, such as one would expect to find in a much larger church. There was also a tablet to Edward Kay-Shuttleworth, who was commemorated here rather than, as had originally been intended, at St. Mary, Bourne Street (see Chapter 4).

Even the hymn books at St. Swithun, and also at St. Mary Ashbury had on their covers gold leaf embossed representations of their respective patron saints, designed, of course, by Travers. It was certainly unusual to provide country parishes with such books, which bound together the English Hymnal and the English Catholic Hymn Book.

In Peter Anson's *Fashions in Church Furnishings 1840-1940*,[1] there is one of his characteristic line drawings of the interior of Compton Beauchamp church, complete with a 1920s lady with cloche hat, and a canopy which

Device of St. Swithun, Compton Beauchamp (used on hymn books)

was not in fact ever installed. However, the work there fits in well with the church and adds a distinction it did not have beforehand. It is more than a period piece, and it should be preserved. Unfortunately, in the last two years the tabernacle has been removed from the high altar and now stands empty in the vesting chapel. Further, it appears that the remainder of the fittings will require attention if they are not to deteriorate.

Samuel Gurney is buried in the churchyard at Compton Beauchamp.

GURNEY WAS ALSO ANXIOUS TO embellish the church at Ashbury, a larger village some two miles from Compton Beauchamp. Here too there were a number of different schemes. The church of St. Mary is also mediaeval, and lies in the centre of the village; it is much larger than St. Swithun, Compton Beauchamp.

The work that was actually carried out at Ashbury was the refurnishing of the north chapel in 1927; the dedication is to St. Hubert, and it is a memorial to Evelyn, Countess of Craven, who had lived nearby (See Plate 24).

Travers separated the chapel from the nave by a turned wooden screen, and access is through a gate in it. The large window has painted glass in the lower half showing a scene of St. Hubert and the stag. The reredos and

St. Mary Ashbury: design for chapel of St. Hubert

Design for high altar, Ashbury

altar are extremely attractive in their simplicity. This rectangular reredos has a black and gilded frame and contains a small rood. On the altar are two small gilded wooden candlesticks. Included are two frontals, one in red, and one in black for requiems. Above is a relief of St. Hubert similar to that of St. Swithun at Compton Beauchamp. The original drawing showed panelling around the chapel, but that was never installed.

In 1927 Travers also prepared a design for the high altar at Ashbury. It was a charming ensemble with a reredos of Our Lady holding the infant Jesus, set within riddels and surmounted by the usual boy cherubs. On the altar were two candlesticks. This scheme, which would have given the church great dignity, was unfortunately never taken up; nor was a third design, for a War Memorial chapel. That was to have consisted of a simple English altar and rectangular reredos within plain iron riddels and curtains. However, on the altar was to stand a large baroque tabernacle and two matching candlesticks. To the left of the altar was to be a memorial triptych of St. George, which was identical to that in SS. Peter and Paul, Mitcham.

TRAVERS AS DESIGNER IV

NEAR TO ASHBURY AND COMPTON BEAUCHAMP, but in Wiltshire, is the ancient and attractive town of Cricklade. The tower of the church, which is dedicated to St. Sampson, dominates the skyline. It was built in the first year of the reign of Mary Tudor, and has been much embellished since.

One of the patrons of the living in the 1920s was the Duke of Argyll, a founder member of the SSPP, and it is more than likely that Travers received the commission from this connection and as a result of the work he had done for Samuel Gurney at Compton Beauchamp and Ashbury. There were incidentally some of the last ritual disturbances in the country at Cricklade about the time the work was done.

Travers designed around 1929 two altars and three windows for this fine church. Betjeman describes the altars as 'comely' and indeed they enhance the building. The high altar is one of Travers' best surviving English altars. It has riddel posts supporting boy cherub candlebearers rather than the more usual angels. The reredos has now faded to salmon pink from terracotta, and is made to represent leatherwork; in the centre is a Jesuit IHS device within a large sunburst. As at Godmanchester later, the materials used were appropriate for the grandeur of the surroundings, and the work has lasted well.

High altar, St. Sampson, Cricklade with original two candlesticks, as installed c 1929

Although the original drawings showed only two large silver baroque/deco candlesticks and no crucifix (because there was a crucifixion scene in the window above), in fact what was later provided on the high altar were six gilded plaster baroque candlesticks and a matching crucifix. Two of these are still in position with the crucifix, and the two original deco candlesticks stand in niches in the lady chapel on the south side of the chancel.

The lady chapel altar is similar but on a smaller scale; the reredos is rectangular and blue, containing a stylized border, and with bas relief rood figures on it, and again has lasted well. On the mensa are two square based dumpy candlesticks to a design used later at St. Edward, Corfe Castle, and also illustrated in the Abridged Anglican Missal, 1941.

Both these altars were praised in the English Churchman's Kalendar, which often lauded Travers' work in the 1920s and 30s. It called the high altar pillars 'sufficiently elaborate to be artistically worth while, which is more than can be said of many modern sets of riddel posts,' and called the lady chapel altar 'an excellent example.'

In the north aisle is a window of St. Nicholas on board ship, a design used by Travers on many occasions. This particular window is however reported to have been one of his favourites, and certainly the colours

Lady chapel altar, St. Sampson, Cricklade, as installed c 1929

Design for window of St. Nicholas in church of St. Sampson, Cricklade, 1929

remain vibrant. Of particular charm are the representations of the sun and of the wind, the latter as a cherub blowing the ship along. The window is signed and dated 1929, but must have been relettered after that date, as a second dedicatee was added later.

At the western end of the north aisle is a single lancet window of St. Christopher, which is a memorial to the son of a former vicar who was drowned whilst on a holiday outing. Opposite in the south aisle is a small window of Our Lady and the infant Jesus backed by an emerald green tree of life, identical to that at Tyneham.

In 1938 Travers exhibited at the Royal Academy a design for an east window in this church, showing the Fall and Redemption of Man with a crucifixion rood in the centre, showing the cross sprouting into the tree of life, Adam and Eve being expelled from the Garden of Eden, and a nativity scene. The Hand of God sends forth his spirit from above. This window is above the high altar, and was in fact installed at the same time as it, despite not being exhibited until much later.

DURING 1935 MARTIN TRAVERS BEGAN his work for St. Martin, Liss (Longmoor Garrison Church), which was the headquarters of the Transport Branch of the Royal Engineers, and their successors the Royal Corps of Transport. This work continued until his death, and involved not only furnishings but also a large number of significant windows. Although not strictly a country church, it was certainly not urban.

This work began with the design of a most striking Art Deco triptych reredos depicting Our Lord standing on the world, against a reddish background, with familiar detail in silver gilt, but on this occasion including a stylized grenade in each corner with the Royal Engineers' motto 'Ubique'. It thus had an alternative meaning, showing Christ's message spreading light throughout the world. This was a memorial to those members of the Corps who had been killed in the First World War. Travers also provided a new frontal in red and gold and a set of altar furniture in silvered wood. He then superintended alterations to the roof and the insertion of new steel columns to hold it up, thus enabling the reredos to be seen more clearly from all parts of the church (See Plate 25).

In 1937 there followed a square stone font in more modern style than usual for him, with plain cover.

The reredos was commissioned after the local corps commander found that the regiment had an unexpected surplus of funds which had been mislaid. However it so impressed the Army authorities that at the luncheon to celebrate the dedication of the reredos, on 26th April 1936, it was decided by them and by the senior railway officers present to commission a series of memorial windows, and again to instruct Travers[2].

There were eventually 10 windows, given by railway companies and other statutory undertakings to commemorate their staff who had died in the two wars, and the first eight were designed by Martin Travers.

The first four were given by the main railway companies in memory of their staff who had died in the First World War, and each incorporated the patron saints of two cathedrals on the system, and the coats of arms of representative cities and towns. The Southern Railway window featured Our Lady, patroness of Salisbury, and St. Augustine, to represent Canterbury. The London Midland & Scottish window featured St. Mungo of Glasgow and St. Alban; the London & North Eastern Railway showed St. Andrew for Edinburgh and St. Peter of York. Finally the Great Western Railway

Design for memorial windows to G.W.R. and L.P.T.B. for St. Martin, Longmoor Camp, dedicated 1939

Design for memorial windows to L.N.E.R. and L.M.S. for St. Martin, Longmoor Camp, dedicated 1939

window depicted St. David of Wales and St. George. Each window showed also the relevant cathedrals and coats of arms, as well as being lettered in Travers' usual clear way. The fifth window was given by the then London Passenger Transport Board and showed St. Paul and St. Edward the Confessor. These first five windows were dedicated in May 1939.

During the Second World War many transportation troops from all over the world served at Longmoor, including in particular Canadians. When peace came the Canadian National and Canadian Pacific Railways offered another window in memory of their staff who had died. Travers depicted on this window St. Lawrence, and the arms of all the Canadian provinces (which he also used at Bramshott, nearby). This window was dedicated in April 1948. The seventh window was that for the Port of London Authority, showing St. Nicholas, patron saint of sailors, but on this occasion without the ship in his hand which featured in so many other Travers windows; this was dedicated in July 1949, so Travers never saw the finished glass. The final Travers window was to the Movements Control Service and the Royal Engineers (Transportation), and featured St. Christopher carrying the Christ child, another of Travers' motifs; this was also dedicated posthumously, in this case in September 1949.

Travers also designed fine stone plaques for the church, to staff of the Great Western and Southern Railway reserves, in about 1948.

Two further windows in the same genre were subsequently inserted, one to the new Royal Corps of Transport and one to the Inland Water Transport section of the Royal Engineers. They, and a very fine rose window featuring the arms of the Royal Corps of Transport, were designed by Lawrence Lee, and the first two certainly derive a great deal from Travers.

Longmoor in fact had more Travers windows than any other single building. In 1977 however the Royal Corps of Transport vacated Longmoor and moved to Leconfield, East Yorkshire. They took with them much of the contents of the church.

It is perhaps the ultimate irony so far as Travers' work is concerned, bearing in mind his strongly anti-militaristic views, that one of the best collections of his work is on an army base; access by the public is very restricted indeed and subject to close security. A former parachute packing station was adapted as the new church for the Royal Corps of Transport and in this unpromising situation are now displayed the windows, the reredos, the font, and the plaques. The RCT subsequently became part of the Royal Logistic Corps, and Leconfield is now the Army School of Transport.

The new building has a low ceiling and walls which are not of great strength. The windows have therefore been installed on wooden frames, five on each side of the church, within the walls, so that they are backlit by artificial means. However the restricted amount of room available means that they run from floor to ceiling in a stunning display which is unmatched anywhere else, and where also they can be seen close up.

Behind the altar, which is now pulled out, the reredos stands on the east wall. At Longmoor it stood on the altar, but at Leconfield the restricted height means that it too runs from floor to ceiling, thus dominating the church even more. Unfortunately, two beams run into the east wall at ceiling height and small portions had to be cut out of the reredos in order that it could be accommodated, and they also prevent the outer sections being closed during Lent as was previously the custom. However the reredos is in splendid condition. The frontal is no longer in existence, and the altar furniture was replaced by a later set by another designer, which was taken to Leconfield. The font (now undrained) and its cover and the plaques are also in the new church. A visit to this site shows Travers' later work at its very best.

FATHER MAURICE CHILD WAS, WITH Samuel Gurney, the moving spirit behind the SSPP. Child is often referred to as the 'enfant terrible' of Anglo-

Catholicism, because of his sarcasm and sense of humour, but his organizational powers were obviously considerable. He was a curate at Bourne Street until 1923, and was a librarian at Pusey House, Oxford, for a short time, before becoming General Secretary of the Anglo-Catholic Congress in 1925. He held that position until the merger of the Congress and the English Church Union with effect from 1st January 1934, the achievement of which was Lord Halifax's last contribution to ecclesiastical matters, and thereafter took on an equivalent position with the new body, the Church Union, until 1940.

From 1935 to 1950 Child was rector of Cranford, in what was then Middlesex, and for the first five years he obviously combined that with his role in the Church Union.

Child was an important figure and it is unfortunate that so little has been written about him. He was distrusted by some because of his irreverence, although apparently Lord Halifax became very attached to him, and entrusted to the SSPP the task of printing for him the First Prayer Book of Edward VI. There is a description of him in *Asking for Trouble* by Bruno Scott James (1962), an autobiography written by a former Nashdom monk who went over to Rome[3]. He says:

> He [Child] was a fine preacher with a very attractive voice, and he had great charm of manner, but he sometimes liked to affect a rather bizarre and not very clerical dress that did not appear to further his apostolate. Nevertheless, he did good work among delinquent young men, over whom he was said to exercise a somewhat salutary influence.'

The church of St. Dunstan at Cranford qualifies as a country church, despite its proximity to London, by virtue of its location, and also of its situation when Father Child went there. It is on the approach to the now-demolished Cranford House, and until the construction of the M4 motorway, was isolated. The area did not really become absorbed into London until the post-war construction of Heathrow Airport, although there was some development along the Bath Road, away from the old village, and that required a new church, dedicated to the Holy Angels, which was actually just over the border into the modern borough of Hounslow.

St. Dunstan Cranford is a small brick church with a number of magnificent tombs; it was lit by gas until well after the Second World War. The work that Travers carried out there was amongst his last in the baroque pastiche style which had been so popular 10 to 20 years before, but of course Child had not previously had a parish of his own in which to express his own preferences.

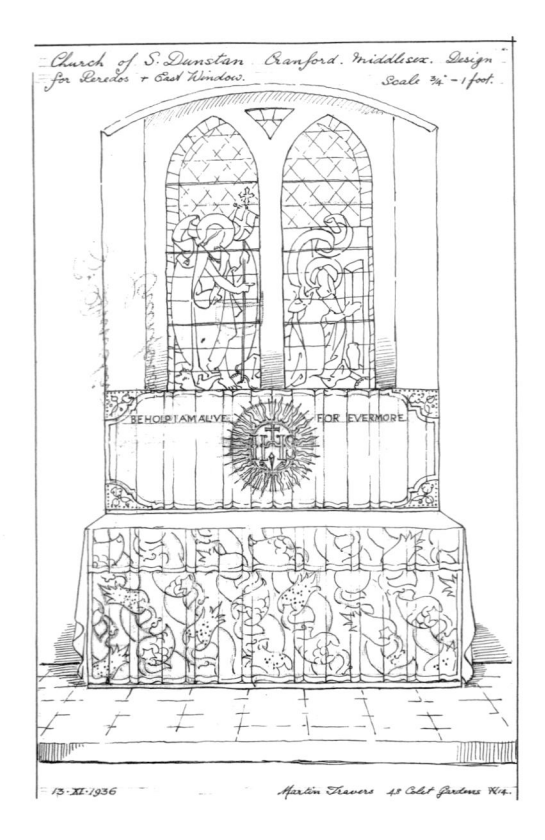

St. Dunstan Cranford: design for high altar

Travers produced several schemes for St. Dunstan's, and in 1936 he installed the high altar and its terracotta coloured reredos, which incorporated a tabernacle, which can convert to a throne for exposition by sliding the roof forward over the doors. Four baroque candlesticks were included with a crucifix. Attached to the altar is a double-sided frontal in gilded and painted wood. Above hangs a splendid octagonal canopy, matching the frontal, and complete with wooden pendant tassels (See Plate 20).

The year before Travers had designed a processional cross for the church, which appears to have been the first piece of work for the parish.

Travers then remodelled the chancel arch and placed two cherubs and cartouches above it. He made new communion rails and repositioned them, and also provided a new gallery at the west for the choir and organ. This restoration and refurbishment apparently necessitated the closure of the church for a time in 1936–7.

St. Dunstan Cranford: interior

In 1939 he provided new sacristy accommodation 'on the cheap'; this is now in very poor condition with an inadequate damp course and leaking roof.

1941 saw him design a statue and plinth of Our Lady with an extraordinarily tall canopy above, which has been moved since, but remains in the church. He also designed a tabor for exposition of the Sacrament in silver gilded wood with a large painted angel's head on the front; it looks very theatrical and is in many ways a throwback to Travers' earlier work. Finally in 1944 and 1945 respectively Travers designed memorial tablets for the church.

He considered Cranford his best work. It fits in well with what was there previously, but it is perhaps less striking than Compton Beauchamp, although better preserved. It has been suggested that Travers was, as usual, dilatory in finishing the work at Cranford, and that others were brought in to complete it.

In complete contrast to St. Dunstan was Holy Angels, which was built in 1935 as a corrugated iron mission. In 1940 it was provided with its own

Interior, Holy Angels, Cranford, in converted Rodney Hut, 1943

priest, but in 1941 it burned down and was replaced the following year by a converted Rodney hut. Travers however created within this unpromising situation an ultramontane sanctuary, from designs dated 1943. Across the eastern end he placed a screen, forming a sacristy behind, and in front was a baroque altar complete with six baroque candlesticks and a rood. On either side stood a single pillar topped with a boy cherub holding a candlestick. The detail was altered during the course of the life of the building, which itself burned down in about 1965. A new, striking, brick-built church was constructed in about 1970 with the same dedication but in a different location.

There could hardly be a better example of Travers' versatility than the two sets of furnishings in Cranford.

ONE OF TRAVERS' MORE COMPREHENSIVE refurnishings during his later period was at St. Mary Magdalene, Littleton, then in Middlesex but now in Surrey. The incumbent was Revd Samuel Porter, who had been a curate at St. Matthew's Westminster in 1928, the year after the Frank Weston memorial chapel had been installed by Travers.

Father Porter wanted the beautiful small mediaeval church at Littleton to take on a more Catholic appearance. A church had in fact stood on the site since 1135, and for about 170 years until 1308 had been served by the Benedictine monks from nearby Laleham Abbey.

Travers' first design for this church was a cross for the gable in 1935, but from 1939 to 1943 he produced a series of designs in order to further

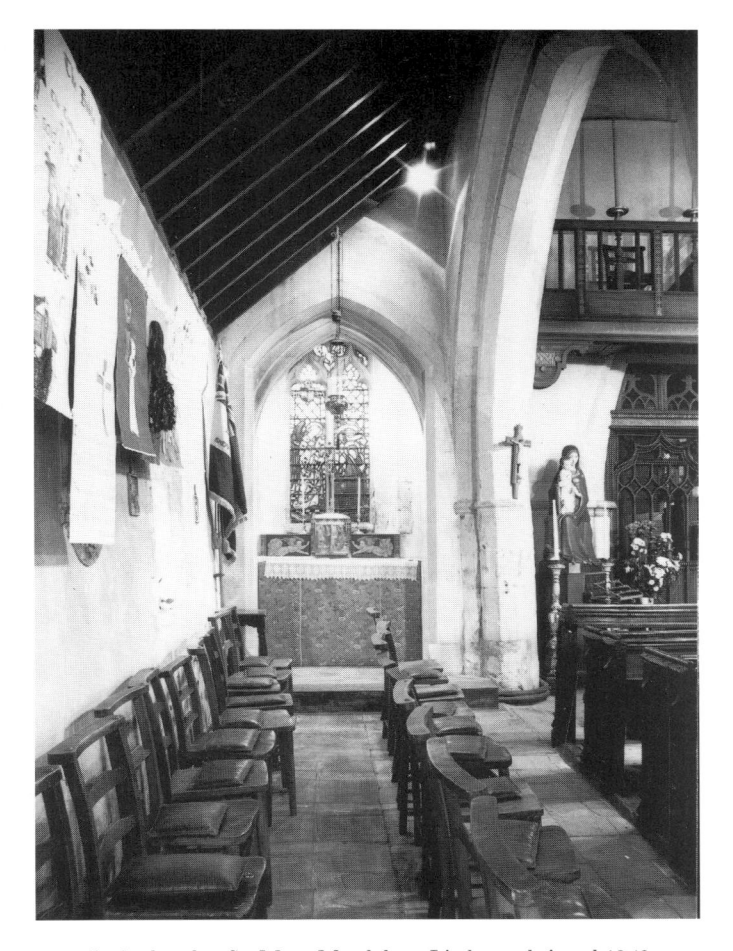

Lady chapel at St. Mary Magdalene, Littleton, designed 1942

Father Porter's vision. In the north aisle he installed a small window of St. Benedict in 1939, commemorating the monks from the Abbey. During the following year he carefully altered the appearance of the chancel by adding a rood loft above the Tudor chancel screen, complete with figures and six candlesticks. 1941 saw a design for a lectern, and at the end of the north aisle he erected in 1942 a tiny lady chapel within the window arch.

A shallow gradine decorated with an angel in flight on either side of a gilded tabernacle is set below the window sill. This forms a backing to a stone shelf altar. The sill acts as a further gradine and displays the candlesticks, and a window depicting the Annunciation acts also as a reredos; the crucifix is attached to the central tracery.

This is an imaginative scheme for such a confined space and if St. Augustine Queen's Gate boasts Travers' largest reredos, St. Mary Magdalene Littleton can proudly lay claim to his smallest.

In 1942 Travers designed the statue and plinth of the Blessed Virgin Mary and, for the high altar, a reredos and six wooden baroque/Deco candlesticks with matching crucifix. Unfortunately the reredos later suffered from woodworm and had to be removed but the crucifix and candlesticks remain.

St. Mary Magdalene Littleton: drawing of interior

Travers also embellished the font cover with a dove design, and in 1943 provided the choir stalls with new oak desks with linenfold panelling including two return stalls for the clergy. At about this time a confessional was formed out of an old pew in the north west corner of the church.

The total effect of his work at Littleton is harmonious and pleasant and it remains in good condition.

Travers had in fact designed a sanctuary scheme for the nearby All Saints, Laleham, in the 1920s, which involved a small English altar, crucifix and two candlesticks; the work was installed in 1926 but later removed.

He also in 1933 built a choir and clergy vestry at another nearby church, St. Nicholas, Shepperton, and in 1942 prepared drawings for a sanctuary reordering and alterations to the chancel screen, but that was not taken up.

THE LAST EXAMPLE OF A COUNTRY CHURCH to be given extended treatment here is St. Edward King and Martyr, Corfe Castle, on the Isle of Purbeck. This part of the country was familiar to Travers from his earlier work in Tyneham.

Corfe Castle is something of a picture postcard village, and most of it is now owned by the National Trust. It is of course dominated by the ruins of the castle itself. The church is mediaeval, but was substantially reconstructed in 1859. One feature of the reconstruction was the erection of steps to the sanctuary. Both the sanctuary and the chancel were floored with coloured glazed tiles, and the east wall behind the altar was also tiled. Later a screen was erected.

William York Batley became Rector of the village in 1938, and during his incumbency extensive works were done to the church, under the supervision of Martin Travers.

The first work which Travers designed was in 1938, and involved the design of a wooden screen to the north chapel, which was dedicated to the Holy Spirit. Subsequently, Travers furnished the chapel with a simple English altar with a wall-hung altar cross and two dumpy silver gilded wooden candlesticks, to the same design as those at Cricklade. In the drawings was a tester displaying the Holy Spirit as a dove, but this was not executed. The chapel was dedicated in 1942. The east window in the chapel was designed by Travers in memory of Marjorie Graves, but, unusually, was commissioned during her lifetime. On 19th August 1943 Miss Graves wrote to local antiquary Dr. Dru Drury that she was altering her will in order to provide that £400 be left to the Church for the purpose of providing the window, to be designed by Martin Travers; in the event of Travers predeceasing her, the money was to go to the restoration fund. She says: 'It will be a great honour to meet Mr. Travers – you will know how much I look forward to this opportunity because he represents stability in an unstable world.' Two months later she sent details of her ancestry to Dr. Dru Drury, for eventual incorporation in the window. The design was dated 17th December 1943, and as executed shows the coat of arms in the corner of the Annunciation scene, with the Holy Spirit as dove above, with good strong colours and fine lettering.

In that chapel is kept a Mothers' Union banner, also designed by Travers in 1943, showing Our Lady with the Child on a pink background surrounded by gold.

Earlier, in 1939 Travers designed a characteristic font cover for the church, together with oak seats around the baptistery and under the

Chapel of Holy Spirit, St. Edward, Corfe Castle, as originally designed, 1942

tower. The cover is gilded with elaborate 'arms' representing the holy water of baptism, and the Holy Spirit as dove hangs above from the ceiling. This work was done in 1940. It bears some similarity to a contemporaneous design for St. Stephen, Battersea.

At the end of the war, it was decided to reorder the sanctuary. Miss Graves was still alive, and obviously very impressed by Travers. On 2nd May 1946 she wrote to Mr. York Batley with a cheque for £500 to assist in the restoration. She asked that her money be used specifically for the rearrangement of the east window 'according to the magnificent design by Mr. Martin Travers' which she said she had had the privilege of seeing recently. She continued: 'I need not tell you how truly I appreciate this opportunity to be associated, however indirectly, with the work of this great Artist (sic, with capital letter).'

Coincidentally, on the same day in 1946 Dr. Eeles wrote to Dr. Dru Drury, praising the work in the chapel. He said that 'the highest praise' was due to Travers for his work, and that he looked forward to a similar transformation in the sanctuary. This was forthcoming in 1947. Travers had the screen

East end, St. Edward, Corfe Castle, as originally designed in 1947

removed, altered the floor levels, took out the tiles, and repaved with local Purbeck stone. In addition, he carried out the rebuilding of the east window in accordance with the design with which Miss Graves had been so impressed. This is indeed one of his cleverest designs; the tracery of the window was altered so that there were 4 instead of 3 lights. Travers reused the existing glass, but designed the two small end panels at the bottom of the window, and the large panel on the right in the middle, to tone in. It is only on close inspection that the new work can be seen.

In front of that window, Travers installed a simple English altar with large silver plated Caroline cross and candlesticks. The cross was designed for use in processions and was on a wooden plinth to match the reredos. There were riddel curtains around the altar and a deep terracotta reredos with text. Unfortunately, in about 1991 the riddel curtains and reredos were removed in order that westward celebration could take place. Travers also designed a frontal with monograms of ER.

Travers produced trundles for candles, which hang above the sanctuary choir, a fine lozenge shaped memorial to John MacD. C. Wilson (1920–43), and a brass beadle's mace depicting St. Edward.

Just three days before his death, Travers wrote to Dr. Dru Drury with an outline for a ewer. At his death, the major work had been carried out at Corfe Castle, but he was in the process of carrying out other work. A war memorial plaque and a list of rectors were both said to have been sufficiently far advanced in drawing to be followed by others, and they were indeed later finished. In addition, he had in hand a processional cross, wood but silvered and gilded, which he had designed in 1947. On 13th September 1949 Travers' former pupil Douglas Purnell wrote to say that he was prepared to take on the cross, and would use the same craftsman as Travers would have done, and indeed it was subsequently made. It bears some resemblance to the work at St. Helier for the Queen. It does not look as though the ewer was ever completed.

Corfe Castle is an important example of Travers' versatility, showing design and reordering within the existing church. It is a great shame that the sanctuary arrangements have been altered, but there remains a great deal of quality to be seen.

This is one of the significant monuments to Travers' later years and well illustrates the developments in his practice during the period after 1935.

CHAPTER 7

Travers as Designer:

V THE LATER YEARS 1939–1948

This chapter covers both the Second World War and the years thereafter. It might be thought that church furnishings ceased to be required at time of War, but in fact that was not the case. Travers continued to be in demand, and some new work was commissioned. Indeed, even before the end of the war, work was being commissioned by way of memorial, such as at Bramshott and Burghclere in Hampshire.

The end of the war brought with it not only a renewed demand for memorials, such as had occurred at the end of the First World War, but also a tremendous need for restoration of damaged churches. Much of Travers' earlier work had been lost by enemy action, but there is no doubt that had he lived on the early 1950s would have been busy for him. He had by the post war period achieved a considerable degree of respectability; he designed work for Queen's College Oxford, and Ely Cathedral, none of which was executed, and for Gibraltar Cathedral, some of which was done after his death. He also designed a cross for the bombed Temple Church. However, perhaps the most prestigious commission was from the then Queen, for candlesticks and a crucifix for St. Helier Church, Jersey, to commemorate the liberation of the island from the Germans, and that was carried out. Travers had progressed from being a suspect Anglo-Catholic ecclesiastical stage dresser almost to the centre of the Establishment; his early death prevents us from knowing what would have followed. His willingness to adapt

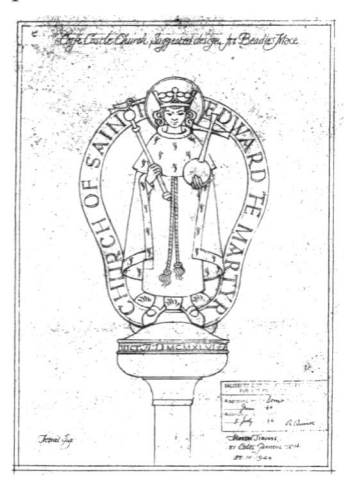

Design for beadle's mace, Corfe Castle

178

in accordance with the wishes of his clients lead one to believe that he would have been able to come to terms in due course to the needs of the Liturgical Movement, however unlikely a prospect that appears at first glance.

In about 1938–9 Travers designed an altar for the chapel of the Kent & Canterbury Hospital, a new wing of which had just been built. As originally installed, this had a reredos with pleated wood effect and a Christus Rex figure on it, and above was a tester. On the altar were two characteristic squat wooden candlesticks. There is a painting in the chaplaincy of the altar in that condition. In 1948 Travers added altar rails, but at some point thereafter the chapel was moved into a new area of the hospital, and although the altar itself and the rails remain in place, the reredos, tester, and candlesticks have all disappeared.

In about 1940 he was involved in another hospital chapel, this time in the Victorian Dudley Road (now City) Hospital, Birmingham. He was asked to design a reredos and backing in the apse for the chapel as a memorial. This is a little known piece of work but quintessential Travers. No other artist could have carried it out, and it is instantly recognizable. The triptych is decorated with his rope designs, the blue backing has stars on it, and in front of the backing is the symbol of the Holy Spirit against a sun.

Among commissions carried out by Travers in 1939 was work at Holy Cross, Greenford. Here, as the suburbs moved out, the old parish church was too small for the requirements and so a new church was built adjoining the old, which in turn became a chapel. Travers provided an altar for the old church with the Ten Commandments on the reredos, rather in the Wren style, with a Christus Rex, and two gilded matching candlesticks on a small altar with a Laudian frontal.

At St. Stephen's Battersea, between 1939 and 1942, Travers installed a gothic pre-cast stone font with a pyramidal cover decorated in one of his usual knot designs. An alternative design which he produced for the font cover had four scrolls on top, which on closer inspection turn out to represent the water of baptism coming from a shell finial; a similar cover was made for Our Lady of Warnford, Hampshire. He installed a simple ogee shaped reredos within two riddels and this was bordered with the knot design once again; in the centre was a silver gilded crucifix. The oak altar and sanctuary rails were also to his design but the statue of St. Stephen and tabernacle were made later by Francis Stephens, although in the Travers style.

Sadly, in 1977 St. Stephen's was closed and became the Pentecostal 'Assemblies of the First Born'. The contents were dispersed, but the altar, rails and crucifix were taken to the nearby Christ Church, a modern building

St. Stephen Battersea: high altar, 1940 (conical light fittings added later)

erected in 1959, together with the statue of St. Stephen. They fit well in the atmospheric little building. The reredos and font cover were bought and stored by Mr. W.P. Anelay, then the Chairman of the York Diocesan Advisory Committee, for further use within that area, but after a very long period in which no home could be found for them, have recently been passed by him, together with a reredos from St. James, Watford, for use in St. George, Headstone, Harrow. The Battersea reredos, in characteristic terracotta colour with the wood simulating drapery, is now in the lady chapel at Harrow; the holes where the crucifix was attached are still in evidence but the crucifix itself is in the north chapel at Christ Church. The font cover, which bears a dedication to Father Coleman, former vicar of St. Stephen, and has a dove beneath, is to be repainted in sympathetic style for St. George.

In 1939 Travers prepared three designs for St. Mark, Swindon New Town, which involved refurnishing the sanctuary, rearranging the existing rood figures, and a wall tablet. However, with the outbreak of war the schemes were not carried into effect and the only work which was actually done was a striking east window, showing Christ in Glory, which was put in after Travers' death.

Strange as it may appear, the outbreak of the Second World War seems in general to have had relatively little effect on Travers' practice. Parishes continued to order work, and some schemes which were in the course of production were continued, such as at Cranford and Littleton.

Indeed, one scheme for which Travers had produced drawings just before the war, for a screen with rood at St. John, South Collingham, Nottinghamshire, produced a sheaf of correspondence with various ecclesiastical dignitaries objecting to the form of the screen on the basis that it was too southern for the area; Travers initially stood his ground, but one can hardly believe from the letters that the future of the country was at stake at the time. In due course, he did agree to change the design and the screen was erected to modified plans drawn in 1940; it is of wood, and there is a decoration of small stars attached to it. It is to the memory of Albert James Maxwell, vicar of the parish 1907-37, and has above it a typical Travers rood with a sun motif behind the crucified figure.

In the correspondence about South Collingham is a PS on a letter from Travers to Dr. Eeles, enquiring whether the latter had ever been to Combe Hay, Somerset, to which the artist was about to travel to prepare memorial tablets. There are indeed fine stone tablets and a hatchment in that church as designed by Travers, to the Smart family, and throughout the years memorial tablets continued to form part of his practice.

In 1940 Travers also returned to Clifton Campville, Staffordshire, where he had made a lectern in 1919 and had also prepared drawings for the lady chapel in 1922. On this occasion he enlarged the high altar and redesigned the sanctuary. Although further works have been carried out to the church since that time, the sanctuary remains substantially as redesigned by Travers.

Travers also designed a further window for St. Michael and All Angels, Cheriton, Hampshire, in 1940. He had already provided four aisle windows for this church around 1920, and when his then patron, Mrs. Mary Augusta Phipps Egerton, herself died, he was asked by her sisters to commemorate her. The window is at the east end of the north aisle; it was not installed until 1946, and shows Our Lady, but in the right hand light is the deceased herself in mediaeval costume. The result is more charming than might be thought; it stops just short of bad taste.

1940 also saw a design for a pulpit for St. George, Headstone, where earlier he had installed the large east window in 1937. This pulpit was in quasi-Jacobean style with a sounding board depicting the holy dove; it was installed the following year, and paid for by the Mothers' Union. In 1947 the same church wanted to install its own design of reredos for the high altar, but the Diocesan Advisory Committee was firm in advising that Travers should be consulted. In fact, however, Travers was too busy to take on the commission, and it was handed on to via Faith Craft to his assistant John Crawford, who had carried out much of the carving for Travers for many years. The design, showing the Epiphany, came to the church in December 1947, about seven months before Travers' death, and Crawford also made some very fine screens for the lady chapel. The work is almost indistinguishable from Travers' own, both in quality of design and in execution; even the lettering is similar. This church has recently acquired other Travers work from Battersea, as described above, and Watford, as described in Chapter 9, and has also commissioned new statues designed by Francis Stephens. It is a place where Travers' work is clearly cherished, unlike nearby Northolt, and these recent additions are a welcome development.

The additions are coherent, not least because all the work dates from the same period, 1937–41, when Travers was leaning towards Art Deco with less emphasis on Baroque; the total restrained effect is very pleasing.

The bombing, especially in London, was destroying many churches in which Travers had worked. The war also prevented some of his schemes being put into effect at all. For St. Paul, Bow Common, in East London, he had designed a new high altar with reredos and altar cross in 1939 and 1940. A land mine fell on the church on 20th September 1940, which led to it being closed, and on 19th March 1941 the church was burned out after further bombing. It seems certain that Travers' work was never done.

In fact 1941 was much the quietest year of the war for Travers' practice, although he did produce a scheme for the comprehensive internal refurbishment of St. Mary, Norwood Green, Southall, very near Cranford, which was never taken forward.

One of Travers' last works in the East End of London was the sanctuary reordering of Holy Trinity, Shepherdess Walk, Hoxton, in 1942, following war damage in which the east window had been blown out. The church is a typical example of Gothic Revival by Railton, and during the inter war years the parish priest had been the well known Father Kenrick, who had translated the English Missal. He had also been in the first group of pilgrims after Father Hope Patten had revived the devotion at Walsingham.

At Holy Trinity, Travers designed a simple rood which was intended to fit into the five blocked up lancets of the east window. Above the chancel arch was an IHS sunburst plaque in gilded wood, and a similar plaque at the top of the centre lancet showed the Hand of God. Further down was a small circular representation of the Holy Spirit as a dove and below this was a baroque crucifix. In the adjacent lancets were figures of Our Lady and St. John. A simple rectangular reredos stood beneath the window behind the high altar, on

Holy Trinity Hoxton: interior facing east

which stood six baroque candlesticks and a tabernacle. The frontal was of standard Roman pattern. The whole effect was striking in its simplicity and bore witness to Travers' gift of concise and skilful draughtsmanship, but unfortunately it was not installed. What appeared in the church was a rood with its figure on a base in front of the window, a stone altar with no frontals, and a large flat simple rectangular frame enclosing the rood. This supports curtains used to veil the crucifix at Benediction. Somehow the frame spoils the original simplicity and the rood would have looked better without its base. It was built partly of plywood and now is to be restored. Above the chancel arch and above the reredos are the circular plaques.

In the following year, 1943, Travers designed a hatchment as a memorial to Father Kenrick; other hatchments were also erected at the same time and are by him, and there are some later additions by others. There is also a Travers confessional in the church with tall Corinthian pilasters; it was formerly in St. Mary, Bourne Street, and was to be included in his unused scheme for that church's extension in 1924.

Holy Trinity Hoxton has a large number of shrines although no other work by Travers.

Organ case at St. John, Bethnal Green, 1948

Apart from the angular organ case and the possible attribution of an aumbry shaped like a church spire at St. John Bethnal Green (1948), the furnishings at Hoxton are all that remains of Travers' work in the East End, where once Anglo-Catholic churches dominated the landscape.

Another London church for which work was designed in 1942 was St. Peter, Acton Green. Travers had designed a very elaborate surround for a niche recess around a statue of the Sacred Heart in 1925, but although many other Counter-Reformation style furnishings were put into the church, this was not. Although that drawing does not include the detail of a statue, the Sacred Heart image, which is now in a plain niche in the south wall, is almost certainly by him. In 1942 he designed a new high altar, an organ gallery, and also a backing for the shrine of Our Lady of Walsingham. The parish priest of the church at this time, Father W.G. de Lara Wilson, was a great supporter of the Walsingham devotion, and had also himself been a curate at Bourne Street when Travers was carrying out work to the high altar in that church. The image of Our Lady of Walsingham is set in a baroque niche surrounded by twelve stars and surmounted by two cherubs holding a cartouche inscribed with a MAR monogram. It may be that it was the same niche for which the 1925 surround was proposed. Travers' organ gallery, at the west end, is wooden and fairly plain. The drawing for the high altar shows two alternative designs on the same plan, with variations both to the reredos and the ornamentation at the side of the altar. The work was carried out but the reredos has since been removed: the present altar has no reredos but six large candlesticks and a crucifix to Travers' design on a gradine behind the altar. At either side are volutes as shown on the left hand side of the original plan.

An important commission, which began in 1942, was for the church of St. Mary, Northolt, in what was then Middlesex. This is a small mediaeval church with an interesting history. Each of its rectors between 1231 and 1875 also held the See of London; several became Archbishop of Canterbury, including the High Church William Laud, who was beheaded in 1645.

In the early 1940s a new rector, Gordon Lewis Philips, arrived; he had trained at Kelham and became a regular contributor to 'The Fiery Cross Magazine', then appearing under the auspices of the Church Union. He embellished the building with the furnishings required to give it a more Catholic appearance. Travers began in 1942 by remaking the font cover using timber from the existing seventeenth century cover, and sculpting the base from a stone which stood beneath the bowl and encased the original damaged base.

During 1943 Travers produced designs for the Chapel of St. Stephen, giving it a proper altar, two gilded candlesticks, and a crucifix. Above were a figure of St. Stephen and the text from his martyrdom; in this chapel Father Phillips reserved the Sacrament. Travers' original design for this chapel showed a kneeling figure of St. Stephen in a typical continental style of dalmatic. Both this and the text of the martyrdom were to be stencilled on the wall, but in fact what appeared was the semi-relief figure made from a standard mould with plinth. His drawing included a single iron riddel bracket to the left of the altar, on which was a single candlestick and a curtain, which would have had the effect of screening the altar from the rest of the church.

Design for chapel of St. Stephen, Northolt

For the high altar, Travers formed a triptych by adding two side panels to a painting of the Adoration of the Magi which had been given by a parishioner and which has variously been attributed to the Flemish, Dutch, and Spanish Schools. On the new panels he painted the text of the Magnificat and in each outer corner a winged putti head. All was toned down for antique effect.

1945 was the tercentenary of Archbishop Laud's death and Father Philips commissioned Travers to make a hatchment which commemorated both the fact that Laud had been Rector of Northolt and that of his death in 1645. It depicts the arms of three of the four dioceses which he held, namely St. David's, London and Canterbury.

Travers also made for the church a plinth for flowers under the statue of Our Lady, and a crucifix.

Design for high altar, St. Mary, Northolt

Later, in 1947 he produced a complete scheme for the chancel of St. Mary Northolt, which showed the lower part of the sanctuary and chancel to be panelled. On the high altar were four baroque candlesticks and the painted crucifix, which now hangs by the pulpit. Behind was the triptych referred to above, and on the right side of the east window hung the Laud hatchment; on the left was another existing monument. Dominating the north wall of the chancel was a large painted and gilded relief of Our Lady crowned as Queen of Heaven and standing on a crescent moon being supported on a wrought iron bracket. The whole concept was original and delightful, but unfortunately it was not completed. It may well be that the same design for the relief of Our Lady was used for Old St. Pancras when the restoration work there was done at about the same time. In fact the statue of Our Lady in Northolt church is a small plaster figure, not by Travers, on a bracket between the chapel and the chancel arch.

Over the last few years the work done by Travers in the chancel has been dismantled and various changes have been made to the church furnishings without full appreciation of its architecture and history. The triptych has been moved to hang on the south wall by the main door, where it is out of place. The chapel of St. Stephen has also been dismantled and the only altar in the church stands at the chancel steps facing westward. It is on a vivid orange patterned carpet and the former chancel now has a pine room-divider and pot plants. This is one case where the dignity of Travers' furnishings has been completely lost.

In 1942 Travers designed a lady chapel for the Evangelical church of St. Mary, Loughton, Essex. It was in fact not installed until after the war and was blessed by the Bishop of Barking on 31st March 1946; it was given by Ernest Griggs in memory of his wife who died in 1939. The chapel is by no means Travers' most distinguished piece of work, but it is interesting as showing how he adapted his usual style for a parish without

Design for chapel, St. Mary, Loughton, Essex

the traditions with which his work is normally associated. The altar has a reredos, which is a plain board but with the central third raised, and has on it a sun motif with 'IHS'. In gold on black in elaborate Gothic lettering are the words 'Ye are justified in the name of Lord Jesus by the Spirit of Our God.' Behind is a cross, not a crucifix, on the wall with INRI in a scroll and the initials of the four Evangelists at the extremities.

Travers also designed in 1942 a sculpted figure of Our Lady with the Holy Child, which was placed over the High Altar at the sumptuously furnished Abbey Church at Beaulieu, Hampshire, where it remains, in fine condition. A similar relief was provided after the War for Romsey Abbey.

At this time, he also became involved with the churches at Hawkinge, Kent. The vicar, Revd Shaw Page, had been known to him previously at West Wickham, also then in Kent, and had moved from there to Hawkinge. It will be remembered that Travers' friend Sedding had been

Design for reredos, Hawkinge, Kent

buried at West Wickham, and Travers had designed an internal vestry wall and tablets there in 1934; the wall was removed in 1961 when a new vestry was built. In 1942 Father Page's son was killed in action, and his wife died at about the same time. Travers painted and gilded the existing wooden reredos in unmistakable style and erected a memorial tablet to the two of them, by which time the rector had moved on. It is interesting to note that the repainted reredos at West Wickham, which has an Agnus Dei symbol, is very similar to an unexecuted design for a chapel in St. John Maddermarket, Norwich, produced almost 30 years before.

There were then two churches in the village of Hawkinge, St. Michael and All Angels, an ancient church on a hill outside and well away from habitation, and St. Luke, a Victorian church on the main road amidst the houses. In 1942 Travers designed for the old church, St. Michael, an altar, rood and candlesticks as a memorial to one H.L.P. Boxer, who died that year. The retable had a sunburst and the words 'All Nations should come and glorify thy Name,' with a crucifix painted on. The effect was rather more Italianate than Baroque. The correspondence also indicates that Travers repaired the Royal Arms and a textboard for the church for his expenses only.

That church was subsequently made redundant and sold for housing; the whereabouts of the furnishings is unknown.

It also appears that in 1942 St. Luke Hawkinge was damaged by the fall of a bomb, and the vicar made an appeal for funds for a new church to replace it, which Travers designed for him. However, the appeal must have fallen on deaf ears because the church was not rebuilt then; it lasted until the 1950s when it was affected by fire, and was finally replaced in 1958.

One of Travers' least known schemes was for Holy Trinity, Wyke Champflower, Somerset, but this demonstrates well his ability to assimilate his work to that which was there before. The Wyke church is only 46 feet long, and is completely hidden from the road, as it is behind the Manor House, to which it is joined and of which it was originally the private chapel. The building is dated 1624 and is an extraordinarily atmospheric survival.

Wyke has always been within the parish of the adjoining town of Bruton, but Travers was consulted in 1942 by Revd D.R. Pelly, who had retired to the Manor. On 8th October 1942 a faculty was sought for Travers' designs to extend the altar, reposition a Ten Commandments board from the north wall to form a reredos and place a crucifix on it, erect hangings behind, provide two silvered wooden candlesticks and a frontal for the altar, remove a box pew and replace it with a parson's seat, restore the acorn terminals on the pews, place a new font within the church, form a new doorway in the west wall and incorporate a room from the manor house as a sacristy, and rewash the walls, and this was granted in 1943. Unfortunately, shortly after that Pelly died and although most of the work had been carried out, neither the new entrance and incorporation of the sacristy nor the hanging behind the altar had been done, and the new font had been deferred. Travers designed Pelly's grave slab with an elaborately carved cross, which was later copied for the adjoining grave of his wife, who died many years later. She however paid for a new stone font by Travers in memory of her husband, and this is dated 1945. The existing Seventeenth Century wooden cover was used.

The woodwork designed by Travers used some wood from the one box pew which was removed, and the whole of the work fits exactly in scale and execution with its surroundings. All the work is still there, although the candlesticks are not now generally used.

In 1943 Travers began designing war memorials again, although of course the war was still at a critical stage. At The Ascension, Burghclere, Hampshire, he produced a fine north aisle window in memory of Richard Ford Rew Elkington, 1918-43, who had been killed in action. The window depicts St. George the Martyr and St. Richard of Chichester.

At nearby St. Mary the Virgin, Bramshott, he designed three fine lancet windows showing the arms of the Canadian provinces to commemorate the encampment of forces from that country on Bramshott Common in both world wars, with Our Lady and the Child in the centre light, and the Hand of God above. He also made up a new chancel north window by reusing an existing figure on a new background.

At Christ Church, Radlett, Hertfordshire, he designed and produced a tablet in stone with gilded badge and inscription to Flying Officer Leslie Manser VC.

At All Saints, Fulham, where he had worked before, he produced in 1943 a scheme for new clergy seats in memory of two members of the choir who had been killed. However, although a faculty was obtained, the work was not carried out at that time, and a modified scheme by another architect was used in 1951.

Another project at this time was for windows at St. Leonard, Chesham Bois, Buckinghamshire, on which there is some detailed information available in the form of an article written by Hugh Salmond for the *Journal of the British Society of Master Glass Painters* in 1970-11[1]. Travers suggested that the east window be rebuilt using not only fragments which had been taken from the pre-existing east window and stored because of the war, but also glass from elsewhere. Some members of the parish objected, but Travers demonstrated his ideas to a meeting and carried the day. He was then asked to design a completely new west window, which he did; the lettering in that window is rather angular and unlike his usual style, but still enhances the church. It shows Our Lord's appearances after the Resurrection.

In 1944, new work continued to be commissioned. The Community of the Resurrection had been bombed out of their London priory at 39, Pont Street, early in the war. On 8th September 1944 their new priory at 8, Holland Park, Kensington, was opened, and the newsletter reported 'Mr. Martin Travers carried out the work with his usual distinction.' The work was in fact a high altar with baldachino around and above it, a crucifix on the wall and a statue of Our Lady on the wall, which may be the one which he was asked by the Community to modify for the chapel in early 1945. Another altar had a bas-relief of Our Lady similar to the one designed for Northolt and the one actually in Old St. Pancras, and a crucifix.

Interior of Priory of St. Paul, Holland Park, 1944–5

The Community vacated Holland Park in 1968. The statue of Our Lady was taken to the retreat house at Hemingford Grey, Cambridgeshire, and the bas-relief of Our Lady together with crucifixes, candlesticks and memorial tablets designed by Travers are now in the Community's Priory of St. Michael in Burleigh Street, Covent Garden.

The ethos of the work at Holland Park was classical rather than baroque, and the Community was certainly going through a 'Roman' phase at that time.

At St. Thomas, Oxford, the church where Father Wodehouse had previously introduced Italianate furnishings whilst a curate, Travers designed, in 1944, a statue of Our Lady and a parclose screen. The screen was never put in, but the gilded and painted statue of Our Lady and the Holy Child is among his very best. It was a recognition of the ministry of Father Jalland at that church; he had previously been a patron of Travers while at St. Luke, Swindon.

Poster for St. Thomas the Martyr, Oxford

Also in 1944, Travers designed a characteristic backing for a stone image of Our Lady in the side chapel at St. Francis of Assisi, Great West Road, Isleworth. The otherwise bare church by Shearman was enhanced by a finely detailed terracotta coloured wooden canopy with sun device and spire above.

A well-known Catholic parish in Kent is St. Barnabas, Tunbridge Wells. In 1938 Father William Torrence retired as vicar and was replaced in February 1939 by Father Frank Steel, who commissioned Travers to carry out refurbishment works in St. Stephen's Chapel and the Lady Chapel. These commenced with designs in 1944.

Travers embellished the existing reredos in St. Stephen's Chapel at St. Barnabas. The reredos is in Gothic style and contains figures of St. Augustine of Canterbury, St. Lawrence, St. Stephen, and St. Clement; he heightened it and made the four statues for it. On the altar stands a painted wooden crucifix and two baroque square based silver candlesticks. A frontal in terracotta red fabric containing a black IHS sunburst and stylized applique border of pomegranates was also provided. Two hatchments were designed and they would have hung on either side of the chapel window, but they were never executed (See Plate 27).

The lady chapel was far more ultramontane. The reredos was designed as a vast frame for a Seventeenth Century painting of Our Lady. It contains semi-reliefs of the Four Doctors of the Church, St. Augustine, St. Gregory, St. Hieronymus (Jerome), and St. Ambrose. All the panels are again bordered with stylized pomegranates much favoured by Travers at this time. On the stone gradine stand six wooden baroque candlesticks, and below on the altar are two square based candlesticks together with a domed tabernacle. It appears in fact that the six candlesticks were a later addition, for a photograph immediately after the works were completed does not include them. The design for this scheme originally included an open wooden turned screen enclosing the chapel and dividing it from the chancel. It incorporated a gate at the rear in front of the sacristy door, which would have been extremely inconvenient. Around the top were stencilled the words 'Verbum Caro Factum Est.' This screen was never in fact constructed, but in 1947 Travers designed and installed a shallow octagonal tester, which hangs above the altar and which depicts the sevenfold gifts of the Holy Spirit proceeding from a dove (See Plate 26).

It was at one time thought that Travers made a few alterations to the high altar reredos by installing a large Oberammagau crucifix and painting two panels in pale blue and stencilling Latin inscriptions upon them; four shields appeared at the same time on the lower half. However, recent research has shown that this work was in fact carried out by Milner & Craze.

There can be no better example of Travers' unwillingness to be labelled and of his versatility than his work at this church, where he was able almost simultaneously to carry out work in the Gothic and Baroque styles.

At St. James, Bushey, Hertfordshire, Travers designed a chapel in 1944 at the east end of the north aisle with unmistakable reredos of deep red with a stylized robed and crowned Christ looking almost Orthodox. The altar is used for a 'youth chapel' and there are texts on either side in lozenge shaped tablets with equally unmistakable lettering.

Travers was engaged by the church of St. Catherine, Preston North Without or Preston-next-Faversham, Kent, to prepare several sets of

Design for sanctuary, St. Catherine, Preston Next Faversham

drawings for alterations to the church. These drawings show that he had a major transformation in mind and this would have involved the parish in vast expense, including the construction of a stone parclose screen. The high altar as shown was an English altar with simple reredos and crucifix attached. His typical stylized border of pomegranates in gold and black surrounded it and two wooden candlesticks stood on the mensa. The riddels are modern in style and have neither cherubs nor angels. Oak communion rails were included. The following year he designed a lady chapel for the north aisle, which included an altar with a triptych behind and two candlesticks. Above was a crowned statue of Our Lady. This chapel would have been divided from the nave by a stone screen. In 1947 a set of drawings appeared for a rood beam across the chancel arch above a new screen with its own loft.

Eventually, most of these plans had to be abandoned as the cost was far too high and only the high altar and communion rails were executed, together with an attractive rood beam across the chancel arch, and a Bishop's chair in the sanctuary, which was in memory of a local man killed in the war. He also designed the parish war memorial on the north wall. The total effect is pleasing even without the completion of all the scheme. He may also have designed a pulpit, which was later removed from the church, and the crowned statue of Our Lady may be his.

The trustees of the Shrine of Our Lady of Walsingham own a preparatory school, Quainton Hall, in Hindes Road, Harrow. The headmaster for many years was Father Eyden. Travers was asked by him in 1945 to design a war memorial for the school chapel, and did so. This remains in use at the school. It appears that the backing to the image of Our Lady of Walsingham, which stands on the memorial, has been repainted subsequently. The chapel also possesses a shrine of St. Francis and a high altar with large crucifix and tabernacle, and a reversible frontal, which are all clearly of the Travers' school, although they may have been executed after his death.

Travers was also asked to design a memorial to Father Eyden's mother at Walsingham itself. He produced a design for the Chapel of the Seven Sorrows, which is actually outside the main shrine buildings and forms part of the Via Dolorosa. The Chapel, which is an extremely confined space, contains a small altar, the frontal of which has teardrops on a black background, and a bas-relief of Our Lady as Mater Dolorosa in the place of the reredos. A similar frontal design had been used some years earlier at St. Augustine, Queen's Gate. Unfortunately, the interior of the chapel suffers the effect of damp and wet because it is often open to the elements, and although redecorated from time to time is again in need of attention at the time of writing.

It is interesting that Travers did so little at Walsingham, which was in many ways the culmination of the Back to Baroque Movement. The only work by him there is the chapel referred to, a rood placed at the top of the staircase in the main shrine, next to the altar of the Coronation of Our Lady, in memory of Mary Pyle-Bridges, which had been left in his workshop when he died, and also possibly a large crucifix to a similar design to that at Quainton Hall, which is in one of the guest rooms. It may be that Father Hope Patten preferred to employ Milner & Craze as architects because of personal connections; it may also be that he disapproved of Travers' agnosticism and irregular (by his standards) personal life.

Also in Norfolk in 1945, Travers returned to Norwich for further work. The church of St. Matthew, Rosary Road, Thorpe Hamlet, was an undistinguished Victorian building outside the City Centre. He provided a wooden high altar with Agnus Dei sign and rood with figures for the church after designing them in 1945. In about 1982 the Victorian church was closed and converted to housing, and a striking new church opened in Telegraph Lane West. Although the design was modern, many of the fittings from the former church were moved to the new building, including a series of windows by Travers' pupil Lawrence Lee. Fortunately, the altar and rood figures were also moved. The altar is now free standing, and the

Interior of the old church of St. Matthew, Thorpe Hamlet, Norwich, showing rood and high altar, carried out c 1947

rood figures are now hung on a whitewashed wall immediately behind it, where they look most effective. The church is a fine example of the union of old and new, and the Travers fitments contribute materially to the success of the building.

The rood figures were one of a number which Travers was installing in various churches across the country at this time. The following year for example he designed roods for All Saints, Westbrook, in his home town of Margate, and SS. Peter and Paul, Old Town, Bexhill-on-Sea.

In 1945 Travers produced two drawings for a simple low triptych below the east window at St. Mary, Ticehurst, Sussex. One showed Our Lord in alb and stole holding chalice and paten with texts pertaining to Holy Communion. The other showed Our Lady with the infant Jesus and the text 'His name is called the Word of God', and also depicted the Annunciation. The drawings also included two large wooden candlesticks and new communion rails. This second scheme was the more colourful and perhaps appropriate for a church dedicated to St. Mary, but the parish chose the former,

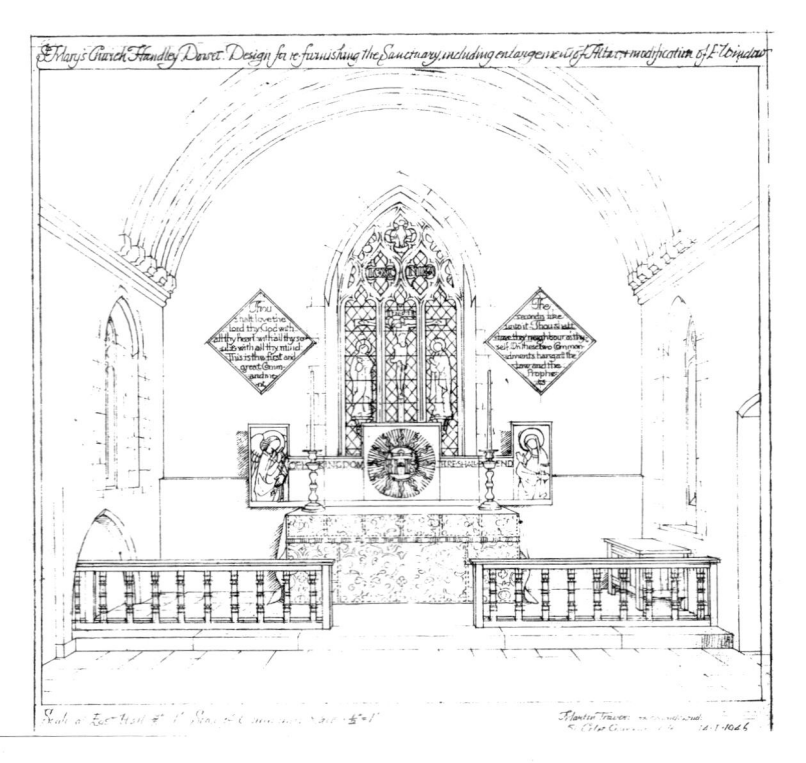

Design for sanctuary, St. Mary, Sixpenny Handley

with the communion rails, and this was installed in about 1947 in memory of Francis Fitzgerald Hart and Anthony Gilbert Hart (See Plate 30).

In the same year, 1945, Travers produced a scheme for St. Mary, Handley (now known as Sixpenny Handley), Dorset, which was very similar to the second scheme for Ticehurst, and included the same wooden candlesticks. However instead of the Virgin and Child at the centre of the triptych was an IHS sunburst with the angel Gabriel on the left door and Our Lady on the right. Sanctuary rails were included, as were two hatchments of the summary of the law, which hung on either side of the east window. In fact the finished hatchments have the words of the Magnificat in Latin. Unfortunately the triptych has been moved so it is next to the font, but could be returned to its original position, thus completing a charming and inexpensive scheme for a small country church.

Also in 1945, Travers designed a rather run of the mill Christus Rex, altar candlesticks and communion rails for Christ Church, Upper George Street, Luton, which was closed in 1976 and subsequently demolished.

There were rather fewer windows being put in at that time, but in the same year Travers did design a set of windows for the baptistery at the famous church of St. Barnabas, Pimlico, which is now a daughter church to St. Mary Bourne Street.

In 1946 however a number of churches did require windows. Some of these were as a result of bomb damage: Travers designed the east window of the crucifixion at the rather dull Christ Church, Ware, Hertfordshire, to replace a window blown out, and also rebuilt the west window from fragments. Others were new projects all together, and at this time a new tendency was taking hold in his glass. Instead of the clear glass around the subject, which had been a feature of his work since the Tyneham window designed in 1925, he began on occasion to use soft colours as background. This can be seen in the east window of Our Lady and the Holy Child at St. Mary, North Mymms, Hertfordshire, designed in 1946, also to replace a window damaged in the war, where the insipid background detracts from the strong colours of the subject. Another designed at this time was the east window of St. Andrew, Buckland, Kent, installed in 1949 after his death.

At SS. Peter and Paul, Wadhurst, Sussex, a war memorial chapel was designed in 1946 with a triptych of the Resurrection, and a memorial panel in the window. It included an open wooden screen, a Laudian covered altar on which stood two baroque candlesticks, and a wooden priest's bench. The work was carried out in 1947, and in fact Lawrence Lee painted the triptych, the only piece of work he carried out for his employer other than in stained glass. Unfortunately, the current Florentine frontal is not in keeping with the original designs; Travers had intended a real silk brocade frontal with fringing. However the scheme is otherwise substantially complete and is in very good condition.

Another commission for a memorial chapel at this time was the refitting of the Hastings memorial chapel at St. Giles, Stoke Poges, a church which receives a very great number of visitors because of its connections with the poet Gray. The chapel was provided with a new altar with characteristic sun device on the reredos, and the window above is dated 1947 and signed both by Martin Travers and by his chief assistant Lawrence Lee. Other windows were reconstructed from old glass. This chapel is, like the rest of the church, in exceptionally good condition and well visited.

Travers was, as has been said, becoming much more a part of the ecclesiastical establishment. During the last years of his life he received a considerable quantity of work from Faith Craft, the furnishing arm of Faith House. In addition he received commissions such as a pewter memorial tablet for Eton College, which was done. He designed an altar and furnishings for Queen's College Chapel, Oxford, but this was not carried out: the College had certainly asked him to report on the condition of their stained glass, which he did, by letter dated 13th December 1946, but have no record of asking him to design a new sanctuary! The Temple Church had been almost completely destroyed in the War, but he designed a cross in 1944 at a time when it was hoped that it could be reused temporarily. In fact, rebuilding took many years. In other places, such as the now demolished Roman Catholic Church of St. George, Norwich, Travers died before he could make any significant progress on work he had designed.

Travers visited Ely Cathedral in 1946 and supplied designs for a new east window in the lady chapel. Unfortunately, the Dean and Chapter did not adopt these plans as they regarded the project as too expensive: further, they appear to have returned the final plans to the artist, and at some point thereafter they have disappeared. However, Lawrence Lee retained a preliminary coloured draft, which shows that there would have been no fewer than 15 lights depicting a variety of saints. This is a tantalizing 'might have been': there is little doubt that Travers' work would greatly have enhanced the magnificent setting for which it was intended.

The most prestigious commission to proceed at this time however was undoubtedly that from H.M. the Queen, for the silver painted wooden crucifix and matching candlesticks for the high altar of St. Helier Church, Jersey, the incumbent of which is always the Dean of the island. These are fine items, although they do not entirely fit with the décor of the remainder of the church. They are inscribed as a donation from Her Majesty, and were seen by the present Queen when she visited Jersey in 1989. They were a gift to the island in order to commemorate its liberation from the German occupation in the Second World War (See Plate 32).

In 1947 Travers returned to Old St. Pancras, a church for which he had provided a trompe l'oeil backing to a tabernacle in about 1925. The church had been damaged in the War, and he carried out a rearrangement of the sanctuary (which has since been rearranged again), and designed and executed a plaster tympanum with dove effect and a very striking bas-relief of Our Lady, which may have been intended for St. Mary Northolt, and certainly was similar to that installed in the Community of the Resurrection's Priory in Holland Park, although the St. Pancras image has lost its surround. He also designed a rood and pulpit for this small but homely church, which were never executed.

Old St. Pancras was not the only church which required remedial work after the War. Travers also prepared plans for the refurbishment of St. Jude, Courtfield Gardens, South Kensington, the vicar of which was then Revd H.W. Beck, who had previously been concerned with Travers when he was at St. John, Harrow. Here the nave walls were whitewashed, the altar was rather crudely extended by 1'6" at each end by adding a panel, and silver gilt candlesticks were provided rather similar to those in Jersey. The reredos was altered by the addition of a new section, and it appears that curtains were hung; the brackets remain, but not the curtains. He also moved some figures to replace a window which had been blown out. It is proposed to remove the whitewash from the walls of this large church, and in any event it is crumbling in places already.

Another site to which Travers returned after the war was Tonbridge School. Here, in 1947 he designed a screen as a memorial for the Second World War, and in 1948 an altar in the antechapel. By this time the scheme from 1925 for the west door with its series of panels describing the memorial windows and the reredos, had finally been executed. Each panel was linked to another by an intricate knot design culminating in a golden tassel. Unfortunately, all this was lost in the 1988 fire.

It will be recalled that during the war Travers had designed and made a bas-relief of Our Lady and the Holy Child for Beaulieu Abbey. In 1947 he designed a similar relief together with riddel posts and furnishings below for the high altar at nearby Romsey Abbey. That again is very high quality work, worthy of its noble surroundings.

Travers also carried out post war work at St. Mark, Herston, Swanage, not far from Corfe Castle, where he designed the centre light only of the east window, showing Our Lord with chalice and paten. He also designed for this small church an English altar with hangings and two candlesticks, and hanging lights on either side; on the altar was to be a small rood panel in front of the curtain. He also designed a font cover, but no work was done other than the window.

At this time he carried out works to the existing rood screen at the fine church of St. Michael, Mere, Wiltshire, which included a rebuilding of the parapet; the loft had been restored rather clumsily in the early years of the twentieth century. In addition he designed and constructed a wooden screen between the nave and the tower, with fine lettering and a characteristic Travers cartouche of dedication. He also designed a new altar for St. Lawrence, Tinsley, Sheffield, with a long stepped reredos around a rood,

Unexecuted design for work at St. Lawrence, Tinsley, 1947

and fine figures of St. Lawrence and St. Stephen. Unfortunately, this work was not carried out, and when the sanctuary at Tinsley was reordered, in 1953, it was to a different scheme.

It is clear that during the last years of his life Travers was beginning to carry out more work in the Gothic idiom, although not strictly in the sense that his former master Ninian Comper, shortly to be knighted, would have approved. This can be demonstrated by his work at St. Barnabas, Tunbridge Wells, and by an unexecuted design for St. Andrew, Harrow Road, Sudbury, for a war memorial reredos.

In 1948 Travers also designed a new gothic triptych for St. Saviour, Pimlico. It had been intended to create a lady chapel out of the north chapel in the church. The triptych contained the Annunciation in the centre and on the doors were St. Mary Magdalene, King Edward the Confessor, St. Stephen, and St. Peter. This did not materialize, but Travers did add rood figures to the church's Gothic Revival high altar reredos and also a text beneath. Somehow the final result is not very satisfactory, in that the diminutive rood figures seem to perch precariously on top of the gothic pinnacles. St. Saviour had also commissioned a large statue of Mary based on one in Bruges and this was made in about 1942.

Travers of course died on 25th July 1948, and thus very little if any of the work designed by him earlier that year was completed under his direct supervision. In addition of course, there were ongoing projects such as Corfe Castle where part of the work had been done and the rest was in train. It is in many cases very difficult to entangle when exactly at this time work was done, and by whom.

Travers had been assisted by the same basic 'team' for some years – Alf Noe was the decorator and gilder, John Crawford was technical assistant and the carver, and Lawrence Lee was the assistant in relation to stained glass. Crawford had worked for Travers since about 1924 and Lee since about 1931, and Lee succeeded Travers in his teaching post at the RCA. Crawford also taught there from 1926 to about 1954, rather surprisingly in stained glass rather than in wood, and apparently had carried out some restoration of old glass on his own account even before joining Travers.

It is sometimes said that Lawrence Lee was in partnership with Travers, but that is not in fact correct: he was his assistant and he recalls the very clear distinction between the two of them.

Another former assistant of Travers was Douglas Purnell. He had worked with him before the war, but after the war he set up on his own at 6, Wellesley Grove, Croydon.

In 1948 Travers designed windows for St. Nicholas, Chislehurst, St. John, Harrow, St. Martin, Longmoor Camp, Liss, and SS. Peter and Paul, Leominster, Herefordshire. All these schemes were carried out; the Leominster window, showing a vision of Our Lady and the Child from the Revelation, was finished by Lawrence Lee after Travers' death, and is signed with the initials of both of them. Lawrence Lee was always punctilious in ensuring that the initials of all those involved appeared on a window.

Travers prepared a scheme for woodwork in Chelsea Methodist Church, which was almost the only example of a commission from a non-Anglican source, but appears not to have been carried out.

In June 1948, seven weeks before his death, Travers prepared a small but effective scheme for the little church of All Saints, in the tiny hamlet of Tudeley, near Tonbridge. It had an east window of the Resurrection flanked by two plaques of the Summary of the Law, and below hung a simple dossal curtain on a pole. To this was attached a crucifix and the altar below was in a conventional style with panelled frontal. New communion rails were also included. Unfortunately the window did not materialize, probably because of Travers' untimely death and the amount of work in train at that time, but an altar is said to have been installed, and then removed some years later. This church is best known for the windows by Marc Chagall, which in the 1960s and 70s were hailed as a masterpiece, but had the Travers scheme been executed it would have given the church a greater warmth than now exists; the sanctuary is now very cold and bare.

The last drawings dispatched by Travers before his death appear to be those for SS. Peter and Paul, Temple Ewell, Dover, which are dated 20th July 1948. They relate to sanctuary furnishings and an east window, and the work was carried out posthumously. The east window shows a rood scene and remains in good condition.

Another piece of work carried out after Travers' death was at St. Michael, Helston, Cornwall, where he had designed a rood set and screen, both of which were installed in 1952. The rood set is in standard form and was obviously created in the same moulds which he had used for several other commissions, but the screen was most unusual. The church was built in the eighteenth century, and Travers produced a classical screen to tone in with the building; the screen had four columns and a pediment, with four candlesticks above, and stood in front of the rood beam itself. Unfortunately, in 1972 the screen was taken out of the church completely, and the rood set was moved on to the north wall; it looks striking against the white but is somewhat incongruous in that position and it is a great

Rood and screen, St. Michael, Helston, erected posthumously in 1952

shame that the changes were permitted. It is not clear who carried out the work after Travers' death, but it is clear that his designs were used and that he had received the original commission.

The attribution of work at this time is made more difficult because Travers had certain standard designs and moulds, as has become apparent from the discussion of his work, and his disciples were able to use them to carry out work. Also of course, having been trained by him they were obviously influenced by the work he had done. It is extremely difficult to distinguish the late work of Travers from the early independent work of Lawrence Lee, such as the Epiphany window in the lady chapel of St. Margaret, Leigh-on-Sea, Essex, which Lee himself said was 'obviously by a disciple of Martin Travers'[2]. St. Mary Aldermary in the City on the other hand has a fine east window of the crucifixion, carried out by Lawrence Lee but to Travers' designs.

At St. John the Baptist, Tunstall, Kent, a hanging rood using plaster figures designed by Travers was installed by a former assistant of his, Francis (later Revd Francis) Stephens, as late as 1967. The figures had been stored for many years in a cellar, until they came to the attention of John Betjeman, who was instrumental in seeing them used.

The difficulties of attribution of work at this time can be illustrated also by the high altar, reredos and tabernacle of St. Gregory the Great, Horfield,

Bristol. This work has usually been attributed to Travers himself. However, there is a considerable file of papers in the Council for the Care of Churches, which makes it clear that the work was done by the Faith Craft cooperative, which had been founded by Wilfred Lawson in 1921. They said on 29th July 1948 that they had been 'working closely with Martin Travers of late', having just heard of his death, but this work was given to Travers' assistant John Crawford and Travers himself had no dealings with it. It proved controversial because some on the Diocesan Committee thought that the proposed work was substandard; in fact it is likely that the real objection was theological, as John Crawford had worked for Travers for so long and was well known in his own field. The work was actually carried out in 1949 or 1950.

For some time after Travers' death work furnishings continued to be made in the same idiom either by his former staff or by others, especially Faith Craft. Perhaps the clearest example of that is at St. Silas, Pentonville, where in 1949 a comprehensive scheme was devised for a new high altar and rails, a Sacred Heart shrine, and a backing for the shrine of Our Lady. In the event, only the backing for the shrine of Our Lady was made, and that has subsequently been adopted for the shrine of Our Lady of Walsingham. This was in fact designed by Francis Stephens for Faith Craft.

Douglas Purnell designed the fine baroque reredos and much other work at St. Augustine, Tonge Moor, Bolton, in the style of Travers, and he also carried on with Travers' work at Gibraltar Cathedral, as to which see Chapter 8. Purnell did other work in Lancashire also, all in the style of Travers, particularly a hanging rood at St. Aidan, Bolton (a daughter church of St. Augustine), side chapel reredoses at St. Stephen, Lever Bridge, also in Bolton, and St. Catherine, Burnley, and a high altar and domed tabernacle for St. Peter, Blackburn (now demolished).

Not a great deal seems to be known of Purnell; Canon Roger Davison, who was at Tonge Moor when much of the work was done, remembers him as a small, somewhat diffident man, who in later years was to be found working in the Art & Book Shop near Westminster Cathedral, which supplied many Anglican churches as well as Roman with tasteful antiques of various sorts.

Chapter 8

Travers as Designer:

VI WORK ABROAD

One of the more unusual features of Martin Travers' practice was that geographically his work was concentrated in the South East of England. He worked mainly in Greater London, the suburbs of what were then Middlesex and Surrey, and also in Hampshire, East Anglia, Kent, and Berkshire. He was, perhaps unexpectedly, not much employed by the great Anglo-Catholic churches in Brighton. There is however also a considerable amount of his work in the West Country, especially in Somerset and Wiltshire, but virtually nothing north of the Trent. He did no work in the great cities of the north, other than windows for Stand Unitarian Church near Manchester (destroyed in the Second World War), and the windows in St. Augustin, Tynemouth, are many miles from his nearest other church. The only work he appears to have carried out in Scotland was a fine crested plaque in the Episcopal Church in Peebles, there is very little in Wales, and despite the family connections, nothing in Ireland.

However, there is some little-known work abroad.

It is obviously more difficult at long distance to collate information about work which may or may not have been carried out some years ago, and which is many thousands of miles away, than it is to visit a church in, say, Surrey.

In certain places, especially New Zealand, a great deal of information has come to light in relation to his work which may not generally be known in this country. In others, there is very little which can be included.

In Europe, Travers was directly concerned with three separate projects, all for the Church of England, the first two of which both date from 1927. For the Church of the Nativity, St. Jean de Luz, France, he designed a reredos. The church has long since closed, and it appears there are no relevant faculties or the like, so it cannot be said with any certainty whether or not

Christ's Chronicle: The Heavenly City

the work was ever carried out. Travers certainly visited the church himself on one of his trips abroad, and drew up measurements in his notebook. In fact, he had family connections in the area as his mother's sister lived in the town for many years, and it may be because of that link that he was asked to design the work. It can however be said without fear of contradiction that any work which was done is not there now.

The position with the church of St. George, Madrid, is very different. There were and are a considerable number of English people living in Madrid, who wanted their own church. Spanish law at the time however prohibited the holding of property by religious organizations other than the Roman Catholic Church, so it was necessary that the building be treated as diplomatic property and called the Embassy Chapel. In fact, it was and is a focus for expatriates in the city. The actual church is a somewhat peculiar building designed by a local architect not, as is often the case with chaplaincies abroad, to look as much like an English country church as possible, but rather in the style of a small Spanish mission.

Travers' work inside was very extensive. In effect he was asked to furnish the church ready for use, including providing some stained glass windows. Other windows were added subsequently as funds became available.

Over the south door is a characteristic Travers memorial plaque on a deep red background edged in gilt, to William Edgar Allen (1837–1915), who left money to enable the church to be completed. The pews, pulpit, kneeling desk and lectern are all by Travers and all of high quality. Of particular interest are the pulpit, which has volutes, carved patterns and the IHS symbol facing the congregation, and an elaborate double-sided lectern, with carved tassel patterns on the corners. Travers also designed the gilded font cover, which is more restrained than many of his covers, but adds some colour to the church. The altar has no great distinction and the sanctuary arrangements have been altered to allow westward celebration. Travers also designed the sanctuary windows, the middle three of which are all memorials. The centre east window features St. George and the Dragon, but on this occasion there is a variant from his usual design: St. George is shown on horseback. Although it appears that Travers produced designs for the window over the south entrance plaque, and also the windows of St. Patrick and St. Andrew in the nave, these were executed later by a Spanish firm.

There is thus a very considerable quantity of Travers woodwork in this church, and, unusually, much of it has remained in original condition.

Travers' other work in Europe was in relation to the Cathedral of the Holy Trinity in Gibraltar[1]. This classical building is the mother church of the Anglican Diocese which is now called Gibraltar in Europe. Following the Second World War, the then Bishop, H.J. Buxton, made an appeal for funds which he called 'Saying thank you to Malta and Gibraltar', designed to provide improvements for the pro-Cathedral in Valletta and the Cathedral in Gibraltar. Various works were planned for Gibraltar, most of which involved extensions for ancillary use which did not in the end take place, although new vestries were built. In 1946 Bishop Buxton resigned and was replaced by Bishop C.D. Horsley, once of St. John, Upper Norwood; it was he who instructed Travers, but the latter was consulted in relation to the interior alone.

In 1947 Travers designed a seal for the bishop, and the next year, shortly before his death, he designed a chancel screen with rood and with two altars below, in front of the chancel arches, and iron screens across the two side aisles. Above was to be a tympanum rather similar to that used in St. John, Greenhill, Harrow. He also produced designs for the sanctuary.

The work designed by Travers would have been extremely expensive, and none of it was done in his lifetime. In fact, of his original design all that was carried out were the side screens, which have an elaborate IHS design above their respective entrances.

The visitor however will see on either side of the high altar a side altar and each has behind it an unmistakable Travers design in bas-relief. The altars are however at the east end of the respective aisles, and not where Travers had planned them. The north chapel has Our Lady, the south St. George slaying the dragon, and each of them is behind an iron screen, as mentioned above, which was part of the original design. There are hatchments of the Annunciation in the lady chapel. The high altar has a large reredos with cross and figures in niches, which again look like Travers' work; even more like his work is a plaque in the sanctuary to Bishop Hicks.

The answer to the apparent puzzle is that all this work was actually carried out by Travers' former pupil Douglas Purnell, who took on the project after Travers' death, but applied his master's principles and designs to the work. There is no mention in the guidebook of Travers himself.

In the middle of the renovation work, on 27th April 1951, there was a huge ammunition explosion in Gibraltar, which blew out all the windows of the Cathedral and caused much other damage to the building. It appears that during the course of that year much of the work being done had to be carried out again, but the Cathedral could be used again by Christmas 1951.

The photographic evidence suggests that the side screens, which were made in Ronda, Spain, were inserted in late 1951, but certainly before the new chapels, which were dedicated on Christmas Eve 1952. The reredos was also made locally to Purnell's designs, and appears to have been erected shortly after the explosion, at about the same time as the screens.

The Cathedral is maintained in immaculate condition and in addition to the Travers/Purnell work there are a number of interesting monuments.

In addition to the three places in Europe already mentioned, Travers was involved indirectly in relation to the chaplaincy at All Saints, Milan. It appears from the surviving correspondence that the then Bishop of Gibraltar had spoken to Travers about the shape of the windows in the apse of the church; then however the chaplain proposed inserting some particularly low quality glass designed locally. The Archdeacon had previously been vicar of St. Andrew, Catford, where he had employed Martin Travers, so on 11th January 1929 he wrote and asked for his advice. The reply came back the next day, and ruffled a few feathers. Travers wrote that all three schemes proposed were 'exceedingly bad'. He continued:

> Unfortunately the artist appears to have not the remotest understanding of the medium, but is intending to make a realistic picture in glass without any regard to the leading bars, etc., which are essential to the practical studies of any serious window ... I cannot see any point in depicting a definate (sic) personality such as S. Peter by a mere costume study of an Arab.

This was a typically acerbic report; the misspelling is also characteristic.

Information on Travers' work in Africa is not easy to garner. In South Africa, it appears that he designed apse windows for St. Martin de Porres, East London in 1919, and many windows for St. John, Durban, in 1922. These included glass showing St. Martin and St. Gregory and also clerestory windows of Our Lady. For St. Saviour, East London, at an unknown date, he designed a very large window of the Crucifixion with soldiers in uniform on both sides. It is possible that St. Martin and

Design of windows for St. John, Durban, 1922

St. Saviour are the same church; there was certainly a St. Saviour in East London at that time. Travers' notebooks also indicate that he designed furnishings for churches in Johannesburg and Pretoria, without further details. It is not clear whether any of this work survives.

Travers certainly designed a baldachino suitable for an East African church in the 1920s, but it does not appear that this was ever built. He did in 1930 design a baldachino and a memorial slab for Zanzibar Cathedral as the African tribute to Bishop Weston, having already of course designed the memorial in St. Matthew, Westminster. It is not clear what the present position is in relation to this.

In Asia, he designed a high altar for the former cathedral in Colombo, Sri Lanka, in the 1920s, but investigations on this have been inconclusive. He also appears at some date unknown to have designed an altar for the former Anglo-Catholic mission church of St. Michael, Polwatte, Colombo, but it is not clear whether this work was ever executed. Certainly Travers is likely to have met the then Bishop of Colombo, Mark Carpenter-Garnier, at the 1933 Anglo-Catholic Congress.

He also designed a series of windows for Bishop Cotton School, Simla, India, in 1936, some of which were a memorial to the Bishop himself, and others showed Our Lady and St. Thomas, Apostle of India. This work was carried out, and remains in the school chapel.

In the Americas, Travers designed in 1920 a memorial cross for an unspecified site in Bermuda, but there are no further details. In 1931 he exhibited a design for stained glass for Christ Church Cathedral, Victoria, British Columbia, near where his granddaughter was in practice as a stained glass painter herself. The cathedral was built in 1926, but it does not appear that his work was ever carried out.

There is however one very interesting and well-documented piece of work by Travers in North America, and it appears to be his only work in the United States. In 1930 the University of Rochester, in the north of New York State, moved to a most impressive riverside campus from its previous location in the city. One of the buildings erected was the Rhus Rhees Library, a classically designed building looking out on to the main quadrangle. The library was provided with a recreational reading room, in which a log fire was kept burning, and all text books and note books were excluded. This was the gift of Francis R. Welles, and Charles A. Brown, both alumni of the University, and was luxuriously furnished by them. Mr. Brown was a lawyer and book collector who died in 1938. His daughter, Meredith, was born in 1899 and died, with one of her brothers, in an aeroplane crash in 1925. Her husband and widower, Ralph Fisher Skelton, was an artist and a friend of Martin Travers. He himself was killed in another aviation crash in 1929, when he was piloting his own plane, but he left provision in his will for a window to be erected in memory of his wife, and this is what Travers designed.

We are told that the window was received from London 'just in time to be installed on the day before the opening of the dedication ceremonies', which, for Travers, was remarkably punctual.

The window is in fact a variation on the 'Tyneham' theme without the religious content. The same tree as is found in so many windows by Travers, with the same twists in its trunk, is said here to be a sapling ash tree and to symbolize youth. Instead of a Virgin and Child beneath it, there is a fountain of knowledge, around which some cherubic young children play, and the fountain runs into the river of life. The theme is life in and beyond the University, and in the background can be seen the city and a mountain range, the latter to show achievements. The window bears the superscription 'To the memory of Meredith Brown Skelton, 1899–1925'.

The window is still in the reading room in good condition and is valued by the University (See Plate 31).

In the Antipodes, Travers designed in about the 1920s a hanging rood for St. George's Cathedral, Perth, Western Australia, but this was never executed.

In New Zealand however, Travers carried out two exceptionally well-documented commissions, both of interest and one of real significance.

Travers had been an exact contemporary at Tonbridge with Guy Brown, who was later ordained and changed his surname to Bryan-Brown. Bryan-Brown came from a clerical family, and proceeded from school to Downing College and then Ridley Hall in Cambridge. He was ordained deacon in 1909 and priest in 1911, and initially taught at Glenalmond, before in 1913 taking up a position as Chaplain to Christ's College, Christchurch, New Zealand. He appears to have been a muscular Christian, and had been awarded a hockey blue at Cambridge. He was as well known in the school for his sporting prowess as for his religious activity. However in August 1916 he left the school to become Chaplain to the 3rd Battalion, Canterbury Regiment of the New Zealand Armed Forces, and was killed in action on the Western Front on 4th October 1917[2].

Bryan-Brown had been a popular figure in Canterbury and money was raised for a window in his memory in the College chapel.

Travers produced a design dated 25th June 1925, the faculty was granted later that year, and it was installed on 7th August 1927. It remains in place.

The window shows the deceased as Sir Guy de Brienne dressed in the style of a crusader, with lance and sword. The College magazine observed that the fact that Bryan-Brown played for the Crusaders at Cambridge (the University cricket second team) gave an additional point to the figure. It bears a similarity to the four windows in St. Michael and All Angels, Cheriton, Hampshire, dated about 1920, depicting the four deceased nephews of the donor, all in armour. At the top of the Christchurch window are the arms of Tonbridge School and the University of Cambridge. Around the figure are typical Travers decorations of beads and tassels.

This is an interesting window, and unusual for Travers, although the symbolism has not lasted as well as many of his and it has a dated feel to it.

Travers' other window in New Zealand has a most convoluted history behind it[3].

The Great Hall of what was Canterbury College (University) and is now the Christchurch Arts Centre has a large five light window on the north wall. Following the First World War, as early as 1919 the idea of a war memorial to commemorate the dead of the College was mooted. By 1920 it had been decided that this should take the form of a window. In 1923 the governors of the College began looking for an artist, and despite considerable local pressure, they passed over New Zealand designers in favour of British. J.P. Gabbatt, former professor of mathematics at the College, had returned to England in 1922, and he was asked to select an artist. In 1924 he recommended Travers and in July of that year he came up with a design. Gabbatt had suggested as a theme 'To gain life, life must be given, with special reference to the life of the University', but Travers modified this to 'sacrifice in the pursuit of knowledge.' He drew a female figure of Knowledge at the top of a mountain, with six attendants, representing Courage, Truth, Peace, Justice, and Humanity. On the pathway leading to the top of the mountain were famous people who had died or been persecuted in the quest for knowledge, including Cook, Darwin and Scott but also Galileo, Leonardo da Vinci, Dante, and Columbus. In the centre were Socrates and Plato, and at the foot were human figures fighting off two red dragons, which represented Ignorance and Brutality. This design was shown in *The Studio* magazine in 1925[4].

The first design was not universally favoured in Christchurch, not least because it contained so little reference to the war it was supposed to commemorate. The College wrote to Travers on 25th May 1925 asking him to submit a second design 'embodying to some extent the spirit of devotion and

Original design for Christchurch, New Zealand, prior to revision to include soldiers in uniform

sacrifice that characterised the efforts of those connected with Canterbury College in the World War.'

In mid 1926 Travers sent a further design, which featured a variety of historical figures relevant to the motif of sacrifice on a triumphal arch, with St. George on horseback fighting a dragon above. He told the College that they could have St. Michael instead of St. George if they wished, or Our

Lord on the White Horse of Revelation; Travers' touchiness when his work was questioned is apparent yet again.

By this time the College had set up committees and sub-committees to deal with the window; there was a certain amount of dithering, but they finally decided that the first design, if modified, was preferable to the second. Professor James Shelley, professor of education at the College and a leading art critic in Christchurch, had been brought on to the committee, and he sent a handwritten list of guidelines and a sketch to Travers. Some members of the committee were anxious that the figures on the window were all from British imperial history, and in particular that figures from German and Austrian history should be avoided, but Shelley, although he was a member of the Imperial British Society, put forward the name of Beethoven amongst others.

These recommendations were received by Travers in April 1927. Nothing happened for a year, and so the College asked Professor Wall, professor of English, to make enquiries while he was in England in May 1928. Travers apparently said that it would be ready within a month or two, but in fact eighteen months later, in late 1929, the College had still heard nothing and sent an urgent telegram. Travers promised the revised design would be ready in January 1930, but in fact it arrived in July of that year.

By November 1930 it had been approved and only two minor recommendations were made, both of which are interesting in the light of further developments later. It was suggested that the only Maori in the design, who is shown in a position of deference, should be standing, and further that one of the soldiers should be depicted as a Maori. Neither suggestion was adopted by Travers, who indicated in January 1931 that the window should be ready in 18 months. There does not appear to be any real reason why in the event the commission was so long delayed, although of course during the next few years Travers' first wife was ill, and then she died in 1934. However, in late 1935, by which time Travers had carried out a large number of commissions at relatively short notice for other places, he said that he hoped to dispatch the window by the end of that year. Again, that proved wildly optimistic. On two occasions, members of the College teaching staff on leave in England had been sent to see Travers, and on 26th April 1937 the College resolved to contact the New Zealand High Commission in London to threaten legal action. At this point, six years after his design had been approved, Travers asserted that he had been having difficulty in finding authentic portraits of some of the subjects. However, it appears that firing of the glass eventually began in August

1937, and in April 1938, 14 years after Travers was first instructed, he told the College that the window was on its way. It arrived in time to be dedicated on 27th September 1938, at which time of course the next World War was very much on the horizon. Travers indeed exhibited the design at the Royal Academy in 1940, when of course the next war was well under way. In May 1945 he wrote asking for the final instalment of his fees now that the war was over. The Registrar waited 4 months before beginning his response 'I regret the delay ...'

Fiona Ciaran, the leading New Zealand authority on stained glass, thinks that the completed window includes the greatest number of portraits of any English window of the twentieth century.

As finally completed, the window has in the centre oculus the Spire of Aspiration, springing from the Tree of Life. On either side are the arms of Canterbury College and of New Zealand. The main part of the window shows a mountain with, at its summit, Humanity sheltering young children, who represent future generations. Below are Action, drawing his sword, Justice, seated and holding scales and sword, Truth with mirror, and Thought, an elderly philosopher. Extensive silver staining was employed in relation to this part of the window, resulting in pale yellow and gold as the predominant colours. Above the mountain is the Southern Cross. On the mountain stand various distinguished figures from history, arranged in groups, and in the bottom of the picture New Zealand soldiers defend the mountain against a red hydra, which represents brutality and ignorance. In the far right of the window a gold-digger examines some nuggets, a nurse tends a wounded soldier, and Bishop Selwyn gives a Bible to a Maori warrior, who bends his knee. The figures from history are as follows:

(i) Those involved in service by war: Robert Clive, James Wolfe, King Alfred the Great, King Richard the Lionheart, Nelson, Wellington, Francis Drake, and Henry Lawrence, seventeenth century Puritan;

(ii) Those involved in service by peace: Pitt, King Henry VI, Elizabeth Fry, Edward Gibbon Wakefield, Scott of the Antarctic, and Captain Cook;

(iii) Those involved in service by thought: William of Wykeham, Shakespeare, Chaucer, Wren, Purcell, Caxton, Reynolds, Florence Nightingale, Roger Bacon, thirteenth century scientist, Harvey, Darwin, Newton, Faraday, Watt, and Selwyn.

The total effect is overwhelming rather than aesthetically pleasing. The window also suffers from the defect which was immediately apparent in 1924, namely that it does not immediately strike the observer as being a war memorial.

It is not clear whether or not Travers simply lost interest in the window, but it does not reflect well on him that he failed to deal with matters expeditiously, or to communicate properly with his clients.

The window has recently been the subject of some controversy. While to some it may seem as a charming period piece, to others the attitude of deference struck by the only Maori in the picture is regarded as demeaning, and the window was vandalized because of that. It has been repaired however, and remains in place; indeed postcards are available with a key to the persons described on the reverse. There is great interest in it locally.

Chapter 9

Travers as Church Builder

It would be idle to pretend that Travers' reputation rests on his work as a church builder, as opposed to decorator and furnisher. However, he was involved in a number of projects which have interest, even if some consider that the end results were sometimes less than satisfactory.

Travers of course was not a member of the RIBA. In certain cases that meant that he had to collaborate with a registered architect in order that his designs be accepted. In the building of churches between the wars, he

Good Shepherd Carshalton Beeches: drawing of exterior by Travers

worked with T.F.W. Grant, who translated Travers' sketches into working drawings, and after the war, in the restoration of the war-damaged church of Holy Trinity, Lamorbey, he worked with E.B. Musman.

It is clear that there have been severe problems with damp and water penetration at least at Emmanuel Church, Leyton, and the Good Shepherd, Carshalton Beeches, but it seems rather hard to blame Travers for this when he was a designer, not an architect.

The real problem was that there was great pressure at this time to produce cheap churches for the suburbs. The Incorporated Church Building Society published a volume entitled *New Churches Illustrated* in 1937, which shows 52 churches erected during the years 1926 to 1936, including three in which Travers was concerned. In the preface the editor commented 'It is much to be regretted that architects should sometimes be asked or expected to design churches for a sum far below an essential minimum'[1].

In 1926 Travers and Grant prepared a preliminary sketch for the church of St. Andrew, Felixstowe, which they exhibited at the 1929 Royal Academy, but the design was not adopted.

THE FIRST ACTUAL CHURCH BUILDING with which Travers was concerned was St. James, Elfrida Road, Watford. This was a relatively new church, the nave and aisles of which were built by A.M. Durrant during the period 1910-16. It was constructed in brick and had Romanesque windows and arches. Durrant served in the First World War with the Royal Engineers, was awarded the Military Cross, and was killed in action on 5th December 1916.

As early as 1925 the parish were considering a chancel extension, and needed an architect who would be in sympathy with the church. Travers was recommended to them, and he and Grant were chosen to carry out the extension, which they did with considerable skill; the faculty for that was dated 1927, and the drawings are not in Travers' usual style, presumably being produced primarily by Grant. They built a brick chancel which blended in perfectly; the clerestory of the existing nave had a single window to each bay, and the aisles had two, but Travers and Grant gave the new chancel a Renaissance flavour by changing the rhythm so that in the clerestory there were three windows per bay, creating a simplified version of a Venetian window, with a central round headed light flanked on either side by flat-topped ones. Outside on the roof, where the chancel and nave meet, they placed a small lead covered cupola, which stands on coupled wooden columns; this distinguishes the building as a church to the casual passer-by, although it is hardly a landmark.

Interior of St. James Watford before replacement of the reredos: work designed 1927

The interior of the church was whitewashed leaving the stone facings. Travers provided many fittings, including an altar, which was furnished with a plain cross and two baroque candlesticks as well as a painted and gilded wooden frontal. He included oak communion rails and choirstalls. The parclose screens, which incorporated friezes of winged cherubs' heads, were similar to those in the lady chapel at St. Saviour, St. Albans. Four star shaped embossed plaster light fittings, which directed the light towards the altar, hung in the sanctuary: although these are thought of as being characteristic of Travers, they were used by Maufe at St. Saviour, Acton, in 1925 and Travers worked at that church on windows in 1927, so he may in fact have taken the idea over from that distinguished architect.

In 1930 Travers returned and designed and installed at the east end of the south aisle a two light memorial window to Amy Hastings, showing the Three Kings bringing their gifts to the Mother and Child.

In 1931 he designed a memorial plaque to his predecessor as architect, Arthur Michael Durrant. This was surrounded by a garland and hung on the south wall.

The reredos which Travers originally provided for the church appears from the photographic evidence to have been of wood, but lacking any decoration. Its outline had redolencies of Baroque styling. In 1939 he was called back to do further work, and under the east window he provided in substitution for the earlier work a tall but simple painted and gilded reredos with a border of stylized tassels and volutes. The centre depicted the seven fold gifts of the Holy Spirit and was somewhat similar to that at St. Matthew, New Kent Road. He also designed new light fittings with silk cylinders around the bulb and a striking new pulpit with a tester above and four columns supporting the tester. The faculty for all this work was dated 1939, and the reredos was certainly installed, but it is not clear whether the other work was done. Certainly in 1950 a new pulpit designed by another was installed as a war memorial.

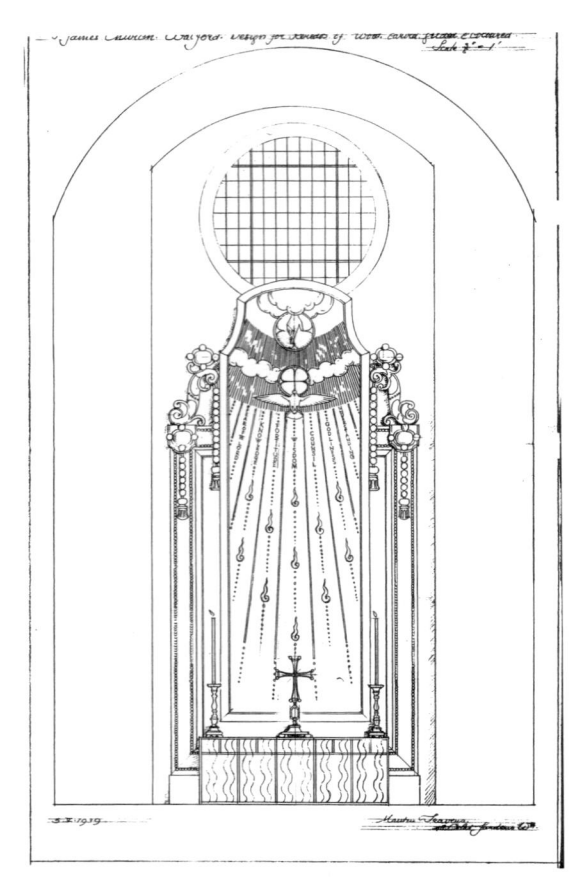

Design for replacement reredos, St. James, Watford

The church was an interesting example of Travers adapting his ordinary style to fit the requirements of his clients: there was no great Catholic tradition in the parish, and the result was a pleasant, rather understated, interior.

The church is an unobtrusive building in a side street. It had a short life for the purpose for which it was intended, as in about 1973 it was declared redundant and the parish was merged with that of St. Mary, Watford. The building was deconsecrated and sold to the Hertfordshire County Council for use as part of the adjoining Field Junior School. Fortunately a proposal that the entire site including the church and the school be cleared and a new school be built was rejected by the Governing Body. The contents of the church were scattered far and wide, but some have been traced.

The altar itself was taken to St. Mary, the ancient parish church of Watford out of the area of which the new parish had been created originally. The pews (not by Travers) were used in the new Roman Catholic Church of Our Lady Immaculate and St. Andrew, Hitchin, and it was said at the time that the contractors working on that building took the choirstalls and other Travers furnishings; these cannot now be located. The altar rails were modified for use in Holy Trinity, Bishop's Stortford, and the reredos was sold to Mr. Anelay of York to join his Travers work from Battersea (see Chapter 7); it has recently been given to St. George, Harrow for further use.

Unfortunately, the centre section of the reredos, on which the characteristic decoration could be seen, was made of a linoleum type material, which has cracked over the years and made it unusable. Some parts of the decoration from the outside of the reredos have however been used on the east wall at St. George, behind the Crawford reredos, and some are on the west wall. The tablet which protruded at the bottom of the reredos to hold the altar cross at Watford has been removed and is now used to elevate the crucifix at Harrow.

The plaque in memory of Durrant was left in the church and remains, but the stained glass windows have been removed and have not been traced.

IN 1927 TRAVERS AND GRANT designed a nave and new tower for the church of St. Mary, Liss, Hampshire. That design was again not accepted, and the church was finished by Maufe in about 1930, but Travers did subsequently provide both an altar and windows for the church.

IN 1928 TRAVERS AND GRANT designed the church of the Good Shepherd, Queen Mary Avenue, Carshalton Beeches, which is featured in *New Churches Illustrated,* and about which there is much information in the parish history[2]. This church was built in 1929-30 and Lord Halifax laid the foundation stone on 26th June 1929. It was intended as a daughter church to All Saints, which is in the old village of Carshalton, and replaced a previous mission church of the same name; Father Hope Patten had been curate in charge of the mission 1920 to 1921, under the well-known

Exterior of Church of Good Shepherd, Carshalton Beeches, as originally built, 1930

Papalist Father W. Robert Corbould, whose incumbency stretched from 1919 to 1958. Curiously, Travers was never employed to carry out fittings at the parish church, although Comper carried out a major refurnishing scheme there.

Father Corbould wanted the new church dedicated to St. Francis of Assisi (some say to St. Francis de Sales), but on this issue he gave way to local feeling and the old name was reused.

The church of the Good Shepherd is certainly distinctive. It was built in a loose expression of the Spanish Mission style; it is interesting, not only that Travers had travelled extensively in Spain, but also that shortly before this project he had provided extensive furnishings for the British Embassy Chapel in Madrid, which was built by a local architect in the style of a mission. The style is rare in this country, although in the early 1920s Paul Waterhouse built the Convent of the Incarnation for the Sisters of the Love of God at Fairacres, Iffley Road, Oxford, in a similar vein.

John Betjeman refers to the Good Shepherd as 'Essoldo moderne in a Hispano-Italian baroque style with clever stained glass. Displeasingly decayed but the essential quality of the design should not be ignored.' (The decay has been remedied since that was written).

The church is of brick, limewashed inside but now with brick visible

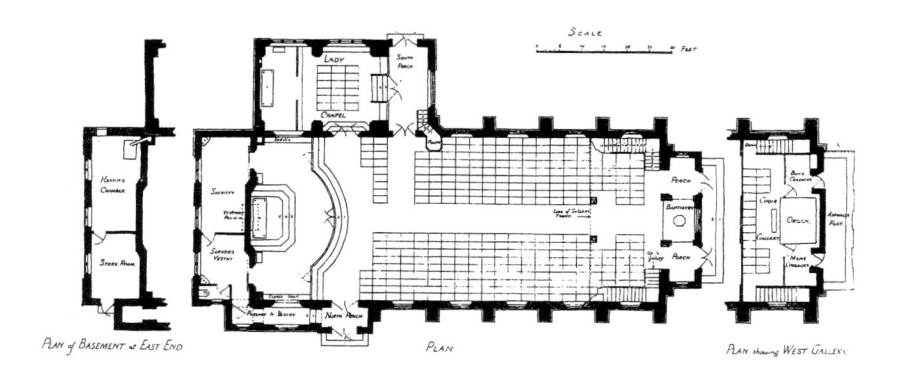

Plan of Good Shepherd Carshalton

outside after the removal of the rendering, with rectangular metal 'Crittall' type windows. The roof is supported on steel principals and is covered with copper, with a large Spanish style bellcote on the west gable. There was no damp proof course, and the buttresses, which are a distinctive feature of the external design, are hollow and useless, so the church has suffered from damp from the time it was built. It is interesting that the total cost of the structure was only £6060, and of the fittings £700. Unusually, the bill for the church was cheaper than the estimate.

In due course the damp problems required a major restoration, which was carried out in 1985.

The ceiling is moulded pre-cast plaster and was originally stencilled in a baroque design, which has now unfortunately been painted over following a reordering in 1984. The floors are of wood block. Under the high circular east window hangs an enormous Italian-style rood above a simple wooden reredos resembling a type of pleated leatherwork. The Jesuit IHS monogram is the central design and is surrounded by a sunburst. The reredos and altar originally stood within riddel posts supporting Travers' usual boy cherub candlesticks. The use of riddel posts in this Spanish setting was odd, but probably reflects the feelings of the Southwark Diocesan authorities. On the altar were six baroque candlesticks and a crucifix.

In 1952 part of the roof blew off in high winds. In 1967 the church suffered a fire in the vestries following vandalism, after which the riddels and cherubs were removed and the altar pulled forward in order to allow celebration from the westward position. Other improvements were carried out to the vestries themselves, and a circular disc showing the hand of God with an alpha and omega was taken from the top of the rood and set above

High altar of Church of the Good Shepherd, Carshalton Beeches, as originally constructed

the round window. Unfortunately the previous, typical, red and gold horizontal stripes on the vestry doors, which resembled curtains, were not replaced.

In the east wall, on the north side of the altar, is a simple baroque aumbry designed by Travers. This had to be the method of reservation in the Diocese of Southwark at a time when the Advisory Committee would not have sanctioned a tabernacle on the high altar. The Committee included Travers' advocate Dr. Eeles, but it is unlikely that he would have approved of a tabernacle. It was only two years after the rejection of the 1928 Prayer Book.

A lady chapel was designed for the south side of the church, and is shown on the plans, but was not built owing to lack of funds. Travers also designed a priest's house, which again was never built. Very recently (2000–1) the parish has completed an extension to the church with a chapel which, although not as designed by Travers, is not out of harmony with the existing building.

The church was lit with Travers' usual embossed plaster light fittings in the form of stars similar to those at St. James, Watford and St. Matthew, New Kent Road; these have now been removed, as they became dangerous.

Travers gave the window of St. Nicholas to the parish and opposite, in the south wall, is another window by him showing Our Lady crowned Queen of Heaven standing with a crescent moon under her feet. In the south west porch is the amusing little window for Father Corbould showing a rook (Cor-) and the cricket bails flying (bowled). The other porch window has the arms of the Bishop of Southwark; following some internal reconstruction this window is now in a lavatory.

The organ is in the west gallery, the front of which, with the altar rails, is of oak, and was originally given a silver grey effect, which was stripped off after the 1967 fire.

The church is no longer attached to the parish of All Saints. Father Corbould refused to allow this to take place during his incumbency; he was a priest of the old school who obviously wanted to keep control of the tradition of the Good Shepherd. After his death, there was a minor cause celebre over the other daughter church, St. Andrew, where the veteran curate, Father R.A.E. Harris, was forced to vacate, after telling Bishop Stockwood that he was prepared to be a martyr for the Catholic Church as he saw it[3]. Father Harris was regarded with some veneration thereafter by some Anglo-Catholics, and his supporters were not pleased when some years afterwards Bishop Stockwood became a Guardian of the Walsingham Shrine.

Good Shepherd Carshalton: window to Father Corbould

At the Good Shepherd there has been a change in churchmanship, and although a fine restoration of the reredos and the hanging crucifix has taken place, the repositioning of the high altar has resulted in a less appealing east end, making the altar seem isolated and no longer part of the sanctuary ensemble.

It remains however a most unusual church and one well worth seeing. The local historian of Carshalton, A.E. Jones, is somewhat dismissive of Father Corbould, saying[4]: 'He lived in an incense-filled world of his own, remote from and uninterested in the everyday life of his parish', but that seems somewhat unfair when considered against his early ministry and the organization required for the building of the new church.

TRAVERS AND GRANT WERE NEXT concerned with the church of the Holy Redeemer, Streatham Vale, which was designed in 1930–1 and built in 1931–2. It was consecrated on 5th March 1932. As with Carshalton Beeches, this was one of the Bishop of Southwark's 'Twenty Five New Churches' for expanding suburbs. The design, showing the interior looking east, was exhibited at the Royal Academy in 1933. The church was a memorial to the Evangelical Clapham Sect, and was designed for worship of that type; since Travers was perfectly prepared to carry out work as required by his patrons, the surprise is not that he was prepared to build this church, but that the clients wanted him, in the light of his reputation as an associate of Anglo-Catholics.

The church looks like a typical building of its age, but the specification was clearly more lavish than the Carshalton church, as it cost £11775, almost twice as much.

Holy Redeemer was built of stock bricks with pre-cast stone tracery in a modified fifteenth century style. There was no dividing arch between the chancel and the nave; the chancel is a continuation of the nave. The roof was again steel covered with copper, and is topped with a classical cupola rather reminiscent of that at Watford, but with solid sides.

There were many typical Travers touches to the church. The hanging lights were more conventional than the stars employed at Watford and

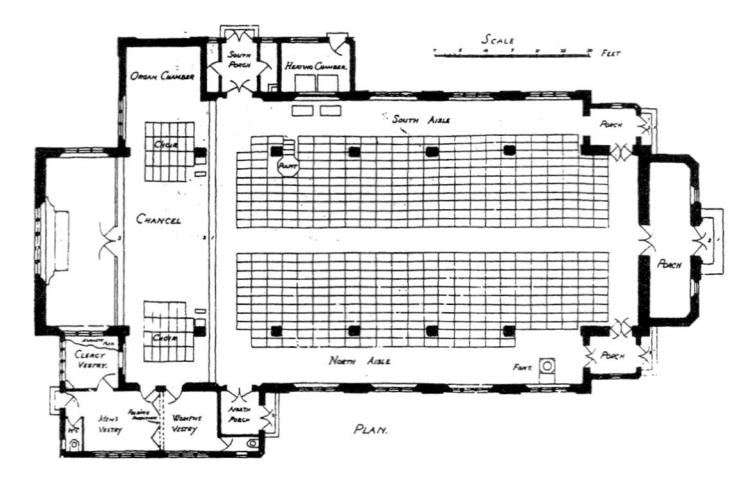

Plan of Holy Redeemer Streatham

North-east exterior view of Church of Holy Redeemer, Streatham Vale, designed 1930–1

Carshalton, but have some baroque feel and were cut from sheet copper. The sanctuary was a modification of Travers' usual style, showing some baroque influence, but with the Ten Commandments on plaques on either side of the clear east window. The reredos was ogee shaped, of pleated wood painted red and gold, with a plain cross on it. There were no candlesticks on the altar. The internal wooden furniture, such as the pews, was all designed by Travers,

Interior of Church of Holy Redeemer, Streatham Vale

save for the lectern which came from elsewhere. The church had no painted glass at all; some windows have oblong panes of different coloured glass, but they hardly add to the décor. Travers anticipated that the east window would in due course be filled with stained glass, but this has never occurred.

The vicarage has volutes on either side of the canopy over the door in a Baroque idiom, but was not built by Travers and Grant, although they produced a design: it was built later by D.E. Nye, a partner of Grant.

The church is largely as built, although the original light fittings and the reredos are no longer there: the text boards remain, as do many of the furnishings.

AT ABOUT THE SAME TIME that the designs for Holy Redeemer, Streatham Vale, were being prepared, Travers was involved on his own account with a most unusual project.

In the first half of the Twentieth Century, many Public Schools had Missions in poorer areas, where the School financially supported activities for the local residents. Cheltenham College had such a mission, in Nunhead in south east London. In 1928 the School made an appeal for new buildings on the site: prior to that time, they owned two semi-detached houses at 29 and 31 Nunhead Grove, behind which was quite a large plot of land, on which stood two club rooms erected on a temporary basis in 1913–4. On the other side of the road they had a lease of premises comprising a further club room, gymnasium, and parish hall, which had been a mission church, all of which were by then somewhat decrepit. The School wanted to build new premises on the freehold plot to bring all the work on to one site. It was originally intended to erect buildings with a projected life of only 30 to 40 years, to save money, and plans were drawn up to that effect by the School architect. However, at some point Travers was consulted: he drew up plans which involved the erection of a permanent building for no larger sum than was contemplated for the temporary buildings suggested by the School architect. In due course the work was done in accordance with his plans, and was opened by the Headmaster and the Bishop of Southwark on 31st March 1932.

Travers designed his new work so that the Mission could continue to use the 1913–4 club room, and so that the Missioner could continue to live in one of the two semi-detached houses on Nunhead Grove. His building consisted of a substantial gym with stage at one end, and a games room with canteen and other ancillary rooms attached. The work was of stock brick and was clearly built to a tight budget: however it had certain

Interior of Cheltenham College Mission, Nunhead, as designed in 1932

interesting features, including an outside covered way joining the various rooms. The gym had Crittall type metal windows, typical of its age.

Between the gym and the old rooms was a small chapel with scout cub room above. During the course of the opening a calvary designed by Travers was taken into the chapel and erected over the altar; the only drawings which appear to have survived relate to the chapel, and the other plans have disappeared. Pictures of the chapel have however survived in the Cheltenham College archives, and they show a typical small rood set over a large wooden tabernacle on a small lace-draped altar in an alcove. There were four Baroque candlesticks on the altar, and a statue to one side.

In fact, the Cheltenham Mission had a short life: during the war there was damage to the buildings, and the College decided to concentrate on work in the town of Cheltenham itself. In due course, in about 1951 the buildings were handed over to Westminster School, and are now Westminster House Club. The two semi-detached houses have disappeared, and the chapel/scout hut part of the complex has been built over. However, the gymnasium and games room remain, although the covered way in front of the games room has been bricked in. The rear of the premises on Banstead Street, which originally looked rather like a suburban cinema, now looks somewhat decrepit because the Crittall type windows have been bricked up, and there is a substantial fence around the building. It is however perhaps Travers' least well known building and not without interest.

RETURNING TO MORE CONVENTIONAL PROJECTS, the third new church built by Travers and Grant was Emmanuel Church, Lea Bridge Road, Leyton, which was designed in 1933 and built in 1935. A model of this church was exhibited at the Royal Academy in 1934. This church was again constructed very cheaply, the total cost being only £5102, with £474 for fittings. Part of the cost was apparently defrayed by local Masonic Lodges, which would not have been very welcome news to some of Travers' patrons; one of Father Fynes-Clinton's bêtes noires was Freemasonry. The cheap construction has yet again resulted in constant problems with damp penetration.

The church is also of brick construction with pre-cast tracery, although considerably less elaborate tracery than was used in Streatham Vale. The window lights here have rounded tops, and the tracery, being of pale stone, stands out against the brick. Around the door frames there is stylized decoration in the stone, with a faint baroque flavour. The roof was not of steel here, but of wood with copper over; however, the copper has since been

Model of Emmanuel, Leyton

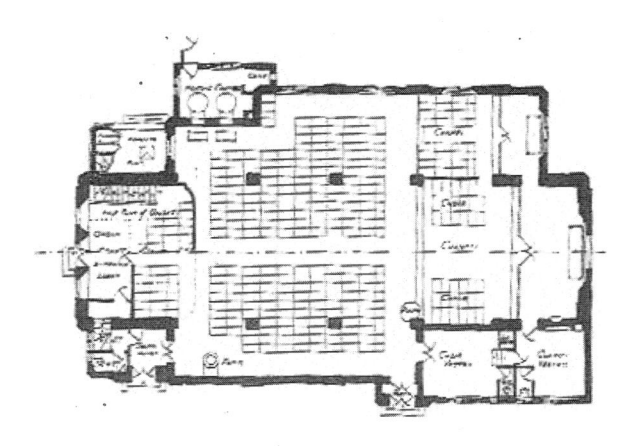

Plan of Emmanuel Leyton

removed. A cupola was planned, but was never added and the aisle roofs were of pre-cast concrete slabs with an asphalt outer covering. Inside the ceiling was pre-cast and identical to that at the Holy Redeemer, as were the light fittings. The church has a high circular window above the altar and an organ in the west gallery, just as at Carshalton.

At Emmanuel Travers installed a large gilded reredos with a plain centre panel; its shape was similar to that used at St. Matthew, New Kent Road, in 1927, but taller. On the side panels to the reredos were characteristic tassel decorations. On the altar stood a plain cross, but no candlesticks, as these were not required.

Unfortunately, the reredos has since been repainted, apparently on the suggestion of the wife of a previous vicar, in a lurid orange and green, with a large wooden cross in front of it. This is particularly unfortunate in that the remainder of the church is relatively untouched. There is a considerable quantity of good woodwork in the pews, choir stalls, and pulpit, and there are two windows by Travers. One of them shows St. George and the Dragon, in the usual Travers

Pulpit, Emmanuel Leyton

depiction, and the other some splendid coats of arms with a dedication to the chairman of the building committee for the church. The church was specifically designed with no windows on the main road side, in order to cut down on noise.

The adjoining vicarage, in Hitcham Road, is also by Travers and again is of cheaply built construction with a flat roof. It is unusual in that his design of domestic premises was so limited. The windows have been replaced.

ALSO IN 1934 TRAVERS CONSTRUCTED for his patron Father Shaw Page of West Wickham a church hall, St. Mary, The Avenue, in rather undistinguished style. This was used for worship until the construction in 1984 of the present church of St, Mary of Nazareth, to which it is now joined. It is again now used as a hall and a false ceiling has been added and a wooden floor laid. However, two plaques from the reredos in the hall are on the wall in the lady chapel above the new church, and there are Travers candlesticks in both that chapel and the main church. The plaques are identical to those produced some years before for St. Matthew, New Kent Road, and St. Luke, Battersea.

It is possible that Travers built another such hall for St. Paul in nearby Caterham, but this is not clear, and the building was in any event demolished in about 1983. There is also a reference to plans for a new parish hall for St. Philip, Reedworth Street, Kennington: certainly the church had a hall, but both have now been demolished. He also designed in 1928 a new two-storey parish hall for St. Matthew, New Kent Road, which complemented his work in the church itself; the hall was built in 1930 by direct labour under Travers' supervision, but has since been demolished.

Travers produced a design for St. Alban, Church Drive, North Harrow, in about 1936 but his design was unsuccessful in the competition and the church, a notable example for its time, was constructed in 1936-7 by A.W. Kenyon. He also designed a mission church for North Mymms, Hertfordshire, in about 1938, but again that was never built.

TRAVERS WAS HOWEVER INVOLVED WITH actual construction at St. John the Baptist, Sheepcote Road, Greenhill, Harrow. Here he added a new and effective modern chancel to an existing rather plain Gothic Revival church. This work was carried out in 1938, and it was intended that he build a tower also, but that was not done before the war broke out, and has never been completed. Circumstances in fact made it impossible to provide a chancel of sufficient length for the height originally intended, so a shallow

Interior of St. John, Greenhill, Harrow, before removal of the screen: work carried out 1938–47

chancel was installed with a roof lower than the chancel arch, and the upper part of the arch was filled in to form a tympanum of Christ in Glory, flanked by Our Lady and St. John, all on a background of stars. A light screen in a simple style and incorporating the pierced knot pattern was placed across the easternmost bay of the nave, thus giving sufficient length to the chancel for the choir stalls. The altar was English in style within riddels and complete with a plain silver cross and candlesticks. The mensa was covered with a Laudian frontal, a type much favoured by Travers.

This was a large commission and is a fine example of Travers' ability to add dignity and grandeur to a rather uninspiring church, the proportions of which made the provision of an inspiring chancel and sanctuary within the site virtually unattainable.

Unfortunately, the church has not been left as Travers left it; in about 1972 the fine chancel screen was removed from the church. The note in the RIBA catalogue to the effect that many of the furnishings have been removed is however inaccurate, as although the altar has been brought into line with modern liturgical practice by removal of the riddels, there is still a great deal of Travers' work in the interior. The north chapel of St. Michael has a fine screen on its west and south sides, which show the quality of the removed chancel screen, and also has a memorial plaque to John William Odell. In addition, there is a characteristic St. Michael and the Dragon window in the chapel. Between the chapel and the high altar is a war memorial tablet, and on the south side an organ screen. The altar rails remain, but the large east window is almost entirely of clear glass, and it is unfortunate that a Travers design was never installed. This is a well kept church in a prominent position in the town centre.

THE LAST CHURCH BUILT BY TRAVERS was St. Cuthman, Whitehawk, Brighton, which was designed between 1936 and 1938 and dedicated in the latter year. The designs in this case bear his name alone.

The building was known in the Diocese of Chichester as 'the Children's Church' owing to the special fund-raising used to pay for its construction. In 1932 the Bishop of Chichester, the Right Revd George K.A. Bell, had started an organisation known as the Sussex Churchbuilders, whose raison d'être had been to provide new churches for poor areas and especially on the housing estates being developed at that time.

For the new development at Whitehawk it had been decided to raise funds for a church from the schoolchildren throughout Sussex. St. Cuthman, the local boy saint from Steyning, was an obvious choice for the patron of the new building, and in addition to the schoolchildren any local companies with the name Cuthman were approached for sponsorship.

By February 1938 there remained a shortfall of £800 and the consecration was due at the end of May that year. A final appeal went out and fortunately the debt was cleared just in time.

The new church seated 350, and by using direct labour cost only £5000 to complete. This included the furnishings and even the organ. However the pews had been procured from the redundant church of St. James, Kemp Town, famous for the ritualistic disturbances during the incumbency of Revd John Purchas; the organ came from the closed church of SS. Mary

Church of St. Cuthman, Whitehawk, as originally designed, 1938

and Mary Magdalene, Bread Street, one of the smaller Wagner mission churches in Brighton. Travers' new sanctuary furnishings were dedicated as a memorial to the late Bishop Southwell, one of the members of the Sussex Churchbuilders.

The Chichester diocesan gazette quoted 'and the future upkeep has not been forgotten, for the church is equipped with a copper roof, which should need no repair for very many years, and with a heating system which is the last word in economy.'

The Bishop of Lewes consecrated the church on Saturday 28th May 1938 amidst much rejoicing and the satisfaction that all of this had been achieved through the prayers and efforts of thousands of children throughout Sussex, over a period of several years. On 2nd July 1938 Bishop Bell preached at a service of thanksgiving attended by representative children from nearly every parish and school in the diocese and the sponsoring companies were also invited to attend.

Unfortunately, St. Cuthman in its original form had a very short life. It was bombed in August 1943 and thereafter, in 1952, completely rebuilt, although a staircase and parts of the original crypt were included in the reconstruction. As with Carshalton, but unlike Streatham Vale and Leyton, it was built to further a Catholic tradition.

Design for memorial chapel, St. Cuthman, Whitehawk

The original church as designed by Travers was an unusual example of a reinforced concrete building, stucco rendered, and complete with a bell tower. Inside was one of his modified baroque/Art Deco sanctuaries. The figures used here have a definite childlike quality, especially St. Cuthman, and the connection with the local schoolchildren must have influenced the designer's thinking.

Three schemes were in fact drawn for this sanctuary. The first was a simple English altar under a tester. It had a rectangular reredos resembling Spanish leatherwork containing rood figures and had a simple narrow border. The corners were decorated to resemble engravings used in leatherwork. Two candlesticks stood on the mensa and candle sconces hung on the east wall on either side of the riddels. Above was an east window of the Resurrection. The second, which was the cheaper scheme and was actually chosen, had no use of stained glass. It included the same reredos, but this time featuring the Jesuit IHS monogram within a sunburst instead of a rood. A more traditional rood complete with Our Lady and St. John was in the blocked window recess above the altar. On either side of the altar were painted and gilded plaques of St. George and St. Nicholas on the left and St. Wilfred and St. Cuthman on the right. Above hung a tester depicting the Holy Spirit. The benches, fittings and pulpit were all included in the design, but no riddel posts were used by the altar.

The third set of drawings was of an altar within riddels under a hanging tester. On the reredos were a Christus Rex, Our Lady, and St. John. Once again there were plaques on each side of the altar, but on this occasion they were of St. George, St. Anne, St. Wilfred, and St. Richard.

Outside on the tower Travers had intended to place a large figure of St. Cuthman. The two designs for this were striking in their simplicity and boldness of line; one showed the saint holding a bell and crook and the other raising a hand in benediction. This idea never materialised, because of the cost.

After the bombing, some fittings were saved. The cross and rood figures, which were originally in the window recess, survived and were rehung on the chancel arch. The crucifix is identical to that at Warnford, Hampshire, from the same period. The plaques from either side of the high altar were also recovered and rehung, and show fine detail, but have more recently been badly affected by woodworm and taken down. A banner of St. Cuthman was also saved and has since been remounted.

This church is much less well known than Carshalton, Streatham Vale, and Leyton, for obvious reasons, and is situated in the toughest estate in Brighton.

IN 1943 TRAVERS DESIGNED A NEW CHURCH to replace the Victorian St. Luke, Hawkinge, Kent, but his plans for that were not adopted: see Chapter 7. There is also a reference to preliminary plans, which have not survived, for St. Joseph, Northolt, a daughter church to St. Mary, where he had carried out a great deal of work in the 1940s (see Chapter 7). It appears that a church of St. Joseph was established in temporary premises in 1942, moved in about 1944, and only had its own proper building in 1969: it is not clear if Travers was involved at all in the early days.

After the war, there was clearly a great deal of work to be done in rebuilding churches damaged by bombing. One such was Holy Trinity, Lamorbey, Sidcup, in what was then Kent. This fine Gothic Revival church, which looks mediaeval at a quick glance, was hit by a flying bomb on 16th October 1944 and almost completely destroyed. On this occasion Travers cooperated with E.B. Musman, FRIBA, in preparing the plans for the rebuilding of the church, which are dated 1945 and 1946. The funds were raised locally, and the church was restored fully to the existing design, with decorated tracery and great attention to detail. Unfortunately Travers died before the rededication, which took place in 1949, and only Musman was available to hand it over to the churchwardens.

However, Travers did design the east window, a fine composition in his later style. It shows Christ in Glory, surrounded by many figures, and with Our Lady and St. John on either side. Above is the Hand of God, the Holy Spirit as a dove, and the seven gifts of the Holy Spirit as tongues of fire. At the very foot of the window are various buildings, including St. Paul's and Rochester Cathedrals. It is marred only by the use of pink and green lozenges of glass instead of the clear glass which Travers had previously favoured. The church is well kept and the window is striking.

Travers also built additions to various churches, such as vestries at Cranford and Shepperton, which are mentioned in the relevant chapters.

Chapter 10

Travers as Graphic Artist

Martin Travers' versatility, which was well demonstrated in his career as a church furnisher and stained glass painter, was also evident in his work as a graphic designer, which was particularly important to him in his earlier years when he was very dependent on work from the Society of SS. Peter and Paul, before his practice received the huge influx of work which resulted from the demand for war memorials after the First World War.

Travers is best known in the graphic field for his book illustrations, and perhaps particularly for the *Pictures of the English Liturgy*. However in certain other, perhaps unexpected, respects his influence has been long lasting.

One aspect of Travers' work was the design of seals for a number of dioceses and other organizations. He designed a seal for the diocese of Portsmouth, and in 1947 a new seal for Gibraltar, which of course was at the same time that he was planning alterations to the cathedral there. At about the same time, he designed a seal for Keble College, Oxford, which is still in use.

Another aspect was the design of what would nowadays be called 'logos'. Travers designed memorial tablets for the Royal College of Medicine in Wimpole Street, but in 1927 he also designed for the Society a Coat of Arms and a Presidential Badge, both of which are still in use today. The Coat of Arms is still used on the Society's notepaper in a somewhat stylized form. In addition, Travers designed in about 1929 a presidential medal or jewel for the Medico-Legal Society, and he also devised a Chapter medal for the Diocese of Southwark.

All these commissions enabled him to display his knowledge of heraldry and the use of heraldic symbols, which is so evident in his stained glass and other architectural work. Although in many ways Travers' work in this field was conservative in conception, he was able to adapt techniques in a fresh, new way, which has enabled his ideas to last.

Cover of Ave, 1925

Travers was also concerned with the design of vestments on a number of occasions. The most famous of his vestments was the First Mass set for Father Humphrey Whitby, discussed in Chapter 4. In addition, in the pre-First World War period, he designed vestments for some of the clergy in Norwich, and one chasuble at least, which came from All Saints Westlegate, is still in use at Mendlesham, Suffolk. He also after the War, provided vestments for Father Ferrier at Shadwell, Yorkshire, and designed items for the Bishops of Carlisle, St. Albans, and Masasi.

The establishment of the Society of SS. Peter & Paul and Travers' early connections with it are dealt with in Chapter 2. There can be no doubt that the work which flowed from that connection was of great importance to Travers in putting his name before many more people; on the other hand

St. Brendan the Voyager, title page

it carried with it the consequence that in the minds of many such people he became identified with the tenets of that Society.

Travers' graphic work is marked by simplicity and bold design. Usually the book illustrations involve one, or at the most two, colours, which makes them easier to reproduce. Obviously there is a certain period feel to them, and the costumes of the laity in particular now have a dated air, but on the other hand the clarity and force of the drawing comes straight through even today. The pictures take the present-day reader back to a period where social attitudes were very different from today: the Empire was still in existence and children still went to church on Sundays. Many of Travers' illustrations depict children in attendance either at the altar or surrounding figures of Our Lord or Our Lady: one striking example was the 1925 cover for *Ave*, the magazine of the League of Our Lady, a predecessor of the present Society of Mary, which was commissioned by Father Fynes-Clinton.

The striking use of black as the dominant colour in illustration, so that the effect was something like a photographic negative, can be seen in the elaborate frontispiece drawn by Travers for the memorial volume to George Sedding. This device was also used in *St. Brendan the Voyager* (1916), *The People's Mass Book* (1921), *An Office of Our Lady* (1925), the picture of *Our Lady of London* (1935), and *The Anglican Missal* (1946) (See Plate 21). It was also employed in the cover of the *Handbook* for the First Anglo-Catholic Priests' Convention (1921). On most occasions he used two colours only, usually black and one other, but rare examples of Travers' use of a number of colours are in the illustrations for *A Prayer Book for Little Children*, by H.R. Baylis (1917), where some of the illustrations are in black, yellow, and blue, and even more strikingly *St. Brendan the Voyager*, which contains some illustrations in four colours, namely black, yellow, blue and green.

Another device used by Travers was in his lettering for the borders and inserts; prepositions and short two or three letter words would be treated as if a monogram and thus space could be saved. This can be seen in the title page of *The Lay of St. Odille* (1915) and in the picture of the offertory in *The People's Mass Book* (1921).

It has been said that Travers was a master of the curved line. This is apparent in his baroque scrollwork, his cherubs, and the intricate knot designs used in the *Anglican Missal* for borders and after paragraphs. These of course also appeared in his reredoses and altar frontals. It is perhaps ironic that he may have used his wife Christine as a model for some of the cherub figures, although the reader of Chapter 1 may well have concluded that she was no cherub.

Title page from the Lay of St. Odille

Travers was also prone to using the same illustrations time and time again, as indeed he did with his stained glass designs. Thus in 1915 the SSPP produced an edition of *Christ's Chronicle* which contained eight illustrations: (1) The Nativity and Seven Sacraments, (2) Our Lady and the Child, (3) Christ in Glory, (4) The elevation of the Host, (5) Two angels and a chalice, (6) Agnus Dei and the Holy City, (7) The Good Shepherd and (8) The Sacred Heart.

These eight illustrations were frequently used in SSPP publications, particularly in the Practical Prayers series and others such as *The Garden of Song*, 1923, and *A Clock of the Sacred Passion*, 1924.

It is also interesting to compare Travers' illustrations not only with modern equivalents, but rather with what else was being produced at that time. By comparison with religious publications of the time Travers' drawings were both simple and striking. Most religious books of the time were sugary, pious, and sentimental. Some of Travers' work is not that far away from being kitsch, but most of it falls well short of the line of bad taste. Some of it is still used today: Holy Trinity, Reading, has service sheets with Travers illustrations on the cover, and St. Thomas, Oxford, has a flyer with a Travers design on it. *Salve*, the magazine of St. Mary Bourne Street, bears on its cover an illustration by Travers of Our Lady holding the church, with cherubs on either side, and the new mass books at St. Barnabas Tunbridge Wells use the gospel plate from *Pictures of the English Liturgy*. For some years St. Nicholas Plumstead have used artwork from the *Anglican Missal* in their parish mass book. *A Manual of Anglo-Catholic Devotion* by Bishop Andrew Burnham (published 2000) contains a number of illustrations from *The People's Rosary Book*[1].

In the 1970s the Church Union issued a set of six 24" by 17" posters of Travers designs of the 1916-21 period, which sold out. They depicted: (1) Our Lady Queen of Heaven, (2) Our Lady Queen of Peace, (3) A crucifix from *Meditations on the Rosary*, (4) The elevation of the Host, from *Christ's Chronicle*, (5) Our Lady of Oxford, from the 1921 Anglo-Catholic Priests' Convention, and (6) The map of Oxford from the handbook for that Convention. Christmas cards were also issued.

Travers' first book illustrations for the SSPP were for the two versions of the Ingoldsby Legends: *The Jackdaw of Rheims* and *The Lay of St. Odille*, both by Richard Barham. These are both paperbacks, in the sense that although beautifully printed they are quite insubstantial and have covers similar to the inner pages. They are both described as being printed at the De La More Press for Samuel Gurney, and sold by the SSPP. Travers then

From the Everlasting Quest, by Margaret Yeo

illustrated three hardbacks for the SSPP, *The Everlasting Quest* and *The Abiding City*, by Margaret Yeo, with a variety of pictures of dragons and castles and also mediaeval figures, real or imagined, and *St. Brendan the Voyager and His Mystic Quest* by James Wilkie (or Wylkie, as the cover has it), with more multi-coloured illustrations. He also illustrated a number of devotional books such as the People's Rosary Book, which contains a number of effective black and white line drawings, *The Altar Book* ('very small, but in large type') and *The People's Mass Book* ('the outcome of the long experience of a priest of the London diocese').

One of the more important collections was *A Garden of Song* by Father Gabriel Gillett, which contains a number of poems. The introduction, by Kenneth Ingram, says: 'Mr. Martin Travers [will not] need a fore-word. It was felt by the editors that there was a special value in collecting some of the best of his work in this single volume so as to make them a more permanent possession. Some of the illustrations have appeared in transitory forms, such as calendars and other occasional publications. All of them blend exactly with the voice of the letterpress, and contribute to the tone of this little treasury of poetry and picture.' Travers' work on calendars and the like has already been mentioned in Chapter 2: the book contains a number of excellent pictures, taken from a variety of sources including *Christ's Chronicle*, *St. Brendan the Voyager*, and *The Everlasting Quest*, one of which is a Crowned Madonna with two cherubs holding the scroll beneath reading 'Alma Redemptoris Mater.' Another illustration shows the Nativity with two small cherubs, one playing the lute and the other struggling with a large cello. Above the stable and around the star are pictures of the seven sacraments, with at the summit a priest elevating the host at an altar with six towering baroque candlesticks. This is an extremely fine, although slim, volume, and now rare.

Alma Redemptoris Mater, from The Garden of Song

17. *Reredos in chapel in St. Saviour, St. Albans, mid 1920s*

19. *High altar, St. Mary, Liss, c 1930*

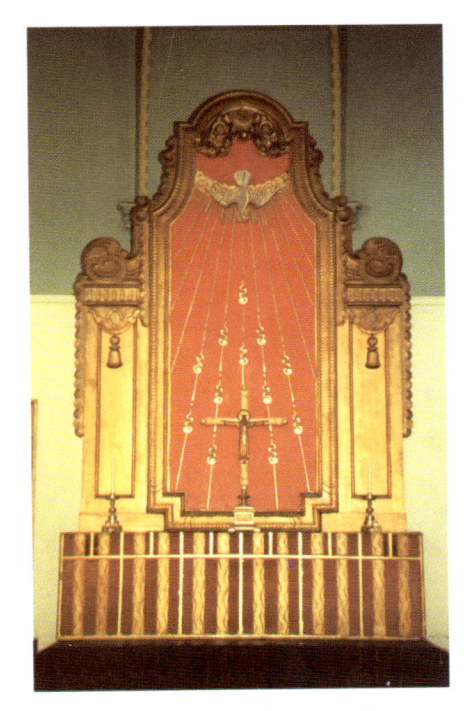

18. *High altar, St, Matthew New Kent Road, 1927*

20. *High altar, St. Dunstan, Cranford, 1936*

21. *Our Lady of London, poster*

23. *Plaque of St. Swithun, Compton Beauchamp, 1937*

22. *High altar and window, St. Swithun, Compton Beauchamp*

24. *St. Hubert chapel at St. Mary, Ashbury, 1927*

25. *Memorial reredos, formerly at St. Martin, Longmoor Camp, now in Leconfield, 1936*

27. *Chapel of St. Stephen in Gothic style, St. Barnabas, Tunbridge Wells*

26. *Lady chapel in Baroque taste, St. Barnabas, Tunbridge Wells*

28. *East window, St. George, Harrow, 1938*

29. *East window in St. Thomas, Camelford, 1938*

31. *Window to Meredith Brown Skelton, Rhus Rees Library, University of Rochester, NY*

30. *High altar reredos, St. Mary, Ticehurst, c 1947*

32. *Altar cross in St. Helier Church, Jersey, given to commemorate the liberation of the island*

The décor of the churches shown was certainly in the earlier period uncompromisingly ultramontane, and the priests have lace albs and Roman vestments. Interestingly, when Travers came to illustrate the Abridged Anglican Missal in 1941 (long after he had ceased to carry out book illustration on a regular basis), the priest was depicted in flowing Gothic vestments. This was published by the Society of St. Peter and St. Paul Trust (1939), as established by Father Whitby after the cessation of the original Society and its associated limited company. As its name indicates, this was a shorter version of the full Missal, also illustrated by Travers and published by the Trust in 1946, although probably planned and drawn before then.

From An Abridged Anglican Missal 1941

In the earlier period, Travers also designed work for the Anglo-Catholic Congress, which is again touched upon in Chapter 2. He produced an illustrated map of 'Catholic Oxford' for the 1921 Priests' Convention, as well as illustrating the *Handbook* and the *Report*. The *Report* for the 1920 Congress was produced by SPCK and is a very sober volume, but in 1923 and 1927 the *Reports* were the work of the SSPP and were more flamboyant in their presentation and typography, with engravings by Quick again. The 1923 volume had on its cover a picture of Our Lady and the Child above a city, which looks very like Travers' work, but in fact is by one West. The 1927 volume had a chalice design, again probably by Travers, and the 1930 and 1933 volumes had the Anglo-Catholic Congress 'logo' of a dove within a cartouche with a stylized sunburst and characteristic Travers teardrops. Various designs for this can be seen evolving in his notebooks.

The 1933 Centenary volume also has an Agnus Dei symbol over the holy city on the title page; this had already appeared over a Poem called 'The Heavenly City' in *A Garden of Song*.

By contrast, in 1922 Travers carried out some line drawings for the Abbey Classics editions published by Chapman & Dodd. There are 24 of these in a numbered series, and the title page, which is the same on each, describes them as being 'ornamented by Martin Travers.' Within the separate volumes are a number of head and tailpieces, which are often repeated from volume to volume. This appears to have been a one off commission, with no ecclesiastical connections.

The books were as follows: (1) Sir James Melville of Halhill: *Memories of his own life*; (2) and (3) William Beckford: *Vathek* and *The Episodes of Vathek*; (4) Sterne: *A Sentimental Journey Through France and Italy*; (5) Cobbett: *Journal of a Year's Residence in America*; (6) Apuleius: *The Golden Ass*; (7) Voltaire: *Candide*; (8) Peter Beckford: *Thoughts on Hunting*; (9) Disraeli: *The Letters of Runnymede*; (10) Voltaire: *Zadig*; (11) and (12) Herman Melville: *Mardi Volumes I and II*; (13) Longus: *Daphne & Chloe*; (14) (15) and (16) John Gay: *Poems, Plays Vol I and Plays Vol II*; (17) Erasmus: *Twenty Select Colloquies*; (18) Petronius: *The Satyricon*; (19) Prior: *Shorter Poems*; (20) Donne: *Devotions and Death's Duell*; (21) and (22) Defoe: *Moll Flanders and Roxanna: The Fortunate Mistress*; (23) Herodotus: *The Aethipoian History*; (24) Johnson: *Journal of a Tour in the Western Islands*.

Another one-off commission came in 1934, when Travers provided a frontispiece, reproduced on the cover, for a small hardback entitled *The Flame of Prayer: a study of the life of prayer in the Church of England*, published by Mowbrays in 1934. Travers' picture was of Lancelot Andrewes kneeling before an altar with Laudian cover. The author of this book was Father E.D. Sedding, the brother of Travers' old pre-war friend George Sedding. Father Sedding had become a prolific author and was by then a member of the Society of St. John the Evangelist.

From time to time it is clear that Travers also continued to design cards and posters and the like, such as a Regina Coeli card for the Community of the Resurrection, although graphic design became less important in his practice as the years went by.

Undoubtedly the most important monument to the particular view of the Faith propagated by the Society of SS. Peter & Paul was the two volume 'Pictures of the English Liturgy', which have already been briefly mentioned in Chapter 2. They can be found in many different forms: part of the confusion in relation to these volumes results from the fact that Volume II, Low

Flame of Prayer, 1934

Mass, was published in 1916, and Volume I, High Mass, in 1922. In addition, *A Picture Book of the Holy Sacrifice for the Children of the Church* (1922), by Father A.H. Baverstock, contains the same drawings as the Low Mass volume, and is in effect a further edition; the cover of at least some of that version says that it is by 'Alban H. Baverstock and Martin Travers.' The position is also complicated by the fact that in 1922 the SSPP issued further volumes entitled respectively *Pictures of the Roman Liturgy* and *Pictures of the American Liturgy*. These both contained pictures for Low and High Mass as used in the separate volumes, but the American volume had two extra plates. The plates could also be purchased unbound, and the SSPP also sold slides of the drawings. In 1923 the Society were advertising the Low Mass volume at the discounted price of 8/6d and the High Mass volume (described as 'probably the most valuable contribution to the study of ceremonial in the English Church that has been published for many years') at 21/–. The Roman joint volume was 30/–, and the American joint volume the same price or alternatively $7. The Lambeth Palace Library has Samuel Gurney's own copies, which were left to it: the High Mass volume has a motif of the Blessed Sacrament on the front and is lettered along the spine, whereas most copies have plainer covers. By 1930 the High Mass volume was available at as little as 5/– and Low Mass at 3/6d, which suggests that they were being remaindered.

The Low Mass volume is simpler than the High Mass; in it all the vestments and the altar are the same in the different plates, but the same yellow and black colouring is used.

The Low Mass volume contained an introduction entitled 'The Lost Opportunity' which was a typical play on words in that it answered an Alcuin Club collection of the same year (Number XIX). This was *Illustrations of the Liturgy* by Clement Skilbeck, himself a stained glass artist, to which Percy Dearmer contributed an introduction styled 'The Present Opportunity.'

The anonymous author of 'The Lost Opportunity' (probably Maurice Child) said: 'The proposed revival (of the Sarum use) has failed, as any movement is bound to fail which begins and ends in studies, and private chapels, and the moderate shrines of the well-to-do. The History of the attempted revival of the 'English Use' is the story of a lost opportunity ... Today the Sarum use barely survives, the Western use spreads widely but with increasing deformities ...'

He went on to say that all of the errors at present found in the Western use 'can be traced to an insufficient knowledge of the principles of the ceremonial involved, together with a determination to treat the Prayer Book Mass as a service read to the faithful instead of an act of sacrifice done before Almighty God.'

There were 13 pictures in the Low Mass volume, depicting respectively the preparation, the Lord be with you, the Collect and Epistle, the Gospel, the Creed, the Offertory, the Sanctus, the elevation of the host, the elevation of the chalice, the priest's communion, the communion of the people, the post-communion and the blessing. It was said that another volume dealing with High Mass would follow 'shortly', but in fact it was to be six years before Volume I appeared.

The High Mass volume, perhaps the quintessential piece of Anglo-Catholic illustrated literature, has no fewer than 29 plates, and in addition there are endplates showing respectively the order of entrance and of exit, which are actually identical! Travers signed the endplates with his initials in the black and white flooring under the beadle's feet.

The cartoons for many of the drawings are to be found in Travers' notebooks of the period, but it is not clear where he drew them. A note before the title page informs the reader that 'The pictures in this book have been drawn from life by MARTIN TRAVERS. The greatest care has been taken to obtain accuracy of detail. And they have been overlooked by many liturgical experts.'

The introduction to the book makes clear the position of its author, presumably again Maurice Child. It is stated as clear beyond peradventure that:

(1) 'The English Mass is a Catholic Rite and is not a Lutheran ordinance. Consequently it will always be interpreted as a Mass, and may be enriched ceremonially and ritually from parent sources.
(2) Such enrichment will tend to approximate our Rite to that of the First English Prayer Book of 1549, which in turn is an English version of the old Roman Mass. That is the surest method of achieving some uniformity.
(3) The Ceremonial will be the simplest form prescribed by the only authority which legislates on such matters, namely the Congregation of Rites in Rome. And that, not so much because it is 'Roman', as because it is the simplest, most convenient, most easily studied, and (to modern minds) most intelligible method of rendering Divine Service. Moreover it is the form adopted (and perhaps adapted) in the vast majority of Anglo-Catholic Churches.'

There then follow notes on the various drawings which follow, including the exhortation under XXV to take the ablutions at the right place, namely after the communion (which was known in Anglo-Catholic circles then as 'tarping'), rather than to follow the 'strange custom' of postponing the ablutions until after the Mass or before the Last Gospel.

The various drawings show the priests in biretta and Roman vestments, the servers in short cottas. All the altars have six Baroque candlesticks with a matching crucifix, of the style that Travers was then turning out. The altar in the Preparation drawing and that of the Censing of the Oblation has six vases for artificial flowers between the candlesticks, and later, at the epistle, four extra candlesticks appear. At the Gospel the servers are carrying disproportionately tall candles which tower over both book and reader. In the drawing of the Creed, the altar has a central crucifix with attached rood figures, again of a type in which Travers specialized at this time.

By the time Travers came to the Sanctus, plate 17, the altar has riddel curtains with a cherub holding a candlestick at each corner, but although

Sanctus from Pictures of the English Liturgy

the note says that it is 'the old English style' it has a baroque Madonna on a crescent moon above and relics on either side of her. In the Agnus Dei drawing an immense reliquary is depicted behind the altar. The following picture, of the Celebrant's Communion, shows a High Mass of Exposition: behind the altar, in the place of the reliquary, is a monstrance with crown above supported on either side by a winged cherub. The Communion of the People shows a simpler altar, but with a domed tabernacle on it. A houseling cloth is held by the five communicants, the only time that the congregation intrudes: one woman wears a long mantilla over her head. There is no picture of the chalice being administered. The final drawing is of the Absolution of the Dead, with the clergy in black vestments and enormous candlesticks around a tall catafalque. This one is signed in the bottom right hand corner.

The plates in this volume are as follows: (1) At the foot of the altar, (2) The preparation, (3) The blessing of the incense, (4) Censing the altar at the introit, (5) The introit, (6) The Lord be with You, (7) The collects, (8) The

Pictures of the English Liturgy: Absolutions of the Dead

Epistle, (9) The Holy Gospel, (10) The beginning of the creed, (11) The Creed, (12) At the Creed, (13) The offertory, (14) Censing the oblation, (15) The lavabo, (16) The confession and absolution at the communion, (17) The Sanctus, (18) The prayer of humble access, (19) The Canon, (20) The elevation of the host, (21) The Pax, (22) The Agnus, (23) The Celebrant's Communion, (24) The Communion of the people, (25) The ablutions, (26) The dismissal, (27) The blessing, (28) The Last Gospel, (29) Absolutions of the Dead.

It is almost impossible to compile a complete list of Travers' book illustrations, particularly because the SSPP went in for quantity, sometimes at the expense of quality, and there were many ephemeral pamphlets. The following are however the most important:

1914: The Jackdaw of Rheims (Ingoldsby Legends), by Richard Barham (SSPP).
1915: The Lay of St. Odille (Ingoldsby Legends), by Richard Barham (SSPP).
The Everlasting Quest, by Margaret Yeo (SSPP).
Christ's Chronicle (SSPP).
Things to Know, in the Practical Prayers series (SSPP).
1916: St. Brendan the Voyager and his Mystic Quest, by James Wilkie (SSPP).
The Abiding City, by Margaret Yeo (SSPP).
Pictures of the English Liturgy, Volume II Low Mass (SSPP).
1917: A Prayer Book for Little Children, by H.R. Baylis (SSPP).
George Elton Sedding: the life and death of an artist and soldier, edited by E.D. Sedding (Letchworth Garden City Press Ltd.).
1920: Bethlem Tableau by C.R. Starey (SSPP).
1921: Handbook for the First Anglo-Catholic Priests' Convention.
Report of the same (both SSPP).
The People's Mass Book (SSPP).
The Altar Book (SSPP).
My Rosary, its meaning and use, by Robert Keable (Travers illustrated the cover only) (SSPP).
Hints to Confessors, by E.S. Maltby (SSPP).
1922: Pictures of the English Liturgy, Volume I High Mass (SSPP).
Pictures of the Roman Liturgy (SSPP).
Pictures of the American Liturgy (SSPP).

A Picture Book of the Holy Sacrifice for the Children of the Church, by A.H. Baverstock (SSPP).
The Abbey Classics Series of 24 books as detailed above (Chapman & Dodd).
1923: A Garden of Song, by Gabriel Gillett (SSPP).
The Anglo-Catholic Congress Books, numbers 1–52 (Travers illustrated the covers only) (SSPP).
Meditations on the Rosary (SSPP).
1924: An Office of our Lady, in the Practical Prayers series (SSPP).
Clock of the Sacred Passion (SSPP).
The People's Rosary Book (SSPP).
1925: John Bull Tracts, numbers 1-96 (Travers illustrated the covers only). (SSPP).
1927: Report of the Anglo-Catholic Congress (SSPP).
1930: Report of the Anglo-Catholic Congress (Catholic Literature Association).
1932: Report of the Second Anglo-Catholic Priests' Convention (ditto).
1933: Report of the Oxford Movement Centenary Anglo-Catholic Congress (ditto).
1934: The Flame of Prayer, by E.D. Sedding, S.S.J.E. (Mowbrays).
1941: An Abridged Anglican Missal (SSPP Trust).
1946: Anglican Missal (SSPP Trust).

'The Offertory' from People's Mass Book

Chapter 11

Travers: A Modern Perspective

At first glance, there can be few more unfashionable choices for a biography than Martin Travers.

There is no doubt that he had a high reputation during his lifetime, and that that reputation was growing when his untimely death occurred. The problem with the regard in which he is held since his death is that a lack of full perception of the breadth of his output has led many to believe that he was simply a poseur who played along with the discredited fantasy world of a few extreme Anglo-Catholics.

It is hoped that what has been set out above goes some way to restoring his reputation, and that it can be seen with the benefit of hindsight that his work contains much of lasting value.

The reaction against Travers' furnishings has partly been because they were often executed in cheap materials. Canon Colin Stephenson in *Merrily on High* (1972) said[1] that Travers 'used his considerable talents in transforming many Anglo-Catholic churches into passable imitations of Italian places of worship except that he worked in papier mâché, which cut the cost but rather gave the impression of a stage set.' It is true that Travers frequently had to cut his cloth according to the means of his clients, but that was at their request not his. He often used gilded silver leaf, where the client could not afford gold. His work in places where there was not much stinting, such as St. Magnus the Martyr in the City, St. Mary Godmanchester, and Romsey Abbey, shows what he could do given the resources. He also developed to perfection the technique of using alternate layers of paint and gilding on wood covered by raised plaster, so that it appeared either like leather or on some occasions similar to pleated material.

However the consequence of using inferior materials is that now, 60 to

80 years after most of his work was done, a number of his chapels and shrines need careful renovation.

The real problem with Travers' baroque pastiche furnishings is not the inferior nature of some of the materials, but the unfashionability of the liturgical and theological ideas which they were designed to further. In the 1920s and 30s, when Travers was producing his baroque pastiches, many Anglo-Catholics believed not only that the Church of England should be moved to a position in which the interior of its churches was indistinguishable from idealized continental (not English) Roman Catholic models, but that the theology taught in them should also be indistinguishable, and that the aim should be corporate reunion. This involved the strict teaching of eucharistic sacrifice by the priest, and that the actual reception of the body and blood of Christ by the congregation was not a necessary part of a solemn celebration – indeed it was to be discouraged. Harry Williams, in his autobiography *Some Day I'll Find You* (1982) refers sarcastically[2] to Anglo-Catholics of that period considering that the three great fundamentals of Christianity were fasting communion, sacramental confession and apostolic succession. Of these, fasting communion was observed in many places with fanatical zeal. The conclusions of the Second Vatican Council effected a revolution in many aspects of Catholic worship, but the revolution had begun earlier; in particular the relaxation on the fasting rules from 1953 onwards seemed to cut the ground from under the feet of many of the older school. The story that Dr. C.C. Keet of St. Clement, Cambridge, put up a notice at that point to the effect that the Bishop of Rome was no longer prayed for in his church, may or may not be apocryphal, but it certainly reflected the reaction of some to the changes on the Seven Hills.

The new liturgical order which resulted from Vatican II should in theory have strengthened the position of Anglo-Catholicism within the Church of England. A vernacular liturgy, communion in both kinds, and a clearing away of some of the mediaeval devotions from the Roman Church, should have meant that union was nearer rather than further away. However, by the time that those changes had been digested Anglo-Catholicism was very much weaker than it once had been. Further it had been diluted by the onset of the Parish Communion, the Church of England's own Liturgical Movement. The Parish Communion became a service which could be used in High, Moderate, and, increasingly after the 1967 Keele Conference, Evangelical, parishes. As benefices of different tradition were united, a new incumbent could celebrate the Parish Communion in each, with perhaps some differences of emphasis. Vestments were no longer regarded as a party sign and were almost universally accepted.

One consequence of the Liturgical Movement was of course that earlier sanctuary arrangements were altered. In some cases this took the form of the pulling out of the altar from its reredos in order that celebration from the westward position could occur. This has resulted in permanent damage to many of Travers' carefully crafted arrangements. In other cases, incongruous temporary altars have been erected in front of the high altar; this at least does not have the effect of destroying that which was there before. The *reductio ad absurdum* of the liturgical reformers can be seen in Bodley's magnificent church of the Holy Angels, Hoar Cross, with its lavish Victorian fittings, in the middle of which stands a small kitchen table which now serves as the altar. The nave altar in St. Augustine Queen's Gate, in front of Travers' enormous reredos, looks equally out of place.

However, the tide of opinion in favour of the new ways was such that appreciation for Travers was all but swept away, and very little was written about him save for occasional references. Anthony Symondson, who catalogued the Travers drawings while employed by the RIBA and was later ordained as a priest in the Anglican Church before joining the Jesuits, was one of the few who remained interested in Travers' work, together with the late Roderick Gradidge, who worshipped at St. Mary Bourne Street and wrote about that church in particular.

Symondson wrote a scathing letter to *The Tablet* (17th August 1974) in response to an overgenerous tribute to Cecil Collins' Icon of Divine Light in Chichester Cathedral, saying that anyone with a passing interest in church furnishings of the twentieth century could see that the work was not original but was 'reminiscent, in design and colour, of the later work of Martin Travers', whom he termed 'the versatile, but agnostic, inventor of Anglo-Catholic Congress baroque.'

Symondson returned to consider Travers further in an article in the *Walsingham Review* in 1977, in which he said[3]:

> [Travers'] work suffers from the obscurity which falls upon men immediately after their death. In recent times it has excited conflicting emotions. The young (or shall we say the more sophisticated among them) regard it with good humoured sympathy; but those of late middle age (although there are exceptions) maintain such antipathetic reactions that their force suggests a deeper cause than that of architecture.

The deeper cause was no doubt the feeling that what Travers' clients represented was a passé and exotic flowering of Anglo-Catholicism which was embarrassing and should be forgotten as soon as possible.

On the other side of this coin is the nostalgia for certainty and for the time when Anglo-Catholicism appeared to be about to take over the Church of England. John Betjeman dwelt on this subject in his verse autobiography *Summoned by Bells*, where he says:

> Those were the days when that divine baroque
> Transformed our English altars and our ways ...

He alluded to the same subject in his poem *Anglo-Catholic Congresses*, in which of course he makes explicit reference to Travers:

> We who remember the Faith, the grey-headed ones,
> Of those Anglo-Catholic Congresses swinging along,
> Who heard the South Coast salvo of incense-guns
> And surged to the Albert Hall in our thousands strong
> With 'extreme' colonial bishops leading in song;
> ...
> Yet, under the Travers baroque, in a limewashed whiteness,
> The fiddle-back vestments a-glitter with morning rays,
> Our Lady's image, in multiple-candled brightness,
> The bells and banners – those were the waking days
> When Faith was taught and fanned to a golden blaze.

Travers' work for the SSPP and his Congress Baroque style has to be seen in the context in which it was carried out. In that context, it can be admired and studied with interest. Much of it is fine of its type, even if it is alien on first glance. It also appears clear, when the whole of his outlook is taken into account, that Travers was not himself promoting the Baroque style. He was prepared to carry out work in accordance with the wishes of his clients, and in the 1920–33 period that involved Baroque pastiches, but his skill was in playing along with the mood of those who were commissioning work from him. He was perfectly able to carry out work in a completely different idiom, as at Holy Trinity, Lyonsdown, which came in the middle of the most intensive output of Baroque furnishings.

One of the main reasons for the unpopularity of and ignorance about Travers' work is that in the mind of those who know of him, his work in furnishing Anglo-Catholic churches is frequently considered to be the totality of his output.

As the reader of this book hopefully now appreciates, Travers' work was far wider in scope and far more influential than that.

Oxford Movement Centenary Congress 1933: reredos in the Albert Hall

His later furnishings are distinguished, identifiable, but within the main stream of conservative minded opinion at the time, and they have aged better than the more exotic work.

Travers' few church buildings are not on the whole memorable. His graphic work is still arresting, although sometimes dated in appearance.

It can be argued however that Travers' more influential contribution to ecclesiastical art lay in his stained glass, and in particular that through his long spell of teaching at the RCA his influence was very much greater than it would have been had he simply been a practitioner.

Travers' stained glass paintings are in a sense timeless. A visitor to a church in which there is one of his windows would almost certainly have some difficulty in deciding its age, unless that visitor had special knowledge. On the other hand, they are in another sense deeply conservative. His disciple Lawrence Lee, in *The Appreciation of Stained Glass* (1977)[4] says that at the most traditional end of the traditional school of glass painting 'the 'Travers School' maintained the historical use of line and tone, which, however bold in its application, often gave an impression of great delicacy at the appropriate distance.' In the same book he says that the real contribution of Travers was to teach stained glass painters to *look* at old glass and to clear desiccated scholarship from their mind. Having adopted that approach, Travers was able, from his deep knowledge of symbolism and of the lives of the saints, to use them in an almost casual way, whereas some of his less talented contemporaries were far too hidebound by artistic protocols, as to which Travers is reported to have said 'These rules do not seem to have been strictly observed, particularly by artists.' His windows have far more vitality than those of his erstwhile master Comper; Travers' figures look like real characters, who feel about what they are doing or seeing. There is often a sense of fun about them, as there was also in some of the furnishings he carried out. On occasion it would be fair to say that the charm on which all who know his work comment comes close to sentimentality, but usually it falls short of it. Some of his work verges on the Mabel Lucie Attwell school of art, but only a minority.

E. Liddell Armitage, in his important book *Stained Glass: History Technology and Practice* (1959) says[5] that Travers and James Hogan (1883–1948), his almost exact contemporary, were 'probably the two most important stained glass artists of the first half of the [twentieth] century.' However, he makes the important point that while all Travers' former pupils retained a profound admiration for him and regarded him as the finest artist of his day in his own particular sphere, his work was not usually found in cathedrals and other places where it would have had a higher profile. Many of Travers' windows are single commissions and they stand on their own. His work at St. Andrew Catford and St. James Riddlesdown is interesting because it shows his development over a long period of time. One of his better sequences was the series of windows at St. Martin, Longmoor Garrison Church, Liss, but that was hardly in the public eye, and is even less so now that it is in Leconfield, East Yorkshire.

While on the one hand Travers was a traditionalist, in the sense that he never incorporated abstract painting into any of his work, on the other hand he was not hidebound by tradition. He worked within the tradition of glass painting, rather than following slavishly what had gone before. Thus, the technical ability which led him to build models and the like was also expressed in the way in which he was always anxious to adopt new techniques involved in glass painting, such as different uses of silver stain.

Lawrence Lee built on what he had learned from Travers to become a very successful stained glass painter in his own right, whose work is found at Coventry Cathedral amongst many other places. He adopted the Travers system of personal control of the studio, in which the artist took a strong interest in every aspect of work from design to finished product.

In his contribution to Armitage's book, Lee said that[6]: 'We are still too near to gain a proper estimate of [Travers'] true worth in the stained glass world, but I believe he will come to be recognized as a most significant artist.' He went on to set out what he had learned from Travers in practical matters, such as the insistence on first class finish of scale designs, the use of photostats rather than hand-drawn cartoons, the use of simple schemes of colour, the commonsense use of leading, so that it became the servant rather than the master of the artist, the rejection of all types of painting which served to promote only naturalistic effects in favour of a simple and direct method of line and tone to express the essentials, the careful selection of colour to give several hues or tones to one area of colour, and the personal control and if necessary personal work at each process. Another well-known glass painter, J.E. Nuttgens, said[7] that the most formative influence on him was Martin Travers 'whose superb sense of design was matched by an instinct for suiting his work to the building.'

Nuttgens had carried out a great deal of work for Travers, and indeed almost certainly actually assisted in painting a high proportion of Travers' best known window designs.

Lee and Nuttgens were however only two of the many pupils influenced by Travers; as well as those he employed, it was his practice to invite some

Design for window, Holy Trinity, Weymouth

students from the RCA to work with him during the holidays, and thus his influence on them went beyond the lecture room. It was a measure of the regard in which he was held that in May 1962, almost 14 years after his death, the Society of Master Glass Painters held a dinner for his friends and associates at which he was fondly remembered.

Travers was a perfectionist, in that each piece, and each commission for stained glass must of necessity be individual, received his personal attention, and each piece was drawn and redrawn until he was satisfied. Even then, changes were often made prior to the actual firing. The draughtsmanship which went into the photostat designs which he used is not only impressive, it has proved of great assistance to those researching his work, as stained glass windows are by their very nature so difficult to photograph. It was Travers himself who devised the technique of blowing up designs photographically to full size, thus preserving their freshness.

On the other hand, there clearly were occasions on which this meticulousness turned into dilatoriness. The New Zealand window was an extreme example, but there were other occasions on which work was delayed and requests by the client became more and more insistent. However, when the work arrived, the complaints normally ceased. On occasion too, members of his staff suffered when Travers insisted that work which had taken many hours was repeated until it was exactly as he required it.

The stained glass windows which Travers designed also came from a wide clientele, in which Anglo-Catholic churches were only one part of his constituency. Undoubtedly personal contacts played an important part in the work, as did his advertising methods: he was able to distribute to prospective clients copies of his photostat designs so they could see what he had done before. That was no doubt one of the reasons why some of his designs were repeated in different places.

The neglect of and ignorance about Travers' work outside of those who feel nostalgic towards the Anglo-Catholic Congresses is shameful. In the otherwise excellent guide to the splendid parish church of Woodbridge, Suffolk, there is no mention at all of the designer of the very fine east window, which dominates the church. In Barham, Kent, the guide says that 'the altar is modern' without any attribution, and fails to mention his wonderful east window at all; similarly he receives no mention in the guide to Burwash church, with its equally excellent east window. In other places, dioceses have disposed of furnishings of his without any proper record of where they have gone, or indeed any sense of their importance.

Travers' work suffered badly in the blitz and in events such as the Tonbridge School Chapel fire, and it is important that what is left is conserved, repaired, and cherished.

He is indeed at the present time an underrated artist, and the aim of this book is to bring his name back before a wider public, and to increase appreciation of his work.

It is as yet too early fully to appreciate the work carried out in churches in the Twentieth Century, but it is, in the view of the authors, early enough to be able to say that Travers was a more important figure than the limited information previously available about him would suggest. It is now more than 50 years since Travers died, and that is sufficient distance to lend enchantment again to his best work.

It does seem that interest in his work is on the increase: the newer editions of Pevsner's *Buildings of England* contain far more references to him than was the case, and in recent years two short handbooks to his work, edited respectively by Leonard Buckley and Father Peter Blagdon-Gamlen, have been published by the Ecclesiological Society.

Chapter 12

A Gazetteer of Travers' Actual and Projected Work

The difficulties inherent in compiling an accurate list of Martin Travers' work have already been alluded to. Not only were many documented projects never actually executed, but also others, which were carried out, have subsequently been destroyed by bombs or later by sanctioned or wanton vandalism. Further, many furnishings have been moved from their original site or broken up. Previous lists of Travers' work have failed to discriminate sufficiently between work that was designed, work that was executed, and work which is still in place. The authors are however conscious that there may well be still more work which is not included below, and of course that there may be errors in the notes. Nearly every piece of work in this country has however either been inspected by one or other or both of the authors, or they have seen up to date photographs of it.

Part I of this gazetteer is a long list detailing work carried out by, projected by, or attributed to, Travers, with notes, but in order to assist the church crawler, there is set out in Part II a short list of extant work in the British Isles, excluding some doubtful or marginal work which is fully noted in Part I.

In each case, London is taken first by boroughs, followed by England by modern counties but ignoring unitary authorities, and then by the rest of the British Isles. In Part I the work abroad is also then set out, followed by miscellaneous work.

PART I
A Comprehensive List

In this part, where the drawings in question are held by the Royal Institute of British Architects this is noted, but no cross-referencing to the plans by num-

Design for window for Stand Unitarian Chapel, Greater Manchester, destroyed in war

bers is given, as the RIBA are in the process of recataloguing all their drawings. Reference is also made to a number of books by abbreviation as follows:

Anson: P.F. Anson: *Fashions in Church Furnishings 1840–1940*, Studio Vista, 1965.

Armitage: E. Liddell Armitage: *Stained Glass: History Technology and Practice*, Leonard Hill Books Ltd., 1959.

Betjeman: John Betjeman (ed.): *Collins Pocket Guide to English Parish Churches: The South*, Collins, 1968 (the northern volume contains no reference to Travers' work).

Clarke: B.F.L. Clarke: *Parish Churches of London*, B.T. Batsford Ltd., 1966.

Cowen: P. Cowen: *A guide to stained glass in Britain*, Michael Joseph, 1985.

Howell and Sutton: P. Howell and I. Sutton: *The Faber Guide to Victorian Churches*, Faber, 1989.

Mee: Arthur Mee: *The King's England*, Hodder and Stoughton, 1937–53, various dates and editions.

Osborne: June Osborne: *Stained Glass in England*, Alan Sutton Publishing Ltd., 1997.

Pevsner: Nikolaus Pevsner and others: *Buildings of England*, Penguin Books, various dates and editions.

RIBA Catalogue: Jill Lever (ed.): Catalogue of the Drawings Collection of the RIBA, Vol T-Z, Gregg International, 1984.

Richardson: K. Richardson: *The 'Twenty Five' Churches of the Southwark Diocese*, Ecclesiological Society, 2002.

Stamp and Amery: G. Stamp and C. Amery: *Victorian Buildings of London 1837–1887*, Architectural Press Ltd., 1980.

(i) London

BARKING
Barking, St. Paul, Ripple Road
The lectern drawn by Travers for this church was never executed: a design by another was used in its place. The church was in any event destroyed in the war.
Drawings in RIBA for an oak lectern, 1933.

BARNET
Friern Barnet, St. James the Great, Friern Barnet Lane
A standard Travers design for war memorial with crucifix in the churchyard, which was carried out; the figure is in good condition but the writing has worn.
Drawings in RIBA for war memorial cross, 1919.

Golders Green, St. Michael, Golders Green Road (now Greek Orthodox)
The design in the RIBA has a relatively small figure at the top of a relatively tall

crucifix, and bears no relationship to the crucifix which is actually in place; it appears therefore that another design was chosen.

Drawings in RIBA for outside calvary, undated.

Monken Hadley, St. Mary
No work was carried out in this church. There is a later window by Francis Stephens in the church in the place for which Travers' design was intended.

Drawings in RIBA for new altar, frontal, reredos and stained glass above, 1948.

New Barnet, Holy Trinity, Lyonsdown Road
There is a great deal of Travers' woodwork in this church, carried out under three faculties, namely: (i) 1925: reredos and oak panelling in rather angular and modernistic style, as memorial to late Vicar, Revd G.E. Gardner, together with curtains, oak credence table, and gilded or silver cross, which was executed, although neither the cross nor the curtains are now in evidence, following reordering in 1992; (ii) 1927: pulpit, new communion rails, communion table all also of oak; (iii) 1931: to remove existing archway at east end of south aisle and to erect carved Austrian oak screen with moulded panels and doors, into clergy vestry, in memory of Arthur Perigal decd. 1879–1931. Windows were installed in 1927 also which are not by Travers. In 1943 he designed the Perigal hatchment, which is in the south aisle chapel, behind the screen. The work is unusual for him and the tone of the church Evangelical, but this church has a great deal of his woodwork, discussed in detail in Chapter 4.

Drawings in RIBA for reredos etc., 1925, for pulpit and altar, undated, for screen, 1931 and for hatchment, 1943.

New Barnet, St. Mark, Potters Road, Barnet Vale
There is a characteristic Travers rood in this church, on the tympanum above the chancel arch, with the supporting figures separate from the crucifix.

Drawings in RIBA for rood, 1945.

BEXLEY

Lamorbey, Holy Trinity, Hurst Road corner
Travers and Musman prepared plans for the restoration of this Victorian church, which was reopened in 1949 after Travers' death. In addition, there is a fine Travers Te Deum east window of Christ in Glory, again installed after his death, although designed by him.

Drawings in RIBA for restoration after war damage, by Travers and E.B. Musman, 1945–6.

Slade Green, St. Augustine, Slade Green Road
This is a similar war memorial design to St. James, Friern Barnet (q.v.). The outside cross was executed and still exists.

Drawing in RIBA for war memorial cross, 1919.

BRENT

Cricklewood, St. Gabriel, Walm Lane
Travers designed a fine window in the north aisle, said by Pevsner to be dated 1927, full of figures in bright colours, showing Christ being taken to be crucified, in memory of Annie Elizabeth Brown, died 21st March 1921.

No drawings in RIBA for this church.

See also: Cowen, p139, Pevsner: *London 3: North West*, p126.

Kilburn, St. John the Evangelist, Rudolph Road
Travers designed a small window in memory of George Martin, parish priest 1901–31, showing a saint with a message coming to him on a scroll from on high. This was installed under a faculty dated 1932, but the church was declared redundant in about 1972 and has been demolished.
Drawing in RIBA for glass, 1932 (wrongly dated as 1923 by Travers).

Sudbury, St. Andrew, Harrow Road
This late design, in more Gothic style than usual for Travers, was never executed.
Drawing in RIBA for war memorial reredos, 1948.

BROMLEY
Bromley, Old Palace Chapel
Travers prepared some drawings for the chapel in what became Stockwell College, but it is not clear whether the work was ever done, and the drawings have been lost.
No drawings in RIBA for this chapel.

Bromley, St. Mary, Church Road, Shortlands
A reredos was installed in the lady chapel in this church and was described by Dr. Eeles in a letter in the Council for the Care of Churches as being the most memorable work in the church, but the church was completely wrecked by bombing in the War.
Drawing in RIBA for reredos in side chapel, 1928.

Chislehurst, St. Nicholas, Chislehurst Common
This south aisle window shows Our Lady saying the Magnificat, with around her four smaller panels showing the Nativity, the Adoration of the Magi, the Presentation, and the Annunciation. It is an excellent well-coloured and detailed window from Travers' last years.
Drawing in RIBA for glass, 1948.

West Wickham, Chapel of St. Christopher, Gates Green Road
A chapel in this hall was opened in October 1935. The parish records indicate that Martin Travers paid for three stained glass windows in the chapel, which were executed by his pupils. Unfortunately the windows deteriorated; parts were used in the door when the chapel was converted into a small room named 'The Old Granary' in what is now The Assembly Halls run by the Coney Hall Trust, but later that glass too deteriorated and was discarded. It is not clear whether Travers designed the chapel itself.
No drawings in RIBA.

West Wickham, St. John the Baptist, Layhams Road
There are plans for the work actually done in this church in the Canterbury Cathedral Archives attached to the relevant faculties, as follows: (i) 1934: for a screen between the north aisle and the nave with two doors, and also tablets to one Anderson and a charity, with the moving of two tablets and the cutting short of some pews; (ii) 1942: painting and gilding to reredos and a memorial tablet to the wife and son of Revd Shaw Page, vicar. Travers' friend G.E. Sedding is buried in the churchyard here near his parents and his father John Dando Sedding carried out much woodwork in the church. The Travers screen was the subject of some controversy when originally designed, and the parish rejected balustrading above it. It was designed to enlarge the vestry and replaced a deal

screen, which had enclosed less of the north aisle. The screen was removed in 1961 when a new vestry was built on; there is now no trace of it. The reredos is of characteristic terracotta colour with Travers' fine lettering and an Agnus Dei symbol, and to the south of it is the lozenge shaped tablet to the Pages. Travers proposed moving the figures from the ends of the reredos and placing them on the wall on either side; this was not done at the time but has been done since. A rood was designed for the mediaeval screen, which in 1991 was itself moved to form a parclose screen between chancel and north chapel, but this was never installed.

There are no drawings in the RIBA, save for the rood, 1942.

West Wickham, St. Mary of Nazareth, The Avenue
Travers designed a church hall, opened in December 1934, and used for worship until a new church was built adjoining it. It has no particular architectural distinction, and is of cheap brick. It is now used for social purposes. Two plaques from the reredos in that hall, showing Our Lady and the Archangel Gabriel respectively, were incorporated into the new church (1984) in the lady chapel upstairs; both the chapel and the main altar have silver gilt wooden candlesticks, apparently by Travers.

No drawings in RIBA.

CAMDEN
Hampstead, St. Mark, Prince Albert Road
This church is sometimes referred to as being in St. Marylebone, but is in fact just in Camden. None of Travers' designs were carried out: Comper's design for the reredos was preferred, and the church was in any event gutted in the War and completely rebuilt.

Drawings in RIBA for children's corner, 1934, and reredos, 1935.

St. Pancras, Holy Cross, Cromer Street
This church has a Travers window of the Good Shepherd, dated early 1920s, in memory of Arthur Crane, died 1920: Our Lord holds a lamp and carries a sheep on his back. His cloak is a fine red rust colour, and although small, this is well executed glass in the north aisle.

No drawings in RIBA for this work.

See also: Pevsner: *London 4: North*, p255; the otherwise excellent history of the parish, M. Farrer and others: *Faithful Cross* (Cromer Street Publications, 1999) does not mention the window.

St. Pancras, St. James, Hampstead Road
There is a design interleaved in Travers' own notebook for this work, which was an open wooden parclose screen; it appears to have been executed in the early 1920s, although there was no faculty, and in any event the church has now been demolished.

No drawings in RIBA for this church.

St. Pancras, St. Pancras Old Church, Pancras Road
Travers carried out two phases of work in this remarkable survival: it is probably the oldest church site in London. In 1925 he designed a tabernacle surround which has a trompe l'oeil effect, appearing to be a concave box; this is in the tower, and after a desecration was repaired and is now used as the shrine of Our Lady of Walsingham (there are no extant designs for this); he may also have removed the galleries, which was work done at that time. In 1947–8 he carried out repair work after the War, which involved

rearrangement of the sanctuary, which has since been again rearranged, a plaster tympanum with dove effect, and a fine bas-relief of Our Lady, which may have been designed for St. Mary Northolt and used to have a sunburst backing. There is a similar image in the Priory of St. Michael, Covent Garden, Westminster (q.v.). A rood loft and pulpit were not installed.

Drawings in RIBA for survey, and repairs and furnishings, including tympanum, pulpit and rood loft, 1947–8.

See also: Betjeman, p278.

West Hampstead, St. James, West End Lane
This church at one time had a Travers altar and reredos, which came from elsewhere and was presented by Evelyn Hayden Green in memory of Mary Pyle -Bridges (*see also* Walsingham, Norfolk). The altar was removed some years ago to the crypt.

No drawings in RIBA for this church.

CITY

Mercers' Hall Chapel, Ironmonger Lane
A war memorial window was designed by Travers for this chapel, but never carried out, despite the design being used widely for publicity purposes. A window by another was installed in 1923, and the Hall was in any event destroyed in the war.

Drawing in RIBA for war memorial window, 1920; a design was also exhibited at the RA, 1927.

See also: Jean Imray: *The Mercers' Hall* (London Topographical Society, 1991), and Journal of the RIBA, 12th December 1931.

SS. Augustine and Faith, Watling Street or Old Change
Travers restored the existing towering C17 reredos at this church and supplied six candlesticks and a crucifix for the new altar in about 1937. The reredos is described after restoration as being ' a rich composition of blue and gold' (Mee). However, the work had a very short life as the church was almost completely destroyed in 1941, and is now used as the Choir School for St. Paul's Cathedral. A faculty was granted in 1939 for further work designed by Travers, including the repair of the floor, the re-erection of a gallery at the west end, the replacement of the organ and pulpit and moving pews; a plan to replace the altar itself was withdrawn, but in any event it seems unlikely that any of this work was carried out, as the War broke out very shortly thereafter.

Drawings in RIBA for decoration of reredos, and for altar and ornaments, 1937–9, and for further restoration, 1939.

See also: Mee, *London*, p331; RIBA Catalogue says that the crucifix was saved and is in St. Paul's, but there is now no record of it there.

St. Edmund the King, Lombard Street
Travers' design for a memorial window was not accepted and a design by another was commissioned. However he later designed a tablet in memory of Revd G.A. Studdert-Kennedy ('Woodbine Willie'), a former vicar, and this was executed and remains in place near the pulpit on the north wall. It is a characteristic well-lettered tablet to a much-loved priest.

Drawings in RIBA for memorial window, 1922, and tablet, 1931. The window was exhibited at the RA, 1926.

See also: T.P. Stevens: *Father Adderley* (T. Werner Laurie Ltd., 1943), p69.

St. Magnus the Martyr, Lower Thames Street
Travers' work in this church is well known and discussed in detail in Chapter 4. Travers restored and adapted the existing furnishings, mostly in 1924–5, reconstructing the reredos with crucifixion group above, and added benches in Bavarian Rococo, a statue of St. Magnus, and communion rails. He reconstructed the chapels of Our Lady and of Christ the King, using doorcases, and designed many fitments for the worship of this famous Anglican Papalist stronghold. In 1931 he added a shrine of Our Lady of Walsingham and in 1935–6 supervised building work in the crypt. The church has survived bombing and fire and the work remains as a monument to Travers' powers; all has been well maintained.

Drawings in RIBA for restoration 1924–8 and for further work to crypt in 1935.

See also: Anson, p323, Betjeman, p263, Clarke, p30, Pevsner: *London 1:City of London*, pp231–3, T.S. Eliot: *The Waste Land* ('inexplicable splendour of Ionian white and gold'), but as that was first published in 1922 it pre-dates Travers' work.

St. Mary Aldermary, Queen Victoria Street
Laurence Lee carried out stained glass in this church, especially a fine east window of crucifixion, to designs of Travers. This remains in place.

No drawings by Travers in RIBA.

See also: Clarke, p37, Pevsner: *London 1: City of London*, pp240–2.

St. Michael Paternoster Royal, College Hill
It seems unlikely that a tablet designed for this church, possibly intended as a Webster Memorial, was ever carried out, as there is no faculty: the church was in any event gutted in the war, and many of the contents were destroyed, and there is now no such tablet.

Drawing in RIBA for tablet containing list of rectors, 1935.

Temple Church
Travers designed a gilded wooden altar cross for the Temple Church after its bombing, at a time when it was hoped that it could be used temporarily. A number of people gave gifts for that purpose: Travers' cross was given by Lord Finlay, a Master of the Bench of the Inner Temple, and son of the former Lord Chancellor. Its whereabouts now are not clear.

Drawing in RIBA for altar cross, 1944.

CROYDON
Purley, St. James, Riddlesdown, off Downs Court Road
Note: In RIBA Catalogue there are separate entries under St. James, Riddlesdown and St. James, Coulsdon, but they are in fact the same church, which was only known as St. James, Riddlesdown, after it became a parish church in 1925.

There is a great deal of Travers work in this church, discussed in Chapters 3 and 5. There are early windows in the aisles, two in the south aisle dated 1916 and one in the north dated 1917. There are two other small undated windows in the north porch. In the lady chapel, from the 1930s, is a 'Tyneham' window with butterflies in memory of Edward Thomas Brown, 1852–1931, and an aumbry and lamp bracket. From the postwar period, the east window is of Christ with chalice and paten with smaller pictures of the Resurrection story along the foot. In addition, Travers designed an English altar of which the cross and candlesticks are in situ together with an Art Deco sanctuary lamp in silver. The north aisle window and the two north porch windows were damaged by vandals in 2001, but will be repaired.

Drawings in RIBA for windows, 1915–6, and for window, reredos and rood, 1946–7.

See also: Richardson, pp120–5

Purley, St. Mark, Church Road, Woodcote Village
In the south aisle, dated 1928, are two Travers windows. The first, in memory of Fanny Kathleen Broadbridge, wife of a former Lord Mayor of London and banker, depicts St. Christopher. This was used some years ago to illustrate the Bank of England's Christmas card. The second, in memory of Thomas James Hicks and his wife, shows Jesus blessing people of many nations. Further along the same aisle is a third Travers window, dated 1931, to William Webb, showing the Risen Christ and St. Peter by the Sea of Galilee.

Drawings in RIBA for windows, 1928 and 1931.

Shirley, St. John the Evangelist, Shirley Village
This scheme for a chapel was not carried out.

Drawing in RIBA for war memorial chapel, 1945.

Thornton Heath, St. Jude, Thornton Road
This design was of the Good Shepherd, similar to that used in Holy Cross, St. Pancras, but this window was not commissioned.

Drawing in RIBA for memorial window, 1931.

Upper Norwood, St. John the Evangelist, Sylvan Road
Travers carried out more work for this church than the preserved designs would indicate. He executed a statue of Our Lady, a blue frontal for the lady chapel altar, a window showing Our Lord, Our Lady, and St. John the Evangelist at the east end of the north aisle, and a chapel which originally had a half relief of St. George above a crucifix on a whitewashed background. The altar has a red frontal. However, the whitewash was subsequently removed, the crucifix moved up, and the figure of St. George moved to the side of the chapel. There is a memorial plaque by Travers in this chapel.

Drawings in RIBA for image, 1935, and window, 1947.

See also: Betjeman, p281.

EALING

Acton, St. Peter, Southfield Road, Acton Green
Travers made the elaborate backing for the Walsingham shrine in the north aisle; this is blue with stars on it, and much later also designed the high altar (now a striking salmon pink) and the candlesticks and crucifix. There was a reredos behind this, which has since been removed. Travers also designed a rather plain wooden organ gallery at the west end. The statue of the Sacred Heart in the south aisle chapel is almost certainly by him, although the elaborate niche design of 1925 was not carried out.

Drawings in RIBA for niche decoration in chapel, 1925, and for (i) reredos for shrine of Our Lady of Walsingham, (ii) high altar, and (iii) organ gallery, 1942.

Acton, St. Saviour, Old Oak Road
This church for the deaf was designed in c1925 by Maufe. Travers provided 7 small well-lettered yellow ochre windows in the lady chapel in memory of Bishop Pereira, who was much concerned with work among the deaf;

these remain in place. The star shaped light fittings and the reredos strongly resemble Travers' work, but in fact are original (save for the addition of the large crucifix) and are by Maufe himself.

Drawing in RIBA for windows, 1927.

See also: *Architectural Review* 1925, p226.

Ealing, Christ the Saviour (formerly Christ Church), New Broadway
In 1935 a faculty was granted for this church for a new oak altar by Travers with Agnus Dei decoration, in memory of Revd L.T. King, vicar 1895–1929, together with alterations to the step levels and repaving; the requiem frontal was also made, but is no longer there. The chancel loft was not made. Travers also designed for this church a triptych with two side panels, which showed Christ extending his blessing in the centre with the signs of the four evangelists around. This was crossed out of the faculty application, as the funds were not available then, but appeared later. The triptych has since been removed and the original Victorian reredos restored. The altar and candlesticks remain.

Drawings in RIBA for frontals, 1935–8, loft, 1935, and high altar, undated.

Greenford, Holy Cross [old church], Oldfield Lane South
In 1939 a new church by Richardson was built in Greenford but the old village church was retained alongside as a lady chapel. The altar has a reredos with the Ten Commandments, like a City Church, with a cross of Christ the King in front of it, and two typical wooden candlesticks.

Drawings in RIBA for reredos and altar ornaments, 1939, and font cover, 1943.

See also: Pevsner: *London 3: North West*, plate 8, which illustrates the work well.

Northolt, St. Mary, Northolt Green
Travers carried out a great deal of work in this small church in what was originally the country. Unfortunately, it has not been sympathetically treated in recent years, and the chapel of St. Stephen has in effect been dismantled. There remain a statue of St. Stephen, a hatchment to Laud, a crucifix, an unusual three-cornered stand, and what was originally a reredos but is now on the south wall; this consists of the Magnificat around an old painting. A new base was made for the mediaeval font, and the cover remade from an early C17 cover. It would appear that the 1947 work (see below) was not done, and in particular that the bas-relief of Our Lady may have been used in Old St. Pancras. Travers also produced preliminary plans for a daughter church of St. Joseph, but it is not clear whether any of his ideas were used in the succession of temporary buildings used with that dedication prior to the establishment of the new church in 1969.

Drawings in RIBA for restoration of font, and seating, 1942, restoration of altar of St. Stephen, 1943, bas-relief of Our Lady, furnishing of sanctuary, and new east window, 1947.

See also: Betjeman, p290, and Pevsner: *London 3: North West*, p187.

Norwood (Hayes), St. Mary, Tentelow Lane
This work was never carried out, despite the note to that effect in RIBA Catalogue; the church is near Cranford, one of Travers' best known schemes.

Drawings in RIBA for comprehensive internal refurnishing, including altar, reredos, communion rails, rood beam, and oak parclose screen, 1941.

GREENWICH
Plumstead, St. Nicholas, St. Nicholas Road
Travers designed a fine Christ in Majesty east window for this church, with on either side lights of St. Michael and St. Nicholas, with ship. It also contains two lights depicting respectively St. George, and St. Joan of Arc. All of these remain, despite extensive bomb damage to the church. A green altar frontal in the church may be by Travers.

No drawings in RIBA Catalogue for this church, but design for war memorial east window was exhibited at RA, 1920, and there are designs in RIBA Photographic Library.

See also: Armitage, p69, Pevsner: *London 2: South*, p281.

HACKNEY
Clapton, St. Thomas, Clapton Common
Travers' designs for high altar, candlesticks, and rood were adopted and installed. The tabernacle and vast throne behind shown on the drawings were never made. The RIBA Catalogue is in error in saying that this church was destroyed in the war: the body of it was damaged, but the east end and the Travers work remain.

Drawings in RIBA for hanging rood, 1920, and tabernacle and throne, 1923.

See also: Pevsner: *London 4: North*, p484.

Dalston, St. Bartholomew, Dalston Lane
A faculty was granted in 1931 for two windows designed by Travers in memory of Revd J.S. Bruhl, one showing St. Bartholomew and one the lion of St. Mark, after an earlier application for stained glass for part only of a window, as designed by another, was refused. The church was closed in 1945, the fittings disposed of in 1953, and it was derelict for many years before being turned into housing. Neither of Travers' windows was of great quality.

Drawing in RIBA for glass, undated, but dated 1931 on faculty.

Haggerston, St. Columba, Kingsland Road (now Christ Apostolic Church (Bethel))
A small hanging rood for the mortuary chapel was designed by Travers in about 1911 and installed, but after this splendid Brooks church was made redundant, the rood was restored and in due course rehung in St. Gabriel, Pimlico (q.v.). Travers also possibly made for this church the delicate wrought iron screen in the chapel, and also a confessional. The church is now used by Pentecostalists.

Drawing in RIBA for rood for mortuary chapel, undated but pre-First War.

Hoxton, Holy Trinity, Shepherdess Walk
In this church the reredos designed by Travers remains, and there is also a confessional with tall Corinthian pilasters, previously in St. Mary, Bourne Street. The reredos is a rood within a frame and cannot be said to be one of his better pieces. There is a roundel above the reredos, and a further roundel above the chancel arch; and on the west (organ) gallery are a series of hatchments, one in memory of Father Kenrick, editor of the well-known English Missal.

Drawings in RIBA for reredos, 1942, and hatchment, 1943.

See also: Pevsner: *London 4: North*, p513 (which wrongly attributes the reredos to another).

Hoxton, St. Mary, Britannia Walk
Travers designed both window and tablet in memory of Nicholas Jessop Devereux,

vicar 1881–1912, probably shortly after his death. These were installed, but the church was bombed in the War and later demolished.

No drawings in RIBA for this church, but photographs of window and tablet.

See also: Mee: London, p737.

Hoxton, St. Saviour, Hyde Road
This bastion of Anglican Papalism, along with many others, in effect opted out of the faculty system and there are no documents at all in relation to Travers' work there in the Diocesan Records. Travers' work is discussed in detail in Chapter 4: between 1919 and 1926 he designed a sarcophagus shaped altar, reredos with rood figures, one-dimensional candlesticks, and other fitments. The church was bombed in 1940 and subsequently demolished; all the Travers fittings were lost. Fortunately, photographs of the interior remain; there is probably no more evocative name for Anglo-Catholics of a certain generation than that of this church.

No drawings in RIBA for this church, but design for altar and reredos exhibited at RA, 1927.

HAMMERSMITH & FULHAM
Fulham, All Saints, Putney Bridge Approach
Although there are a number of designs by Travers for this church (see below), relatively little was actually done by him. The Morison tablet is on the south wall, and on the west wall is the First World War memorial triptych, to which were added later the names of those who died in the last War. The lady chapel was executed by another and none of the 1938 work was carried out. A faculty was granted in 1943 for Travers' design for the 1942 work, which was in memory of two members of the choir who had been killed in the War, but the work was not carried out and a revised scheme by Caroe and Partners was put into effect for the clergy seats in 1951. The high altar was extended later. The candlesticks on it are similar to Travers' designs, but are by Laurence King for Faithcraft, 1949.

Drawings in RIBA as follows: memorial tablet 1927, altar in lady chapel and memorial triptych, 1928, enlargement of high altar and work to chancel screen, 1938, and clergy seats, 1942.

Parsons Green, St. Dionis
This church was the subject of a comprehensive scheme of improvement in English style by Travers, but unfortunately the reredos in characteristic terracotta and with crucifix attached has been moved and now hangs on the south chancel wall; the English altar has in effect been dismantled. The memorial to Father Sinclair and 2 other tablets remain, and there is an unusual font cover of the former church of St. Dionis in the City. The banner also remains, as does the rood loft.

Drawings in RIBA for new altar, reredos, and communion rails, 1932, and for hatchment, 1938, also for alterations to screen, font cover, banner, and memorials, undated.

See also: Anson, p345 (where he incorrectly says this was a Baroque altar), Clarke, p60, Pevsner: *London 3: North West*, p232.

HARROW
Harrow, Quainton Hall School, Hindes Road
A war memorial shrine by Travers is still in place and well used. The figure of Our Lady of Walsingham and its backing on top of the shrine appear to have been repainted.

There is also in the school chapel a plaque to St. Francis and the high altar with reversible frontal and large crucifix, both of which look like Travers' work, but may have been carried out by a follower.

Drawing in RIBA for war memorial shrine, 1945.

Harrow, St. Alban, Church Drive, North Harrow
Travers did not win the competition for this new building and the church was built in 1936 to the plans of A.W. Kenyon, resulting in a distinguished piece of work.

Drawing in RIBA for church, c1936; competition entry.

Harrow, St. George, Pinner View, Headstone.
This church now has a wealth of Travers furnishings. The east window of the Te Deum is one of his larger pieces and shows fine use of colour, but with large areas of clear glass around. The pulpit, dated 1941, is in quasi-Jacobean style with tester; a rather refined piece. The reredos, and matching screens to the south choir aisle bay are by John Crawford, Travers' assistant. They are dated 1949, after Travers' death, although Crawford was instructed before the death as Travers was too busy. Recently the church has acquired the reredos from St. Stephen, Battersea (q.v.) in characteristic red 'pleated' wood, but which has lost its crucifix; this reredos is now in the lady chapel. The font cover from that church, with dove beneath, is to be repainted for this church. In addition, the church has acquired the reredos from St. James, Watford (q.v.); that proved unusable as it was, as the main part of it was in a linoleum-type material and had cracked. However the tablet which held the cross in Watford is now beneath the crucifix here, and parts of the decoration from the reredos are behind the Crawford reredos here, with other parts on the west wall.

Drawing in RIBA for pulpit, 1940; design for east window exhibited at RA, 1938.

See also: Armitage, p69, Mee: *Middlesex*, p98, Pevsner: *London 3: North West*, p260.

Harrow, St. John the Baptist, Sheepcote Road, Greenhill
Travers completed the east end of this church, including a tympanum over the chancel arch, but the tower got no further than the base before the outbreak of the war. However the note in RIBA Catalogue that most of the furnishings have been removed is misleading. Although the fine light screen was taken down in about 1972 and the riddel posts to the high altar have also disappeared, there remain a fine screen to the north chapel, an organ screen, the Odell tablet, the war memorial tablet, and a St. Michael window in the north wall of the chapel. The tympanum is in good condition.

Drawings in RIBA for completion of east end, 1937, altar, 1938, tablet, 1941, screen font cover and text boards, 1944, war memorial tablet, 1947, chapel of St. Michael and glass, undated.

See also: Mee, *Middlesex*, p98, Pevsner: *London 3: North West*, p260.

HILLINGDON
Cranford, St. Dunstan, Cranford Park
Travers considered his transformation of the interior of this small brick church with its many monuments as his best work. It is interesting not only in that it was commissioned by Father Maurice Child, an important figure in the Anglo-Catholic world of the time, but also because by the time it was carried out the Back to Baroque style was well past its zenith. There are many striking features of the furnishings, especially the crowned statue of Our Lady with extremely tall canopy, and the tabernacle in the reredos. There are screens and many smaller features such as the hymnboards. Travers also

added the vestries, which have always leaked; his last work was a small scroll to an airman killed in the war. The work is discussed further and at length in Chapter 6.

Drawings in RIBA for processional cross, 1935, reredos and tabernacle, 1936, chancel screen, 1938, vestry alterations and pulpit, 1939, statue of Our Lady, Royal Arms and tabor, 1941, and tablets, 1944 and 1945.

See also: Betjeman p288 (whose dating is wrong), Pevsner: *London 3: North West*, p311 (an improvement on the first edition of *Middlesex*, which ignored all the Travers work completely), and Victoria County History of Middlesex, Vol III, 1962, p185.

HOUNSLOW
Bedford Park, St. Michael & All Angels, Bath Road
This well known Norman Shaw church was just around the corner from Travers' house at the time he was commissioned to design the altar and reredos in the Chapel of All Souls at the east end of the south aisle. In the south wall of the chapel is a fine window of 1915, dated and signed, showing St. George slaying the dragon over London, with recognizable buildings including St. Paul's Cathedral and a local house, and a memorial tablet to Robert Haynes Barrow, priest, with dedication inside and writing outside as well; the inner doorcase to the south door is also by Travers. The east window is not by Travers (although it may have been designed by him) but is c1952 by Lawrence Lee. The processional cross is also attributed to Travers.

Drawings in RIBA for altar and reredos for chapel, 1914.

See also: Pevsner: *London 3: North West*, p408, Stamp and Amery, p158.

Cranford, Holy Angels, Bath Road
This was a temporary church in a Rodney Hut, which dated from 1942 and was burned out in about 1965. Travers designed a rather angular reredos, which was later modified by having the cherubs removed from the side of the altar; the line was also simplified. It was a great contrast to his work in the other Cranford church, St. Dunstan (q.v.).

Drawing in RIBA for tabernacle, reredos, and pulpit, 1943.

See also: Victoria County History of Middlesex, Vol III, 1962, p 186.

Osterley (Isleworth), St. Francis, Great West Road
The stone statue of Our Lady in this rather bare church by Shearman is backed by a terracotta canopy with sun device and spire above, unmistakably by Travers.

Drawing in RIBA for canopy to image above lady chapel, 1944.

ISLINGTON
Barnsbury, St. Clement, off Bride Street
The Travers lady chapel window here depicted Our Lady with the Child and at her feet two cherubs, one playing the lute and the other the pipes. In the side lights were St. Clement, holding the church, and two others. The whole was in oblong panels with little left clear. The church is now used for housing, and the window was stolen after redundancy but before conversion. The altar was also by Travers.

Drawing in RIBA for glass and furnishing of lady chapel, undated but pre–1917; window also exhibited at RA, 1915.

Clerkenwell, Holy Redeemer, Exmouth Market
This church has a copy of Travers' stations of the cross from St. Augustine, South

Kensington by his assistant John Crawford, dated c1935, and also a reredos to the shrine of Sacred Heart, which was adapted by Travers himself, in particular by adding sections at the sides.

No drawings for this church in RIBA.

Islington, Paget Memorial Mission, Randell's Road
In this extraordinary survival of an Edwardian mission chapel in a derelict area is much arcaded panelling with cartouches inscribed V[iolet] P[aget] which Pevsner: *London 4: North*, p663, says are 'probably designed by Travers, pupil of [Beresford] Pite'. These certainly look like Travers' work and are probably his first recorded piece.

No drawings for this in RIBA.

Pentonville, St. Silas, Penton Street
This church has a chapel of Our Lady of Walsingham, which looks very like the work of Travers and is sometimes attributed to him. In fact however this shrine was originally designed for a large statue of Our Lady, and was part of a comprehensive scheme for refurnishing of the church with new high altar and communion rails and shrine of Sacred Heart, of which only this was executed. It was dated 1949, shortly after Travers' death, and was designed by his pupil Francis Stephens in the Travers style; the faculty was granted in 1950.

No drawings in RIBA for this church.

KENSINGTON & CHELSEA
Chelsea, Chelsea Methodist Church, Kings Road
This was an unusual commission for Travers; apart from Stand Unitarian Church, near Manchester (q.v.), it represents his only involvement with Nonconformity. The work designed was in wood, with a central pulpit over the holy table. It appears unlikely that it was ever carried out, and in any event the church is now in smaller accommodation on the same site.

Drawing in RIBA for pulpit, holy table, communion benches, lectern and hymnboards, 1948.

Holland Park, Priory of St. Paul, 8, Holland Park
The former London priory of the Community of the Resurrection at 39, Pont Street, was damaged in the blitz. On 8th September 1944 the new priory at Holland Park was opened and it was said that 'Mr. Martin Travers carried out the [internal] work with his usual distinction.' On 12th January 1945 Travers was asked to adapt the existing statue of Our Lady for the chapel and later that year to do other work. There was a high altar with baldachino and crucifix on the reredos, and a statue of Our Lady on the wall, probably the one which was modified. Another altar had a bas-relief of Our Lady similar to that in Old St. Pancras, and a crucifix; these are now in the Priory of St. Michael, Covent Garden, Westminster (q.v.). The statue of Our Lady is in St. Francis House, Hemingford Grey, Cambridgeshire (q.v.).

Drawings in RIBA for arrangement of chapel, 1944, and for image of Our Lady and memorial, 1945.

See also: P.F. Anson, *Call of the Cloister*, (SPCK 1964), p133.

Notting Dale, St. Clement, Sirdar Road
Travers designed a First World War memorial window for this church, and this is at the west end of the north aisle. The two light window shows Our Lord and a kneel-

ing soldier, as at Broadstone, Dorset and other places. It is possible that there were statues by Travers in this church at one time, but none now remain.

No drawings in RIBA for this church.

Notting Hill, All Saints, Talbot Road
This church has work designed for it and also work designed for St. Columb, Notting Hill (q.v.). The lady chapel designed by Travers was bombed out in the war. The reredos from the Sacred Heart chapel is now on the north transept wall; the statue is by Dupont of Bruges. There is a picture of it in its original position in *Survey of London*, Volume 37 (North Kensington). In the south transept is the war memorial altar and reredos of St. George, which was originally in St. Columb, with typical Travers pleated designs.

Drawings in RIBA for reredoses in Lady Chapel and chapel of Sacred Heart, 1937, and for screen, 1938.

See also: Betjeman, p274, Clarke, p104, Howell & Sutton, pp73–4, Pevsner: *London 3: North West*, p454.

Notting Hill, St. Columb, Lancaster Road (now Serbian Church of St. Sava)
Travers designed a three light window for the baptistery, the centre light of which depicted Our Lady and the Holy Child on a crescent moon, rather like his window at All Saints, Norwich (q.v.). The baptistery has recently been pulled down and the fate of the windows is not known. The gravestone was to Father George Lovelace and was carried out but its location is uncertain; the altar is now in All Saints, Notting Hill.

Drawings in RIBA for windows, c1915, gravestone, 1928, and altar, 1931. A cartoon for the central baptistery window was exhibited at the RA, 1922.

See also: Clarke, p112, Pevsner: *London 3: North West*, p467.

South Kensington, St. Augustine, Queen's Gate
This work is discussed at length in Chapter 4. Travers completely refurnished the interior of Butterfield's church, and it is now dominated by the enormous reredos, a variation of a design originally proposed for Holy Trinity, Reading. In addition, Travers modified the pulpit and designed the internal memorial to the departed, frontal, pulpit, rails, tester, and stations of the cross, then the backing for a shrine, and the side altar; the east window was designed by him and executed after his death. The reredos excites conflicting emotions, but some regard it as Travers' greatest monument.

Drawings in RIBA for kneeling desk below war memorial, 1925, reredos and rood, reversible frontal, and communion rails, 1928, tester, 1929, and reredos in the Lady Chapel, 1938.

See also: Anson, pp321–2, Betjeman, p272, Clarke, p109, R. Gradidge: *Back to Baroque* (Twentieth Century Society, 1992), Howell & Sutton, p79, Pevsner: *London 3: North West*, p456, Stamp & Amery p116, E & W. Young: *London's Churches* (Grafton Books, 1986), p73.

South Kensington, St. Jude, Courtfield Gardens
Travers superintended the post-war restoration of this church, which included whitewashing the polychromatic interior, and he also lengthened the altar, inserted a new section at the foot of the reredos and provided silver gilded wooden altar ornaments. The altar hangings have since been removed. He also transferred figures from another window to replace the destroyed east window.

Drawings in RIBA for enlargement of high altar with new ornaments and hangings, 1947.

See also: Pevsner: *London 3: North West*, p458; *Survey of London*, Vol 42, p375.

LAMBETH
Clapham, Holy Spirit, Narbonne Avenue
This church has a triptych dated c1933 with a statue of the Holy Child, which is now folded away in the sacristy out of use. It appears that it also had lady chapel candlesticks by Travers, but these have disappeared. Travers is said to have embellished the rood (1936) and there is a fine banner by him (1939). There is a pulpit with an elaborate bracket above it, which looks as if Travers worked on it: all these improvements were carried out during the incumbency of Father J.H. Humphries (1931–9), formerly of St. Andrew Battersea (q.v.).

No drawings in RIBA for this church.

Kennington, St. Agnes, Kennington Park
This famous church was demolished after the Second World War and a small replacement provided. The new church has a crucifix, two candlesticks and a statue of Our Lady by Travers, all from the old church, in it. In the old church, Travers provided in addition a wooden retable, a prayer desk in front of the rood, and curious angel stencilling to the roof, as well as carrying out work to the chancel levels and so on. In 1926 he had to appear before the Chancellor with the parish priest in order to obtain for the church a faculty for two further altars, to St. George and St. Joan of Arc, which were installed in front of the screen. The rood was not by Travers, but was cleaned by him; it is now in St. Peter, Streatham (q.v.).

Drawings in RIBA for rearrangement of chancel levels, alterations to the high altar, rearrangement of organ, and decoration of chancel roof, 1925.

Kennington, St. Philip's Church Hall, Reedworth Street
Travers designed a hall for this church: it is not clear whether his design was ever used, but in event the church and hall have now been demolished.

No drawings in RIBA for this building.

Streatham, St. Peter, Leigham Court Road
The large hanging rood by Temple Moore from St. Agnes Kennington is now in this church; this has wrongly been attributed to Travers, but his notebook of the time shows clearly that he only cleaned it and did not alter it.

No drawings in RIBA for this church.

Streatham Vale, Holy Redeemer, Churchmore Road
The entire church was built by Travers and Grant in a restrained style, and is discussed at length in Chapter 9. Travers designed all the interior furniture: since it was a memorial to the Evangelical Clapham sect the décor is restrained, and included the Ten Commandments on either side of the ogee shaped reredos. The church itself is in modified C15 style of stock brick.

Drawings in RIBA for entire church, 1930–1, by Travers and Grant. Design showing interior looking east was exhibited at the RA, 1933.

See also: Anson, p323, Clarke, p272, Pevsner: *London 2: South*, p389, Incorporated Church Building Society *New Churches Illustrated*, 1937, p106, and Richardson, pp156–163.

Vauxhall, Clarence Club
Travers is said to have designed an altar and ornaments for the Clarence Club, but no

further details have been found of the club or its fate, save that it no longer exists. It was probably connected to St. Peter, Vauxhall.

No drawings in RIBA.

LEWISHAM

Catford, St. Andrew, Sandhurst Road

This church has a large collection of Travers glass, which is of particular interest in that it shows his development over the years. The east window shows Christ in Majesty with many other saints around, and the lady chapel windows King David, Our Lady and St. Teresa. There are other windows of the Infant Christ, St. Michael, Simeon, and St. Ambrose.

Drawings in RIBA for war memorial east window, 1920, lady chapel window, 1922, and window in south aisle and clerestory windows of chancel, 1935; the east window was exhibited at the RA, 1921.

See also: Armitage, p69, Betjeman, p273, Clarke, p248, Cowen, p141, Mee: *London*, p826 (where he refers to 'gloriously coloured glass of outstanding beauty') and Pevsner: *London 2: South*, p413.

Catford, St. Lawrence, Catford Road

This church was demolished in c1970 and a new church was built. Revd F. Raynes, a former curate, took the Travers reredos to St. Paul, Woodford Bridge (q.v.). The reredos was a plain board with gilded edge and rood figures, well lettered, in memory of two former parishioners named Cossins.

Drawings in RIBA for lady chapel reredos, 1932.

Lewisham, St. Mary, Lewisham High Street

Although the designs preserved were only for a prayer desk, in fact in about 1934 Travers designed a complete lady chapel for this church, including a reredos with a Raphael Madonna against a typical golden pleated wood background, with gilded wood cross and candlesticks. The prayer desks were at one time in front of the altar. Unfortunately, in a reordering in 1996 the reredos was fixed to the ceiling of the north transept, where it remains. The prayer desks are still in the church and the altar furnishings are in the vestry.

Drawing in RIBA for prayer desk, undated.

MERTON

Mitcham, SS. Peter & Paul, Church Road

This church has a war memorial shrine of St. George and the dragon, as seen in many other places, with tablet to Douglas Drewett.

Drawing in RIBA for war memorial, c1920; design also exhibited at RA, 1928.

Wimbledon, St. John the Baptist, Spencer Hill

This church has a very fine altar and screen with two doors in it and St. John the Baptist above, erected as a memorial to a parishioner who was killed in the First World War; the predominant colour is turquoise/green.

Drawing in RIBA for altar, reredos and screen in north aisle, 1923.

NEWHAM

East Ham, St. Bartholomew, Barking Road

A faculty was granted in 1936 for Travers' design for a partition screen in wood, and it may be assumed that it was put in, but the church was burned out by incendiary bombs in the War and all the fittings were lost. It was rebuilt, but later demolished and there is a modern replacement. It has been said that there was a design for a font cover here, but the drawing appears to have been for St. Mary Magdalene, East Ham (q.v.).

Drawing in RIBA for partition screens at west end of nave, 1935.

East Ham, St. Mary Magdalene, High Street South
The font cover in this mediaeval church is certainly not by Travers and there is no bell bracket. No work was done for this church, and any such work as was done for St. Bartholomew, East Ham (q.v.) was lost in the War.

Drawing in RIBA for font cover and bell bracket, 1937.

REDBRIDGE
Woodford Bridge, St. Paul, The Green
This church had the reredos from St.Lawrence, Catford (q.v.), which was somewhat incongruously hung on the west wall of the church, out of keeping with the remainder of the furnishings. In early 2002 the church was reordered and the reredos removed and auctioned. Despite the best efforts of one of the authors, it went to a dealer for sale for domestic use.

No drawings for this church in RIBA.

RICHMOND
Twickenham, St. Mary, Church Street
A faculty was granted for vestry alterations by Travers, but in fact the work was not done at that time, and was carried out much later to a different design.

Drawing in RIBA for vestry alterations, 1946.

SOUTHWARK
Newington, St. Matthew, New Kent Road
Travers completely remodelled the interior of this previously rather dull church; his work included encasing the arcade columns, adding clerestory windows, and closing off the apse with a new reredos, the whole described in RIBA Catalogue as 'typically resourceful and theatrical.' The new reredos depicted the Holy Spirit sending out tongues of fire to the Christus Rex figure. The work is described in detail in Chapter 5; Travers reused many of the existing furnishings in order to save money, such as using the old screen to make new parclose screens. The church has recently been demolished; the reredos has been taken to St. Agatha, Landport, Portsmouth (q.v.) for further use. In 1930 a hall was built to Travers' design.

Drawings in RIBA for survey, 1926, lowering aisle roof, casing iron columns, screens and new altar, 1927, frontal and tablet, 1935, and rood, 1937.

See also: Clarke, p252 and Pevsner: *London 2: South*, p576.

Nunhead, St. Antholin (now St. Anthony), Nunhead Lane
Travers' work in this church was quite extensive, but lasted in that form for only a short time as the church was bombed and gutted in 1940. He not only restored the reredos, but also pulled it forward, and installed new communion rails, flanking walls, alteration to steps, and the removal of an iron chancel screen. Following the gutting, the church was completely rebuilt and Laurence King again restored the reredos. The crucifix is by Travers and the outside calvary also remains in position, albeit dilapidated: the

figure has disappeared from it. At the time of writing, it is said that the reredos is yet again to be restored and altered to be placed in another new building.

Drawings in RIBA for restoration of reredos, 1937, for screens etc., 1938, and outside calvary, 1939.

See also: Pevsner: *London 2: South*, p613.

Nunhead, Cheltenham College Mission (now Westminster House Club), Nunhead Grove
Although the drawings which survive simply relate to the chapel, in fact Travers designed an entire complex for the Cheltenham College Mission, behind two semi-detached houses at 29–31 Nunhead Grove which have since been demolished. The complex included a gymnasium/stage, and games room, as well as a chapel and scout accommodation. In 1941 the College pulled out of south east London, and in 1950 it was taken over by Westminster School. The chapel part of the building is no longer there, but the gymnasium, backing on to Banstead Street, remains, although the windows have been bricked up.

Drawing in RIBA for chapel interior, 1930.

See also: C.H. Pigg (Ed): *Cheltenham College Register 1919–51* (Cheltenham College, 1953); T.S. Pearce: *Then and Now* (The Cheltonian Society, 1991).

Southwark, All Hallows, Pepper Street
This work, to the altar and reredos, was never taken forward, and the church was in any event bombed out.

No drawings in RIBA for this church, but design for altar and reredos exhibited at RA, 1935.

Southwark, Cathedral of St. Mary Overie
It has been said that it was only because of an 'administrative mistake' that this glass was not commissioned; Travers did much other work in the diocese but not in the Cathedral, which has glass by both Comper and Lawrence Lee.

Drawing in RIBA for glass for lady chapel, 1916.

Southwark, Holy Trinity, Trinity Church Square
Travers transformed the interior of this church with a window in grey, yellow and gold glass to represent the Trinity, other windows, and a high altar with riddel arrangements. Above was an octagonal canopy. The work is discussed in detail in Chapter 5. In 1973 the church was gutted by fire and all the furnishings were lost, although the photographic evidence suggests that the glass had already been removed by that time. It is now a recording studio.

Drawing in RIBA for high altar etc., and also for vase, 1928.

See also: Betjeman, p279, Mee, *London*, p692, Pevsner, *London 2: South*, p575.

Walworth, St. John, Larcom Street
This church has behind the high altar the repainted reredos designed by Travers for the Good Shepherd, Borough Green, Kent (q.v.); in front of it are Comper altar furnishings.

No drawings in RIBA for this church or for this work.

Walworth, St. Peter, Liverpool Grove.
The side altar of this church was provided with a reredos showing St. Christopher and the Holy Child. The church was bombed and the work destroyed. The chapel was

rebuilt, c1953, in Travers' style but not copying the original. There is a cartouche of cherubs over the door to the chapel, which is particularly reminiscent of Travers, but is not original.

Drawings in RIBA for reredos, 1929.

SUTTON

Carshalton Beeches, Church of the Good Shepherd, Queen Mary Avenue.
This extraordinary Spanish mission style building, with constant damp problems, was built too cheaply. However, as Betjeman says 'the essential quality of the design should not be ignored.' The projected lady chapel and priest's house were never built, and the furnishings have been altered since its construction. The church has an enormous Italian rood above the altar, and originally had the combination of an English altar with baroque crucifix and six candlesticks. Travers also provided four windows, Our Lady and St. Nicholas in the main church and two small glasses for the Bishop and the Rector in the entrance. In 1967 there was a fire in the vestries, which led to considerable changes, especially to the sanctuary, and the loss of some of Travers' work. Subsequently the characteristic light fittings were removed on safety grounds. In 2000–1 a lady chapel was built as part of a large extension to the church, which has not affected the Travers design at all. After a period in which it had rather been neglected, the church is now well cared for again. This building is discussed in detail in Chapter 9.

Drawings in RIBA for complete church by Travers and Grant, 1928, and for painted glass, 1930.

See also: Anson, p323, Betjeman, p269, Pevsner: *London 2: South*, p646, Incorporated Church Building Society: *New Churches Illustrated* (1936), p94, Richardson, pp21–6, and A.E. Jones: *From Mediaeval Manor to London Suburb: an obituary for Carshalton* (author, 1976) on Father Corbould.

St. Helier, St. Peter, Middleton Road
The chapel of St. Francis in the church was never completed and no work was done here by Travers. One drawing is wrongly labelled as St. Andrew Morden instead of St. Peter Morden (sic) although they bear the same date, but that must be a slip of the pen as there has never been a St. Andrew, Morden, and in any event this church is just in Sutton.

Drawings in RIBA for furnishings and decorations in Chapel of St. Francis, 1939–41.

See also: Richardson, p138.

Sutton, St. Barnabas, St. Barnabas Road, Newtown
The Travers window in this church is in the south aisle, is of the Annunciation, and is in memory of Fanny Mary Smith deceased. It bears some resemblance to the window at Fordwich, Kent (q.v.): whitewashing was also carried out under the same faculty, and presumably under Travers' direction. In this case it has improved the interior appearance of the church.

Drawing in RIBA for window in chapel, 1934.

TOWER HAMLETS

Bethnal Green, St. James the Great, Bethnal Green Road
This work was a very fine scheme, but was not been carried out, and the church had a very simple high altar with curtain behind; in any event the building is now closed.

Drawings in RIBA for altar and reredos, 1924.

Bethnal Green, St. John, Cambridge Heath Road
Travers designed for this church the somewhat crude organ case with dove of the Holy Spirit, which is still in place. In addition, there is an aumbry topped by a Wren spire, similar to the cover at St. Dionis, Parson's Green, which is almost certainly either by Travers or one of his followers.

Drawing in RIBA for installing organ, 1948.

Bow Common, St. Paul, Burdett Road
Travers' design for the former church appears never to have been executed as it was overtaken by the war. The church was hit by a land mine in September 1940 and burned out in March 1941; a radical new church was constructed after the war.

Drawing in RIBA for high altar, reredos and altar cross, 1939–40.

Limehouse, St. John the Evangelist, Haley Street
A faculty was granted in 1938 for work to this church: Travers designed an extension to the high altar, a two sided frontal of oak, carved and coloured, a plain reredos with draped effect and large crucifix, and a canopy above rather like a pelmet cover. There was also a plaque to Revd C.H. Walters and Sister Mary Agatha SSM, and a scroll to Walters. The work had a short life as the church was bombed in 1941 and later demolished.

Drawing in RIBA for reredos and frontal, 1936.

Limehouse, St. Peter, Garford Street
Travers provided a crucifix and two candlesticks for this church, which were donated by then incumbent, Father C.C. Hordern, in memory of a parishioner killed in the Second World War. When the church closed in about 1968 they were returned to the donor, but are now in private hands.

No drawings in RIBA for this church.

Poplar, All Saints, East India Dock Road
The Travers churchyard cross remains in place, although now worn; there is a photograph of it in the RIBA photographic collection. Travers designed a striking reredos with Pieta design for the south aisle chapel, but it is not clear, despite extensive research, whether it was ever built; there was certainly no faculty. In any event the church was badly damaged in c1941 and rebuilt in c1956; there is no internal work by Travers to be seen.

Drawing in RIBA for war memorial chapel, and churchyard cross, 1919.

WALTHAM FOREST
Leyton, Emmanuel, Lea Bridge Road
This church remains in reasonably original state, although the copper from the roof has been removed, and behind the high altar now is a brightly coloured wall. However, there are two good windows, and the original wooden furnishings are still there; the outside is as built. There is virtually nothing baroque about the building at all, save for some stylised external decoration, and it was clearly built of stock bricks on the cheap. The adjoining vicarage in Hitcham Road is also by Travers: the original metal windows in it have been replaced.

Drawings in RIBA for complete church by Travers and Grant, 1933, and model was exhibited at RA, 1934.

See also: Anson, p323, Incorporated Church Building Society: *New Churches Illustrated*, pp42–3; also *Victoria County History:* Essex VI, 1973, pp222–3, where it is said that this was built with assistance from Masonic Lodges.

Walthamstow, St. Peter, Woodford New Road
In this church, the rather plain altar and a fine coloured tablet to Sir Thomas Courtenay Theydon Warner, 1857–1934, are by Travers. The frontal is no longer there. The planned alterations to the façade were never carried out, but it appears clear that Travers superintended the removal of the galleries and whitewashing in 1936–7.

Drawings in RIBA for oak communion table and frontal, 1935, altering the façade, 1939, and for memorial, undated.

See also: *Victoria County History:* Essex VI, 1973, p292.

WANDSWORTH
Balham, St. Mary, Balham High Road
This door in the south transept has above it an elaborate and well-lettered board in memory of J.J. Jones, and this remains.

Drawing in RIBA for doorcase with board above, 1933.

Battersea, Christ Church, Battersea Park Road
This church was built only in 1959, but on the closure of St. Stephen, Battersea (q.v.) the altar and rails by Travers were moved here, together with the crucifix from the high altar reredos, which is now in the north chapel, near a statue of St. Stephen which is in fact by Francis Stephens in the Travers style. There was also a sacrament house by Stephens.

No drawings in RIBA for this church: see St. Stephen, Battersea.

See also: Clarke, pp197–8, Pevsner: *London 2: South*, p667.

Battersea, General Hospital Chapel
It seems likely from a reference in Travers' own notebook that this simple reredos, showing the Virgin and Child and rather similar to Winforton, Herefordshire (q.v.) was in fact executed, probably before the First World War. The Hospital has been demolished.

Drawing in RIBA for reredos, undated.

Battersea, St. Andrew, Dashwood Road
Although the designs retained are only for the sanctuary, Travers in fact completely refurbished the whole interior of the church in 1928–30. The work is described in detail in Chapter 5, but involved a new reredos depicting the Resurrection, a new double-sided frontal for the high altar, the refashioning of a door frame to make a new reredos for a side altar, a new frontal for that, and a large sacrament house. The entire church and all the furnishings were destroyed by bombs in the War and never rebuilt.

Drawings in RIBA for high altar and reredos, 1927.

Battersea, St. Luke, Ramsden Road
This work was amongst Travers' most sumptuous of the period. The fine high altar communion rails are complemented by the extensive work in the lady chapel, including a fine triptych of Our Lady with side panels on the walls, rails, and a sunburst above. The silver wood candlesticks are no longer on the lady chapel altar. In addition there is a screen to the chapel and a window of King David with his lyre. At the west end is an

elaborate font cover. All this work remains in good condition. Mee describes the font cover as 'soaring upward like a miniature temple of gold.'

Drawings in RIBA for screen and other work including window in lady chapel, communion rails for high altar, and font cover, 1925–8.

See also: Clarke, p197, Mee: *London*, p791, and Pevsner: *London 2: South*, p663.

Battersea, St. Stephen, Battersea Park Road

This work as set out below was carried out, but in about 1977 this church was declared redundant and became the Assemblies of the First Born. Some of the furnishings were taken to Christ Church, Battersea (q.v.), but the reredos (without its crucifix) and font cover were sold to W.P. Anelay, then the Chairman of the York Diocesan Advisory Committee, for possible use in that diocese. He stored them for many years, but in 2000 they were given to St. George, Harrow (q.v.).

Drawings in RIBA for reredos, communion rails, and tablets, 1939, and font cover, 1940.

Tooting, St. Paul, Welham Road, Furzedown

Travers produced two similar designs for three light east windows, one for this church (built 1925) and the other for St. Andrew, Langley Mill, Derbyshire. The design for the latter was in fact used here and there; it shows Christ in Glory in the middle light, as did the other design, but it obviously omits the dedication appropriate to Langley Mill. It was restored in 1952 after bomb damage.

Drawing in RIBA undated for east window; there is a further similar design for Langley Mill, Derbyshire, 1936.

See also: Richardson, p74.

Wandsworth, St. Andrew, Garrett Lane

This church has a south aisle window of the Presentation, in memory of Douglas Tudor Craig, vicar 1899–1937; unfortunately it is now partly obscured by subsequent alterations to the internal structure.

Drawing in RIBA for window, undated.

See also: Clarke, p277, Pevsner: *London 2: South*, p701.

WESTMINSTER

Covent Garden, Priory of St. Michael, Burleigh Street

The London Priory of the Community of the Resurrection has various items by Travers from the former Priory of St. Paul, Holland Park, including a splendid bas-relief of Our Lady, similar to that in Old St. Pancras but retaining its circular backing, candlesticks, and crucifixes. On the stairs are memorial hatchments to Charles Gore and to the Community.

No drawings in RIBA for this building: see Priory of St. Paul, Holland Park.

Paddington, St. Mary Magdalene, Rowington Street

This famous and magnificent church in which Comper had already carried out notable internal work was further enhanced by the altar, frame to painting above it, and tabernacle designed by Travers in Baroque style for the east wall of the south transept; he also provided a most striking outside calvary with volutes at the foot of the cross.

Drawings in RIBA for lady chapel altar and communion rails, 1922–3.

See also: Pevsner: *London 3: North West*, p677, Stamp and Amery, p100.

Paddington, St. Paul, Harrow Road
This church was destroyed by bombing in 1940. Travers' assistant Noe left certain notes about his work, which are now in the Council for the Care of Churches. In them he says that an altar or painted reredos was made for this church and used until its destruction.

No drawings in RIBA for this church.

Pimlico, St. Barnabas, off Pimlico Road
This church has Travers windows showing the baptism in the Jordan, the casting out of Eden, the Annunciation, etc.

Drawing in RIBA for baptistery window, 1945.

See also: Betjeman, p282.

Pimlico, St. Gabriel, Warwick Square
The small hanging rood, designed by Travers for the mortuary chapel at St. Columba, Haggerston, was refurbished after the redundancy of that church, and is now in the south aisle of St. Gabriel.

No drawings in RIBA for this church: see St. Columba, Haggerston.

Pimlico, St. Mary, Bourne Street
Travers' work at this church is very well known, and is discussed in detail in Chapter 4. His work however is less extensive than appears at first sight, as the pencil specification in his notebook makes it clear that he was asked to reuse materials wherever possible; his skill with the high altar was to modify the existing work in such a way that it looked completely different. The shrine of Our Lady Queen of Peace was to be the first of a number of such shrines, but his overall plan did not take effect. In 1922–3 Travers designed an extension to the church, but in 1924 the parish chose Goodhart-Rendel's competition design. Travers continued to design the Holy Redeemer shrine in 1925, but that was not commissioned.

Drawings in RIBA for tablets, 1918 and 1919, high altar and reredos modifications and tabernacle and funeral candlesticks, also 1919, sedilia 1922, extension of church, undated but 1922–3, frontal 1924, and shrine of the Holy Redeemer, 1925. A design of an image and shrine was exhibited at the RA, 1924.

See also: Anson, p322, Betjeman, p283, Clarke, p191, Stamp and Amery, pp126–7, B. Brindley: *Infinite Riches in a Small Room* (parish, 1970s), R. Gradidge: *Back to Baroque* (Twentieth Century Society, 1992), and N. Price (ed.): *Streets of Heaven* (parish, 1999).

Pimlico, St. Saviour, St. George's Square
The Gothic-influenced design for the chapel was never carried out. However there is a statue of Our Lady by Travers based on one in Bruges, and he also carried out some stencilling to the reredos of the high altar and added some rather incongruous small rood figures on top of it.

Drawings in RIBA for furnishing chapel at east end of north aisle, 1948.

St. John's Wood, All Saints, Finchley Road
In 1933 a faculty was granted for an English high altar with plain reredos, and the floor of the sanctuary, and especially the steps, were rebuilt. This was an example of work carried out by Travers which was not distinctive in any way. The church has been demolished.

Drawing in RIBA for altar and reredos, not dated.

St. Marylebone, Royal College of Medicine, Wimpole Street
This was one of Travers' few secular commissions. He designed a characteristic tablet to Mildred Beatrice Williamson, and a simple tablet to another. Certainly the Williamson tablet is no longer on display in the College. Travers' other connections with the Royal College were in the long term more important: in 1927 he designed the Coat of Arms and Presidential badge, both of which are still in use.
Drawing in RIBA for tablets, undated.

Westminster, Christ Church, Victoria Street
This church was demolished after war damage. A faculty for sanctuary apse windows by Travers is dated 1927. The best description of the work is in Mee: *London* at p 90, where he says that an unknown benefactor gave the vicar £1600 in cash for them, and they were 'most attractive portraits on a light background': Christ giving keys to Peter, on one side St. Oswald with raven, St. Elizabeth, St, Stephen and St. Alban, on the other St. Mary Magdalene, St. Edward Confessor with the Abbey, St. Francis and St. Longinus. The aisle window, of which the design is in the RIBA, was of the Madonna and child.
Drawing in RIBA for aisle window, undated.

Westminster, St. Matthew, Great Peter Street
Travers carried out extensive work in this well-known church, which was prominent in the Anglo-Catholic Congresses; it is discussed in detail in Chapter 4. The altar and reredos to Bishop Weston, with its large crucifix, was in the south aisle and the wall plaque in characteristic style was on the south wall. Travers also designed a large tabernacle and a benediction throne in Baroque style, and altered the existing rood with characteristic decorations. In 1977 the church was badly damaged by fire and the rood was lost, but the Weston chapel furnishings were saved; they are now under the tower, where they are easily visible but no longer fulfil their original function. The tabernacle also remains.
Drawings in RIBA for altar and reredos in Chapel of Holy Name, 1926, alterations to rood, and wall monument to Bishop Weston, undated, book and missal stands, 1930. The designs for the altar and reredos in memory of Bishop Weston were exhibited at the RA, 1929.
See also: Anson, p322, Betjeman, p283, Clarke, p187.

(ii) Provinces

BEDFORDSHIRE
Bedford, St. Paul, St. Paul's Square
Travers designed a Te Deum west window for this church, in memory of Canon Woodard, but his design was not accepted and a window by another was inserted in 1930.
Drawing in RIBA for window, 1928.

Dunstable, Priory Church of St. Paul
Travers visited this church on 12th February 1948 and thereafter appears to have prepared drawings (now lost) for rearrangement of the chapel of St. John the Baptist, but this was not carried out.
No drawings in RIBA for this church.

Flitwick, SS. Peter and Paul
In May 1948 Travers designed a small wooden lozenge-shaped plaque for the west wall of this church, which recorded the names of those who had died in the Second World War. The plaque was installed in 1949.
No drawings in RIBA for this church.

Luton, Christ Church, Upper George Street
In 1946 a faculty was granted for work in accordance with designs by Travers, namely to remove the top step under the altar, to erect a Christus Rex figure on the wall behind the altar, and to provide four new altar candlesticks and new communion rails. The scheme gave some distinction to an otherwise rather undistinguished building. However in 1976 the church was made redundant and it was subsequently demolished. The redundancy report refers to the candlesticks as being 'Faith Craft 1950' but in fact they were by Travers.
Drawings in RIBA for altar ornaments and communion rail, 1945.

BERKSHIRE
Chavey Down, Heathfield School Chapel
There is something of a mystery about the statue of Our Lady as designed, but Travers undoubtedly provided for the school chapel a small rood set, and also altar figures, all of which remain in use.
Drawing in RIBA for statue of Our Lady in niche, undated.

Clewer, Chapel of Community of St. John the Baptist
A Travers statue was made for the Community, and having been in Clewer for many years, in 2001 it moved to their new home at Begbroke, Oxfordshire.
Drawing in RIBA for statue of Our Lady, 1936.

Clewer, St. Stephen, Vansittart Road
The church has a similar statue to that previously in the nearby Community.
No drawing in RIBA for this church.

Eton, Eton College Chapel
A Travers tablet, inscribed to C.R.W-T., E.V.S., E.W.P., and H.E.E.H., is in the ante chapel.
Drawing in RIBA for pewter memorial tablet, 1946.

Reading, Holy Trinity, Oxford Road
Travers designed a huge baroque reredos for this extraordinary church, which was originally a proprietary chapel, built in 1826. However the reredos was never installed here, but the design was modified for use in St. Augustine, South Kensington (q.v.). In more recent years the church has been filled with a variety of furnishings from eclectic sources by the former vicar, the late Canon Brian Brindley. These included the Pugin screen from St. Chad's R.C. Cathedral, Birmingham, and an altar from St. Paul, Oxford, with a Belgian tabernacle which by the use of a key device turns to become an exposition throne; Travers designed the gradine and side extensions to this altar, and probably the candlesticks. The gradine and its candlesticks now begin to show their age. In the (liturgically) north chapel are the former high altar and matching credence tables by Travers from Nashdom Abbey, together with a large crucifix and six three sided candlesticks, which can be turned to show gold, red, or black as appropriate.

Drawing in RIBA for reredos for this church, undated.

South Ascot, All Souls
Although Travers designed a reredos for the lady chapel in this church, this was not installed. He did however design a surround for a piece of C16 Flemish carving above the tabernacle, and this was dedicated in 1937. The tabernacle itself was there when Travers surveyed the church. The present reredos, of antique Spanish leather, was installed in 1964.

Drawing in RIBA for tabernacle surround and reredos, 1937.

See also: Betjeman, p115, where it is incorrectly stated that the south chapel is by Travers.

Speen, Elmore Abbey
The Benedictine Community has taken statues by Travers of Our Lady and St. Benedict to their new abbey; both were originally in Pershore, and then moved on with the brothers to Nashdom and thus to Elmore. The statue of Our Lady is a maquette of that in St. Mary, Bourne Street; it was made in about 1922 and the crown was replaced in about 1956.

No drawings for this building in RIBA, but see Nashdom, Buckinghamshire.

See also: *Jubilee Book of the Benedictines of Nashdom*, (Faith Press, 1964).

BRISTOL
Horfield, St. Gregory, Filton Road
There are a high altar with fittings, reredos, and tabernacle in this church which have been attributed to Travers. In fact however, extensive correspondence in the Council for the Care of Churches makes it clear that these were carried out by John Crawford, Travers' former assistant, in 1949, after Travers' death, although in his style.

No drawings in RIBA for this church.

See also: Betjeman, p120 (where the attribution to Travers is incorrect).

BUCKINGHAMSHIRE
Burnham, Nashdom Abbey
Martin Travers had already designed a statue of St. Benedict and one of Our Lady (a maquette of the statue of Our Lady Queen of Peace at St. Mary, Bourne Street) for the Benedictine Community when they were at Pershore Abbey. In 1926 they moved to Nashdom and he converted the 'Noble Saloon' to a chapel in the most ultramontane taste. The altar had a canopy and two console tables and the candlesticks were three sided with different colours on each side so that they could be revolved according to the use required. The canopy was renewed in 1962. In 1987 the Community moved to Speen, Berkshire (q.v.). The high altar, without canopy, but with credence tables, is now in Holy Trinity, Reading (q.v.). Travers also designed a chapter house reredos to back an Italianate altar donated by his patron Father Whitby; they were sold to St. Agnes, Ullet Road, Liverpool, but never used there and are thought now to be in private hands.

Drawings in RIBA for high altar and rearrangement of chapel, 1924.

See also: Anson, p323, *The Jubilee Book of the Benedictines of Nashdom* (Faith Press, 1964).

Chesham Bois, St. Leonard
This church has two fine windows, one a reconstruction, neither of which is actually

signed by Travers. The west window shows Our Lord's appearances after the Resurrection and is an original piece of work with rather odd angular writing in place of the usual beautiful lettering. The east window is a clever reconstruction by Travers of old glass.

Drawings in RIBA for east and west windows, 1943–5.

See also: Pevsner: *Buckinghamshire*, p242, and H. Salmond: in *Journal of British Society of Master Glass Painters*, 1970/1, Vol 14, no 5.

Hedgerley, St. Mary
Travers prepared designs for this church but the work was not done: there is no screen at all in the building. He died shortly after the last designs were done.

Drawings in RIBA for alteration of altar and screens etc., 1946–7.

Iver Heath, St. Margaret
This church has a very fine 'Tyneham' style window of Our Lady with tree behind an English altar with gilded and pleated reredos and text, all by Travers. In early 2002 the reredos was dismantled and stored, spoiling the effect intended. The vestry was not built at that time; the porch is certainly an addition, and may be by Travers.

Drawings in RIBA for furnishing the sanctuary, painted glass for east window, new vestry and south porch, 1932.

Stoke Poges, St. Giles
Travers was asked to refit the Hastings (south) chapel at this well-kept church, which has many visitors because of its poetic connections. The work was in memory of John Stuart Devereux, who was killed in action in 1944.

The chapel was provided with a new altar with characteristic sun device on the reredos and the crucifixion window behind is signed by Travers and Lee. Other windows were reconstructed.

Drawings in RIBA for chapel and windows, 1946–7.

See also: Pevsner: *Buckinghamshire*, p652.

CAMBRIDGESHIRE
Cambridge, Holy Trinity, Market Street
No work by Travers was ever carried out in this church.

Drawing in RIBA for chancel panelling, 1938.

Ely, Cathedral of the Holy Trinity
Travers visited Ely Cathedral in 1946 and produced drawings for the east window to the lady chapel. Unfortunately the Dean and Chapter did not adopt the designs, on the grounds that the project would have been too costly, and the plans have disappeared, save for some preliminary drawings in the possession of Lawrence Lee.

No drawings in RIBA for the cathedral.

Godmanchester, St. Mary
Martin Travers was baptised in this church, and also buried there. In the south chapel of St. Anne is an excellent English altar, reredos and communion rails all by him. The reredos is typical of his work: red, of pleated design, and with a crucifix on it. There is a wall scroll also of typical pattern recording that the work was done in memory of the Tillard family. On the floor of the chapel, within the rails, is a clear tablet to Travers, which commemorates that he designed the altar and reredos.

Drawings in RIBA for altar, 1937.

Hemingford Grey, St. Francis House
This is a retreat house run for the Community of the Resurrection, which now has in its chapel the statue of Our Lady adapted by Travers for the Priory of St. Paul, Holland Park, Kensington (q.v.).
No drawings for this building: *see* Priory of St. Paul, Holland Park, Kensington.

Huntingdon, The Priory
This is something of a mystery. Travers designed a window showing a cherub on the back of a bat flying over a mediaeval town. A photograph of the design in the RIBA has written on the back 'stained glass window at The Priory, Huntingdon.' However, the priory in Huntingdon was demolished some centuries ago: there is a house called 'The Priory' in West Street, Godmanchester, which adjoins Huntingdon, and has one round window, but that window is now glazed with clear glass. It is not clear whether this design was ever in it.
Drawing in RIBA of roundel window, undated.

Littleport, St. George
This church has a fine Travers window in the north aisle, signed and dated 1934, which depicts the appearance of Our Lord after resurrection, with text 'by the breaking of the bread …'. The window is in memory of Charles Crayfield Defew, died October 1932; unfortunately a vestry wall has been inserted in the church which partly obscures the glass.
Drawing in RIBA for window, 1932.

CHESHIRE
Alsager, St. Mary Magdalene, Crewe Road
No work by Travers was ever carried out in this church.
Drawing in RIBA for painted glass, undated.

Ashton on Mersey, St. Mary Magdalene, Moss Lane
Travers designed a window for this church in memory of Sarah Alice Johnson. No such glass was put in, and an altar rail was given in her memory instead; there is nothing to indicate that is by Travers.
Drawing in RIBA for glass, 1926.

Runcorn, St. Michael and All Angels, Greenway Road
This red sandstone church near the Mersey bridges has two fine early windows by Travers in the south aisle, both war memorials from the First World War. One shows St. Joan of Arc and St. Michael the Archangel with a dragon, the other St. George and St. Nicholas of Myra; the latter is signed and dated 1921. Between them is a plaque commemorating the dead of the parish. The chapel designed by Travers was not installed, and the plaque to the Young Men's Society on the west wall appears not to be his.
Drawings in RIBA for chapel, 1919, for one window, 1920, and for two plaques, undated.

CORNWALL
Camelford, St. Thomas of Canterbury
The east window of this church is one of Travers' most successful designs. The church

was dedicated in 1938 and his first design was rejected. His second design illuminates the whole of the small building. It shows Christ on the Cross in Glory, St. Mary Magdalene at his feet, St. Thomas holding Canterbury Cathedral, and St. John supporting Our Lady of Sorrow. This variation on the usual rood formation works extremely well and this little known piece of work deserves to be much better appreciated.

Drawing in RIBA for glass, undated.

Helston, St. Michael
Travers designed for this church a rood set, which is now on the north wall, but was originally on a beam across the chancel. The rood set is of standard design but beneath it was a fine and most unusual classically inspired screen by Travers with pediment and four columns, which set off the C18 church well. The screen and rood were in memory of William Claude Coleman, and were erected in 1952, well after Travers' death, presumably by one of his pupils. Unfortunately, the screen was taken out in 1972 and the rood moved.

No drawings in RIBA for this church.

Marazion, All Saints
This church has two phases of work by Travers. In the first, he dealt with the organ gallery and vestry beneath; this has been altered since, and in any event is not a piece of great interest. He also designed a wooden screen between the north aisle and the nave. In the later phase he furnished a chapel in the north aisle with a large crucifix between two enormous white painted candlesticks; the backing has been removed and the crucifix is now on the wall. In addition, the chapel has a statue of Our Lady and communion rails and a lozenge shaped slate tablet by Travers with an inferior addition above it.

Drawings in RIBA for vestry, organ gallery and screen, 1938, altar in north chapel, communion rails, image of Our Lady, and memorial tablet, 1944.

See also: Pevsner: *Cornwall*, p113, and H. Keast: *The Catholic Revival in Cornwall 1833–1983* (Catholic Advisory Committee for Cornwall, 1983), p24.

Mawnan, SS. Maunanus and Stephen
In 1938 a faculty was granted to remove many images and the like from this church. Travers then prepared a scheme of refurbishment for the church, most of which could not be carried through because of lack of finance; the first part, which was done, was to install screens for a new organ. In August 1939 Dr. Eeles wrote that Travers was putting in 'good and simple fittings', in response to complaints that work was wrongly being carried out. Travers' plans for an enlarged altar with English hangings and plain cross (not crucifix) on the backboard and wrought iron candleholder above were not executed; nor were his plans for a new ceiling with characteristic stars in the chancel. He redesigned the pulpit on a wooden base in lieu of the existing stone one, but that also was not done.

Drawings in RIBA for altar area and for pulpit, undated.

Newlyn, St. Peter
This small church in a fishing port has a remarkable high altar and reredos. Travers designed a reredos with Our Lady and the Child on it, which was installed without them. A considerable amount of work was done in this church by the then incumbent, Revd Allen Wyon, who in place of the Travers design carved a large crucifix for the

reredos, underneath which is a terracotta representation of the Last Supper. Travers' pleated reredos is topped by an elaborate tester above which is further ornamentation, dominating the church. In addition, he made a font cover with dove symbol and a representation of the waters of baptism, and encased the west end in a wooden organ gallery, on which there is a Christus Rex figure.

Drawings in RIBA for high altar, organ gallery, tester, communion kneelers for side chapel, and font cover, 1937–9.

See also: Pevsner: *Cornwall*, p126, H. Keast (see under Marazion), p24.

DERBYSHIRE
Burbage, Christ Church
The faculty for this work is dated 1925. Travers designed a fine coloured window showing rood figures in his earlier style with the symbols of the crucifixion around; the window remains in place.

Drawing in RIBA for war memorial window, undated.

Derby, St. Anne, Whitecross Street
No work by Travers was ever carried out in this church, although a fine Baroque scheme was designed.

Drawing in RIBA for reredos and tabernacle, 1924.

Langley Mill, St. Andrew
Travers' design for the three lancet east window at Langley Mill was used both here and at St. Paul, Furzedown, Tooting (q.v.); there are insignificant differences between the two. In the centre light is Christ in Glory over a City, with his supporters in the side lancets.

Drawing in RIBA for glass, 1936, exhibited at RA 1935.

Swanwick, St. Andrew
This well-known and justly praised war memorial east window was designed by Travers for the Warham Guild. It has some similarities in style to that at St. Augustin, Tynemouth (q.v.). It shows Christ with Our Lady and St. John, with towers beneath.

Drawing in RIBA for window, 1919.

See also: Armitage, p69, Osborne, p127, Pevsner: *Derbyshire*, p336

DEVON
Buckland Monachorum, St. Andrew
No work by Travers was ever carried out in this church: the design, showing St. Andrew holding the church, was never taken forward.

Drawing in RIBA for east window, 1947.

Washford Pyne, St. Peter
This very remote church has a fine gilded wooden tablet by Travers to the dead of the First World War, on the north wall of the chancel, carried out about 1920.

Drawing in RIBA for tablet, undated.

DORSET
Bournemouth, St. Stephen, St. Stephen's Road
Travers designed a very fine large wooden statue, carved and gilded, in a shrine, with extremely tall cover. It is just to the south of the chancel arch in this splendid church.

Drawing in RIBA for statue of St. Stephen, 1936.

Broadstone, St. John the Baptist, Macauley Road
This church has a fine detailed war memorial west window by Travers, showing various saints and a kneeling soldier and sailor as found elsewhere. There is strong colour and very little clear glass, and it is signed and dated 1920. In the chancel is a memorial tablet, 1921, with elaborate lettering.

Drawing in RIBA for glass and tablet, 1920–1.

Corfe Castle, St. Edward
Travers did a great deal of work in this church, including some which was unfinished at his death, and this is discussed in detail in Chapter 6. In 1938 he designed a screen and altar set for the north chapel and in 1942 this was dedicated. The following year he designed a font cover, and in 1943 a memorial window of the Annunciation to Marjorie Graves, for the chapel. The work included a comprehensive rearrangement in about 1947, involving removal of an existing screen, altering floor levels, and moving the Royal Arms. In addition, he reordered the sanctuary with a new high altar and redesigned the east window with new tracery to include both old and new glass. In 1991 the riddel posts and reredos were removed from the altar, spoiling the original effect. In addition, Travers designed a banner, trundles, mace, tower benches, and two tablets, one a war memorial. A list of rectors and one of the tablets were almost completed at his death and were finished later, and Douglas Purnell made the processional cross to Travers' design.

Drawings in RIBA for various furnishings and glass, 1938–47.

See also: Armitage, plate 53, and Pevsner: *Dorset*, p167.

Gussage All Saints, All Saints
Travers designed a stone lozenge-shaped memorial tablet to Arthur Savile Beresford Freer, vicar 1901–36, which is on the south wall of the chancel in this church; the typography is, as usual, unmistakable.

No drawings in RIBA for this church.

Shillingstone, Holy Rood
Travers visited this church in 1948 and prepared drawings (now lost) for an altar, which was never taken forward.

No drawings in RIBA for this church.

Sixpenny Handley, St. Mary
This church has a Travers reredos showing the Annunciation and a sunburst, which unfortunately has now been moved from the sanctuary and hung in the baptistery at the back of the church; there are also two hatchments with the Magnificat in Latin, in their original places on either side of the altar. Travers' candlesticks are kept in the vestry.

Drawings in RIBA for alterations to sanctuary, 1946–7.

Steeple, St. Michael
In the 1920s Travers visited this church, and subsequently provided a simple reredos for the high altar. The reredos has since been removed and is now in the tower in a dirty condition, and generally inaccessible. It may be that at one time the reredos from Tyneham (q.v.) was here.

Drawing in RIBA for reredos, not dated.

Swanage, St. Mark, Herston
The centre light only of the east window in this small church is by Travers and shows Our Lord in blessing, holding a chalice, with the usual fine lettering. The altar furnishings and font cover were not commissioned.

Drawings in RIBA for east window, work in the sanctuary, and font cover, 1947.

Tyneham, St. Mary
The Travers glass in this church is very well known and its importance is discussed in Chapter 5. The east window shows Our Lady and the Holy Child under a tree, with a butterfly in the background, and much clear glass. The window was given in memory of Grace Draper by her husband Warwick Draper of Sheepleaze, Worbarrow Bay. Unfortunately Travers' reredos, which was brought back to the church after its reopening by the Army, was not restored to its proper place, but has been hung on the west wall in the gallery: it is a simple dark red board with crucifix. This window was one of Travers' own favourites.

Drawings in RIBA for chancel furniture, 1925; the design for the altar and window were exhibited at the RA, 1927.

See also: Armitage, p69 and plate 52, Mee: *Dorset*, p269 ('a most beautiful window of our time'), Osborne, p94, also L.M.G. Bond: *Tyneham, a lost heritage*, (Longmans 1955), p101, and P. Wright: *The Village that died for England* (Jonathan Cape, 1995), passim.

Weymouth, Holy Trinity, Town Bridge
The east window of the lofty north aisle of this church has a Travers design of Our Lady as Stella Maris on board ship, put in under a faculty of 1947 to replace a window damaged in the blitz. It is an original and striking piece of glass, which shows Our Lady and the Child on the ship, apparently in Weymouth Harbour, with the church of Holy Trinity featured.

Drawing in RIBA for window, 1946.

Wyke Regis, All Saints
The work at this site was part of Father Humphrey Whitby's patronage of Travers. He commissioned him to design memorials to Sir Arthur Otway, Bart., Henrietta Otway, and (Henrietta) Evelyn (Marianne) Whitby, his grandparents and mother respectively. Father Whitby himself was also buried in the churchyard; he died shortly after Travers himself. The gravestones to Father Whitby's grandparents and mother remain, although they are worn. Sir Arthur Otway's gravestone has an Agnus Dei symbol; his wife has a lily and cross on her stone. Mrs. Whitby's stone has a distinguished rood carving on it. In addition, there was a tall cross in the graveyard to Sir Arthur and Lady Otway on an elaborate plinth. Although the carved plinth remains, the cross has disappeared.

Drawings in RIBA for graveyard cross and gravestones, 1915–6.

ESSEX
Corringham, St. Mary
In 1938 Travers supplied a crucifix for the wall behind the high altar for this church, with characteristic dedication scroll. The scroll remains, but the crucifix has disappeared. In 1939 he supplied a statue of Our Lady with plinth; the statue has been remounted but the church still has the plinth. There are designs with the faculties.

No drawings in RIBA for this church.

See also: Betjeman, p186.

East Donyland, St. Lawrence
In about 1970 the reredos from Minster Abbey was installed in this church. Travers did not design that reredos, but he carried out work on it in 1934 (q.v.). The reredos was sold in 1998 and is thought no longer to be in the country.
No drawings in RIBA for this church, but see Minster-in-Sheppey, Kent.

High Easter, St. Mary the Virgin
This church has a Travers east window of three lights given by Edward Gepp, vicar 1903–16, son of Edward Gepp, vicar 1849–1903. The window is in fine colours with realistic figures and animals and has an appealing sense of light. They lights are (i) the Annunciation, (ii) the Nativity and (iii) the Presentation in the Temple. In bottom right is 'MT 1931'. An alternative design was for a Tyneham style window.
Drawing in RIBA for glass, 1931.

Loughton, St. Mary
Travers designed an oak screen (not carried out) and a memorial chapel (installed in 1946). There is a simple altar with a reredos with sun motif and words of scripture, with cross (not Crucifix) behind; the tone of the parish is Evangelical. This is not one of Travers' more memorable pieces, but remains in place.
Drawing in RIBA for memorial chapel and oak screen, 1942.

Stanford-le-Hope, St. Margaret
In 1939 Travers renovated the north aisle altar in this church and provided it with a new cross (not crucifix) and candlesticks in silvered wood, with a new dossal and frontal. The church has since been considerably altered for the worse internally and the altar itself and its furnishings have disappeared, although on the windowsill is a notice recording that the cross and candlesticks on the altar were given in memory of Emily Russell (died 1928) the wife of the then rector.
No drawings in RIBA for this church.

Stanstead Mountfitchet, St. Mary
This church (which is redundant, but still consecrated) has a Travers stone cartouche to Arthur William Blyth in the south aisle.
Drawing in RIBA for cartouche, about 1928.

GREATER MANCHESTER

Bolton, St. Augustine of Canterbury, Ainsworth Lane, Tonge Moor
This church has the following furnishings which are or may be by Travers: a crucifix on the reredos and a cartouche with title of church in north west porch, obtained 1963 second hand and relettered. However it also has many furnishings by Travers' pupil Douglas Purnell: war memorial triptych and altar frontal (1949), reredos in Travers' style (1952), high altar (1962), images of St. Augustine and Sacred Heart, shrine of Our Lady of Walsingham, sacristy crucifix (said to have been designed for Gibraltar Cathedral), and hatchment (deceased died 1944). There is also a hanging crucifix at St. Aidan, a daughter church, dated 1952 or later.
No drawings in RIBA.

Stand (near Whitefield) Unitarian Chapel, Ringley Road
This glass work was carried out and was then destroyed in the War. There was a window showing Faith Hope and Love, to Archibald Winterbottom and his wife, and also a window with a text and the mildest of baroque flavours, including a cherub beneath

the text. The chapel was destroyed in 1940 and rebuilt in American Meeting House style in 1955, with a new window to the Winterbottoms. It was Travers' only work for the Unitarian Church.

Drawings in RIBA for glass, undated.

See also: G. Hague *The Unitarian Heritage* (published by Unitarian Heritage, 1986).

HAMPSHIRE
Beaulieu, The Blessed Virgin & Holy Child
This bas-relief of Our Lady with her Child and a dove, very similar to that in Romsey Abbey, is above the High Altar and is in good condition.

Drawing in RIBA of sculpted figure of Our Lady, 1942.

Bentley, St. Mary
Travers' notebook indicates he designed altar ornaments for this church, and there is a pair of wooden candlesticks which could be his in the lady chapel.

No drawings in RIBA for this church.

Bentworth, St. Mary
In the north aisle of this church is a tablet by Travers of which there is a photograph in the RIBA. It is in dark stone with gold lettering and is in memory of Gordon, Victor, and Cecil Gordon-Ives showing the family crest at the top and the badges of the Coldstream and Scots Guards at the bottom. The Gordon-Ives family were friends of Travers' friend George Sedding.

No drawings in RIBA for this church.

Bramshott, St. Mary the Virgin
In this church Travers provided three fine lancet windows in the east wall of the chancel, featuring the arms of the Canadian provinces, to commemorate the encampment of Canadian forces on Bramshott Common in both wars, and also a new window on the north wall of the chancel, which reused an existing figure but placed it on a new background. The work appears to have been carried out in 1945 and was paid for by money from Canada.

Drawings in RIBA for two windows, 1943.

Brockenhurst, St. Nicholas
This New Forest church has three panels by Travers, the first two in one window on the north side of the nave and the other in the next window. They are (1) to one Gill, vicar 1917–24, showing St. Nicholas in a schooner with the arms of the Isle of Man (the deceased's home), signed and dated 1926, (2) to Captain Gandy, showing a map of Africa with the Union Castle line flag and the arms of the Cutlers' Company, installed 1932, above (1), and (3) to H.N. Bowden-Smith showing St. Francis preaching to the birds, signed and dated and installed 1936.

Drawings in RIBA for windows, 1931–4.

See also: Mee: *Hampshire*, p96.

Burghclere, The Ascension
This church has a window by Travers in memory of Richard Ford Rew Elkington, who was killed in the Second World War; there is nothing to suggest that the adjoining altar is by Travers.

Drawing in RIBA for window for and altar, 1943.

See also: Armitage, p69.

Cheriton, St. Michael & All Angels
This church has two separate phases of work by Travers. In about 1920 he was commissioned by Mrs. M.A.P. Egerton to commemorate four nephews of hers, all of whom had been killed in the First World War. In the nave are the windows to Geoffrey C.S. Pratt, John F. Egerton, Basil R.F. Christy, and Stephen E.F. Christy, all dressed as mediaeval knights, and each representing a virtue (Honour, Loyalty, Duty, and Courage respectively). Each window has scenes from the Bible, the Mort d'Arthur, and various lives of the Saints. In 1946 the east window of the south aisle was dedicated, to Mrs. Egerton herself. It shows the transformation of his style over the years, but is of particular interest in showing the deceased herself in mediaeval dress in the right hand light.

Drawings in RIBA for nave windows, undated, and for Egerton window, 1940; design for nave windows also exhibited at RA 1920.

See also: Armitage, p69.

Droxford, St. Mary and All Saints
This church has a three light window of Our Lady by Travers in the lady chapel, which is in memory of Revd Stephen Bridge and his wife; it shows also St. Francis, St. Wilfrid, St. Stephen and St. George and is dated 1938.

No drawings in RIBA for this: design for window exhibited at RA, 1938.

See also: Osborne, p145.

Liss, St. Martin (Longmoor Garrison Church)
Longmoor Garrison was the headquarters of the Transportation Branch of the Royal Engineers and their successors, the Royal Corps of Transport. The church was built in 1931 and in the 1935–9 period Travers designed a reredos, frontal and altar furniture, altered the roof to permit the reredos to be seen properly, installed a font, and prepared five windows in memory of the dead of the First World War from the railways and London Transport. After the war he added another three in similar style, and some plaques, and later still another two were added by Lawrence Lee. This was the largest collection of his glass in one place, and is discussed in detail in Chapter 6. In 1977 the reredos, font, and all the windows moved to the new location of the Army School of Transport at Leconfield, East Yorkshire (q.v.).

Drawings in RIBA for war memorial reredos, font, alterations to roof, and windows, 1935–48.

See also: Armitage, p69, Lee: *The Appreciation of Stained Glass* (Oxford University Press, 1977), p93, and The Institution of the RASC and RCT: *Memorials Register* (Institution, Camberley, 1998).

Liss, St. Mary, Station Road
Plans by Travers and Grant for completion of the main body of the church in 1927 were not taken forward. However, in about 1930 Travers designed further work which was put into effect; this was an English altar with triptych reredos showing a gilded bas-relief of Our Lady and the Child. This remains today in fine condition, and is of course near the similar reliefs at Beaulieu and Romsey. At some point Travers carried out stencilling on the tower roof, and in 1942 designed two small windows; that to Enid Sedgwick, depicting Our Lady and St. Anne, is particularly good. The other is to her husband Sidney Newman Sedgwick.

Drawings in RIBA for tower and completion of nave, with Grant, 1927, for high altar, undated (c1930) and for windows, 1942.

See also: Anson, p346 (where he wrongly refers to this as a Baroque altar), Pevsner: *Hampshire*, p319.

Portsmouth, St. Agatha, Landport
Father Dolling's old mission, now a 'continuing church', has the reredos and lily crucifix from St. Matthew, New Kent Road, Southwark (q.v.).
No drawings in RIBA for this church.

Portsmouth, St. Stephen, Buckland
This church, which was destroyed by bombing in the Second World War, had a great deal of Travers glass, including a war memorial east window in characteristic style of 1921, with much colour and little clear glass, showing Christ on horseback with many soldiers; there were also windows of Our Lady and of St. Luke, the latter in memory of a local doctor, and work in the sanctuary. All was lost in the air raids.

Drawings in RIBA for windows, rood, reredos, and enlargement of high altar, 1921–32; designs for lady chapel window exhibited at RA 1921, for east window at Royal Scottish Academy, 1922, and for west window at RA, 1923.

References: Armitage, p69.

Romsey, Abbey of St. Mary and St. Ethelflaeda
This important building has a fine English altar by Travers with bas-relief of Our Lady above, very similar to that at Beaulieu (q.v.). This shows what Travers' best work can look like when cared for properly.

See also: Armitage, p69, Betjeman, p221, and Pevsner: *Hampshire*, p485.

Drawing in RIBA for high altar and bas-relief above, 1947.

Ropley, St. Peter
There is no Travers glass in this church.
Drawing in RIBA for window, undated.

Silchester, St. Mary
This church has a Tudor screen but no modern figures; Travers did no work there.
Drawing in RIBA for rood, 1942.

Warnford, Our Lady
The drawings do not reflect that which was actually carried out by Travers in this isolated church in parkland. It has a typical large hanging crucifix above the mediaeval screen, a small Christus Rex, now on the north wall above a war memorial, and a simple square wooden font cover, which is now unused and kept in the tower.

Drawings in RIBA for enlargement of altar with new crucifix, hanging rood and new screenwork, 1937.

HEREFORDSHIRE
Leominster, Priory Church of St. Peter & St. Paul
This church has a Lady Chapel window which is dated 1948, showing a vision of Our Lady and the Child. It is said to have been begun by Travers and finished after his death by Lawrence Lee, who was always meticulous over ensuring that the proper signature was on windows; this bears the initials of both of them.

No drawings in RIBA for this church.
See also: Osborne, p153, Pevsner: *Herefordshire*, p227

Winforton, St. Michael
This small and remote church has a fine and important early reredos by Travers; there is a draft bill dated 1915 in his notebooks, which dates it. The reredos was well restored in 1994, and shows a relief of Our Lady on an ogee shape, with lettering on either side, and curtains with rods and prickets at the edges.

Drawings in RIBA for reredos, undated.

HERTFORDSHIRE
Ayot St. Lawrence, St. Lawrence
There are a number of tablets in the church but nothing at all by Travers to Alice Catherine James, as designed.

Drawing in RIBA for tablet, 1926.

Bishop's Stortford, Holy Trinity, South Street
This church now has the altar rails from St. James Watford, (q.v.); they were modified for it.

No drawings in RIBA for this church.

Bishop's Stortford, St. Michael, Windhill.
This church has an ancient screen, but Travers' work to complete it was never carried out.

Drawing in RIBA to complete mediaeval chancel screen with rood, 1946.

Bushey, St. James
This church has at the east end of the north aisle a typical Travers reredos of the time, terracotta in colour with a stylised crowned and robed Christus Rex. On either side are texts in hatchments.

Drawing in RIBA for altar, 1944.

Cheshunt, Bishops' College Chapel
Travers certainly provided an altar set and other figures for the College chapel. The College was closed in 1969 and the altar set and a Madonna are now in St. Mary, Cheshunt (q.v.); a painted figure of Christ dated 1945 is in St. Albans Abbey (q.v.). It appears that decorative work to the chapel was also carried out.

Drawing in RIBA for decoration of chapel and for altar ornaments, not dated.

Cheshunt, St. Mary the Virgin, Churchgate
Some furnishings from the College chapel were taken from there to the parish church opposite: there is a small Travers Madonna and child, and a fine silver altar cross and two candlesticks. The church also has a hanging Christus Rex (dated 1952 and of the Travers school, in memory of A.F. Winnington-Ingram), and antique Baroque standard candlesticks, the origin of which is unknown.

No drawings for this church in RIBA.

Hitchin, Holy Saviour, Radcliffe Road
This little-known church by Butterfield has a whitewashed chancel, which is said to have been done by Travers. The stars on the ceiling may also have been by him. The lady chapel reredos is by Wilfred Lawson for Faith Craft, 1933, and is indistinguishable

from Travers work of that era: Lawson (b1893) was a contemporary of Travers and was also a stained glass painter as well as the founder of Faith Craft.
No drawings in RIBA for this church.
See also: Howell & Sutton, p55, Pevsner: *Hertfordshire*, pp 199–200.

North Mymms, St. Mary, North Mymms Park
This church has a Travers east window showing Our Lady and the Holy Child, dated 1948, in good colours but with rather an insipid background of coloured lozenges. It does not appear that the sanctuary was rearranged at that time. In 1938 Travers designed a mission church as a daughter to this, but it was never built.
Drawings in RIBA for window and rearrangement of sanctuary, 1946, and for mission church, 1938.

Potters Bar, St. Mary, The Walk
Travers designed for this very fine church a reredos and also a hanging rood as a war memorial, but the work was never done: the church has neither reredos nor rood.
Drawing in RIBA for reredos and rood, 1945.

Radlett, Christ Church
This church has a tablet by Travers to Flying Officer Leslie Manser VC, in stone with coloured and gilded badge and inscription.
Drawing in RIBA for memorial tablet, 1943.

St. Albans, Abbey and Cathedral of St. Alban
Above the altar of the persecuted in the north transept is a painted figure of Christ on a cross but holding the Blessed Sacrament, dated 1945, in characteristic style. This came from Bishops' College, Cheshunt (q.v.).
No drawings for the cathedral in RIBA.

St. Albans, St. Saviour, Sandpit Lane
This church has a Travers lady chapel with characteristic Congress-style reredos reaching upwards, and with tabernacle inside it. The chapel is screened with high wooden railings. There are also windows in the south wall of the chapel and two memorial priest's desks.
Drawings in RIBA for lady chapel windows and high altar, 1924–8 and for priest's desks, 1931; screen work for chapel exhibited at RA, 1931.
See also: Pevsner, *Hertfordshire*, p316.

Ware, Christ Church, New Road
Travers designed an east window of the crucifixion and other scenes to replace a window destroyed in the War; he almost certainly rebuilt the west window from fragments. Neither is particularly inspiring and the church is similarly depressing.
Drawing in RIBA for proposed east window, 1946.

Watford, St. James, Elfrida Road (now Field Junior School)
Although the RIBA holds only plans for a window and the pulpit, in fact Travers' work was far more extensive and there are other plans with the faculties. In 1925 Travers was recommended to finish the construction of this church, which at that time had no chancel. He and Grant designed the extension with cupola and Travers designed many of the fittings. The work is described in detail in Chapter 9. The faculty for the chancel

and additional aisles was dated 1927; the architects modified the designs for windows when they added the chancel. Inside, there was originally a plain wooden reredos, but in 1939 this was replaced by a reredos of painted and gilded wood, the tall centre panel representing the seven fold gifts of the Holy Spirit and enclosed by a picture frame and stylised tassels and volutes; a pulpit was also designed at that time. Travers also designed oak choirstalls, communion rail, altar, north and south chancel screens with friezes of winged cherubs' heads, cross and candlesticks. In the chancel were four gilt stars within a circle hanging in the chancel; they concealed the light fittings directed towards the altar. In 1930 Travers designed and executed a window of the adoration of the Magi at the east end of south aisle as a memorial to Amy Hastings, and in 1931 a memorial tablet to the original architect. The church was made redundant in c1973 and now forms part of Watford Field Junior School. The disposal of contents is deal with in Chapter 9, but see also Holy Trinity, Bishop's Stortford and St. George, Harrow.

Drawings in RIBA for painted glass and pulpit, undated.

ISLE OF WIGHT
Ryde, All Saints, West Street
It seems probable that Travers oversaw the repair of clear glass windows at the church; later Lawrence Lee designed new glass for the church.

Drawing in RIBA for repair of glass after war damage, undated.

KENT
Barham, St. John the Baptist
This church is well known for the lancet window to the south of the porch, which has Travers' memorial window of St. George killing the dragon, to the 23rd Signals, full of colour with especially vivid red. Near it is a plaque to the regiment by him. However, more spectacular, and in a different style, is the 1925 east window depicting Our Lady with cherubs around her against an uncluttered background, with beneath it pictures of the life of St. John the Baptist. Equally spectacular is the English altar with Travers reredos, in predominantly green, with fluted columns for riddel posts. There is a further plaque in the vestry. This is one place of pilgrimage for devotees of Travers, and it is disturbing that the guide does not mention his name.

Drawings in RIBA for windows, panel frontal, altar, and communion rail, 1920–3; memorial window exhibited at RA, 1920.

See also: Armitage, p69, Osborne, p159, Mee: *Kent*, pp32–3, (who speaks of a 'fine window of St. George' by Travers and a 'magnificent east window by the same artist'), and Pevsner: *East Kent*, p136.

Bilsington, SS Peter and Paul
Travers' design for a rood was not accepted, but he did execute a hatchment in memory of the lawyer Sir Arthur Fairfax Charles Coryndon Luxmoore, 1876–1944, which is on the south wall, in need of some restoration.

Drawings in RIBA for rood and hatchments, 1945.

Borough Green, Good Shepherd
Travers designed a pleated reredos for this church, which is now in St. John, Walworth (q.v.). A frontal was also made, but disintegrated some years ago.

No drawings in RIBA for this church.

Buckland, St. Andrew
The rood was never installed, but in 1949 the glass designed by Travers was put into the east window; it shows Our Lord, flanked by saints, extending his blessing.
Drawings in RIBA for rood and window, 1946–7.

Canterbury, All Saints, Military Road
This church was formerly the Garrison Church but in 1975 it became a parish church; the Travers reredos from the nearby St. Gregory the Great was moved here and is now in the chapel behind the high altar. It was originally behind the altar but is now opposite it. It is ogee shaped, and shows Our Lady and the Child on gold against a blue background with gold stars.
No drawings in RIBA for this church.

Canterbury, Canterbury and East Kent Hospital Chapel
As originally installed, this was an altar with a reredos with pleated wood effect and a Christus Rex figure, a tester, and two candlesticks. There is a painting of this in the Chaplaincy; subsequently Travers supplied communion rails. The chapel furniture has been moved since then, and although the altar itself and the rails remain, the reredos, tester, and furnishings have disappeared.
Drawings in RIBA for altar, reredos and choir screen, 1938, and for oak communion rails, 1948.

Canterbury, St. Gregory the Great
It appears that at one time there were drawings in existence in relation to this church, as Noe lists it in a typewritten list in the Council for the Care of Churches. The date is not known, but was probably in the 1940s. In 1975 on the redundancy of this church the lady chapel reredos was removed to All Saints, Canterbury (q.v.).
No drawings for this church in RIBA.

Folkestone, Eversley School
Eversley (or Eversleigh) School was built as a boarding school in about 1910, and had a chapel. Travers designed distinctive stained glass windows showing SS. Francis and Catherine, but it appears that these were never made.
Drawings in RIBA for painted glass, 1927.

Fordwich, St. Mary the Virgin
The east window of this church is of the Annunciation, with a disproportionately large Angel Gabriel, in memory of Revd Richard Hitchcock, rector 1893–1931, similar to that at St. Barnabas, Sutton (q.v.). A ray of light extends down from the emblem of God at the top. This church is held by the Churches Conservation Trust, but access is readily available.
Drawings in RIBA for window, 1936.

Goudhurst, St. Mary the Virgin
It does not appear that any work was actually carried out by Travers here.
Survey drawings in RIBA, 1944.

Hawkinge, St. Luke
There were two churches in Hawkinge, St. Michael, the old church out of the village, and St. Luke, Victorian, and on the main road. Revd Shaw Page, a previous patron of Travers while at West Wickham, Bromley (q.v.) moved to Hawkinge after the death of

his wife and son, to whom Travers prepared memorials in his former church. St. Luke, Hawkinge, was damaged in the War and Travers designed a new church to replace it. However, this work was never carried into effect; the church lasted until a fire in the 1950s and was then replaced in 1958 by a small and tawdry modern building to serve this large village. Nothing appears to remain which emanates from Travers.

Drawing in RIBA for new church and parish room, 1943.

Hawkinge, St. Michael and All Angels.
This was the old church at Hawkinge. Travers designed for it an altar, rood, and candlesticks as a memorial to H.L.P. Boxer, died 1942. The retable had a sunburst and the text 'All Nations should come and glorify thy Name'; the crucifix of the rood was painted on boards, and the total effect was somewhat Italianate. Travers also agreed that for expenses only he would repair the Royal Arms and textboard. This church has been made redundant and has now been sold for housing; it is not clear what has happened to the furnishings.

Drawing in RIBA for altar and furnishings, 1942.

Ickham, St. John the Evangelist
Travers designed a gilded reredos for this church, but his design was passed over. The faculty for the alternative is dated 1924, which enables Travers' drawing to be dated roughly.

Drawing in RIBA for reredos, not dated.

Maidstone, Mangravet Parish Hall
Travers and Grant designed a very pleasant altar and reredos for this hall, used for worship prior to the construction of a church. It appears that the hall is no longer there.

Drawing in RIBA for altar and reredos by Travers and Grant, 1928.

Margate, All Saints, Westbrook
This church, in Travers' own home town, has a hanging Christus Rex rood in memory of Canon H.L.L. Hubbard, with his initials at the foot.

Drawings in RIBA for rood, 1946.

Meopham, St. John the Baptist
This church has three tablets to members of the Smith-Masters family. Two are straightforward brass plates of no particular distinction, but a photograph of them is in the Travers collection at the RIBA. The third, in memory of sons of the family killed in the First World War, is in wood, red with lettering and is in the Travers style. In his own notebook he indicates in a note in 1922 that he has designed 3 tablets at Meopham.

No drawings in RIBA for this church.

Minster-in-Sheppey, SS Mary & Sexburga
In this church Travers devised a scheme which won over the parish. The original intention was to remove the large C18 reredos to the tower. Travers suggested that it be improved by painting dark red and gilding and by removing bad lettering. In addition, he put in a new altar and cross and candlesticks. He also restored the old chancel screen, of which only the base then remained. A new section was also added to the north end of the communion rails. However, faculties were obtained in 1964 to remove the reredos (which eventually went to East Donyland, Essex (q.v.)) and in 1969 to move the screen

across the tower entrance, where the reredos was originally to go. In due course new candlesticks were provided and there is now little trace of his work.

Drawings in RIBA for altar, reredos and restoration of chancel screen, 1934.

Petham, All Saints
This is something of a mystery. The church was gutted by fire in 1922, and Travers designed an altar, reredos and two lancet windows to replace the lost work. His notebook indicates that the work was done, but it was not: a rival's scheme was preferred.

No drawings in RIBA for this church.

Preston North Without or Preston-next-Faversham, St. Catherine
This church, very near Faversham Station, was the subject of many drawings but not all of the scheme was carried out. In particular, no stone screen was built. However, there is a fine rood on a beam, and behind that the high altar has a typical Travers reredos of the time, and a pair of his candlesticks. These were erected to the memory of John Hankins Martin, vicar 1912–38. In the sanctuary is a bishop's chair by Travers, made in memory of a local man killed in the Second World War, and above the lady altar is a Virgin and Child also attributed to Travers. In addition, there is a Caen stone war memorial on the north wall by him.

Drawings in RIBA for alterations to sanctuary, new stone parclose scheme, chancel screen, rood, bishop's chair, chapel and war memorial, 1944–8.

Rusthall, St. Paul
This church has the westernmost window in the south aisle by Travers. It depicts St. John the Evangelist and is in memory of Louis Marshall, 1899–1917. The window shows a roundel at the top with the sign of St. John the Evangelist, and below the saint himself; at the foot are the disciples at the empty tomb, with dedication. There is also a plate beneath, probably by Travers. It is dated from the notebooks to pre–1923, although the style looks later.

Drawings in RIBA for window, not dated.

Stoke, SS Peter & Paul
This church has a war memorial chancel screen with cross above, all in plain wood, designed by Travers for the Warham Guild.

Drawings in RIBA for screen, 1919.

Temple Ewell, SS Peter and Paul
The drawings for this church were dated 20th July 1948, i.e. five days before Travers' death. The glass was installed to Travers' design in 1950. It has three main panels consisting of Christ crucified with Our Lady and St. John on either side and a circular window depicting Christ in Majesty above. The faculty granted hatchments on either side of the window, a reredos with Agnus Dei, and a simple altar and rails. The sanctuary has since been refurnished, but the candlesticks are still in the church, at the west end.

Drawings in RIBA for sanctuary furnishings and glass, 1948.

Tonbridge, School Chapel
There were three schemes here (see below): the 1909 scheme was not executed, but the 1925 reredos was, and formed one of Travers' most impressive pieces, in his old school. It showed Christ breaking the bread at Emmaus. In 1947–8 he carried out further work in the form of a doorway memorial and an altar in the antechapel. Unfortunately all this work was lost in 1988 when the chapel burned down.

Drawings in RIBA as follows: for reredos etc., in style of Comper, 1909, for reredos in more Baroque style, 1925, and for war memorial screen, 1947, and altar, 1948.

See also: Osborne, p167, where she refers to the glass as being by Travers, whereas in fact it was by Christopher Whall, and H.D. Furley (ed): *Tonbridge School Register 1861–1945* (Rivingtons, 1951).

Tudeley, All Saints
This church, which is now well known for its windows by Chagall, could have had a Travers window, but the full scheme by him, drawn very shortly before his death, was not taken up. An altar with permanent frontal is said to have been installed, and then removed some years later. It is, however, clear that Travers designed the electrical installation, which was carried out after his death.

Drawings in RIBA for refurnishing sanctuary, 1948.

Tunbridge Wells, St. Barnabas, Stanley Road
In this church, Travers carried out two contrasting pieces of work. In St. Stephen's Chapel he reconstructed the reredos and had four figures made for it, the whole being Gothic in style; he also designed a fabric frontal for the altar. In the lady chapel, the reredos, which was designed as a frame for a Renaissance painting, has semi-relief figures, and later a tester was added. It was thought that he had carried out work to the high altar at the same time, but recent research has shown that this was not so.

Drawings in RIBA for alterations to reredos in St. Stephen's Chapel, 1944, and to lady chapel, 1946–7.

See also: Howell & Sutton, p119 'After the Second World War, Martin Travers was commissioned to work in both Gothic and Baroque: by him the Lady Chapel was transformed in the Ultramontane taste while his high altar and the reredos of St. Stephen's chapel are disciplined Gothic.' (The high altar is not in fact by him).

Tunstall, St. John the Baptist
This church has a hanging rood, which was left unfinished at Travers' death and was stored for almost 20 years in a cellar. After interest by John Betjeman, this was completed by Francis Stephens and installed in 1967 in memory of a young man who had died. The rood is in fine condition and adds great distinction to the church.

No drawings in RIBA for this church.

See also: Pevsner: *West Kent*, p476.

Ulcombe, All Saints
This church has a statue of Our Lady, which was in Travers' studio when he died and was subsequently presented in memory of Gertrude Jeffrey.

No drawings in RIBA for this church.

LEICESTERSHIRE
Medbourne, St. Giles.
Travers' design was not chosen for this church, which has a fine window by Powell & Sons dated 1946.

Drawings in RIBA for memorial window, 1943.

NORFOLK
Haddiscoe, St. Mary
This remote church has a Travers window in the south aisle, signed and dated 1932. It

shows Our Lady with the tree of life behind, and the Holy Child and another figure with the church in the background. There is characteristic lettering on the dedication to the flower painter Mia Arnesby-Brown, died 1931.

Drawings in RIBA for window 1931.

See also: Cowen, p152, Mee: *Norfolk*, p161 calls the window 'the loveliest thing in the church'; Osborne, p186.

Norwich, All Saints, Westlegate Street
This church previously had the window of Our Lady which is now in St. John Timberhill (q.v.) and is probably the first completed window by Travers. The church also had a frontal, which is now in Wicklewood, Norfolk (q.v.), and a chasuble, which is now in Mendlesham, Suffolk. The church is now redundant but remains open as a social centre.

Drawings in RIBA for altar frontals and vestments, 1909–12.

Norwich, St. George's Roman Catholic Church, Fishgate
This was Travers' only known project for the Roman Catholic Church. He visited the church on 9th April 1948 and subsequently prepared drawings (now lost) for a crucifix and dossal. It does not appear that the work was carried out and in any event the church has since been demolished.

No drawings in RIBA for this church.

Norwich, St. John Maddermarket
This church was much enhanced under the incumbency of Canon Busby. The design for an altar prepared by Travers very early in his career was not taken up, but it seems that he was commissioned to gild and stencil with writing and with lilies the lady chapel altar and reredos, which appear to be of continental origin. There is also stencilling over the north door, and it seems also that Travers altered the lectern, which again was brought into the church. In addition, the high altar crucifix, which came from St. George, Tombland, is attributed to Travers. This church is held by the Redundant Churches Fund, but is open some afternoons.

Drawings in RIBA for altar, 1909.

Norwich, St. John Timberhill.
This church was an excellent window of Our Lady and the Holy Child on a moon, removed in 1976 from All Saints Westlegate (q.v.), and erected in this church in the south aisle. This is a very early piece of Travers glass, probably the earliest: the draft is in his notebook for c1909. The church also has a fine statue of Our Lady, said to be from very late in Travers' career.

No drawings in RIBA for this church.

Norwich, St. Julian, King Street
It seems probable from surviving information and from the lack of a faculty that no furnishings by Travers were introduced into this church; there may have been some vestments. The church was severely damaged in the Second World War and later rebuilt.

Drawings in RIBA for screen, lectern and vestments, 1909.

Norwich, St, Matthew, Telegraph Lane West, Thorpe Hamlet
Travers designed a high altar and rood with figures for the Victorian church of St. Matthew, Rosary Road. When the new church was built, in a striking quasi-Scandinavian style, c1980, the crucifix and rood figures were removed and hung on the wall behind the

high altar, which also moved; the high altar is of wood and has an Agnus Dei picture on it. The rood figures stand out well on the white background.

Drawings in RIBA for former church of St. Matthew: high altar and rood loft, 1945, and other alterations, 1947–8.

Thurne, St. Edmund
This remote Broadland parish has a typical Travers window of its era, with medallions of St. Edmund and Our Lady.

Drawings in RIBA for window, 1934.

Walsingham, Shrine of Our Lady
The Walsingham shrine has comparatively little work by Travers. However, Father Eyden, headmaster of Quainton Hall School, Harrow (q.v.) commissioned Travers to design, in memory of his mother, the outside Chapel of Seven Sorrows. The small altar has teardrops on a black background, with a bas-relief of Our Lady as Mater Dolorosa in the place of a reredos. It is not in a good state because often open to the elements. At the top of the staircase next to the altar of the Coronation of Our Lady are placed three rood figures in memory of Mary Pyle-Bridges (died 1973), which was a piece left in Travers' studio on his death and subsequently restored.

Drawings in RIBA for chapel of Seven Sorrows, undated.

Wicklewood, All Saints.
This church has a Travers altar frontal from All Saints, Westlegate, Norwich, (q.v.).

No drawings in RIBA for this church.

NORTHAMPTONSHIRE
Kettering, St. Mary, Fuller Street
This church has a small Travers window depicting the Coronation of Our Lady high up on the west wall.

Drawings in RIBA for painted glass, 1925.

See also: Journal of RIBA, 12th December 1931.

Kettering, SS Peter & Paul, Sheep Street
This church has a very fine north chapel by Travers enclosed within a wooden painted screen. In the chapel are two small rails with kneelers. The altar itself is of no great interest, but on it is a large gold painted tabernacle with a cross on top and sun behind; on either side are figures on the reredos. There is a lettered railing on the reredos, and behind is Comper glass.

Drawings in RIBA for chapel, 1920.

NOTTINGHAMSHIRE
Collingham South, St. John the Baptist
This church has a fine wooden chancel screen, in good condition, dedicated to the memory of Albert James Maxwell, vicar 1907–37. Above it is a typical hanging rood with 'flat' figures of Our Lady and St. John; there are roundels at the extremities of the cross. There was great controversy over this work at the time it was originally proposed, with Travers being asked to design a more Gothic form. It would appear that he did eventually bow to the pressure, although he placed some stars on the underside of the screen as a mark of individuality.

Drawings in RIBA for screens, 1939–40.

See also: Pevsner: *Nottinghamshire*, p105; he dates the screen as 1940, but it was probably carried out after the war as the RIBA have a card of thanks to Travers dated 1947.

OXFORDSHIRE

Ashbury, St. Mary
At this church, formerly in Berkshire, Travers designed the North Chapel in memory of Evelyn Countess of Craven, who lived nearby at Ashdown House.

It has an altar with a rood on the reredos, two candlesticks, and above a representation of St. Hubert. To the right, on a shelf, is an empty tabernacle. There is also screenwork. Travers designed a high altar also, which was never in fact executed; nor was his design for a war memorial chapel.

Drawings in RIBA for Craven Chapel, high altar and reredos, 1926–7.

See also: Anson, p323, Betjeman, p111 and Betjeman and Piper: *Murray's Berkshire: an Architectural Guide* (J. Murray, 1949), p114.

Begbroke, Chapel of Community of St. John the Baptist
The CSJB moved here in 2001 from Clewer, Berkshire, and brought their statue of Our Lady by Travers.

No drawing in RIBA for this building, but see Clewer.

Compton Beauchamp, St. Swithun
This is one of Travers' outstanding works, and he believed that it was his second best scheme after Cranford. All the work was carried out on behalf of Samuel Gurney and is set out in detail in Chapter 6. It includes the high altar, tabernacle (now empty and in the vestry), plaque of St. Swithun with rain, side screens, altar rails, lady chapel, plaque to Edward Kay-Shuttleworth, and font cover; also a fine east window.

Drawings in RIBA for high altar and furnishings, rood loft, altar rails, pulpit, and grill, undated, and for wall plaque to St. Swithun, 1937.

See also: Anson, p323, Betjeman, p112, and Betjeman and Piper: *Murray's Berkshire Architectural Guide*, 1949, p121, where it is said that there is a 'golden altar by MT [and] lofty pillaried font cover'; also Gurney: *Isabel, Mrs. Gurney, later The Lady Talbot de Malahide* (Jarrolds and Simpkin Marshall, 1935).

Oxford, Queen's College Chapel
It is clear that Travers in fact did no work of furnishing in the Chapel of Queen's, although he undoubtedly advised the College at this time about the state of the windows.

Drawings in RIBA for extension of altar and reredos etc., 1946.

Oxford, St. Edward's School, Woodstock Road
Although the drawings are titled for the dining hall, in fact this Travers window is in the Warden's House. It is dated 1930, shows St. Edward, and was a gift from Mr. and Mrs. H.C. Brooke-Johnson 'as a mark of their love for the school and to commemorate [Mr. Brooke-Johnson's] term as President of the SES Society'.

Drawings in RIBA for window, 1930.

Oxford, St. Paul, Walton Street
This small classical building was converted by Father Roger Wodehouse into a passable imitation of a French or Belgian parish church. The reredos which was drawn was never constructed, but after Father Wodehouse's departure Travers designed a gradine and the high altar was extended with volutes on either side. It is probable that he

designed the baroque candlesticks and crucifix. The high altar, complete with ingenious mechanism for turning the tabernacle by means of a key into a benediction throne, is now in Holy Trinity, Reading (q.v.).
Drawings in RIBA for reredos, 1926, and for enlargement of high altar, 1945.
See also: Anson, p322.

Oxford, St. Thomas the Martyr, Becket Street
This church, which had also been partly refurnished by Father Wodehouse (see St. Paul, Oxford), has a fine gilded and painted statue of Our Lady and the Holy Child by Travers, rather similar to that in St. John Timberhill, Norwich (q.v.). The parclose screen was never put in.
Drawings in RIBA for statue and parclose screen, 1945.

SOMERSET
Bath, The Ascension, South Twerton
This large early work by Travers forms the east window of this church. It was damaged in the War, but rebuilt thereafter. It shows the Ascension with fine strong characterisation, and with a walled city (possibly Stralsund in Germany) beneath. There is much use of yellow and a great deal of clear glass around the figures, akin to much later work. The reredos in this church was painted c1921, but not by Travers: it was carried out by Christopher Webb.
Drawings in RIBA for window, 1912.

Bicknoller, St. George
This church has a Travers window in good condition immediately to the south of the altar. It is a virgin and child in blue and red, in memory of Violet Lena Vernon.
Drawings in RIBA for window, 1936.

Blackford, Holy Trinity
This is not Blackford near Wincanton, as the RIBA Catalogue indicates, but Blackford near Wedmore. For this exceptionally ugly 1820s church Travers designed an east window and a very early simple reredos with crucifix. The work by him was not commissioned, but since the faculty for the inferior scheme chosen was dated 1920 his work can be dated, and it was a forerunner of many more.
Drawings in RIBA for altar and glass, undated.

Chesterblade, St. Mary
In this minute church is this very early Travers work showing the Nativity of Our Lord, signed and dated 1913. The characterisation is splendid and the window is described in lyrical terms by Mee: *Somerset*, at p115 thus: 'The tracery is filled with golden-haired angels in silvery robes, and angels below are raising a blue veil to reveal the Madonna and her Child at Bethlehem, with smiling shepherds about her and a shepherd boy looking on wonderingly with a lamb in his arms. One of the richly winged angels seems to be rocking the child.'
Drawings in RIBA for window, 1912, and design exhibited at RA, 1913.

Combe Hay, Church (no dedication)
This church has two stone Travers tablets on north wall with arms between, all well executed, in memory of John Cass Smart, Mabel Ellerby and others.
Drawings in RIBA for memorial tablets, 1940.

Curry Rivel, St. Andrew
In 1915 the north aisle of this church was reconstructed, in memory of a former vicar, but no glass was in the end put in, by Travers or anyone else.
Drawings in RIBA for window, undated; design for part of aisle window exhibited at RA, 1915.

Drayton, St. Catherine
This church has a very fine Travers window showing Our Lady surrounded by local crafts, all vigorously depicted, on the north wall of the north aisle. In addition however there is a suspended rood figure with the supporters at the foot of the arch, altar ornaments, including a Christus Rex, and a hanging trundel above the altar; there are also tablets on either side of the altar.
Drawings in RIBA for window, 1939; design for window exhibited at RA, 1936.

East Brent, St. Mary
On the north side of the chancel, this church, well known for its Tractarian disputes in the C19, has a Travers window in memory of Preb. Archdale Palmer Wickham, vicar 1911–35, depicting his interests in cricket and butterflies, with good detail; it is signed and dated 1939.
Drawings in RIBA for window, undated.

Martock, All Saints
This church has a Travers high altar cross and candlesticks, given in memory of Preb. Wickham, who was at Martock before East Brent. The cross is dated 1941, and resembles that at Drayton (q.v.). There is a dedication tablet on the wall, which is said not to be by Travers, but looks like his work.
No drawings in RIBA for this church.

Nettlecombe, St. Mary
This remote church, next to Nettlecombe Court, has a typical Travers east window dated 1935 in memory of Sir Walter John Trevelyan and his daughter Urith, with a picture of the Court and Church. It has a Tyneham like figure of Our Lady with tree and also a depiction of the four seasons. In addition, there is a simple reredos with rails at side, and at that time (1935) the old stone altar was replaced; the ensemble is also like Tyneham and a hideous Victorian reredos was replaced. There is also a possibility that two gilded candlesticks in the church are by Travers.
Drawings in RIBA for altar and reredos, undated; design for east window exhibited at RA, 1935.

North Perrott, St. Martin
Travers designed an east window for this church, but it was never executed and the window remains clear glass.
Drawings in RIBA for window and tracery, 1946–7.

Wedmore, St. Mary
It appears that Travers at some date unknown drew plans for a screen for this church, but the work was never done.
No drawings in RIBA for this church.

Wyke Champflower, Holy Trinity
Travers drew up a scheme for the restoration of this small church on behalf of Revd

D.R. Pelly, who then lived in the adjoining manor house. He carried out work to the interior, lengthening the altar, repositioning a board to form a reredos, and providing a new crucifix and candlesticks. He then renovated the pews and provided some new woodwork. Pelly then died before the completion of the work, and Travers designed his grave slab; he then designed a new stone font in his memory. There are no drawings for the work save those with the faculty, and the drawings for the grave have been lost, although Noe refers to them in a list in the Council for the Care of Churches.

No drawings in RIBA for this church.

STAFFORDSHIRE
Clifton Campville, St. Andrew
Travers initially designed a wooden lectern carved as war memorial with cherub on top, and that remains in the church. In about 1922 he supplied two standard candlesticks, and then designed a lady chapel altar and window, neither of which was in fact executed. In 1940 he designed alterations to the high altar involving its lengthening, which were carried out.

Drawings in RIBA for lectern, 1919, and for high altar, 1940.

SUFFOLK
Aldeburgh, SS. Peter & Paul
Travers' design for this church was not accepted and an alternative by A.K. Nicholson was used.

Drawings for memorial chapel, 1930.

Denston, St. Nicholas
This unspoiled country church has a fine Travers memorial window, dated about 1932, to Algernon Charles Windham Dunn-Gardner, showing St. Nicholas holding Denston church in his hands and on either side smaller representations of St. Nicholas as patron of children and of sailors respectively, with heraldic devices beneath.

Drawings in RIBA for window, undated.

See also Mee: *Suffolk*, p123

East Bergholt, St. Mary
Travers' design for the oak screen to the north aisle chapel (where the organ now is) in this large Suffolk church had a Baroque flavour to it which would not have accorded with the rest of the furnishings. An alternative design by an unknown third party was accepted.

Drawing in RIBA for oak screen, 1937.

Felixstowe, St. Andrew
This scheme was not accepted.

Drawings in RIBA for new church by Travers and Grant, 1926, and preliminary sketch for church exhibited by them at RA, 1929.

Great Waldingfield, St. Lawrence
Travers' scheme for a high altar reredos was never executed. However, although the faculty itself is lost, it appears that a faculty was granted in 1948 for his work in the south aisle, which was a simple altar and triptych of the Annunciation. The triptych was stolen c1980. The altar and rails are unexceptionable; the tablet referring to the triptych looks as though it could be by Travers.

Drawings in RIBA for masking the existing high altar reredos and for altar and reredos for south aisle, 1945.

Kentford, St. Mary
It appears that at some date unknown Travers prepared designs (now lost) for stained glass at this church, but no work was carried out.
No drawings in RIBA for this church.

Thurston, St. Peter
This church is mentioned in Noe's list of Travers' drawings in the Council for the Care of Churches, but the plans are lost and there is no work by him in the church. It may be that he put in a design for the east window of the south aisle, which was blown out in the war and replaced by a new window by Powell & Sons.
No drawings in RIBA for this church.

Woodbridge, St. Mary
This fine town church has an excellent Travers east window showing the Adoration of the Magi with much clear glass around. The wise men are clearly characterised and Our Lady has a typical deep blue cloak. The window is clearly dated 1930 and signed.
Drawings in RIBA for window, undated.

See also: Betjeman, p373, where he says 'The interior has been wonderfully improved of late by a beautiful East window by Martin Travers', Osborne, p224 (wrongly dating the work as 1909), and Pevsner: *Suffolk*, p498, wrongly dating it as 1929.

SURREY
Caterham, St. Paul's Church Hall
In a list compiled by Noe this appears, and Travers built a similar hall at nearby West Wickham, but it is not clear whether he built this hall, which in any event has been demolished.
No drawings in RIBA for this church.

Haslemere, St. Christopher, off Wey Hill
This important Arts & Crafts church has a St. Christopher window by Travers, 1935, and a hanging rood, possibly installed after Travers' death but certainly to his design.
Drawings in RIBA for window, 1935, and rood, 1947.

Hersham, St. Peter
This church by Pearson has an unsigned window of the Presentation by Travers in memory of Catherine Hamilton (1860–1944); it is the west window of the south aisle, in an area now screened off. There is the usual fine detail and the Hand of God above.
No drawings in RIBA for this church.

Laleham, All Saints
In 1926 a faculty was granted for a Travers reredos in Tyneham style with 'Sic enim Deus dilexit Mundum' on it, and also a crucifix with two wooden gilded candlesticks. In 1965 the crucifix was deleted from the faculty and a faculty granted for continued use of altar without candlesticks. Yet a further faculty in 1972 authorized removal of the reredos and its replacement by a curtain. All the Travers work has therefore now disappeared.
Drawings in RIBA for reredos and rearrangement of sanctuary, not dated.

Limpsfield Chart, St. Andrew
No faculty was granted for this work and there is no sign of it.
Drawings in RIBA for reversible altar frontal, 1935 and 1938.

Littleton, St. Mary Magdalene, Squires Bridge Road
Travers' work at this church is set out in detail in Chapter 6. The interior of this mediaeval church was transformed by skilful adaptation of what was already there. Travers carried out alterations to the Tudor screen, including placing a typical rood and candlesticks on it, set up a fine statue of Our Lady with candlesticks on either side, made a font cover with dove design, provided a reredos, six candlesticks and a crucifix for the high altar, a window of St. Benedict in the north aisle, and a minute chapel made up in a window arch at the east end of the north aisle, with a tabernacle and a window of the Annunciation. The high altar reredos has since been removed.
Drawings in RIBA for alterations and furnishings, 1935–43.
See also: Betjeman, p290.

Shepperton, St. Nicholas, Church Square
In 1933 a faculty was granted to add a vestry for choir and clergy on to south transept, as designed by Travers. This is not a piece of work of any great interest. In 1942 Travers prepared a more comprehensive scheme for the interior, which was not carried through, and the interior remains as it was.
Drawings in RIBA for vestry, 1932, and alterations to chancel screen, 1942.

SUSSEX (EAST)
Bexhill, SS Peter & Paul, Old Town
This church has a Travers rood high up on the tympanum, very similar to St. Mark, Barnet Vale (q.v.).
Drawings in RIBA for rood, 1946.

Brighton, Annunciation, Washington Street
This church was the recipient of a typical Travers Congress style high altar, which remains in position.
Drawings in RIBA for altar, tabernacle etc., 1925.
See also: H. Hamilton Maughan: *Some Brighton Churches*, (Faith Press, 1922), which shows the church before this work was done.

Brighton, St. Cuthman, St. Cuthman's Close, Whitehawk
This church designed by Travers was dedicated in 1938, but was bombed in August 1943. The crucifix was left standing and is above the chancel arch, with rood figures. There are also two wall plaques, showing St. George and St. Nicholas, and St. Richard and St. Cuthman respectively, which were originally either side of the altar. There is also a banner, which has been remounted.
Drawings in RIBA for church and furnishings, 1936–8.

Burwash, St. Bartholomew
This church has a very fine Travers triple lancet east window, signed and dated 1928. The centre light shows Our Lady with the Holy Child, the north light St. Bartholomew, and the south St. Richard of Chichester. There is a great deal of detail, and typical Travers cherubs. The windows are in memory of Richard Linnington Martyn-Linnington, vicar of the parish from 1909 until his death in 1925.

No drawings in RIBA for this church.

Hove, All Saints, Eaton Road
This church has four Travers windows in the south chapel, depicting respectively the Annunciation, the Incarnation, the Three Kings, and the Presentation in the Temple. There are two small windows in the porch showing the patron saints of England, Wales, Scotland, and Ireland. The windows are in memory of Canon Peacey and his wife Ellen. The date is 1932.

Drawings in RIBA for windows, undated.

See also: D. Robert Elleray: *The Victorian Churches of Sussex* (Phillimore, 1981) at plate 152 and Mee: *Sussex*, p214.

Hove, St. Patrick, Cambridge Road
This work was not done and there is no Travers work in the church.

Drawings in RIBA for rearrangement of south chapel, 1924.

Northiam, St. Mary
The east window of the south aisle is by Travers in memory of 'G.F. 1880–1937'; it shows the Nativity with a background of an oast house and sheep, making it look as though the birth had taken place in the local countryside. Unfortunately a choir vestry has been placed in front of the window, but it remains visible. The window was subsequently slightly altered to include the name of the widow of the man originally commemorated.

Drawing in RIBA for window, 1937.

St. Leonard's, St. Peters Grange
These premises are an old people's home, which from 1897 to about 1963 was run by the Community of St. Peter, Woking. There was a chapel at the premises. Travers did not do the original work, but it is possible that he carried out alterations to the reredos. The altar was removed to St. John's Church, St. Leonard's, in 1963, but the reredos was not removed.

Drawing in RIBA for cherubim for reredos, 1942.

Ticehurst, St. Mary
This work by Travers was carried out in c1947 and was donated by Mrs. Margaret Terry in memory of her father, Revd Francis Fitzgerald Hart (1868–1942) and her brother Revd Anthony Gilbert Hart (1916–44). Mrs. Terry gave a striking reredos with a central panel of Christ holding a chalice and blessing, and trompe l'oeil effects, together with candlesticks, a set of altar frontals, and a memorial hatchment on the south wall of the sanctuary. The candlesticks are still in existence but not on show, but the reredos is well kept.

Drawings in RIBA for enlargement of high altar and associated work, 1945.

Wadhurst, SS Peter and Paul
The chapel at the east end of the south aisle has a triptych of the Resurrection designed by Travers, but in fact painted by Laurence Lee. It shows in the centre panel Our Lord emerging from the tomb with sleeping soldiers on either side, and in the outer panels texts in the usual fine lettering. The total effect, as with a number of his works at that time, was Italianate rather than Baroque. There is a wooden screen at the side with priest's stall and a memorial inscription in the window opposite.

Drawings in RIBA for war memorial chapel and for altar frontal, 1946–7.

TYNE & WEAR
Tynemouth, St. Augustin, Jackson Street
This church has a magnificent Travers east window with 4 lights, as a war memorial. The dates are said to be centre light 1922, outer lights 1925, and oculus, at top, 1927. In the centre is Our Lady robed and crowned in the sun's rays, with a sceptre of lilies and the Christ Child, a design used in advertisements in Anglo-Catholic Congress literature. At the base, is a Pieta. This design is of great significance in that it was exhibited at the 1925 Paris Exhibition: see Chapter 1. In the left light are St. George and St. Augustine, in the right, St. Nicholas of Myra and St. Oswald. In the oculus, the Risen Christ in Glory, perhaps more reticent in manner, with the inscription IC XC NIKA. The window also features the kneeling soldier and sailor as seen in St. John, Broadstone, Dorset (q.v.).

No drawings in RIBA for this church.

See also: Cowen, p195, *The Studio*, Vol 85 (1923), p133.

WEST MIDLANDS
Birmingham, St. Aidan, Herbert Road, Small Heath
Travers designed early lady chapel windows for this church, but they appear not to have been installed.

Drawings in RIBA for window, 1912.

Birmingham, Chapel of Dudley Road (now City) Hospital
In this Victorian hospital Travers designed a very typical triptych with Our Lady and the Infant Jesus decorated with ropes and other designs. Behind, in the apse, he placed stars on a blue background, in front of which is the Holy Spirit against a sun. This is a little known piece of work, but well preserved.

Drawings in RIBA for reredos and treatment of apse, 1940.

Birmingham, St. Mark, Washwood Heath Road
This work was not carried out.

Drawings in RIBA for Chapel of St. George and rood etc., 1946.

WILTSHIRE
Amesbury, SS Mary & Melor.
This work was not carried out.

Drawings in RIBA for window, undated.

Bulford, St. Leonard
This church has a Travers tablet to Brig. Gen. Harold Eustace Carey, 1874–1944. It is on the north wall of the church, opposite the entrance; it is oblong in shape and bears a crest.

Drawings in RIBA for memorial tablet, 1945.

Chute Forest, St. Mary
This remote church, which is now redundant, has a lozenge shaped memorial tablet in slate by Travers to Frank George Fowle, 1884–1942, with the usual fine lettering. The RIBA Catalogue wrongly indicates that this tablet is in St. Nicholas, Upper Chute.

Drawings in RIBA for memorial tablet, 1945.

Cricklade, St. Sampson
This work is discussed in detail in Chapter 6. In this church is much good work by Travers including two fine altars, the High Altar in faded terra cotta and the Lady Chapel altar in blue. The High Altar has the characteristic IHS sunburst device, and the Lady Chapel altar has 'flat' rood figures. The church also has the St. Nicholas window, Travers' own favourite, in the north aisle, dated 1929, but partly relettered later. The window is signed and shows St. Nicholas at sea in ship with sun, and cherub for wind. In addition there are three other windows, one of St. Christopher (in memory of the vicar's son, who drowned), the second of Our Lady with the tree of life, and the third the great east window.

Drawings in RIBA for high altar and glass above and also St. Nicholas window, 1929; design for east window exhibited at RA, 1938.

See also: Anson, p323, Armitage, p69 and plate 51, Betjeman, p401, who says ' recent work by Martin Travers has produced good painted glass, comely altars and other fittings;' Mee: *Wiltshire*, p121 and Osborne, p94.

Mere, St. Michael
In this church, Travers designed a tower screen, lettered in typical fashion and with his characteristic dedication scroll. He also carried out work to the restored rood loft, especially the parapet, to improve it. The rood figures are not his.

Drawings in RIBA for restoration of rood loft, vestry screen and tower clock, 1945–7.

Swindon, Christ Church, Cricklade Street, Old Swindon
For this church Travers provided a north transept window in memory of Fitzroy Pleydell Goddard, Lord of the Manor of Swindon, who died in 1927. It has three coats of arms and a view of Liddington from Goddard's house. It is a most unusual window, in that there is no religious content: most of the window is landscape.

Drawings in RIBA for window, 1930.

See also: Cowen, p201, Betjeman in L.V. Grinsell and others: *Studies in the History of Swindon* (Swindon Borough Council, 1950) at p180, Pevsner: *Wiltshire*, p506 and Victoria County History, Wiltshire, IX, 1970, p148.

Swindon, St. John the Evangelist, Aylesbury Street
This was a daughter church of St. Mark, and was demolished about 1957. It is not entirely clear whether or not the design for the Travers rood was actually carried out, but it seems that it probably was. There is no record of any faculty.

Drawings in RIBA for rood, 1947.

Swindon, St. Luke, Broad Street
In 1926 Travers designed a crucifix for the new south aisle chapel for this church. The altar has since been replaced, but the crucifix is now part of a war memorial on the south wall. In 1928, he was commissioned to refashion the existing rood, which was on a beam, and to render it suitable for hanging. He reused the existing figures, but provided a new cross, which hangs today in the church.

Drawings in RIBA for hanging existing rood, 1928.

Swindon, St. Mark, Faringdon Road
The three Travers schemes for this church (see below), which were in memory of Canon Ross, were not taken up at the time because of the outbreak of the war, but the new east window was installed after the war was over. The window shows Christ in Glory with

the signs of the four evangelists around him and the Hand of God above. The Christ figure is surrounded by a golden oval. This is the outstanding piece in the church, and it is unfortunate that the full scheme was not implemented.

Drawings in RIBA for refurnishing sanctuary and new east window, 1939.

YORKSHIRE (EAST)
Hessle, All Saints
This large mediaeval church was indeed altered in about 1947–8, but the work was carried out by other architects, and Travers' scheme was not used.

Drawings in RIBA for rearranging interior and screen and south aisle chapel alterations, 1947.

Leconfield, St. Martin, Normandy Barracks Garrison Church (Royal Army School of Transport)
In 1977–8 the Royal Army School of Transport moved to this site from Longmoor Camp, Liss, Hampshire (q.v.). The work is discussed fully in Chapter 6. The present building, which is a former parachute packing station adapted as a church, has all ten memorial windows from Longmoor (8 by Travers and 2 by Lee) along the sides on inner walls, backlit. The reredos has been adapted also and is now on the east wall. In addition there are the Travers font and plaques from Longmoor. The whole is very well maintained: access is however by appointment only and even then is not easy and is subject to stringent security checks.

No drawings in RIBA for this church, but see Longmoor.

YORKSHIRE (SOUTH)
Tinsley, St. Lawrence
The Travers drawings for this church show that an elaborate reredos with saints on either side was proposed. However, in fact the work was not carried out, and the sanctuary was not refurnished until 1953, and then to another scheme.

Drawings in RIBA for refurnishing of sanctuary, font cover and side windows, 1947.

YORKSHIRE (WEST)
Horbury, House of Mercy Chapel
Travers designed an elaborate high altar with towering tabernacle for the Sisters of St. Peter, but this does not appear to have been executed. Subsequent photographs show the high altar as having two successive designs of crucifix on a framed reredos, the second of which looks like a Travers piece or a copy of one, as do the candlesticks, but this has not been verified. The Sisters have since moved out of the old convent.

Drawings in RIBA for high altar and reredos, 1923.

Ilkley, St. Margaret
This Travers window is signed and dated 1937. It shows Our Lady and the Christ Child, and on either side St. Hilda of Whitby, with seagull, and St. Margaret of Antioch, with the church in her hands.

Drawing in RIBA of window, 1936.

See also: Cowen, p217.

Shadwell, St. Paul
This is a small church with a disproportionately large Travers Baroque style reredos covering the east end. It has a baldachino, and two figures of SS. Peter and Paul on

either side. The reredos has been considerably altered since its installation in 1924. The altar was pulled out from the reredos in 1962. The colours were 'toned down' about 1967 when a general reordering took place in which the tabernacle was removed. The candlesticks were used for a time in Holy Trinity School, Bury, Greater Manchester, but are now in private hands.

Drawings in RIBA for different forms of reredos, 1924.

See also: N. Yates: *Anglican Ritualism in Victorian Britain 1830–1910*, (Oxford University Press 1999), pp361–2. He says 'Between 1920 and 1927 (Father Douglas) Ferrier had installed, in what was a very small building, a large clothed statue of Our Lady and a new baroque reredos, designed by Martin Travers, the favourite architect of the anglo-papalist Society of St. Peter and St. Paul, which included a tabernacle for reservation.'

South Kirkby, All Saints

This church had a Travers requiem altar of sarcophagus shape with hangings, dating probably from the 1930s. The hangings were later replaced by copies made by Watts & Co., and the altar was taken out of the church some years ago, made portable by the addition of wheels, and used for a time in Holy Trinity School, Bury, Greater Manchester: it is now in private hands.

No drawings in RIBA for this church.

(iii) Remainder of British Isles

SCOTLAND
Peebles, St. Peter, Eastgate

This church has a memorial tablet by Travers to Dugald Charles Bremner, died 1922, with crest above, of which there is a photograph in the RIBA.

No drawings in RIBA for this church.

WALES
Cardiff, St. Stephen, West Bute Street

Travers made two designs for this dockside church in memory of a local shipowner. One showed SS. Nicholas and Oswald, and was chosen for the window near the west door, the other St. Nicholas with his ship, which was rejected. The church is now closed. It was a recording studio and is now a hall for functions, but the windows remain.

No drawings in RIBA but design for window exhibited at RA, 1922.

See also: Cowen, p223.

Clydach Vale, St. Thomas

This church has a Travers war memorial triptych, c1921, which remains in place in good condition.

No drawings in RIBA for this church.

Llangynfelin (near Borth), St. Cynfelin

This small church near Aberystwyth has a lancet window of Our Lady by Travers in the south wall. There appears to be no faculty in relation to it and the date is uncertain.

No drawings in RIBA for this church.

Llantilio Pertholey (near Abergavenny), St. Teilo
The church has a Travers bronze tablet with enamelled crest, to W.H. Thomas, of Tredilion Park, Monmouthshire, died 1914, on the north wall, to the left of the chancel screen.

Drawings in RIBA for tablet, undated, and not attributed to this church.

Manordeifi (Maenordeifi)(near Cardigan), St. David
This church has a painted oak reredos by Travers in deep blue and gold in Renaissance/Baroque style, dated 1923, and given in memory of John Vaughan Colby, died 1919; it shows the three women at the tomb. There are side pillars with arms of Colby and St. David, which was intended to be the beginning of matching panelling across the east wall.

No drawings in RIBA for this church.

CHANNEL ISLANDS
Jersey, St. Helier Church
This important commission to Travers was for a cross and candlesticks in silver painted wood. They were given to Jersey by the then Queen in 1947 to commemorate the liberation of the island, and are so inscribed. It also appears that the present Queen saw the set on her visit to Jersey in 1989.

Drawings in RIBA for ornaments, not dated.

See also: Armitage, p69.

(iv) Overseas

AUSTRALIA
Perth, St. George's Cathedral
It appears from information from the Cathedral that no rood was ever executed.

Drawing in RIBA for hanging rood, undated.

BERMUDA
Location unclear
It is not clear whether any such work was ever carried out.

Drawing in RIBA for memorial cross, 1920.

CANADA
Victoria, Christ Church Cathedral, British Columbia.
It does not appear that this work was carried out.

No drawings in RIBA, but design exhibited at RA, 1931.

FRANCE
St. Jean de Luz, Church of Nativity
This church has long since been closed. Further, it appears that there are no relevant records at all as to furnishings or the like. Travers certainly visited the church; his aunt lived in St. Jean de Luz.

Drawing in RIBA for reredos, 1927.

GIBRALTAR
Gibraltar, Cathedral of the Holy Trinity.
The chancel screen with its altars below was never installed, but there are two side chapels, on the north to Our Lady and on the south to St. George, with plaster and bas-relief to Travers' designs. There are also iron screens on either side with IHS motifs which accord exactly with his drawings. The work was carried out after Travers' death by Douglas Purnell in 1951–2; Purnell also designed the reredos in Travers' style and a plaque to Bishop Hicks. There are also characteristic tassel decorations on the organ case, the origin of which is not clear, and hatchments of the Annunciation in the lady chapel, which are by Purnell.

Drawings in RIBA for chancel screen and rood with altars below the loft and iron screens across aisles, and also for refurnishing sanctuary, 1948.

See also: D.L. Simpson: *Holy Trinity Cathedral Gibraltar*, a comprehensive but unpublished draft book dated 1948 and later revised, in the Guildhall Library, City of London.

INDIA
Simla, Bishop Cotton School Chapel
There were a number of windows designed by Travers for this school, including a memorial to Bishop Cotton himself, and pictures of Our Lady and St. Thomas, Apostle of India. This work was done and remains in position.

Drawings in RIBA for windows, 1936.

NEW ZEALAND
Christchurch, Christ's College
This work is discussed in Chapter 8. The window by Travers, showing Revd Guy Bryan-Brown dressed as a knight in armour (as with the contemporary windows at Cheriton, Hampshire (q.v.)) is still in the School.

Drawing in RIBA for window, 1925.

See also: Fiona Ciaran: *Stained Glass Windows of Canterbury*, University of Otago Press, 1998, W136, Don Hamilton: *College! A History of Christ's College*, 1996, passim.

Christchurch, Christchurch Arts Centre (formerly Canterbury Arts College and then University of Canterbury)
This elaborate window by Travers was, as set out fully in Chapter 8, ordered as a war memorial in 1925 and designed by 1930, but was not despatched until 1938. It shows The Service of Humanity by Action and Thought with many portraits. It has in recent years been vandalised as it was thought condescending to Maoris.

No drawings in RIBA for this work, but design exhibited at RA, 1940.

See also: *The Studio*, Vol 89 (1925), p217, Armitage, p70, Fiona Ciaran: *Stained Glass Windows of Canterbury, New Zealand*, University of Otago Press 1998, W105 and Glyn Strange in *New Zealand Historic Places* No 70, September 1988.

SOUTH AFRICA
Durban, St. John
It seems likely that 5 windows were made by Travers for this church, including those of St. Martin and St. Gregory and also some rather unusual clerestory windows. The present position is not known.

Drawings in RIBA for windows, 1922.

East London, St. Martin de Porres/ St. Saviour
There is a picture in the RIBA of a design by Travers of a crucifixion with soldiers around, which is labelled St. Saviour, East London, which may or may not be the same church. Otherwise this is somewhat obscure.
Drawing in RIBA for window, 1919.

SPAIN
Madrid, St. George
This church, built as the Embassy Chapel in Spanish Mission style, has a wealth of furnishings by Travers, including much of the woodwork. This includes the pews, pulpit, kneeling desk, lectern and painted font cover. There is a tablet over the south entrance to a benefactor, and a number of windows around the sanctuary. Other windows were designed locally at a later date.
Drawings in RIBA for furnishings and glass, 1927.

SRI LANKA
Colombo, [former] Cathedral
There is no evidence to suggest that this work was ever done.
Drawing in RIBA for high altar, undated.

Colombo, St. Michael, Polwatte
There is a record of a drawing of an altar for this Anglo-Catholic mission church, but it is not clear whether it was ever carried out.
No drawings in RIBA for this church.

UNITED STATES OF AMERICA
Rochester, University of Rochester, New York State.
This glass was executed and is still there. The work is a memorial to Meredith Brown Skelton, 1899–1925, and was given by her husband, who himself died in a plane crash in 1930. The donor, Ralph Fisher Skelton, was an artist and a friend of Travers. His wife was the daughter of one of the benefactors of the library. It is said that the window arrived the day before the opening. It shows a familiar 'Tyneham' tree with a fountain in the foreground and no religious content.
Drawings in RIBA for windows, 1929.

ZANZIBAR
Zanzibar Cathedral
The designs were for the memorial to Bishop Weston. It appears probable that this work was carried out, but there is no up to date information.
Drawings in RIBA for baldachino and memorial slab, 1930.

(v) Miscellaneous Work

(a) GRAVESTONES
There are records of the following additional gravestones:
Brompton Cemetery, London: Headstone to Father J.C. Howell of St. Mary Bourne Street.
Chiswick Cemetery, London: Headstone to Elizabeth Elen Houghton.
East Sheen Cemetery, London: Headstone to Revd Samuel Edmond Clarke, 1923.

Hounslow Cemetery (St. Nicholas), London: Headstone, deceased unknown.
Liphook Cemetery, Hampshire: Headstone, photographed c1944.
Wanstead Cemetery, London: Headstone for W.J.H. Jones, 1932.

(b) DOMESTIC WORK
Houses
Barkway, Hertfordshire: no trace has been found of a house in this village, said to have been called The White House.
Laleham, Surrey: mention is also made of house here for A. Simpson.

Domestic Glass etc.
London, Dulwich, 56, Overhill Road: living room window, pre First World War: this property no longer exists.
London, Ealing, 22, Montpellier Road: music room window, 1921: this property no longer exists.
London, Kensington: glass for unknown address in Normand Road.
London, Westminster, 26 Welbeck Street: electric lamp: no further information known.

PART II
A Short List of Extant Work

In the case of Part II four abbreviations are used, namely B for building work, F for furnishings, including internal tablets, G for glass, and M for tombstones and outside war memorials and the like.

(i) London

BARNET
Friern Barnet, St. James the Great: M
New Barnet, Holy Trinity, Lyonsdown: F
New Barnet, St. Mark, Barnet Vale: F

BEXLEY
Lamorbey, Holy Trinity: B G
Slade Green, St. Augustine: M

BRENT
Cricklewood, St. Gabriel: G

BROMLEY
Chislehurst, St. Nicholas: G
West Wickham, St. John the Baptist: F
West Wickham, St. Mary of Nazareth: B F

CAMDEN
St. Pancras, Holy Cross: G
St. Pancras, St. Pancras Old Church: F

CITY
St. Edmund the King: F
St. Magnus the Martyr: B F

CROYDON
Purley, St. James, Riddlesdown: F G
Purley, St. Mark, Woodcote Village: G
Upper Norwood, St. John the Evangelist: F G

EALING
Acton, St. Peter, Acton Green: F
Acton, St. Saviour: G
Ealing, Christ the Saviour: F
Greenford, Holy Cross [old church]: F
Northolt, St. Mary: F

GREENWICH
Plumstead, St. Nicholas: G

HACKNEY
Clapton, St. Thomas: F
Hoxton, Holy Trinity: F

HAMMERSMITH & FULHAM
Fulham, All Saints: F
Parsons Green, St. Dionis: F

HARROW
Harrow, Quainton Hall School: F
Harrow, St. George, Headstone: F G
Harrow, St. John the Baptist, Greenhill: B F G

HILLINGDON
Cranford, St. Dunstan: F

HOUNSLOW
Bedford Park, St. Michael & All Angels: F G
Osterley (Isleworth), St. Francis: F

ISLINGTON
Clerkenwell, Holy Redeemer: F
Islington, Paget Memorial Mission: F

KENSINGTON & CHELSEA
Notting Dale, St. Clement: G
Notting Hill, All Saints: F
South Kensington, St. Augustine: F G
South Kensington, St. Jude: F

LAMBETH
Clapham, Holy Spirit: F
Kennington, St. Agnes: F
Streatham Vale, Holy Redeemer: B F

LEWISHAM
Catford, St. Andrew: G
Lewisham, St. Mary: F

MERTON
Mitcham, SS. Peter & Paul: F
Wimbledon, St. John the Baptist: F

SOUTHWARK
Nunhead, Cheltenham College Mission (now Westminster House Club) B
Nunhead, St. Anthony: F M
Walworth, St. John: F

SUTTON
Carshalton Beeches, Good Shepherd: B F G
Sutton, St. Barnabas: G

TOWER HAMLETS
Bethnal Green, St. John: F
Poplar, All Saints: M

WALTHAM FOREST
Leyton, Emmanuel: B F G
Walthamstow, St. Peter: F

WANDSWORTH
Balham, St. Mary: F
Battersea, Christ Church: F
Battersea, St. Luke: F G
Tooting, St. Paul, Furzedown: G
Wandsworth, St. Andrew: G

WESTMINSTER
Covent Garden, Priory of St. Michael: F
Paddington, St. Mary Magdalene: F M
Pimlico, St. Barnabas: G
Pimlico, St. Gabriel: F
Pimlico, St. Mary: F
Pimlico, St. Saviour: F
Westminster, St. Matthew: F

(ii) Provinces

BEDFORDSHIRE
Flitwick, SS. Peter & Paul: F

BERKSHIRE
Chavey Down, Heathfield School Chapel: F
Clewer, St. Stephen: F
Eton, Eton College Chapel: F
Reading, Holy Trinity: F
South Ascot, All Souls: F
Speen, Elmore Abbey: F

BUCKINGHAMSHIRE
Chesham Bois, St. Leonard: G
Iver Heath, St. Margaret: F G
Stoke Poges, St. Giles: F G

CAMBRIDGESHIRE
Godmanchester, St. Mary: F
Hemingford Grey, St. Francis House: F
Littleport, St. George: G

CHESHIRE
Runcorn, St. Michael and All Angels: F G

CORNWALL
Camelford, St. Thomas of Canterbury: G
Helston, St. Michael: F
Marazion, All Saints: F
Mawnan, SS Maunanus and Stephen: F
Newlyn, St. Peter: F

DERBYSHIRE
Burbage, Christ Church: G
Langley Mill, St. Andrew: G
Swanwick, St. Andrew: G

DEVON
Washford Pyne, St. Peter: F

DORSET
Bournemouth, St. Stephen: F
Broadstone, St. John the Baptist: F G
Corfe Castle, St. Edward: F G
Gussage All Saints, All Saints: F
Sixpenny Handley, St. Mary: F
Swanage, St. Mark, Herston: G
Tyneham, St. Mary F G
Weymouth, Holy Trinity: G
Wyke Regis, All Saints: M

ESSEX
Corringham, St. Mary: F
High Easter, St. Mary the Virgin: G
Loughton, St. Mary: F
Stanstead Mountfitchet, St. Mary: F

HAMPSHIRE
Beaulieu, The Blessed Virgin & Holy Child: F
Bentworth, St. Mary: F
Bramshott, St. Mary the Virgin: G
Brockenhurst, St. Nicholas: G
Burghclere, The Ascension: G
Cheriton, St. Michael & All Angels: G
Droxford, St. Mary and All SS: G
Liss, St. Mary: F G

Portsmouth, St. Agatha: F
Romsey, Abbey: F
Warnford, Our Lady: F

HEREFORDSHIRE
Leominster, Priory Church of St. Peter & St. Paul: G
Winforton, St. Michael: F

HERTFORDSHIRE
Bishop's Stortford, Holy Trinity: F
Bushey, St. James: F
Cheshunt, St. Mary the Virgin: F
Hitchin, Holy Saviour: F
North Mymms, St. Mary: G
Radlett, Christ Church: G
St. Albans, St. Saviour: F G
Ware, Christ Church: G
Watford, St. James (now Field Primary School): B

KENT
Barham, St. John the Baptist: F G
Bilsington, SS Peter and Paul: F
Buckland, St. Andrew: G
Canterbury, All Saints: F
Canterbury, Hospital Chapel: F
Fordwich, St. Mary the Virgin: G
Margate, All Saints, Westbrook: F
Meopham, St. John the Baptist: F
Minster in Sheppey, SS Mary & Sexburga: F
Preston North Without, St. Catherine: F
Rusthall, St. Paul: G
Stoke, SS Peter & Paul: F
Temple Ewell, SS Peter and Paul: F G
Tunbridge Wells, St. Barnabas: F
Tunstall, St. John the Baptist: F
Ulcombe, All Saints: F

NORFOLK
Haddiscoe, St. Mary: G
Norwich, St. John Maddermarket: F
Norwich, St. John Timberhill: F G
Norwich, St, Matthew, Thorpe Hamlet: F
Thurne, St. Edmund: G
Walsingham, Shrine of Our Lady: F

NORTHAMPTONSHIRE
Kettering, St. Mary: G
Kettering, SS Peter & Paul: F

NOTTINGHAMSHIRE
Collingham South, St. John the Baptist: F

OXFORDSHIRE
Ashbury, St. Mary: F
Begbroke, CSJB: F
Compton Beauchamp, St. Swithun: F G
Oxford, St. Edward's School: G
Oxford, St. Thomas the Martyr: F

SOMERSET
Bath, The Ascension, South Twerton: G
Bicknoller, St. George: G
Chesterblade, St. Mary: G
Combe Hay, Church: F
Drayton, St. Catherine: F G
East Brent, St. Mary: G
Martock, All Saints: F
Nettlecombe, St. Mary: F G
Wyke Champflower, Holy Trinity: F M

STAFFORDSHIRE
Clifton Campville, St. Andrew: F

SUFFOLK
Denston, St. Nicholas: G
Great Waldingfield, St. Lawrence: F
Woodbridge, St. Mary: G

SURREY
Haslemere, St. Christopher: F G
Hersham, St. Peter: G
Littleton, St. Mary Magdalene: F G

Shepperton, St. Nicholas: B

SUSSEX (EAST)
Bexhill, SS Peter & Paul: F
Brighton, Annunciation: F
Brighton, St. Cuthman, Whitehawk: F
Burwash, St. Bartholomew: G
Hove, All Saints: F
Northiam, St. Mary: G
Ticehurst, St. Mary: F
Wadhurst, SS Peter and Paul: F G

TYNE & WEAR
Tynemouth, St. Augustin: G

WEST MIDLANDS
Birmingham, Dudley Road (now City) Hospital: F

WILTSHIRE
Bulford, St. Leonard: F
Chute Forest, St. Mary: F
Cricklade, St. Sampson: F G
Mere, St. Michael: F
Swindon, Christ Church: G
Swindon, St. Luke: F
Swindon, St. Mark: G

YORKSHIRE (EAST)
Leconfield, St. Martin (Garrison Church): F G

YORKSHIRE (WEST)
Ilkley, St. Margaret: G
Shadwell, St. Paul: F

(iii) Rest of British Isles

SCOTLAND
Peebles, St. Peter: F

WALES
Cardiff, St. Stephen (closed): G
Clydach Vale, St. Thomas: F
Llangynfelin, St. Cynfelin: G
Llantilio Pertholey, St. Teilo: F
Manordeifi [Maenordeifi], St. David: F

CHANNEL ISLANDS
Jersey, St. Helier Church: F

Footnotes

CHAPTER I

1 Anthony Symondson in an article in *Walsingham Review* 63, 1977, reproduced in P.G. Cobb (Ed.): *Walsingham* (White Tree Books, 1990), refers to Travers as having been born in Norwich. So does the section on Travers in J. Lever (Ed.): *Catalogue of the Drawings Collection of the RIBA, Vol T–Z* (Gregg International, 1984).
2 See H. Montgomery-Massingberd (Ed.): *Burke's Irish Family Records* (Burke's Peerage, 1976), pp1128–9.
3 See H.D. Furley (Ed.): *Tonbridge School Register 1861-1945* (Rivingtons, 1951), p303.
4 On the College see C. Frayling: *The Royal College of Art, One Hundred and Fifty Years of Art and Design*, (Barrie & Jenkins, 1987), passim.
5 N. Pevsner: *Buildings of England: London 4: North*, (Penguin Books, 1998), p663.
6 See A. Symondson: *Sir Ninian Comper: the last Gothic Revivalist* (RIBA Exhibition Catalogue, 1988).
7 John Betjeman in *Architectural Review*, 85, p79.
8 L. Lee in P.E. Blagdon-Gamlen: *Martin Travers, a handlist of his work*, (Ecclesiological Society, 1997), p16.
9 F. Stephens in *idem*, p20 and privately.
10 Micheal Mac Liammoir: *All for Hecuba, an Irish Theatrical Autobiography*, (Methuen, 1946), p205.
11 Micheal Mac Liammoir: *Enter a Goldfish, Memoirs of an Irish Actor, Young and Old*, (Thames and Hudson, 1977).
12 C. Fitz-Simon: *The Boys, a biography of Micheal Mac Liammoir and Hilton Edwards*, (Nick Hern Books, 1994), p40.
13 *Enter a Goldfish*, p32.
14 *Enter a Goldfish*, p25.
15 *Enter a Goldfish*, p153.
16 *Enter a Goldfish*, pp153–4.
17 *Report on the Present Position and Tendencies of the Industrial Arts, as indicated at the International Exhibition of Modern Decorative and Industrial Arts, Paris, 1925*: Department of Overseas Trade, 1927)
18 See for example: F. Scarlett and M. Townley: *Arts Decoratifs 1925: A Personal Recollection of the Paris Exhibition* (Academy Editions, 1975).
19 *All for Hecuba*, p205.
20 *Enter a Goldfish*, pp190–1.
21 *All for Hecuba*, p229.
22 C. Lycett Green (Ed): *John Betjeman: Letters, Volume 1, 1926 to 1951*, (Methuen, 1994), p288.
23 *idem*, p287.

CHAPTER TWO

1 Peter F. Anson: *Fashions in Church Furnishings 1840–1940*, (Studio Vista, 1965).

2 J. Embry: *The Catholic Movement and the Society of the Holy Cross*, (Faith Press, 1931), p309.
3 R.A. Knox: *A Spiritual Aeneid*, (Burns Oates, 1958), p62.
4 S. Gurney: *Isabel Mrs. Gurney afterwards The Lady Talbot de Malahide 1851–1932*, (Jarrolds and Simpkin Marshall, 1935).
5 Quoted in E.W. Kemp: *N.P. Williams: a memoir and some sermons* (SPCK, 1954), which contains a great deal of material on the SSPP.
6 It is tantalizing to think that Travers may have designed these altars, but the evidence is against it, in that his notebooks do not refer to the church. There is contemporary evidence that work was carried out to the high altar in St. James the Less in about 1911 by an architect called T. Rogers Kitsell, and he may have done the work in St. Michael also. In fact St. Michael, West Hoe, is very little documented; it appears to have been closed and turned into a factory for a number of years in the 1930s, and was reopened in 1948 after St. James the Less had been bombed. It then became a daughter church of St. Andrew, Plymouth, until being made redundant again about 1995. The building still stands. The note in Pevsner's *Buildings of England: Devon* at p654 that the altars were installed in St. Michael, Albert Road, Devonport, is an error.
7 E.D. Merritt: *The Erratically Drafted Memoirs of Edmund Douglas Merritt*, (Arthur's Press Ltd., 1951), p84.
8 Anson, *op. cit.*, p327.
9 Merritt, *op.cit.*, p85.

CHAPTER THREE

1 E.D. Sedding: *George Elton Sedding, the life and work of an artist soldier*, (Letchworth Garden City Press Ltd., 1917), p119.
2 *The Studio*, Volume 85, p133.
3 A. Hughes: *Rivers of the Flood*, (Faith Press, 1973), p44.
4 *Jubilee Book of the Benedictines of Nashdom 1914–1964*, (Faith Press, 1964), p40.

CHAPTER FOUR

1 See also N. Price (ed.): *Streets of Heaven: 125 years in the parish of St. Mary's Bourne Street*, (St. Mary's Bourne Street, 1999), passim.
2 T. Ashurst in *Streets of Heaven*, *op.cit.*, p125.
3 B. Brindley: *Infinite Riches in a Little Room* (St. Mary Bourne Street, undated), p8 and L. Buckley: *Sir Ninian Comper and Howard Martin Otto (Otho) Travers: a Belated Tribute*, (Ecclesiological Society, 1992), p27.
4 See B. Doolan: *The First Fifty Years, a History of the Catholic League 1913 to 1966*, (Crux Press, 1966), passim.
5 H.A. Wilson: *Received with Thanks*, (Mowbray, 1940), passim.
6 E. & W. Young: *London's Churches*, (Grafton Books, 1986), p73.
7 G. Stamp and C. Amery: *Victorian Buildings in London 1837-1887* (Architectural Press 1980), p116.

CHAPTER FIVE

1 L.M.G. Bond: *Tyneham: a lost heritage* (Longmans, Dorchester, 1955, republished by Dovecote Press, 1984), p101 in Dovecote edition.
2 H. Hamilton Maughan: *Some Brighton Churches* (Faith Press, 1922).
3 T.P. Stevens: *Cassock and Surplus: Incidents in Clerical Life, mainly in London*, (T. Werner Laurie Ltd., 1947), p65.
4 B.F.L. Clarke: *Parish Churches of London*, (B.T. Batsford Ltd., 1966), p252.

5 J. Betjeman: *Collins Pocket Guide to English Parish Churches: The South*, (Collins, 1968), p279.
6 *Idem*, p373.
7 J. Betjeman in L.V. Grinsdell and others: *Studies in the History of Swindon*, (Swindon Borough Council, 1950), p180.

CHAPTER SIX
1 *Op. cit.*, p324.
2 See: the Institution of the RASC and RCT: *Memorials Register* (Institution, Camberley, 1998).
3 B. Scott James: *Asking for Trouble*, (Darton Longman Todd, 1962), p34.

CHAPTER SEVEN
1 H. Salmond: *Martin Travers Pays a Visit*, in *Journal of British Society of Master Glass Painters*, 1970/1, volume 14, number 5.
2 L. Lee quoted in P. Cowen: *A Guide to Stained Glass in Britain*, (Michael Joseph, 1985).

CHAPTER EIGHT
1 See in particular D.L. Simpson: *Holy Trinity Cathedral Gibraltar*, a comprehensive but unpublished history in the Guildhall Library, London: it was originally dated 1948 and later revised.
2 F. Ciaran: *Stained Glass Windows of Canterbury, New Zealand*, (University of Otago Press, 1996), W136, and D. Hamilton: *College! A History of Christ's College* (1996).
3 Ciaran, *op.cit.*, W105 and G. Strange in *New Zealand Historic Places*, number 70, September 1988.
4 *The Studio*, Volume 89, p217.

CHAPTER NINE
1 Incorporated Church Building Society: *New Churches Illustrated* (ICBS, 1937), preface.
2 See: J. Moore, D. Parsons, and B. Tuffield: *The Church of the Good Shepherd* (parish, 1980).
3 M. Stockwood: *Chanctonbury Ring, an autobiography* (Hodder & Stoughton, 1982), pp103–4.
4 A.E. Jones: *From mediaeval manor to London suburb: an obituary for Carshalton*, (author, 1976), p121.

CHAPTER TEN
1 A. Burnham: *A Manual of Anglo-Catholic Devotion* (Canterbury Press, Norwich, 2000); there is a short note on Travers at pp xx–xxi by J.W.S. Litten, who quotes from *Pictures of the English Liturgy* as if Travers had written the notes to it: whoever did write it, Travers certainly did not.

CHAPTER ELEVEN
1 C. Stephenson: *Merrily on High*, (Darton Longman Todd, 1972), p55.
2 H. Williams: *Some Day I'll Find You, an autobiography*, (Mitchell Beazley, 1982), p96.
3 A. Symondson in *Walsingham Review*, 63, 1977, reproduced in P.G. Cobb (Ed): *Walsingham* (White Tree Books, 1990).
4 L. Lee: *The Appreciation of Stained Glass*, (Oxford University Press, 1977), p90.
5 E. Liddell Armitage: *Stained Glass: History, Technology and Practice* (Leonard Hill Books, 1959), p68.
6 L. Lee in Armitage, *op.cit.*, p196.
7 J.E. Nuttgens in Armitage, *op.cit.* p200.

Index

PERSONS

Argyll, Duke of 36, 163
Arnesby-Brown, M. 132, 316, Plate 10
Atlay, Revd M.E. 80, 100, 102

Baker, Revd W.G.V.C. 36, 38
Barham, R. 256
Batley, Revd W.Y. 175, 176
Baverstock, Revd A.H. 251, 257
Baylis, H.R. 244, 256
Beck, Revd H.W. 201
Bell, Rt. Revd G.K.A. 236
Betjeman, J. 7, 27, 29, 82, 120, 131, 163, 205, 224, 261, 290, 316
Blackham, R.J. 29
Blagdon-Gamlen, Revd P.E. 64, 268
Bloxam, Revd J.F. 91
Bonkowski, C. (née Travers) 30
Brindley, Revd B. 77, 88, 297
Brown, G. (later Bryan-Brown, Revd G.) 5, 213, 214, 332
Buckmaster, M. 29
Buckley, L. 88, 268
Busby, Revd W. 59, 317

Candlish, J (née Travers) 26
Carlyle, Revd A. 34
Chase, Revd C.R. 33
Cheetham, Revd E. 46
Child, Revd M. 34, 35, 36, 38, 39, 41, 45, 46, 102, 158, 168, 169, 252, 253, 282
Comper, J.N. 7, 9, 10, 15, 64, 75, 104, 111, 139, 150, 203, 264, 274, 289, 290, 315
Corbould, Revd W.R. 16, 93, 224, 227
Cornibeer, Revd A.E. 80, 100
Crawford, J. 107, 111, 182, 203, 206, 282, 283, 298
Crowley, A. 19

Davison, Revd R. 206
Deakin, Revd C.R. 43, 44, 80, 102, 103, 104
De Lara Wilson, Revd W.G. 185
Dru Drury, G. 28, 175–7
Durrant, A.M. 220, 222, 223

Edwards, H. 17, 30
Eeles, F.C. 103, 111, 126, 152, 181, 226, 273, 301
Egerton, M.A.P. 64, 181, 307

Eliot, T.S. 46, 93, 276
Eyden, Revd M. 196, 317

Ferrier, Revd D. 76–8, 243, 329
Fynes-Clinton, Revd H.J. 60, 93, 95, 96, 97, 98, 232, 244

Gardner, Revd G.E. 98, 272
Gillett, Revd G. 247, 257
Goodhart-Rendel, H.S. 84, 86, 87, 88, 104, 295, P5
Gradidge, R. 261
Grant, T.F.W. 220, 223, 228, 230, 232, 286, 290, 292, 308, 311, 314
Graves, M. 175–7, 303
Gurney, S. 11, 34, 38, 39, 82, 155, 156, 158, 160, 161, 163, 168, 246, 252, 319

Harwood, E. 11
Havard, Revd W.T. 122
Hobbes, Revd A.J.F. 145, 155
Hogan, J. 264
Horsley, Rt. Revd C.D. 209
Howell, Revd J.C. 36, 38, 79, 82, 84
Humphries, Revd J.H. 121, 142, 286

Jack, L.E. 89, 91
Jalland, Revd T.J. 130, 193

Kay-Shuttleworth, E.J. 82, 160
Keable, R. 256
Kilburn, Revd E.E. 89, 90, 91
Knox, Revd R.A.H. 34, 35, 36, 38, 39, 82
Knox, Revd W. 36

Laing, Revd M. 11
Langton, Revd F.E.P.S. 82, 107
Lawson, W. 206, 310
Lee, L. 15, 24, 28, 58, 146, 152, 168, 197, 199, 200, 203, 204, 205, 264, 265, 276, 283, 289, 299, 308, 309, 326, 328
Lethaby, W.R. 5

Maltby, Revd E.S. 256
Maude-Roxby, Revd H. 59
Mac Liammoir, M. 13, 17, 19, 23, 24, 26, 27, 30
Miller, Sir H. 39, 155
Musman, E.B. 240, 272

Noe, A. 28, 107, 203, 313

337

Nuttgens, J.E. 265

Page, Revd S. 189, 190, 234, 274, 313
Pankhurst, S. 5
Parry, S.G. 82, 84
Patten, Revd A.H. 49, 97, 182, 197, 223
Pelly, Revd D.R. 190, 191, 322
Perigal, A. 99, 100
Philips, Revd G.L. 185, 186
Pite, A.B. 5, 6, 9, 25, 284
Porter, Revd S. 172, 173
Purnell, D. 49, 146, 147, 177, 203, 206, 209, 303, 306, 331

Quick, W.M.R. 38, 41

Ross, Revd D.A. 93

Salmond, H. 191, 298
Sedding, Revd E.D. 9, 12, 250, 256, 257
Sedding, G.E. 9–12, 13, 56, 80, 189, 244, 250, 256, 274, 306
Skelton. M.B. 212, 213, 333, Plate 16.
Starey, C.R. 256
Steel, Revd F. 194
Stephens, Revd F. 15, 28, 48, 68, 182, 205, 206, 284, 292, 316
Stevens, Revd T.P. 13, 14, 16, 27, 28, 56, 117
Studdert-Kennedy, Revd G.A. 68, 276
Symondson, Revd A.N. 261

Tiley, Revd J. 114, 115
Travers, C.B.A. (Christine) (née Willmore) 13–15, 17–19, 20, 21, 22, 23, 25, 85, 110, 216, 244
Travers, E.A.O. 2, 22
Travers, H.M.O. (Martin)
 Back To Baroque 31–50
 Birth 1, 3
 Character 15, 267
 Childhood 4
 Church Builder 219–240
 Death 28
 Education 5, 6

Family Background 1
Graphic Artist 241–258
Marriage (1) 13
Marriage (2) 27
Married Life 14, 19, 20, 21, 23
Paris Exhibition (1925) 21, 22, 62, 110
Practice In Early Years 6–11, 51–78
Practice In Later Years 178–206
Practice In Middle Years 21, 110–154
Royal College of Art Teaching 22, 27, 265, 267
Work Abroad 207–218
Travers, H.W. 1, 2, 4, 6
Travers, J.V. (née Stevens) 26, 30
Travers, L.G. (Gertrude) (née Hunnybun) 2, 5,9, 13, 14
Travers, M. 30
Travers, M. (Mollie) (née Jones) 27–30, 112
Travers, N. (Nicholas) 13, 20, 21, 23, 24, 25, 26, 29, 30
Travers, O.B. 5, 13
Travers, O.R. 2
Travers, O.W. 2
Travers, S. (Sally) 13, 20, 24, 26, 27, 29, 30
Travers, V. 2
Tuckerman, Revd G. 104, 109, 142, 143, 144
Twisaday, Revd J.H.C. 150

Weston, Rt. Revd F. 100, 101, 102, 212, 296, 333
Whall, C. 5, 315
Whitby, Revd E.O.H. 10, 11, 12, 36, 38, 39, 43, 55, 60, 75, 79, 80, 81, 82, 85, 87, 88, 243, 249, 298, 304, Plates 2, 6
Wilkie, J. 247, 256
Williams, Revd N.P. 36, 41
Wilson, H. 5, 9
Winnington-Ingram, Rt. Revd A.F. 33, 79, 89, 310
Wodehouse, Revd R. 128, 130, 193, 319, 320

Yeo, M. 247, 256

INDEX

PLACES

Acton
    St. Peter 184, 185, 278, 334
    St. Saviour 126, 221, 278, 334
Aldeburgh, SS. Peter & Paul 16, 322
Alsager, St. Mary Magdalene 300
Amesbury, SS. Mary & Melor, 327
Ashbury, St. Mary 136, 160, 161–2, 319, 338, Plate 24
Ashton-on-Mersey, St. Mary Magdalene 300
Ayot St. Lawrence, St. Lawrence 309

Balham, St. Mary 126, 292, 336
Barham, St. John The Baptist 66–8, 127, 131, 267, 312, 338, Plate 5
Barking, St. Paul 16, 271
Barnsbury, St. Clement 58, 283
Bath, The Ascension 55, 320, 339
Battersea
    Christ Church 179–80, 292, 336
    General Hospital Chapel 60, 293
    St. Andrew 121–2, 293
    St. Luke 122–5, 234, 293, 336
    St. Stephen 179–80, 293
Beaulieu, Blessed Virgin & Holy Child 189, 201, 306, 337
Bedford, St. Paul 296
Bedford Park, St. Michael & All Angels 9, 27, 56, 57, 58, 283, 335
Begbroke, CSJB 319, 339
Bentley, St. Mary 306
Bentworth, St. Mary 306, 337
Bermuda 212, 331
Bethnal Green
    St. James The Great 291
    St. John 184, 291, 336
Bexhill, SS. Peter & Paul 198, 324, 339
Bicknoller, St. George 141, 320, 339
Bilsington, SS. Peter & Paul 312, 338
Birmingham
    City Hospital Chapel 179, 326, 339
    St. Aidan 55, 326
    St. Mark 327
Bishop's Stortford
    Holy Trinity 223, 309, 338
    St. Michael 309
Blackford, Holy Trinity 72, 320
Bolton, St. Augustine 49, 206, 306
Borough Green, Good Shepherd 143–5, 312
Bournemouth, St. Stephen 145, 303, 337
Bow Common, St. Paul 182, 291
Bramshott, St. Mary 178, 191, 306, 337
Brighton
    Annunciation 114–6, 324, 339
    St. Cuthman 236–9, 325, 339

Bristol, St. Gregory (Horfield) 205–6, 298
Broadstone, St. John The Baptist 61, 303, 337
Brockenhurst, St. Nicholas 23, 132, 307, 337
Bromley
    Old Palace Chapel 273
    St. Mary (Shortlands) 126, 273
Buckland, St. Andrew 199, 312, 338
Buckland Monachorum, St. Andrew 302
Bulford, St. Leonard 327, 339
Burbage, Christ Church 127, 302, 337
Burghclere, The Ascension 178, 191, 307, 337
Burnham, Nashdom Abbey 7, 34, 75, 77, 130, 298, Plate 6
Burwash, St. Bartholomew 131, 325, 339
Bushey, St. James 195, 310, 338

Cambridge, Holy Trinity 299
Camelford, St. Thomas of Canterbury 152, 300, 337, Plate 29
Canterbury
    All Saints 312, 338
    Hospital Chapel 179, 312, 338
    St. Gregory 313
Cardiff, St. Stephen 70, 330, 340
Carshalton Beeches, Good Shepherd 16, 72, 119, 219, 220, 223–8, 290, 336
Caterham, St. Paul 234, 323
Catford
    St. Andrew 58, 68–9, 141, 265, 287, 335
    St. Laurence 126, 287
Chavey Down, Heathfield School Chapel 297, 336
Chelsea, Methodist Church 204, 284
Cheriton, St. Michael & All Angels 64, 181, 307, 337, Plate 3
Chesham Bois, St. Leonard 191–2, 298, 336
Cheshunt
    Bishops' College Chapel 310
    St. Mary 310, 338
Chesterblade, St. Mary 11, 55, 56, 320, 339
Chislehurst, St. Nicholas 204, 273, 334
Christchurch, University of Canterbury 15, 214–8, 332
Christchurch, Christ's College 5, 213–4, 332
Chute Forest, St. Mary 327, 339
City of London
    Mercers' Hall Chapel 65–6, 275
    SS. Augustine & Faith 98, 147–8, 275
    St. Edmund The King 68, 276, 334
    St. Magnus The Martyr 60, 93–8, 122, 259, 276, 334, Plates 13, 14
    St. Mary Aldermary 205, 276
    St. Michael Paternoster Royal 276
    Temple Church 28, 178, 200, 276

Clapham, Holy Spirit 142, 286, 335
Clapton, St. Thomas 72, 279, 335
Clerkenwell, Holy Redeemer 10, 107, 283, 335
Clewer
    CSJB 297
    St. Stephen 297, 336
Clifton Campville, St. Andrew 60, 72, 181, 322, 339
Clydach Vale, St. Thomas 62, 330, 340
Collingham South, St. John The Baptist 16, 181, 318, 338
Colombo
    Cathedral 212, 333
    St. Michael (Polwatte) 212, 333
Combe Hay, Church 181, 321, 339
Compton Beauchamp, St. Swithun 82, 128, 136, 145, 155–61, 319, 339, Plates 22, 23
Corfe Castle, St. Edward 28, 114, 164, 174–7, 178, 203, 303, 337
Corringham, St. Mary 305, 337
Covent Garden, Priory of St. Michael 193, 294, 336
Cranford, Holy Angels 171–2, 283
Cranford, St. Dunstan 158, 169–71, 282, 335, Plate 20
Cricklade, St. Sampson 72, 112, 150, 163–6, 327, 340
Cricklewood, St. Gabriel 272, 334
Curry Rivel, St. Andrew 59, 321

Dalston, St. Bartholomew 133, 280
Denston, St. Nicholas 72, 322, 339
Derby, St. Anne 77, 302
Drayton, St. Catherine 141–2, 321, 339
Droxford, St. Mary & All Saints 152, 307, 337
Dunstable, St. Paul 296
Durban, St. John 211, 332

Ealing, Christ The Saviour 107, 138–9, 278, 334
East Bergholt, St. Mary 322
East Brent, St. Mary 141, 321, 339
East Donyland, St. Lawrence 137, 305
East Ham, St. Bartholomew 288
East Ham, St. Mary Magdalene 288
East London, St. Saviour 211–2, 332
Ely, Cathedral 28, 178, 200, 299
Eton, College Chapel 297, 336

Felixstowe, St. Andrew 220, 322
Flitwick, SS. Peter & Paul 296, 336
Folkestone, Eversley School 313
Fordwich, St. Mary 142, 313, 338
Friern Barnet, St. James The Great 60, 271, 334
Fulham, All Saints 130–1, 191, 281, 335

Gibraltar, Cathedral 28, 178, 206, 209–10, 331
Godmanchester, St. Mary 28, 150, 259, 299, 336

Golders Green, St. Michael 271
Goudhurst, St. Mary 313
Great Waldingfield, St. Lawrence 323, 339
Greenford, Holy Cross 98, 179, 278, 334
Gussage All Saints, All Saints 303, 337

Haddiscoe, St. Mary 112, 132, 316, 338
Haggerston, St. Columba 55, 80, 280
Hampstead, St. Mark 7, 274
Harrow
    Quainton Hall School 196, 281, 335
    St. Alban 234, 281
    St. George (Headstone) 153–4, 180, 181–2, 223, 281, 335, Plate 28
    St. John The Baptist 204, 234–6, 282, 335
Haslemere, St. Christopher 142, 323, 339
Hawkinge, St. Luke 190, 239, 313
Hawkinge, St. Michael 189–90, 313
Hedgerley, St. Mary 299
Helston, St. Michael 153, 204–5, 301, 337
Hemingford Grey, St. Francis House 193, 299, 336
Hersham, St. Peter 323, 339
Hessle, All Saints 328
High Easter, St. Mary The Virgin 132–3, 305, 337
Hitchin, Holy Saviour 310, 338
Holland Park, Priory of St. Paul 192–3, 200, 284
Horbury, House of Mercy Chapel 329
Hove, All Saints 116, 325, 339
Hove, St. Patrick 116, 325
Hoxton
    Holy Trinity 88, 182–3, 280, 335
    St. Mary 58, 280
    St. Saviour 9, 89–93, 100, 280
Huntingdon, The Priory 300

Ickham, St. John The Evangelist 15, 314
Ilkley, St. Margaret 142–3, 329, 340
Islington, Paget Memorial Mission 6, 283, 335
Iver Heath, St. Margaret 112, 137, 299, 336

Kennington
    St. Agnes 125–6, 286, 335
    St. Philip's Hall 234, 286
Kentford, St. Mary 323
Kettering, St. Mary 65, 318, 338
Kettering, SS. Peter & Paul 62–4, 117, 318, 338
Kilburn, St. John The Evangelist 133, 273

Laleham, All Saints 114, 174, 324
Lamorbey, Holy Trinity 220, 239–40, 272, 334
Langley Mill, St. Andrew 142, 302, 337
Leconfield, St. Martin Garrison Church 168, 265, 328, 340, Plate 25
Leominster, SS. Peter & Paul 204, 309, 338

INDEX

Lewisham, St. Mary 126, 287, 335
Leyton, Emmanuel 16, 21, 220, 232–4, 292, 336
Limehouse
    St. John The Evangelist 144–5, 291
    St. Peter 291
Limpsfield Chart, St. Andrew 324
Liss
    St, Martin (Longmoor Garrison Church) 166–8, 204, 265, 307, Plate 25
    St. Mary 137, 223, 308, 337, Plate 19
Littleport, St. George 133–4, 300, 336
Littleton, St, Mary Magdalene 172–4, 324, 339
Llangynfelin, St. Cynfelin 330, 340
Llantilio Pertholey, St. Teilo 330, 340
Loughton, St. Mary 188–9, 305, 337
Luton, Christ Church 199, 296

Madrid, St. George 97, 100, 208–9, 332
Maidstone, Mangravet Parish Hall 314
Manordeifi, St. David 74, 75, 330, 340
Marazion, All Saints 152, 153, 301, 337
Margate, All Saints 1, 198, 314, 338
Martock, All Saints 141, 142, 321, 339
Mawnan, SS. Maunanus & Stephen 152–3, 301, 337
Medbourne, St. Giles 316
Meopham, St. John The Baptist 314, 338
Mere, St. Michael 202, 327, 340
Minster-In-Sheppey, SS. Mary & Sexburga 137–8, 314, 338
Mitcham, SS. Peter & Paul 64, 162, 287, 335
Monken Hadley, St. Mary 272

Nettlecombe, St. Mary 112, 141, 321, 339
New Barnet
    Holy Trinity (Lyonsdown) 98–100, 262, 272, 334
    St. Mark 272, 334
Newington, St. Matthew 117–20, 121, 124, 128, 222, 226, 233, 234, 288, Plate 18
Newlyn, St. Peter 150, 152, 301, 337
Northiam, St. Mary 112, 152, 325, 339
North Mymms, St. Mary 199, 310, 338
Northolt, St. Mary 185–8, 192, 200, 239, 279, 334
North Perrott, St. Martin 321
Norwich
    All Saints 10, 54, 243, 317
    St. George (RC) 200, 317
    St. John Maddermarket 10, 59, 190, 317, 338
    St. John Timberhill 54, 317, 338, Plate 1
    St. Julian 9, 10, 55, 317
    St. Matthew 197–8, 317, 338
Norwood, St. Mary 182, 279
Notting Dale, St. Clement 62, 284, 335

Notting Hill
    All Saints 150, 151, 285, 335
    St. Columb 56, 64, 134–5, 150, 285
Nunhead
    Cheltenham College Mission 149, 230–2, 289, 335
    St. Antholin 98, 147, 149–50, 289, 335

Osterley, St. Francis 194, 283, 335
Oxford
    Queen's College Chapel 178, 200, 319
    St. Edward's School 132, 319, 339
    St. Paul 128, 130, 319
    St. Thomas The Martyr 128, 193, 246, 320, 339

Paddington
    St. Mary Magdalene 72–3, 294, 336, Plate 7
    St. Paul 294
Parson's Green, St. Dionis 135–7, 281, 335
Peebles, St. Peter 330, 340
Pentonville, St. Silas 206, 284
Perth, Cathedral 213, 331
Petham, All Saints 51, 53, 72, 314
Pimlico
    St. Barnabas 199, 294, 336
    St. Gabriel 55, 294, 336
    St. Mary 11, 60, 79–89, 102, 158, 160, 183, 199, 246, 294, 336, Plates 9–12
    St. Saviour 203, 295, 336
Plumstead, St. Nicholas 69, 72, 246, 279, 335
Poplar, All Saints 60, 292, 336
Portsmouth
    St. Agatha 120, 308, 337
    St. Stephen 70–2, 308
Potters Bar, St. Mary 310
Preston North Without, St. Catherine 195–6, 314, 338
Purley
    St. James (Riddlesdown) 14, 58, 112, 145–7, 265, 277, 334
    St. Mark (Woodcote) 126, 277, 334

Radlett, Christ Church 191, 310, 338
Reading, Holy Trinity 77, 105, 130, 246, 297, 336, Plate 6
Rochester, University of Rochester 212–3, 333, Plate 31
Romsey, Abbey 201, 259, 308, 337
Ropley, St. Peter 309
Runcorn, St. Michael & All Angels 60, 300, 337
Rusthall, St. Paul 315, 338
Ryde, All Saints 311

St. Albans
    Cathedral 311
    St. Saviour 78, 116–7, 221, 311, 338, Plate 17

341

St. Helier (Jersey), St. Helier 28, 177, 178, 200–1, 330, 340, Plate 32
St. Helier (Sutton), St. Peter 290
St. Jean De Luz, The Nativity 207–8, 331
St. John's Wood, All Saints 295
St. Leonard's, St. Peter's Grange 325
St. Marylebone, Royal College of Medicine 241, 295
St. Pancras
    Holy Cross 62, 274, 334
    St. James 274
    St. Pancras Old Church 117, 192, 201, 275, 334
Shadwell, St. Paul 76, 77–8, 158, 243, 329, 340
Shepperton, St. Nicholas 174, 324, 339
Shillingstone, Holy Rood 303
Shirley, St. John The Evangelist 277
Silchester, St. Mary 309
Simla, Bishop Cotton School 212, 332
Sixpenny Handley, St. Mary 198, 199, 303, 337
Slade Green, St. Augustine, 60, 272, 334
South Ascot, All Souls 145, 297, 336
South Kensington
    St. Augustine 102–9, 138, 196, 285, 335, Plates 15, 16
    St. Jude 104, 201, 285, 335
South Kirkby, All Saints 329
Southwark
    All Hallows 289
    Cathedral 12, 59, 289
    Holy Trinity 72, 120, 289
Speen, Elmore Abbey 77, 298, 336
Stand, Unitarian Chapel 207, 270, 306
Stanford-Le-Hope, St. Margaret 305
Stanstead Mountfitchet, St. Mary 305, 337
Steeple, St. Michael 114, 304
Stoke, SS. Peter & Paul 60, 315, 338
Stoke Poges, St. Giles 200, 299, 336
Streatham, St. Peter 126, 286
Streatham Vale, Holy Redeemer 16, 228–30, 286, 335
Sudbury, St. Andrew 203, 273
Sutton, St. Barnabas 2, 126, 291, 336
Swanage, St. Mark 202, 304, 337
Swanwick, St. Andrew 61, 302, 337
Swindon
    Christ Church 132, 327, 340
    St. John The Evangelist 328
    St. Luke 130, 193, 328, 340
    St. Mark 180, 328, 340
Temple Ewell, SS. Peter & Paul 28, 204, 315, 338
Thurne, St. Edmund 134, 318, 338
Thurston, St. Peter 323
Ticehurst, St. Mary 198–9, 326, 339, Plate 30

Tinsley, St. Lawrence 202–3, 329
Tonbridge, School Chapel 5, 7, 8, 54, 127–9, 201, 268, 315
Tooting, St. Paul (Furzedown) 142, 293, 336
Tudeley, All Saints 204, 315
Tunbridge Wells, St. Barnabas 144, 194–5, 203, 246, 316, 338, Plates 26, 27
Tunstall, St. John The Baptist 205, 316, 338
Twickenham, St. Mary 288
Tyneham, St. Mary 112–4, 116, 127, 165, 304, 337
Tynemouth, St. Augustin 20, 21, 62, 63, 70, 207, 326, 339

Ulcombe, All Saints 316, 338
Upper Norwood, St. John The Evangelist 64, 139–41, 277, 334

Vauxhall, Clarence Club 287
Victoria, Cathedral 212, 331

Wadhurst, SS. Peter & Paul 199–200, 326, 339
Walsingham, Shrine 49, 107, 196–7, 318, 338
Walthamstow, St. Peter 145, 292, 336
Walworth
    St. John 290, 335
    St. Peter 126, 290
Wandsworth, St. Andrew 126, 294, 336
Ware, Christ Church 199, 311, 338
Warnford, Our Lady 152, 239, 309, 337
Washford Pyne, St. Peter 302, 337
Watford, St. James 119, 180, 220–3, 226, 311, 338
Wedmore, St. Mary 322
West Hampstead, St. James 275
Westminster
    Christ Church 295
    St. Matthew 100–2, 172, 295, 336, Plate 8
West Wickham
    St. Christopher, 273
    St. John The Baptist 12, 189–90, 273, 334
    St. Mary of Nazareth, 124, 234, 274, 334
Weymouth, Holy Trinity 266, 304, 337
Wicklewood, All Saints 318
Wimbledon, St. John The Baptist 73, 288, 335, Plate 4
Winforton, St. Michael 59, 60, 309, 338
Woodbridge, St. Mary 131–2, 266, 323, 339
Woodford Bridge, St. Paul 126, 288
Wyke Champflower, Holy Trinity 190–1, 322, 339
Wyke Regis, All Saints 12, 81–2, 304, 337

Zanzibar, Cathedral 10, 212, 333

INDEX

ACKNOWLEDGEMENTS IN RELATION TO PHOTOGRAPHS
Colour Plates (by number)

RW: 4, 5, 7, 8, 9, 10, 11, 13, 14, 15, 16, 18, 19, 20, 22, 23, 24, 26, 27, 30.
RW Collection: 2, 21(Courtesy N. Priestly).
MY: Cover, 1, 3, 6, 12, 17, 25, 29.

Douglas Jones: 28.
Nancy M. Martin: 31.
John Seaford 32.

Black and White Pictures and Line Drawings (by page)

RW: 227
RW Collection: 42, 45, 47, 74, 77, 80, 83, 89, 97 (Left), 129 (Lower), 139, 140, 146, 151, 162, 163, 164, 186, 193, 238, 263
MY Collection: Vi, 18, 53, 57, 61, 63, 64, 65, 66, 69 (Lower), 70, 71, 116, 127, 131, 133, 143, 165, 167, 187, 188, 189, 195, 211, 215, 235, 270
Brighton Local Studies Library: 237
Julia Candlish: 26
Canterbury Cathedral Archives: 67
Cheltenham College: 231
M. Collins: 47 (Lower)
Community of The Resurrection: 192
Corporation of London, Metropolitan Archives: 121, 124
Council for Care of Churches: 8, 16, 56, 58, 69 (Top), 103, 106, 113, 153, 156 (Top), 159, 161, 175, 176, 180, 219, 224, 225, 226, 228, 229 (Both), 232, 233 (Both)

B. Giles: 173, 174
Guildhall Library: 96, 105, 108, 114, 134, 135, 144, 170
Hertfordshire Archives: 99, 222
A.F. Kersting: 171
R. McEwan: 32, 76, 91, 92, 97 (Right), 156 (Lower), 157
D. Miller: 205
National Monuments Record: 101 (Both), 123, 125, 136, 138, 183, 184, 197
RIBA: 47 (Top), 75, 86, 87, 104, 115, 120, 122, 129 (Top), 148, 149, 172, 202, 221
Rector & Churchwardens of St. Magnus The Martyr: 94
Southwark Local Studies Library: 118, 119
Michael Travers: 3, 4
Wiltshire Archives: 178, 198, 266

343